AN
OCEAN
APART

AN OCEAN APART

THE RELATIONSHIP BETWEEN BRITAIN AND AMERICA IN THE TWENTIETH CENTURY

DAVID DIMBLEBY
&
DAVID REYNOLDS

RANDOM HOUSE
NEW YORK

All rights reserved under International and
Pan-American Copyright Conventions.
Published in the United States by Random House, Inc., New York.

Library of Congress Cataloging-in-Publication Data
Dimbleby, David.
An ocean apart.
Bibliography: p.
Includes index.
1. United States—Foreign relations—Great Britain.
2. United States—Foreign relations—20th century.
3. Great Britain—Foreign relations—United States.
4. Great Britain—Foreign relations—20th century.
I. Reynolds, David, 1952– . II. Title.
E183.8.G7D46 1988 327.73041 87-43214
ISBN 0-394-56968-7

Acknowledgment is made to the following for cartoons and illustrations:
Steve Bell, p. 324; Clifford Berryman/Library of Congress, Washington
D.C., p. 132; Daniel Bishop/St. Louis Star-Times, p. 139; British Airways, p. 320; Cummings/Daily Express, p. 206; Garland/Daily Tele-
graph/Cartoon Study Centre, University of Kent, p. 268; Giles/Daily
Express, p. 173; Hall Syndicate Inc./Washington Post, p. 233; Hoover,
p. 114; Jak/Mail Newspapers, p. 339; London University Library, p. 14;
Low/Mail Newspapers, pp. 181, 203; Peter Newark's Western Americana, p. 51; Private Eye, p. 347. Reproduced by permission of: Punch
pp. 22, 43, 80, 87, 250, 321; Stars and Stripes, p. 163; Tribune Media
Services, pp. 75, 99, 142; Universal Press Syndicate/Oliphant, p. 273.

Manufactured in the United States of America
24689753
First Edition

Maps by Alec Spark
Book design by Debbie Glasserman

ACKNOWLEDGMENTS

The idea for this book sprang from the BBC TV and KCET Los Angeles television series of the same name, which was presented by David Dimbleby, with David Reynolds acting as principal historical adviser. Although this is not "the book of the film," many of the interviews conducted and the stories unearthed for the series have provided new insights that have strengthened the narrative.

The television project was conceived by Peter Pagnamenta, who, shortly after work began, was promoted to head the BBC's Current Affairs Department. His place as executive producer was taken by George Carey. The series producer was Adam Curtis, with Peter Salmon and Belinda Giles producing two of the seven films. Blaine Baggett was the producer for KCET. The authors are grateful to all of them for their many valuable contributions to this book. They would also like to thank everyone who played a part in putting together the film series: Linda Parker, production assistant; Nick Catliff, Leonie Jameson, Kerry Platman, Betty Scharf, researchers; Christine Whittaker, David Thaxton, Kevin Brown, film researchers; June Leech, picture researcher; Professor Warren F. Kimball, American adviser.

Our publishers at Random House have coped stoically with text arriving at the last minute—inevitable in a project of this kind—and have been invariably helpful and encouraging under the pressure of producing a complex book at great speed. Our gratitude to Peter Osnos and his staff, particularly Sono Rosenberg. Debbie Glasserman and Nina Ryan were immensely helpful. Ion Trewin and Jane Osborn of Hodder and Stoughton, publisher of the book in Britain, were of great assistance in expediting the American edition. We are also indebted to Paul Dowswell, who found many of the pictures and cartoons, to Alec Spark, who drew the maps, and to Sydney Cohen, who compiled the index. Thanks are also due to our agents Michael Sissons and Peter Matson.

David Dimbleby would particularly like to thank Belinda Giles, who, apart from producing one of the films, assisted him with the book, offering in generous quantities encouragement and criticism; and Carolyn Smith, who not only typed and retyped many drafts of the manuscript, thus allowing joint authorship to become a reality, but who did so with a patience and understanding that twenty years of working with him does not appear to have diminished.

David Reynolds is very grateful to his colleagues at Christ's College for allowing him to monopolize the Fellows' word processor for two years, and to Cambridge friends Dr. John Thompson and Dr. David Cannadine, Professor Bernard Bailyn of Harvard University, and his wife, Margaret Ray Reynolds, who all commented on chapters of his original draft.

Professor John Blum of Yale University generously read the final manuscript, and Dr. John Baylis, Ms. Diane Kunz, Professor Richard Neustadt and Professor Barry Supple were among those who helped with specialist advice.

Crown copyright documents are quoted by permission of the Controller of HM Stationery Office. For other special permissions the authors are grateful to The National Maritime Museum, Greenwich; the British Library of Political and Economic Science; the University of Birmingham; the Borthwick Institute, York; and Yale University Library.

David Dimbleby
December 1987   David Reynolds

CONTENTS

MAPS

INTRODUCTION

The decline of Britain, from the most powerful nation in the world to a small offshore European island, has been as swift as the rise of the United States to occupy the position Britain once held. The two processes were intimately connected. America's rise would have been slower but for Britain's decline.

At the turn of the century Britain ruled over the largest empire ever seen; one-fifth of the globe was under her control. With the empire came ownership of the natural resources needed for industrial manufacture, a monopoly over much of the trade that flowed from it, and mastery of the sea-lanes that provided safe passage for her ships. As America's industry started to expand and seek markets beyond its shores it inevitably came into conflict with this empire. Britain was not much loved. To the United States, which had but recently thrown off the British yoke, she seemed not only arrogant in her assumption of a natural right to supremacy, but tricky and devious too. This hostility was exacerbated by the conviction of all right-thinking Americans that Britain's wealth was immoral, since it was based on colonialism, which reduced millions to servitude.

Britain would not have recognized this picture of herself. In her eyes, she was keeping the peace across great tracts of the earth and raising ignorant peoples to understand and adopt British attitudes to the rule of law, fair government and individual liberty. In the process she had naturally been rewarded with the economic advantages that flowed from her benign rule. The United States was not a serious threat to her position, although it was occasionally an irritant. For the most part America was regarded with amused condescension, a country not yet civilized, in the European sense, but uncouth and raw.

It is remarkable that power has passed from one great nation to another in such a short time without a shot being fired in anger, still less a major war being fought between them. It was not just their own good sense or friendship but other conflicts that have ensured this. The world has been torn apart by war twice in this century. On each occasion Britain has been among the first to enter the fray. In each conflict at the point of exhaustion she has been saved by the United States, and each time, although undefeated, Britain's power has been diminished and her economy weakened.

The United States, on the other hand, emerged from both wars much stronger. As a neutral, America profited from manufacturing the weapons of war for the belligerents while itself remaining at peace. Even after joining the wars, America was protected by vast oceans from the devastation that its allies suffered.

Britain's decline as a consequence of these two wars created the opportunities America sought. Power did not have to be wrested from Britain. It fell into America's hands as a result of her weakness, a transition fraught with misunderstandings, mutual suspicion and occasionally outright hostility. Yet Britain and America were also partners in the two great conflicts, helping to win the victory and impose the peace in ways that shaped our modern world.

Americans sometimes say that they envy Britain "her history," forgetting that her history is their history. The Founding Fathers were British, citizens of British America, who inherited attitudes that left their mark on every aspect of American society. Many of the settlers had first crossed the Atlantic to the New World in order to revive the British tradition of liberty that they felt was being eroded in Britain. They fought against Britain and secured their independence in defense of those same liberties. Liberal values inspired them to create a country more open and more democratic than Britain and to denounce the British Empire long after they had freed themselves from it. But the fact that the two countries shared a liberal inheritance has been more important than their differences over how it should be applied. In this century they have been natural allies in the fight against the threats of Prussian militarism, fascist dictatorship and communist revolution—bound together by a common belief in liberal, capitalist democracy.

The other important element in their common heritage is that both countries speak English. Much is made of the misunderstandings that arise across "the barrier of a common language." Winston Churchill remembered a wartime conference that nearly came to blows because of the opposite meanings of the verb "to table."* But the advantages outweigh any disadvantage. Contact between Britons and Americans has always been easy at every level—military, diplomatic, political and personal. They have been able to establish intimate ties, to understand the other's attitudes, to develop complex relationships without recourse to dictionaries or interpreters. The shared language has linked two cultures as well as two governments. In literature and learning, in films and television, in science, technology and industry, Britain and America have affected each other more closely than any other countries in modern history.

In this book we trace how the complex relationship between Britain and America has evolved during the twentieth century and how it has influenced the world we live in now. To understand this process it is necessary to start at the beginning, with the origins of the United States, long before it became known as a superpower, long before anyone could dismiss Britain as merely an offshore European island.

---

*In Britain "to table" a motion is to put it on the table for discussion; in the United States it means to withdraw it from consideration.[1]

AN
OCEAN
APART

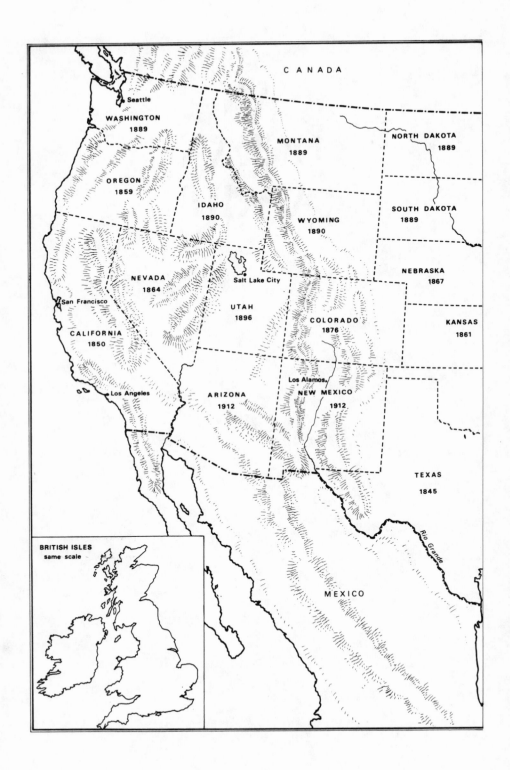

CANADA

Seattle

WASHINGTON
1889

MONTANA
1889

NORTH DAKOTA
1889

OREGON
1859

IDAHO
1890

WYOMING
1890

SOUTH DAKOTA
1889

NEVADA
1864

Salt Lake City

NEBRASKA
1867

San Francisco

UTAH
1896

COLORADO
1876

KANSAS
1861

CALIFORNIA
1850

Los Angeles

ARIZONA
1912

Los Alamos

NEW MEXICO
1912

TEXAS
1845

Rio Grande

BRITISH ISLES
same scale

MEXICO

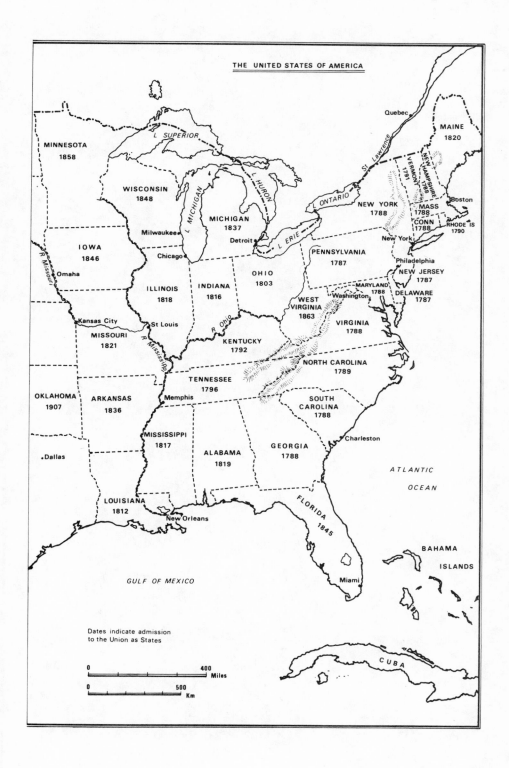

THE UNITED STATES OF AMERICA

Quebec

MAINE
1820

L. SUPERIOR

MINNESOTA
1858

WISCONSIN
1848

L. MICHIGAN

L. HURON

MICHIGAN
1837

L. ONTARIO

St. Lawrence

VERMONT 1791

NEW HAMPSHIRE 1788

Boston

MASS
1788

NEW YORK
1788

CONN
1788

RHODE IS
1790

New York

Milwaukee

Detroit

L. ERIE

IOWA
1846

Chicago

OHIO
1803

PENNSYLVANIA
1787

Philadelphia

NEW JERSEY
1787

R. Missouri

Omaha

ILLINOIS
1818

INDIANA
1816

MARYLAND
1788

DELAWARE
1787

Washington

Kansas City

St Louis

R. Ohio

WEST
VIRGINIA
1863

VIRGINIA
1788

MISSOURI
1821

KENTUCKY
1792

R. Mississippi

NORTH CAROLINA
1789

OKLAHOMA
1907

ARKANSAS
1836

TENNESSEE
1796

Memphis

SOUTH
CAROLINA
1788

Dallas

MISSISSIPPI
1817

ALABAMA
1819

GEORGIA
1788

Charleston

ATLANTIC

OCEAN

LOUISIANA
1812

New Orleans

FLORIDA
1845

BAHAMA

ISLANDS

GULF OF MEXICO

Miami

Dates indicate admission
to the Union as States

0   400
          Miles

0   500
          Km

CUBA

CHAPTER 1

THE STRUGGLE FOR INDEPENDENCE
c. 1620–1865

The *Mayflower* hit the full force of an Atlantic storm a few weeks out from Plymouth. One of its main beams cracked, and the tiny ship, less than one hundred feet long, was forced to drift with the wind for days, tossed to and fro. As they lay in the dark belowdecks, nauseated by the movement and the stench, many of her 102 passengers must have wondered whether their decision to leave England was right. They were an ill-assorted bunch. Some were Pilgrims, Puritans like William Bradford, whose determination to worship their God according to conscience and the Scriptures had led them from their homes in Nottinghamshire first to Holland and finally across the Atlantic. But others were "strangers" to the Pilgrim faith, men and women, mostly recruited by the London merchant adventurers financing the voyage, who were prompted by the depressed economy of England and the lack of opportunity to seek a better life across the ocean. A few of the passengers were not traveling of their own volition. They included family servants and even some young children sailing alone, probably orphans transported overseas to avoid their being a burden on the City of London.

The Atlantic crossing took more than two months. As soon as they made their landfall on the scrubby sand dunes of Cape Cod on November 11, 1620, the free adult males solemnly pledged to "Covenant and Combine ourselves together into a Civil Body Politic, for our better ordering and preservation." But by the time they had found a place fit for habitation, with a good water supply and safe harbor, winter was already upon them, and they did not begin work on the first house, a communal log cabin with thatched roof, until December 25. Over the next three months, Bradford grimly recorded in his history of the colony, "half of their company died, especially in January and February, being the depth of winter, and wanting houses and other comforts; being infected with the scurvy and other diseases which this long voyage and their inaccommodate condition had brought upon them." Bradford's own wife, Dorothy, was one of the early fatalities. In April 1621 the *Mayflower*, which had wintered with them, set sail for England. Despite all their hardships, none of the settlers returned with her, but few could have watched the little ship turn down Plymouth Bay toward the open sea without their hearts sinking. They were now on their own. Behind them was what Bradford called "a hideous and desolate wilderness, full of wild beasts and wild men." And on the other side "there was the mighty ocean which they had passed and was now as a main bar and gulf to separate them from all the civil parts of the world."[1]

The founders of Plymouth Colony were not the first Europeans to encounter the new continent and its Indian inhabitants. In South America, following Christopher Columbus's voyage of 1492, the Spanish and Portuguese carved out their own empires, lured by gold, justifying their cupidity in the name of God. Later, northern Europeans began to leave their mark on the Eastern seaboard of North America. By the beginning of the seventeenth century trading posts were being established by the French on the St. Lawrence River and by the Dutch at New Amsterdam at the mouth of the Hudson. But it was the English who mastered North America. Early settlements along the James River in Virginia (named for Elizabeth, the "Virgin Queen") were followed by the establishment of Plymouth and by a steady influx of migrants during the 1630s and 1640s. Religious persecution, civil war and the collapse of the English cloth trade impelled many to make a leap of faith, hope or even desperation across the ocean into an unknown world. By 1660 Britain's mainland American colonists numbered seventy thousand.

These early settlers named their new settlements after the towns and villages they had left behind: Plymouth, Boston, Ipswich, Newbury, Gloucester. Granted land by a trading company or, later, by a colonial government, they divided it up in the manner they were used to back home. Many Massachusetts settlers had been accustomed to a degree of local self-government in remote villages in Yorkshire or the West Country. They re-created these patterns of life, with compact townships in the midst of open fields farmed in individual lots. There were town meetings, elected leaders and officers with familiar English titles, such as town constable and surveyor of highways. In Virginia and colonies farther south the settlers followed practices typical of other parts of England, such as Suffolk and Essex, with separate farms at some distance from one another, organized by counties and governed through the county court by other familiar English officials, the sheriffs and justices of the peace.

These first settlers were trying to reproduce the ways of life they had known in England but free of the religious, political and economic constraints that had forced them to emigrate. They were Englishmen transplanted, and, in the process, transformed. The institutions they established, such as the Virginia parish or the Massachusetts town meeting, proved very different from their English counterparts. There was no church hierarchy, with land, wealth and power, to keep the local parish in check. There was no rigid political structure of aristocratic landowners and royal government to regiment the life of local townships. Inevitably, some colonists became wealthier and more powerful than the rest, establishing in Southern colonies like Virginia an elite of local gentry, and in ports like Boston and New York a class of wealthy merchants and lawyers. But life in all the colonies, though following English ways, remained freer and less structured than anything in England.

Politics also were English in outward form but different in practice. The constitutions of the colonies were based on the traditions of representative government in England, which had been wrested from the Crown over many generations, particularly at the time of the English Civil War of the 1640s. Each colony was self-governing, owing its allegiance ultimately to the Sovereign. A governor usually represented the King, with an appointed council and an elected assembly taking the place of the two houses of the British Parliament. As the lower houses expanded their powers throughout the colonies they justified themselves by British precedent. The Massachusetts Assembly reminded its governor in the 1760s, "This house has the same inherent rights in this province as the House of Commons has in Great Britain."[2]

The franchise followed the English pattern. Only males who

were owners of freehold property could vote. In England this limited their numbers, but in the colonies most settlers owned their land and so were entitled to vote. The result was a franchise more liberal than anywhere in Europe. Even those who traveled as indentured servants, with their sea passage paid on condition they worked for a master for a period, were often given freehold property when their contracts expired after five or seven years. By 1750 between half and three-quarters of the white male colonists were enfranchised. In England, the most politically advanced European nation, the proportion was still only one in five.

In other ways British America was developing its own distinctive character as the eighteenth century progressed. A majority of colonists were still of English, Scottish or Welsh stock, but the first national census of 1790 revealed that already nearly a third of the white population was non-British, mainly Irish, German or Dutch. One-fifth of the total population was black, mostly slaves imported from West Africa to work on the tobacco and rice plantations of the South.

In 1775, less than two centuries after the first settlements, there were two and a half million people living in eighteen British colonies, which now stretched 1,600 miles down the Atlantic seaboard from the mist-clad Bay of Fundy to the steamy Florida swamps and had begun to push their way into the wild interior. The population of the colonies was already one-third the size of England and Wales.*

The seeds of independence had been sown. The American colonists were freer and more diverse in character than the people of England, and they were growing in numbers and wealth. Yet most still thought of themselves as Englishmen. They certainly had little sense of any common identity as Americans. Their horizons were local, communications primitive. Loyalties hardly extended beyond the immediate community and there were bitter rivalries between individual colonies. New England colonies, such as Massachusetts and Connecticut, influenced by their heritage of Puritanism and local self-government, differed markedly from Southern colonies like Virginia or South Carolina, where the power of the Anglican Church and the big landowners, or planters, predominated. On the

---

*Of these eighteen colonies, thirteen declared their independence in 1776. Of the remainder, East Florida and West Florida were ceded by Britain to Spain in 1783 (and later acquired by the United States), while Quebec, Nova Scotia and Newfoundland formed the nucleus of the future Canada.

edge of the British world, looking back across the ocean for their values and their identity, they were held together by the authority of the British Crown.

To begin with, the colonies were governed indulgently from London, but not out of generosity on the part of British kings, whose priorities lay elsewhere. As long as the American colonies caused no trouble and did not make demands on the British Exchequer their relative independence was tolerated. In the first half of the eighteenth century Britain was more concerned with the struggle for empire between herself and her two European arch-rivals, France and Spain.

While the British were colonizing the Eastern seaboard of America the French were active farther west. They were protecting their fur trade by a line of forts and by alliances with Indian tribes extending from the St. Lawrence River to the Great Lakes, down the waterways of the Ohio and Mississippi rivers all the way to New Orleans. At the outbreak of the Seven Years War (1756–63)—or the French and Indian Wars, as they are known in the United States—the British colonists played their part by attacking the French, who were preventing their expansion westward. A succession of British victories, including General James Wolfe's at Quebec in 1759, secured for Britain all Canada and all the French possessions east of the Mississippi. The peace treaty, signed in Paris in 1763, made Britain the dominant power in North America, and ultimately guaranteed that it would be she, not France, who exerted the formative influence on the future United States of America.

Even at the time the significance of Britain's victory was apparent. Four years after the war was over Edward Gibbon was embarking on his great history of *The Decline and Fall of the Roman Empire*. He planned to write in French, generally accepted as the language of civilization. The Scottish philosopher David Hume dissuaded him: "Let the French triumph in the present diffusion of their tongue. Our solid and increasing establishments in America . . . promise a superior stability and duration to the English language."[3] In 1770 Ezra Stiles, a future president of Yale College, confidently predicted that English would "become the vernacular tongue of more people than any one tongue on Earth, except the Chinese."[4]

British successes in the Seven Years War were not confined to North America. France's navy had been destroyed and her colonies in India conquered. The British Empire had doubled in size, but the costs of its capture and subsequent administration were heavy burdens. The national debt had risen to nearly twice its prewar level, at £130 million, and interest charges of over £4 million had to be found each year. There was no scope for further taxation in Britain, and the government decided that the American colonies, until now virtually free of the burdens of taxation, should contribute to the cost of victory and of the army being maintained in America for the colonists' protection. The various forms of taxation proposed by Britain, whether stamp duties, taxes on sugar or tea, or levies on trade, were not onerous, but they alarmed merchants, lawyers and tradesmen suffering from the postwar economic depression. These professional men argued that since they were not represented in the British Parliament at Westminster it had no right to tax them. Banding themselves into organizations called the Sons of Liberty, they incited mobs to attack the homes and sometimes the persons of the British administrators responsible for collecting the taxes.

The protesters were not looking for independence from Britain. As "freeborn Englishmen" they wanted the principle of "No taxation without Representation," a right won in Britain a century earlier, to be accepted in the colonies. Had wiser policies been pursued by successive British governments the crisis might have been averted. But London reacted firmly to suppress dissent and restore its authority, by insisting that the taxes be paid and by refusing to consult the colonial assemblies. The colonists foresaw a grim future if Britain was successful. She would tap the increasing prosperity of America to finance her European wars and would do so without consent. By 1775 many were convinced that they faced an organized conspiracy to suppress their liberties. In the words of the young Alexander Hamilton, later to be the financial genius of the new republic, the British King George III now had "a settled, fixed plan for *enslaving* the colonies."[5]

After several months of protest, rioting and skirmishes between the colonists and British troops, an entire British army of over thirty thousand men landed near New York to restore order. It was July 4, 1776. On the same day, in Philadelphia, a Congress of the thirteen leading colonies approved a Declaration of Independence, largely written by the Virginian planter Thomas Jefferson. It described in clear, vivid words the nature of the contract between governor and governed, expressing this relationship in the most revolutionary form yet seen. The old political structure of Britain, with its authority derived from the Crown, was rejected in favor of a system in which men would decide for themselves how they would be governed. The traditional rights of freeborn Englishmen, to which the colonists had appealed in the past, were now rejected in favor of an appeal to the natural rights of all humanity:

> We hold these truths to be self-evident, that all men are created equal, that they are endowed by their Creator with certain unalienable Rights, that among these are Life, Liberty and the pursuit of Happiness. That to secure these rights, Governments are instituted among Men, deriving their just powers from the consent of the governed. That whenever any form of government becomes destructive of these ends, it is the Right of the People to alter or to abolish it and to institute new Government. . . .

The Declaration went on to argue that George III's "repeated injuries and usurpations" had imperiled the rights of his people, and concluded "that these United Colonies are, and of Right ought to be, FREE AND INDEPENDENT STATES; that they are Absolved from all Allegiance to the British Crown."[6]

The war for independence lasted seven years from 1776 to 1783. Britain suffered from her extended lines of supply across the Atlantic, from poor generalship, and from impenetrable terrain. Despite George Washington's stalwart leadership, the United States, as they now called themselves, were often short of resources and food, and lacked a clear strategy. But ultimately it was Britain's old enemies, France and Spain, who ensured her defeat by lending their support to the Revolution. France saw an opportunity for harrying Britain in the Caribbean and the Indian Ocean, and even threatened to invade England herself. By 1781 even the Dutch, Britain's old allies, were on the enemy side and the Royal Navy had lost control of the Atlantic. Britain's armies in America were cut off and, after the humiliating surrender of General Cornwallis's troops at Yorktown, were forced to cut their losses and sue for peace. The terms of the peace treaty in 1783 were generous to the new American nation. They acknowledged its independence and granted it borders up to the Great Lakes and the Mississippi.

America won independence as a loose alliance of separate states, but it soon became apparent that they would need a proper national government in order to survive. The Founding Fathers who met in Philadelphia in 1787 to draw up a new Constitution had no intention of replacing one form of tyranny with another, of setting up a powerful central government to dominate them as George III had done. They therefore chose a federal system: the national government was instituted mainly for defense, diplomacy and to meet basic economic needs, such as the provision of a currency and a postal service. State governments retained authority over most areas of daily life. The two houses of the U.S. Congress were also structured to protect the rights of the states. In the House of Representatives populous states were allowed to elect more members, but in the upper house, the Senate, each state, regardless of size, was allowed two senators to protect the interests of minorities.

The new government was a republic. After their experience under George III the Americans were determined to prevent monarchy returning under another name. The president was allowed only limited authority as head of state and commander in chief of the armed forces. To prevent the emergence of a British-style prime minister, whose control over the legislature gave him a relatively free hand to run affairs, neither the president nor any other member of the executive branch of government could be members of Congress. Congress and president were chosen separately, so that a president could never be sure that he would have sufficient support to do what he wanted. And the Congress was given substantial authority of its own—for example, to approve senior executive appointments and, in the case of the Senate, to ratify treaties. This principle of separating the powers of government, ensuring checks and balances between the executive, the legislature and the judiciary, was a profound innovation, and one that would shape America's future history and its relations with Britain. As later British governments were to discover, Congress could prevent an American president from delivering what he had promised.

In name the United States of America was now an independent nation with its own unique government. But in reality it would be many years before America could feel itself truly free of Britain. For the British acted swiftly to restore their control over the seas, temporarily lost in the 1780s. They imposed restrictions on the use of American ships on key sugar trade routes with her colonies in the Caribbean. Britain also retained control of all North America above the Great Lakes, and was slow to withdraw from the forts in the American Northwest that she had conceded in 1783. The states of the new Union, impoverished by war, feared the possibility of a British campaign of reconquest.

The list of American grievances against the British grew when

Britain and France renewed hostilities in the 1790s. Soon Britain was threatened with economic strangulation by Napoleon. She responded ruthlessly to her enemy's attempt to control the seas, claiming the right to board neutral ships and confiscate goods bound for enemy ports. American shipowners, who were prospering from the wartime trade, protested. They were even angrier when Britain claimed the right to seize British-born seamen from these ships and impress them into the Royal Navy, regardless of whether or not they had taken up American citizenship. These irritations were compounded by the clamor from settlers in the American Northwest to attack British Canada, and from Southerners to use the opportunity to push America's boundaries south into Florida, now controlled by Spain, who had become allied with Britain against Napoleon.

In June 1812 the Congress was asked by President James Madison whether Americans should "continue passive under these progressive usurpations and these accumulating wrongs, or, opposing force to force in defense of their national rights, shall commit a just cause into the hands of the Almighty. . . ."[7] Congress decided to declare war on Britain. It was a near disaster for the United States. The attempted invasion of Canada was a failure. The New England states, which had opposed the war, threatened to secede from the Union. In August 1814 British troops even sacked the American capital, Washington, and Madison and his wife barely had time to escape. The British commander, Admiral George Cockburn, found the table at the President's house set for dinner, with wine, in coolers of ice, ready to be served. After availing themselves of the Madisons' unintended hospitality, the British officers selected a few souvenirs, Cockburn taking one of the President's hats and a cushion from his wife's chair, and then left the house to be looted and fired by their soldiers. The new republic was humiliated, but this was just the way of war. The British were taking revenge for the burning of York (now Toronto), which was the capital of Canada.

The transatlantic conflict was a sideshow for Britain compared with the European war, and once Napoleon was defeated, she was ready to make peace. Despite subsequent crises, despite rivalry and suspicion, these two countries henceforth managed to settle their differences peacefully. Few great powers have been so successful. But the war of 1812 gave American nationalism a sharply anti-British edge. The President's house was painted white to cover the

BROTHER JONATHAN *Administering a Salutary Cordial to* JOHN BULL.

American cartoonist Amos Doolittle sees the war as a chance for Jonathan (the U.S.A.) to teach John Bull a lesson. (1813.)

scorch marks, hence its future name, and subsequent British visitors, to this day, are firmly reminded of the reason. Out of the conflict also came a national anthem, "The Star-Spangled Banner," composed at a critical moment during the British siege of Baltimore.

The Napoleonic wars had confirmed the extent of Britain's power. Putting the loss of her American colonies behind her, she carved out a new empire in India, Australia and New Zealand. By the mid-nineteenth century she was producing 40 percent of the world's manufactured goods and importing over a third of the world's trade. Sterling was becoming as acceptable as gold, and the City of London emerged as the main source of international investment. Meanwhile America remained a colony of Britain in economic terms. It had little industry of its own, mainly selling primary products to Britain and buying manufactured goods in return. Between 1820 and 1860 nearly half of America's exports went to Britain, and 40 percent of American imports came from Britain. The trade was largely funded by great British banking houses, such as Barings, which also supplied much of the capital for developing America's transport system: roads, canals, bridges and, above all, the railroads that opened up the West.

Despite independence, then, the young United States lived in the shadow of Britain. America's military and economic weakness dictated a cautious foreign policy. President George Washington in his farewell address of 1796 had warned his fellow countrymen to beware of "the insidious wiles of foreign influence." Europe, he wrote, "has a set of primary interests which to us have none or a very remote relation. Hence, she must be engaged in frequent controversies, the causes of which are essentially foreign to our concerns." Washington did not suggest that America should sever trading connections with other countries. Nor did he rule out temporary alliances at times of crisis. But there should be no extension of these ties. "Steer clear of permanent alliances with any portion of the foreign world," he advised.[8] The policy was defined succinctly by Thomas Jefferson in 1801: "peace, commerce, and honest friendship with all nations—entangling alliances with none."[9]

The first serious test of these precepts came in 1823. In the 1810s Spain's colonies in South America were in revolt. To the delight of many Americans, who saw events there as the next stage of their own revolution of 1776, the Spanish were gradually forced out. But in 1823 there were fears that Spain, supported by France and Russia, might attempt reconquest. Britain, who had developed a profitable trade with these newly independent countries, was keen to prevent Spain's return. Foreign Secretary George Canning suggested to the American president, James Monroe, that they form an alliance to resist the Continental powers.

There followed a lively debate among America's leaders. Two former presidents, Jefferson and Madison, swallowed their suspicions of Britain and urged acceptance of the offer. Jefferson advised that "Great Britain is the nation which can do us the most harm of any one, or all on earth, and with her on our side we need not fear the whole world."[10] But John Quincy Adams, the secretary of state, urged an independent course. "It would be more candid, as well as more dignified," he told Monroe's Cabinet, "to avow our principles explicitly to Russia and France, than to come in as a cock-boat in the wake of the British man-of-war."[11]

The advice was accepted. America remained true to the principle of no entangling alliances, of acting alone. In December 1823, Monroe publicly warned Spain and her allies that "we should consider any attempt on their part to extend their system to any portion of this hemisphere as dangerous to our peace and safety." Although his statement did not apply to "the existing colonies or dependencies of any European power," he warned that interference with a state that the United States of America had recognized as independent would be regarded as "the manifestation of an unfriendly disposition toward the United States." The Monroe Doctrine, as it became known, was of immense importance for the future of American diplomacy. It laid claim to a special area of interest on the American continent, both North and South, in which the United States would brook no interference. It was a warning to the continental powers of Europe and to Britain to keep out, just as the United States promised not to "interfere in the internal concerns" of the Europeans.[12]

The declaration of such a policy from the young nation seemed preposterous. If Spain and her allies had gone to war, the United States could not have maintained the Monroe Doctrine without the help of the Royal Navy. But Britain was gratified that although refusing to join in an alliance, America had at least acted in parallel with her by opposing Spain. Canning claimed later that he had "called the New World into existence to redress the balance of the Old."[13]

The attempt to define American interests and values as the opposite of Britain's was natural for a hypersensitive ex-colony. The Britain from which Americans had rebelled was depicted by them as the land of monarchy, aristocracy and privilege, of imperial oppression and military might, of luxury, frivolity and corruption—in short, as the source of all evils. Thomas Jefferson once called its inhabitants "rich, proud, hectoring, swearing, squibbling, carnivorous animals" and contrasted them with "the polite, self-denying, feeling, hospitable, goodhumoured" people of America.[14] American nationalists wanted their new country to create its own culture to emphasize its separation. Noah Webster, author of the famous dictionary, even called for a new language: "As an independent nation, our honor requires us to have a system of our own, in language as government." He predicted that in time North America would speak a language "as different from the future language of England, as the modern Dutch, Danish and Swedish are from the German, or from one another."[15]

All this was part of the process of building a separate nation, by defining its identify as a New World an ocean apart from the Old. British visitors in the early nineteenth century often remarked on the Americans' inveterate habit of boasting about their nation's real and imagined achievements and deriding everything British. Sydney Smith, the English writer and wit, tried to put them firmly in their place in 1820:

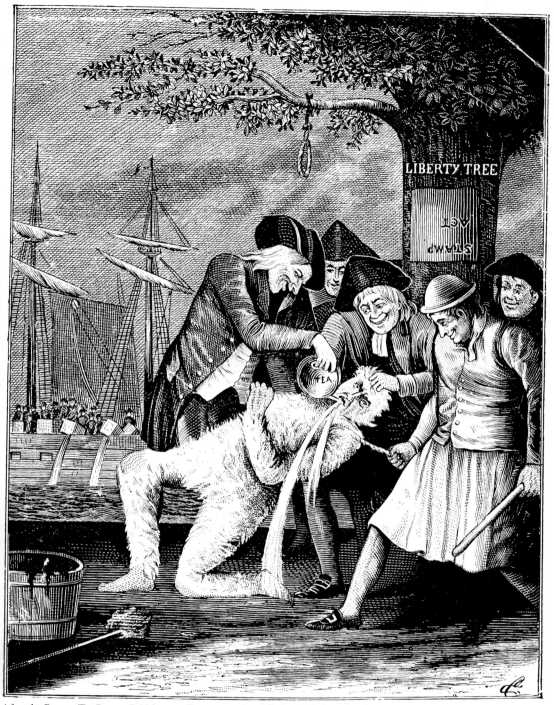

After the Boston Tea Party a British tax collector, tarred and feathered, is forced to drink British tea. Cartoon of 1774. *Peter Newark's Western Americana*

John Trumbull's impression of the signing of the Declaration of Independence. Jefferson in red waistcoat.
Bridgeman Art Library

The beginning of Thomas Jefferson's rough draft of the Declaration of Independence. *BBC Hulton Picture Library*

A Declaration by the Representatives of the UNITED STATE OF AMERICA, in General Congress assembled.

When in the course of human events it becomes necessary for one people to dissolve the political bands which have connected them with another, and to ~~assume~~ ~~sume~~ among the powers of the earth the separate and equal station to which the laws of nature & of nature's god entitle them, a decent respect to the opinions of mankind requires that they should declare the causes which impel them to the separation.

We hold these truths to be self-evident; that all men are created equal, that they are endowed by their creator with certain inherent & inalienable rights; that among these are life, & liberty, & the pursuit of happiness; that to secure these rights, governments are instituted among men, deriving their just powers fro...

Quebec fell to the British in 1759. Canada stayed loyal to the Crown after 1776. *National Army Museum, London*

An artist's impression of the burning of Washington by the British in 1814. *Mary Evans Picture Library*

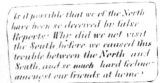

SLAVERY AS IT EXISTS IN AMERICA.

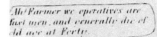

SLAVERY AS IT   **EXISTS IN ENGLAND.**

—THOMPSON—

THE ENGLISH ANTI-SLAVERY AGITATOR.

Defenders of slavery in the American South attack factory slavery in supposedly liberal England (1850).
London University Library

Sargent's portrait of Charles, ninth Duke of Marlborough, and his American wife, formerly Consuelo Vanderbilt. *His Grace the Duke of Marlborough*

J. Pierpont Morgan, Sr. (1837-1913), founder of the great Wall Street banking firm. *BBC Hulton Picture Library*

Automobiles rolling off an early Ford assembly line. *Peter Newark's Western Americana*

Queenstown, 7. Mai 1915.
Der Cunarddampfer „Luſitania" iſt torpediert worden und geſunken.

Admiral Tirpitz, founder of the German navy, gloats over the sinking of the *Lusitania* in this German postcard.
BBC Hulton Picture Library

Some of the *Lusitania's* dead buried in Queenstown, Ireland (May 1915). *BBC Hulton Picture Library*

President Woodrow Wilson (left) and his close adviser Colonel Edward House. *Wilson's photo: BBC Hulton Picture Library / UPI / Bettmann Newsphotos; House's photo: BBC Hulton Picture Library*

New York women campaign for Wilson's reelection (November 1916) on an antiwar platform. *BBC Hulton Picture Library / UPI / Bettmann Newsphotos*

April 2, 1917: President Wilson asks Congress to declare war on Germany. *Imperial War Museum, London*

American troops in London, led by the band of the Welsh Guards (August 1917). *BBC Hulton Picture Library*

General John J. Pershing (left center) and King George V (right center) review American troops. *Imperial War Museum, London*

> In the four quarters of the globe, who reads an American book? or
> goes to an American play? or looks at an American picture or statue?
> What does the world yet owe to American physicians or surgeons?
> What new substances have their chemists discovered? or what old
> ones have they analyzed? What new constellations have been discov-
> ered by the telescopes of Americans? What have they done in mathe-
> matics? Who drinks out of American glasses? or eats from American
> plates? or wears American coats or gowns? or sleeps in American
> blankets? Finally, under which of the old tyrannical governments of
> Europe is every sixth man a Slave, whom his fellow-creatures may
> buy and sell and torture?[16]

To such criticism Americans were acutely sensitive. The English
novelist Frances Trollope commented in 1832 that "other nations
have been called thin-skinned, but the citizens of the Union have,
apparently, no skins at all; they wince if a breeze blows over them,
unless it be tempered with adulation."[17]

But, for all the rhetoric and exaggeration, American nationalists
were right to claim that their country was developing a distinctive
character as the nineteenth century progressed. Even in the colonial period it had attracted many non-English immigrants, and the
flow became more pronounced after independence. Between 1815
and 1860 five million Europeans migrated to the United States, of
whom nearly two-thirds came from Ireland and the German
states, driven out by famine or repression. Many were not Protestants but Roman Catholics, with their own dialects, customs and
religious practices. They settled in the North and Midwest, giving cities like New York and St. Louis a distinctly un-English
character.

Equally unique was the rapid democratization of America. The
Founding Fathers were mostly elitists, who believed that the popu-
lace should be kept in its place. But by the 1830s the old property-
owning franchises had been abolished and nearly all white adult
males had the vote. They were now able to elect not merely members of the U.S. Congress and their state assemblies but also their
head of state, the president. Elections were fiercely contested: in
1840 80 percent of the electorate voted in the battle for the presidency. And around them developed the razzmatazz of electioneer-
ing, with banners, slogans, parades and organized grass-roots
political parties. The idea that ordinary people should choose their

government was an audacious experiment. It was another half-century or more before it began to take root in the monarchies of Europe.

But democracy was more than a system of government. Its egalitarian values permeated the whole of American society. Alexis de Tocqueville, author of the classic work *Democracy in America* and the most perceptive European observer of the pre–Civil War era, considered "the equality of conditions" to be "the basic fact," the most striking "novelty," about the United States.[18] De Tocqueville exaggerated. In the big cities of the Northeast the top 1 percent of the population owned about a quarter of the wealth in the 1820s. But he was broadly correct, especially about rural areas. Compared with Europe, America was more egalitarian, its social structure less ossified. There was no hereditary aristocracy dominating national politics and social life. The greater availability of land enabled people to move around more easily and to shape their own fortunes. Even Americans entering what in Britain would be called domestic service retained their "innate sentiment of independence," according to Thomas Grattan, the British traveler. "They satisfy themselves that they are *helps,* not servants—that they are going to work with (not for) Mr so and so. . . . they call him and his wife their *employers,* not their master and mistress."[19]

By the 1830s American-style democracy was becoming an issue in British politics. The emerging middle classes cited the American example in their campaigns for the vote, free trade and a system of publicly financed education. The United States, claimed John Stuart Mill, showed how a country could develop when the middle class was given free rein. He asked his readers in 1840 "whether, with the single difference of our remaining respect for aristocracy, the American people, both in their good qualities and in their defects, resemble anything so much as our own middle class?"[20] Radical democrats like the Chartists went further, claiming that "what democracy is in practice, we are now able to show to the appalled aristocrats. Look across the Atlantic. There we see a great nation springing up as no other people ever did; there we see millions of contented and happy human beings. . . . there we see representative self-government doing for the nation what no other government did or ever can do."[21]

Conservatives countered by indicting America as a horrifying example of a society in which the principle of aristocracy, rule by the best, had been replaced by the pursuit of money and mob popu-

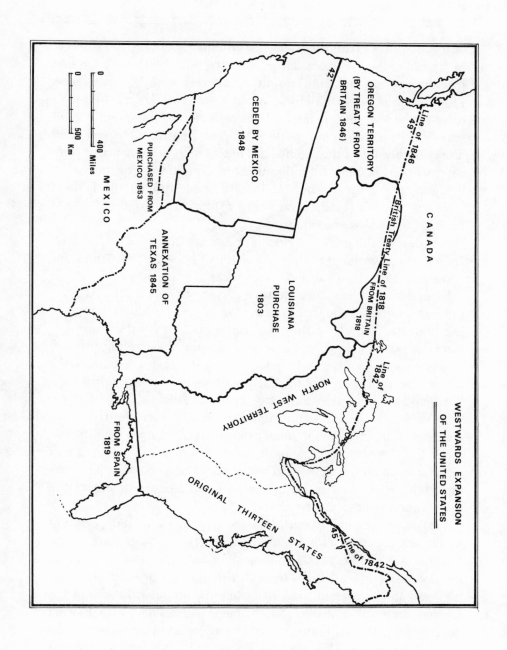

WESTWARDS EXPANSION
OF THE UNITED STATES

OREGON TERRITORY
(BY TREATY FROM
BRITAIN 1846)

CEDED BY MEXICO
1848

PURCHASED FROM
MEXICO 1853

MEXICO

ANNEXATION OF
TEXAS 1845

LOUISIANA
PURCHASE
1803

FROM SPAIN
1819

NORTH WEST TERRITORY

ORIGINAL THIRTEEN STATES

CANADA

Line of 1846
49°

British Treaty Line of 1818
FROM BRITAIN
1818

Line of
1842

45°
Line of 1842

42°

0
500
400
Km
Miles
0

larity. Thomas Hamilton, who toured America in 1830–31, wrote of its politics: "No man can even enter public life without first truckling to the mob, and too often paltering with his conscience. He must profess—often falsely profess—to entertain all the prejudices of the ignorant men by whom he is elected. He goes to Congress with a halter round his neck."[22] And Benjamin Disraeli, then Tory Chancellor of the Exchequer, but soon to become prime minister, warned in 1866: "If a dominant multitude were to succeed in bringing the land of England into the condition of the land in America . . . England, from being a first-rate Kingdom, would become a third-rate Republic."[23]

But despite the growing British debate about democracy, America was still peripheral to Britain's vision of herself. And Americans were not, as yet, concerned about recasting the outside world in their mold. They saw their destiny as lying not across the Atlantic but to the west, in the vast prairies, forests and mountain ranges of the hinterland. In 1800 this was still controlled by the European imperial powers, France, Spain and Britain, and by the original inhabitants, the American Indians. During the next half-century the new republic broke out of the Eastern corridor in which it had been born, and established its authority from the Atlantic to the Pacific. The West, like Britain's empire, was won by bribery, intrigue and war, not to mention the gradual extermination of its Indian inhabitants. But that was not how most Americans saw it. To them it was America's "manifest destiny to overspread and to possess the continent which Providence has given us for the development of the great experiment of Liberty."[24]

France was the first to withdraw from America. In 1803, needing to finance the war with Britain, Napoleon sold Louisiana to the United States. The $11.25 million purchase price was, ironically, mainly raised through loans from British banks. The acquisition, far bigger than the present State of Louisiana, doubled the size of the United States at a stroke. Next Spain was driven from Florida during the 1810s. Its Latin American empire also collapsed, leaving a vast independent Mexican state along the United States' southern and western borders. This was quickly cut down to size by the aggressive expansionist policy of President James Polk. Texas broke away from Mexico and in 1845 was annexed to the United States. War with Mexico followed over border claims, and by 1848 the modern southern boundaries of the United States had been virtually fixed. Territory that later became the U.S. states of Arizona, Utah, Nevada, New Mexico and California, all previously part of Mexico, joined the Union.

Britain, alone of the former colonial powers, remained in North America, refusing to relinquish her hold on the Canadian territories. In 1839 there was a war scare over Canada's boundary with Maine. American nationalists sang:

> *"Britannia shall not rule the Maine,*
> *Nor shall she rule the water;*
> *They've sung that song full long enough,*
> *Much longer than they oughter."*[25]

That issue was settled by negotiation in 1842, only to be followed by a new dispute farther west in Oregon Territory. Finally, in 1846, Polk and the British foreign secretary, Lord Aberdeen, agreed that the border between Canada and the United States should follow the forty-ninth parallel, 49 degrees latitude, all the way to the Pacific. Many Americans still resented any British presence in North America, but henceforth the Canadian border was no longer an issue between the two powers.

The United States had grown to nearly three million square miles, fifty times the size of England and Wales. It extended some three thousand miles from coast to coast; on a map of Europe the equivalent journey would be from the Pyrenees to the Ural Mountains. Even before the Mexican war America's population of seventeen million exceeded Britain's, and it was growing at a prodigious rate. De Tocqueville predicted that one day America and Russia would each "hold in its hands the destinies of half the world."[26]

But could this vast country hold together? Or would the United States tear itself apart? Those questions became central to American politics in the 1850s, for the great expansion to the Pacific had reopened an old and bitter argument about whether slavery would be permitted in the new territories of the West. The crisis led to a civil war that could have permanently divided the United States into two separate countries. It was not, at least initially, an issue of morality, a struggle for the rights of black people, but a battle for political power.

Slave owning, once widespread throughout America, was by

"WHAT! YOU YOUNG YANKEE-NOODLE, STRIKE YOUR OWN FATHER!"

The British magazine Punch *ridicules America's impertinence in standing up
to Britain over Oregon in 1846.*

1850 confined to the Southern states, where it had become essential
to the big cotton plantations on which the wealth of the Southern
aristocracy depended. Few Northerners endorsed the rights of
blacks to be free and equal citizens of the United States. On the
contrary, many opponents of slavery, including Abraham Lincoln,
thought the best solution to America's race problem would be to
deport former slaves to Africa. Northerners were more concerned

about what they called "the slave power": slavery supported what seemed to them a fossilized social and political system. Its aristocratic, hierarchical nature seemed inimical to the egalitarian, democratic values that Northerners believed set America apart from Europe. A new "Republican" party emerged in the North in 1854 to champion these principles under the slogan "Free soil, free labor, free men."

To allow slavery into the West would be an offense to Republican ideals. It would also compete with the opportunities there for white labor. New slave states would increase the support for aristocratic values in the U.S. Senate, where each state had two senators, regardless of size, and where the South would therefore be able to block the wishes of the Northern majority. Southerners, too, were concerned about the balance of power in Washington. If free states made up more than two-thirds of the Senate, slavery could be abolished by an amendment to the Constitution. Although three-quarters of white families in the South did not own slaves and therefore did not have a direct stake in the system, they were convinced that emancipation would mean racial violence and social revolution, sweeping away the rights of all whites. A Georgia newspaper called the Republican party "hideous, revolting, loathsome, a menace . . . to Society, to Liberty, and to Law. . . . its decrees but the will of a wild mob."[27]

By 1860 one Southern senator commented that relations between Northerners and Southerners in Congress had virtually ceased to exist. "No two nations on earth are or ever were more distinctly separated and hostile than we are here. . . . How can the thing go on?"[28] In November 1860 the Republican Abraham Lincoln won the presidential election, almost entirely thanks to Northern votes. North and South were so estranged by now that many Southerners were convinced that this heralded the total abolition of slavery. Immediately the states of the Deep South announced their secession from the Union, claiming the same rights to form a government as their forefathers had asserted against Britain in 1776. When Lincoln used force against them in April 1861, the upper South, led by Virginia, joined the rebellion. The Confederate States of America was born.

Britain's role in the war that followed was denounced throughout the North. She began by declaring her neutrality, arguing that the ethical issues behind the war were unclear. In 1861 the Unionists did not claim to be conducting an antislavery crusade. Lincoln

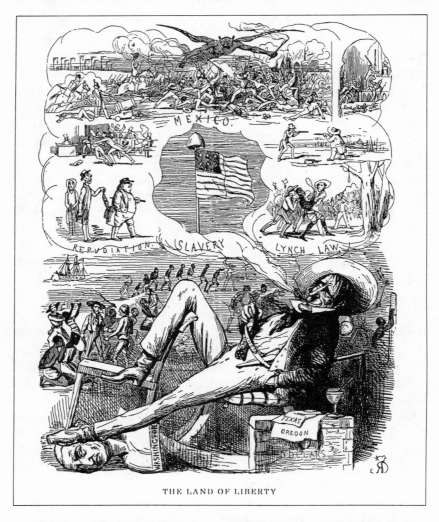

THE LAND OF LIBERTY

A British cartoonist of the mid-nineteenth century scoffs at America's claim to moral superiority.

began his inaugural address with the pledge "I have no purpose, directly or indirectly, to interfere with the institution of slavery in the States where it exists."[29] Many English liberals, including Gladstone, saw the South's cause as a war for national liberation like the recent secession of the Italian states from Austria's Hapsburg empire. "They are fighting not for SLAVERY but for INDEPENDENCE," insisted William Squier, a Unitarian minister in Preston, England, an active supporter of the antislavery movement.[30]

There were practical as well as moral objections to Britain's supporting the North. Eighty percent of British cotton, the raw material that kept Lancashire's mills at work and supported a textile industry employing four million people, came from the Southern states. In America Northerners scorned Britain's apparently mercenary motives. A New York magazine parodied her national anthem:

> *God save me, great John Bull!*
> *Long keep my pockets full!*
> *Great John Bull!*
> *Ever victorious,*
> *Haughty, vainglorious,*
> *Snobbish, censorious,*
> *Great John Bull!*[31]

By the end of 1861 the two countries seemed close to war. A Northern warship, the *San Jacinto*, had stopped a British mail steamer, the *Trent*, off Cuba and seized two Confederate diplomats on their way to drum up support in Europe. The captain of the *San Jacinto*, Charles Wilkes, became an overnight hero in the North and was awarded a gold medal by Congress. But British opinion was incensed by the violation of international law and by the affront to Britain's naval supremacy. The prime minister, Lord Palmerston, began a Cabinet meeting by throwing his hat down on the table and telling his colleagues: "I don't know whether you are going to stand this, but I'll be damned if I do."[32] The British government demanded an immediate apology from Washington and the release of the diplomats. As war fever mounted, British reinforcements were sent to Canada and plans were drawn up for an invasion south into Maine. The Union could ill afford a conflict with Britain as well as the Confederacy. Over Christmas 1861 Lincoln's administration backed down. It released the two diplomats and offered an explanation (though not an apology) for Wilkes's action. Palmerston deemed that sufficient, but Northerners were raw at their humiliation.

Britain was engaged in the same deadly game that America had played during the war with Napoleon. The British now wanted to maintain normal commercial business, while the United States was determined to enforce the tightest possible blockade. Britain's continued trade with the Confederacy incensed the North. They were particularly furious at the construction of warships for the South in British yards. The most notorious of these, the *Alabama*, was built by Laird's of Birkenhead in the winter of 1861–62. She sank nearly sixty Unionist vessels in less than two years before herself being destroyed.

A year later, in the summer of 1862, Britain turned from neutrality to covert support for the South. British opinion was appalled by the scale of the casualties in this first modern war, in which the Seven Days' Battle in June had left 36,000 dead or injured. Palmerston, impressed by the South's survival, speculated publicly on whether this was "the moment when it can be thought that a successful offer of mediation could be made to the two parties?"[33] Over the next two months his government explored the possibility of a joint approach with France and Russia to end the bloodbath and secure a negotiated peace. This would have led to two separate American states, the Union and the Confederacy.

But the tide now turned against the South. In September 1862, at the Battle of Antietam, Robert E. Lee's army was forced to end its invasion of the North. In the same month Abraham Lincoln issued a proclamation emancipating all slaves. The practical advantage was the desertion of thousands of slaves from their plantations to join the Unionist armies as guides, spies, road builders and fighting soldiers.

With the South in retreat and the Northern cause assuming a moral superiority in the eyes of the world, no more was heard of British attempts at mediation. The war finally ended in April 1865 with large tracts of the South laid waste and the Confederate states under military occupation. The total death toll was 620,000, greater than the losses America suffered in the first and second world wars combined. The Union, however, had survived, its Constitution intact, its republican values strengthened, its distrust of Britain confirmed. In 1864 the British minister in Washington, Lord Lyons, believed that "three-fourths of the American people are eagerly longing for a safe opportunity of making war with England. . . ."[34] Northern resentment would take several decades to abate.

America had started life as a collection of English settlements on the extremities of the British Empire. In less than two centuries it had broken away from British rule. Yet it took the new nation many decades after 1776 to establish true independence. Economically and culturally America remained almost a British colony. Britain and other European empires hedged it in to the north, west and south. Only with the winning of the West was America great enough to stand alone; only after the South's bid for independence had been crushed was it clear that this vast, prosperous, energetic country could remain united. Now Britain, the world's greatest power, had to face the fact that her errant offspring had grown to maturity. For parent, as for child, it was to prove a difficult process.

CHAPTER 2

LEARNING TO
LIVE TOGETHER
c. 1865–1914

Nineteenth-century Englishmen tended to think of America as a version of their own country. As the Boston writer James Russell Lowell commented in 1869, to them the American was "a kind of counterfeit Briton . . . a kind of inferior and deported Englishman."[1] Americans, on the other hand, were prone to exaggerate the differences. "The youth of America is their oldest tradition," scoffed the playwright Oscar Wilde in 1893. "It has been going on now for three hundred years."[2]

The truth lay in between. America had established its identity as a nation by claiming to be a new country, quite unlike Britain. It did so self-consciously, often aggressively, as children react against their parents. Although the United States developed a distinctive character as the nineteenth century progressed—democratic, a mix of ethnic groups, with a weak central government—there were still obvious family resemblances to the mother country. America had more in common with Britain than with the countries of continental Europe, similarities that were to help the two countries build a closer, more equal relationship as the twentieth century dawned and that laid the basis for their cooperation in two world wars.

In spite of the increasing racial variety of America during the nineteenth century, with immigrants speaking most of the languages of Western Europe, English remained the official language of the United States and newcomers were obliged to learn it. Until the 1890s the largest groups of immigrants were still English speakers, from Ireland, Canada and Australasia, as well as Britain. Every nineteenth-century president was of British stock, except Martin Van Buren (1837–41), whose Dutch family emigrated in 1631.*

A common language and personal ties made possible a steady flow of people and ideas in both directions across the Atlantic, particularly when the steamship, introduced in the 1840s, reduced the voyage from two months to two weeks. Would-be reformers in Britain and America drew particularly close. When, after years of pressure in and outside Parliament, slavery had been brought to an end throughout the British Empire by 1833, the campaigners turned their attention to America. The dying Methodist leader John Wesley had urged William Wilberforce: "Go on, in the Name of God and in the power of His might, till even American slavery, the vilest that ever saw the sun, shall vanish away before you." Across the Atlantic their support was warmly welcomed by American abolitionists. The former slave Frederick Douglass observed that "the growing intercourse between England and this country by means of steam-navigation . . . gives us an opportunity to bring in the aid . . . of those living on the other side of the Atlantic. . . . We entreat our British friends to continue to send in their remonstrances across the deep against slavery in this land."[3]

Equally powerful were the bonds between peace crusaders in 1846, during the crisis between Britain and America over Oregon. Their inspiration was Elihu Burritt, the self-styled "Learned Blacksmith" of Worcester, Massachusetts, who organized a grass-roots protest against the possibility of war. Within six months of its foundation his League of Universal Brotherhood had thirty thousand members in England and twenty-five thousand in America. Mass petitions, known as Friendly Addresses, were exchanged between British and American towns with similar names or similar industries. Replying to one from Manchester, England, four hundred New York merchants wrote: "As a matter of profit and loss, it would be infinitely better that the whole of Oregon should sink into the bottom of the ocean than that two such nations as Great Britain and the United States should go to war about it, to the disgrace of civilization, Christianity, and rational freedom."[4]

---

*Van Buren had the distinction of being the first president born an American citizen. His predecessors, all being born before the War of Independence, began life as British subjects.

The tides of reform and philanthropy that ebbed and flowed across the Atlantic in the mid-nineteenth century showed that the ocean was not an insuperable barrier between the two countries. They were signs of a deeper current pulling America and Britain together in a turbulent world. For both countries increasingly stood out as examples of liberal values in an era when most civilized countries were still dominated by monarchy, aristocracy and a reactionary Church. To be sure, British middle-class reformers had not turned their country into an American-style democracy, nor did they want to do so: even after the 1884 Reform Act only 60 percent of adult men had the vote. But their campaigns to promote parliamentary reform, establish free trade and curb the powers of landowners and the Church of England had made Britain a strikingly liberal country by European standards.

America and Britain rooted their politics and law in the principle of individual liberty and the rights of private property, and the English common law remained basic to the legal systems of most American states. The liberty of the individual was also central to the economic life of both countries. The British and American industrial revolutions were not channeled by national governments to build up a powerful modern state geared to the demands of war, as was happening in Germany, Russia and Japan. Instead they were inspired by individual businessmen, seizing opportunities for profit, creating their own industries, trade and investment within the framework of a free market.

Britain and America were also unusual in the power enjoyed by their legislatures. Although Victorian Britain remained a monarchy, it was a *constitutional* monarchy. The authority of the Queen was now tightly circumscribed by Parliament, particularly the House of Commons, whose MPs represented a majority of the male population. The powers of Parliament were admittedly less extensive than those of Congress over the president, but Britain was much closer to the American political system than to the autocratic monarchies of Europe, such as Germany, Russia or Austria-Hungary, where the legislatures were weak or represented only a privileged minority of the population. All these shared liberal values were soon to prove a potent bond between the two countries.

In 1900 Great Britain seemed supreme. The scramble of the great powers for control of Africa had brought her Egypt, much of East Africa and a vast southern African domain carved out by Cecil Rhodes. At her Diamond Jubilee in 1897 the Queen Empress governed a fifth of the globe. Her subjects were equal in number to the rival empires of France, Germany and Russia combined. A small European island, the size of Wyoming or Oregon, had become the greatest power the world had ever seen.

Britain's political power was matched by her economic strength. She accounted for three-quarters of the world's foreign investment and a fifth of world trade. Despite the extension of the franchise, the old social order remained remarkably tenacious. Aristocrats still dominated the political parties and absorbed the new commercial rich into the landed elite. And the monarchy, instead of declining in public esteem, won new popularity and affection as Victoria's reign neared its end. A puzzled American ambassador marveled in 1897 at the Diamond Jubilee celebrations:

> It was an explosion of loyalty that amazed John Bull himself. What a curious thing it is—that there has been no King in England since Elizabeth of special distinction—most of them far worse than medio-cre—only the foreigner William III of any merit—and yet the mo-narchical religion has grown day by day, till the Queen is worshipped as more than mortal. . . .[5]

Great Britain seemed secure at home as well as omnipotent abroad.

Behind the glittering façade, however, all was not well. Her domi-nance left Britain acutely vulnerable. On every side there were rivals, wanting to share in the pickings of imperialism. The most alarming threat came from the German Kaiser, supported by his High Seas Fleet, but Britain was also at odds with France over North Africa, with Russia over the borders of her Asian empire in Persia and Afghanistan, and with the United States over their rival spheres of influence in the Americas. As Winston Churchill dryly observed, "Our claim to be left in unmolested enjoyment of vast and splendid possessions, mainly acquired by violence, largely main-tained by force, often seems less reasonable to others than to us."[6]

Britain's diplomatic isolation was seriously exposed at the turn of the century. To protect her interests in South Africa she made war on the Boer, or Dutch, republics of the Orange Free State and the Transvaal, incurring the animosity of all Europe. Joseph Chamber-lain, colonial secretary, described Britain as the "weary Titan, stag-gering under the too vast orb of his own fate."[7] It seemed only prudent to reduce the number of her potential enemies. The various disputes that existed between the United States and Britain were of relatively minor importance when set against London's worldwide problems, and the British chose to appease Washington's demands. This benefited America, changing the balance of power in the Western Hemisphere within a single decade and helping the United States to become a major force in the Caribbean and the Pacific.

In London, Anglo-American relations seemed of peripheral importance. Britain was not obsessed with America in the way she would become in the late twentieth century. In the United States, by contrast, relations with Britain were the main issue of foreign policy. It was as if America were trying to define itself in terms of its un-Britishness. Politicians of all persuasions enjoyed "twisting the lion's tail." To Northerners, Britain's behavior during the Civil War still rankled. Claims for compensation for the damage done to Union shipping by raiders like the *Alabama*, built in British shipyards, had been acrimoniously pursued. Gladstone finally accepted arbitration of the issue, and in 1872 Britain agreed to pay $15.5 million in compensation, somewhat outweighing the benefits of having built the ships in the first place.

Americans were also infuriated by the continued British presence in North America. Canada had been given self-government in 1867, as a Dominion under the British Crown. But American politicians still talked of annexing the country. Successive administrations turned a blind eye to raids by the Fenians across the border into Canada that were intended by this Irish-American organization as a way of provoking war between Britain and America, which would help Ireland gain her independence.

There were frequent impassioned complaints about Britain's undue influence within the United States. Three-quarters of the foreign investment in the United States was British, and the scale of Britain's holdings, particularly in railroads, mines and ranches, was a burning issue in the developing West. There were calls for tariffs to keep out British goods and protect infant American industries. One of the leading exponents of such a policy argued that this was "the way to outdo England without fighting her."[8] Farmers protested that the money and commodity markets of London and Liverpool were responsible for the decline of wheat, corn and cotton prices during the depression of 1873–96. Ben Tillman, the ranting, one-eyed leader of the Populist movement in South Carolina, spluttered, "America for Americans, and to hell with Britain and her Tories."[9]

A clear indication that Britain was no longer going to challenge

American interests came over an obscure boundary dispute in
Venezuela—obscure, at least, in British eyes. For decades the Venezuelan government had argued over the line of the jungle border
with British Guiana. It appealed to the United States, citing the
Monroe Doctrine, which had established as a basic tenet of American diplomacy the principle of noninterference in the Americas by
European powers. In July 1895 President Grover Cleveland duly
demanded that the British government submit the dispute to arbitration, adding provocatively, "To-day the United States is practically
sovereign on this continent."[10] Lord Salisbury, the British prime
minister, believed the U.S. note was bluster, and he failed to reply
for four months. When he did, he flatly rejected American interference, arguing that the Monroe Doctrine had no standing in international law.

During the Venezuela crisis of 1895 the New York World *showed Britain hogging the globe.*

Incensed at this dismissal of a sacred precept of American diplomacy, Cleveland sent a special message to Congress on December
17, 1895. America, he announced, would adjudicate the dispute
itself. Thereafter, it would be "the duty of the United States to resist
by every means in its power as a willful aggression upon its rights
and interests" any attempt by Britain to alter the border.[11]

For a few days America was in the grip of war fever. Republicans
and Democrats backed the President. Some talked of invading Canada, while Irish-Americans lined up as volunteers to fight the de-
tested British. The British ambassador told London that Cleveland's
message "had produced in Congress and among the Public a condition of mind which can only be described as hysterical."[12] But then
Wall Street panicked, and share prices plummeted. The churches
spoke out against the talk of war and the administration began to
back down. In London the Cabinet, now preoccupied with the far
graver crisis in southern Africa, where the German Kaiser was
sending messages of support to the Boers, was disinclined to pursue
Salisbury's initially tough response to the United States. The principle of international arbitration of the dispute was reluctantly accepted.

It took three years for the results of the arbitration to be announced. The judgment accepted most of Britain's claims, but this
was not the real significance of the Venezuelan crisis. What mattered was that it had altered the future conduct of Anglo-American
relations. The confrontation and the threat of war concentrated
minds on both sides of the Atlantic, and led to a flood of resolutions,
reminiscent of 1846, insisting that war between Britain and America
was inconceivable. One British petition, with several thousand sig-
natures, summed up what had become an increasingly common
sentiment in both countries: "All English-speaking peoples united
by race, language and religion, should regard war as the one absolutely intolerable mode of settling the domestic differences of the
Anglo-American family."[13]

In January 1897 the two governments signed a treaty agreeing to
submit in future all major disputes to arbitration. It just failed to gain
the two-thirds majority in the Senate required for ratification, but
the widespread public support it received demonstrated the improvement in Anglo-American relations that had taken place.

The rapprochement was further enhanced by the extraordinary
demonstration of pro-American feeling in Britain in 1898. In April
of that year the United States had gone to war with Spain over her

oppressive treatment of the Cubans and her slights to American interests on the island. In the face of almost universal European support for the Spanish cause Britain announced her neutrality and made her pro-American sympathies clear. Within hours of the news that the United States had declared war thousands of red, white and blue streamers decked buildings in London and the British press came out enthusiastically on the American side. American Independence Day, July 4, was celebrated that year throughout Britain.

Just over a year later, the U.S. government returned the favor when Britain went to war in South Africa. American public opinion sided with the Boers in their attempt to defend their republics against the might of the British Empire. When the war was over, the defeated Boer fighters toured the United States reenacting their battles before enthusiastic audiences. The administration, however, bent the rules of its official neutrality to allow an ill-prepared Britain to finance 20 percent of the cost of the war on the U.S. securities market. Hundreds of thousands of pairs of boots and nearly two hundred thousand pack mules were sent to ease shortages in the British Army, while European attempts at mediation were deliberately ignored by the United States.

The United States traded on the atmosphere of goodwill to solve its other outstanding disputes with Britain. These were over the exact line of the border between Canada and Alaska and, quite separately, over the American proposal to build a canal through the Isthmus of Panama, connecting the Atlantic and Pacific oceans. The United States had agreed in a treaty of 1850 that the development of the Panama Canal would be a joint British and American venture. But America's emergence as a major Pacific power during the Spanish-American War made it essential for the U.S. Navy to move from its East Coast to its West Coast ports without making the long journey around South America via Cape Horn. Lord Salisbury was prepared to give up Britain's treaty rights, but, under pressure from the Canadian government, he made the settlement of the disputed Alaskan-Canadian border a precondition.

It took several years to untangle this complicated diplomatic web. In 1899 in return for America's support in South Africa, Britain at last agreed to separate the issues. At this point the U.S. president, Theodore Roosevelt, refused to allow the Alaskan dispute to go to arbitration, a reversal of America's previous insistence that arbitration be accepted by Britain in the Venezuelan dispute. To Canada's chagrin, Britain now chose to put her own relationship with the

United States first, and agreed that a judicial commission, composed
of three American judges, two Canadian representatives and one
British appointee should sit to decide the issue. Under pressure from
London the British delegate consistently voted with the Americans
against the Canadians, who understandably felt aggrieved that their
country's interests were being sacrificed in the cause of Anglo-
American friendship. The dispute was duly settled on American
terms.

As for the canal, a new Anglo-American treaty was signed in
February 1900 allowing America to go ahead with its construction
on condition that the canal would be a neutral zone and unfortified.
Roosevelt and other enthusiastic supporters of America's growing
naval might were unhappy at these restrictions. They forced Secretary of State John Hay to renegotiate the treaty. Eventually all the
U.S. demands for complete freedom of action were conceded and
a new treaty was signed in November 1901. America was now free
to build, operate and fortify a canal for use in peace and war. The
only opposition left was from Colombia, concerned that part of her
territory was to be taken over by the United States. In a shady
maneuver Roosevelt first promoted revolution in Colombia, then
recognized the breakaway republic of Panama, in return for a treaty
giving the United States carte blanche to build and run its canal.
The Panama Canal was eventually opened in August 1914, a few
days after war broke out in Europe.

The United States continued to berate Britain for her imperial
aggression, but by the turn of the century traces of imperialism were
evident in American policy. Central America was becoming what
would now be called an American "sphere of influence," and Britain
supported the United States' new role. When America took control
of the Philippines from Spain in 1898, the London weekly *The
Spectator* commented patronizingly: "She will govern them well
enough, much better than any Power except ourselves, and we have
more of the world's surface than we can well manage. . . . It would
be a relief if another English-speaking Power would take up a
portion of our task. . . ."[14] Cuba, in the wake of the Spanish-
American War, had effectively become a protectorate of the United
States, controlled by American interests and unable to conduct an
independent foreign policy. Over the next few years the United
States also intervened to protect its investments and maintain stability in Haiti, Honduras, Nicaragua, the Dominican Republic and
Mexico.

In justification of this conduct President Theodore Roosevelt added a corollary to the Monroe Doctrine in 1904:

> Chronic wrongdoing, or an impotence which results in a general loosening of the ties of civilized society, may in America, as else-where, ultimately require intervention by some civilized nation, and in the Western Hemisphere the adherence of the United States to the Monroe Doctrine may force the United States, however reluctantly, in flagrant cases of such wrongdoing or impotence, to the exercise of an international police power.[15]

As British influence in the area waned under the pressure of events in Europe, Asia and Africa the United States was declaring its own Pax Americana. For Britain the practical advantage of this growing Anglo-American accord was considerable. Many British politicians saw in it a proper recognition of the common background. Lord Salisbury, a tough, traditional Tory, had little time for sentiment in international affairs and considered America to be an

upstart nation. But his Cabinet had in Joseph Chamberlain an exponent of the "Anglo-Saxon race" theory. "I refuse to speak or think
of the United States as a foreign nation," he told a Toronto audience
in 1887. "They are our flesh and blood." In the euphoria of the
Spanish-American War in 1898 he expressed the fervent hope that
"the Stars and Stripes and the Union Jack should wave together
over an Anglo-Saxon alliance."[16]

Darwin's descriptions of the survival of the fittest were cited in
support of the theory. Britons and Americans, it was argued, shared
unique racial characteristics of intelligence and industry that made
them better than other peoples. They had inherited, from the Dark
Age invaders of Britain, a capacity for self-government. It was their
duty to spread these superior values, to bring enlightenment to
primitive races and to vanquish the inferior Latin, Teutonic and
Slavic peoples who were their rivals. Imperialism was considered
not just a law of society but a law of nature. Superior races must
expand or die. In the words of the Ohio minister, Josiah Strong, one
of America's leading exponents of this thesis:

> It seems to me that God, with infinite wisdom and skill, is training
> the Anglo-Saxon race for an hour sure to come in the world's future
> . . . when the pressure of population on the means of subsistence will
> be felt here as it is now felt in Europe and Asia. Then will the world
> enter on a new stage in its history—*the final competition of races, for
> which the Anglo-Saxon is being schooled.* . . . And can any one doubt
> that the result of this competition of races will be the "survival of the
> fittest"?[17]

In Britain Lord Salisbury's successor as prime minister, A. J.
Balfour (1902–5), was convinced that "the two great co-heirs of
Anglo-Saxon freedom and civilisation" had a common mission.[18]
Americans were "our kin beyond the sea" and the United States'
growing influence in the Americas and the Pacific was desirable.
"The Monroe Doctrine," Balfour stated, "has no enemies in this
country that I know of. We welcome any increase of the great
influence of the United States upon the great Western Hemisphere."[19]

It was a considerable relief to Britain no longer to count the
United States among her potential foes. By 1906 Britain felt able to
withdraw all her forces from Canada and the West Indies. The First
Lord of the Admiralty wrote in 1905: "There is no party in the

United Kingdom nor even in the British Empire which does not contemplate a war with the United States of America as the greatest evil which could befall the British Empire in its foreign relations."[20] With the territorial disputes settled, Britain no longer held the expanding U.S. Navy in her sights, though American admirals were still determined to outbuild Britain. For British leaders, war with the United States had been ruled out. It was, they said in the cliché of the time, "unthinkable." Britain's reaction to a new power flexing its muscles was to accommodate it as long as there was no serious conflict with British interests, particularly since it seemed a country so close in values and kinship to her own. America's growing involvement in the Western Hemisphere was welcomed as an extension of Anglo-Saxon influence.

Britain was less comfortable, however, when that same power expanded economically and threatened to encroach directly on her commercial interests. As the United States' industrial and financial strength grew, American goods flooded British markets, and U.S. capitalists, seeking to expand, started to buy up British companies. At the beginning of the twentieth century the British press was full of dire warnings about the "American invasion" of Britain.

America's industrial revolution began much later than Britain's and did not take off until after the Civil War. With peace came reconstruction, and the railroad was its principal motive force. In 1865 most of America's thirty-five thousand miles of track lay between the Atlantic and the Mississippi, but by 1900 the United States was served by two hundred thousand miles of track, more than in all of Europe put together. Much of the railroad boom had been financed by the City of London, but it had an immediate effect on America's coal, iron and steel production, leading to a fast indigenous development of those industries, where originally the materials had been imported from Britain. With the spread of the electric telegraph and, from the 1870s, the telephone, the United States was becoming a huge national market. Remote farming areas were brought in reach of the big cities and the seaports. American business was now ready to capitalize on the vast scale of the new country.

The industrial revolution in the United States not only outstripped Britain's but took a very different course technologically. America's great innovation was to invent and develop the techniques of mass production, replacing the craftsman, who was responsible for every stage of manufacture, with the production line.

Advertisement in Life *magazine, July 28, 1898.*

Parts for machines, whether clocks, typewriters or sewing machines, were standardized and made interchangeable rather than being produced individually. By World War I Henry Ford was applying these principles with dramatic success on his car "assembly line" in Detroit.

The scale of modern production generated a voracious demand for new capital. Tycoons like John D. Rockefeller in the oil business or Andrew Carnegie in steel virtually ruled their industries, buying out their rivals and taking control of every stage of production, from raw materials to retailing. They could not develop at the speed they required simply by plowing back their profits, unlike the family firms that still dominated manufacturing in Britain. Specialist investment bankers emerged to meet the demand for cash and credit, preeminent among them the Wall Street banker J. P. Morgan. Rapacious for money, power and beautiful women, Morgan was chief banker to the giant conglomerate U.S. Steel, and the organizer of many of the great railroad mergers of the 1880s and 1890s. He arranged most of Britain's loans to pay for the Boer War, and his firm was to play a crucial role in financing Britain's war effort in 1914–18.

By 1913 the United States had replaced Britain as the world's largest manufacturing nation, producing twice as much coal, three times as much pig iron, and five times the quantity of steel. In the 1900s most of this was still absorbed by her domestic market. Britain was a far larger exporter, sending 40 percent of her manufactured goods abroad, whereas America exported only 5 percent. But America's new "trusts," or big business combinations, already being criticized for their wealth and power, needed to expand beyond America's shores, and many turned to Britain, where there was no language barrier.

The first American business to set up on a permanent basis in Britain was Singer. The sewing machine company opened a factory in Bridgeton near Glasgow in 1867. By 1900 there were seventy-five U.S. subsidiaries or jointly owned Anglo-American enterprises in Britain, funded by £10 million of American capital. By 1914 a further seventy companies had arrived. They included H. J. Heinz, introducing processed food to Britain; Henry Ford, opening his first British assembly plant at Trafford Park, near Manchester in 1908; and F. W. Woolworth, beginning to revolutionize the retail trade with "penny markets" in Liverpool, Manchester and Preston.[21]

Among the most prominent arrivals were the electrical industries, a new technology led by the United States. Britain's tramway systems were electrified mostly with American electrical equipment, as was the London "underground" railway system. This led to one of the first of a series of spectacular takeover battles that caught the public eye, as the buccaneers of U.S. industry pitted their wits and strength against British companies.

In September 1900 the Charing Cross, Euston and Hampstead Railway, one of London's many competing underground companies, was acquired by the owner of an empire of street railways in Chicago known as the Chicago Traction Tangle. Charles Tyson Yerkes's recipe for success was to "buy up old junk, fix it up a little and unload it upon other fellows."[22] His activities in Chicago had made him money but many enemies as well, and in 1899 he was forced to sell out and move on. Yerkes's acquisition of a London underground railway company was the first round of a bruising battle to buy and electrify the entire system. Over the next two years he was locked in competition with another syndicate backed by J. P. Morgan, who scented healthy profits to be made under, as well as in, the City of London. The cost of the plans eventually proved prohibitive, however, and after Parliament refused to authorize the necessary legislation, both Yerkes and Morgan were forced to withdraw.

J. P. Morgan was also engaged in a struggle for control of shipping across the Atlantic, trying to wrest passenger and freight trade from British hands. In 1901 he began buying British shipping lines, such as Leyland and White Star, at inflated prices, until his syndicate threatened to dominate not only the shipping business but shipbuilding as well. Even Joseph Chamberlain, a great exponent of Anglo-American cooperation, called "the Morgan Combination . . . a move in a great commercial war," which the British should be "prepared to fight for all we are worth."[23] When it seemed in 1902 that Cunard, the major British transatlantic carrier, might also sell out to Morgan's, Balfour's Cabinet came to the rescue. It agreed to loan Cunard £2.4 million for new vessels and to subsidize their operation. This kind of government support was anathema to many, but radical measures were considered essential to prevent Britain losing control of the North Atlantic.

Tobacco also became the object of takeover fever. In September 1901 James Buchanan Duke, the flamboyant president of the American Tobacco Company, bought up the Liverpool tobacco firm of Ogden's. He then announced that his company had set

MAY 8, 1901.] PUNCH, OR THE LONDON CHARIVARI. 341

JONATHAN SHOPPING.

John Bull. "NOW, MY LITTLE MAN, WHAT CAN I DO FOR YOU?"
Master Jonathan. "WAL, GUESS I'LL BUY THE WHOLE STORE!"

["American millionaires agree to purchase the Leyland Line (Mediterranean, Portugal, Montreal and Antwerp) Fleets. A meeting of shareholders has been called in order to confirm the arrangements."—*Vide* "*Daily News,*" May 1.]

Bernard Partridge in Punch *(1901) on the Americans buying up Britain.*

aside £6 million to capture the entire British and Continental ciga-
rette markets. His approach was direct: "Hello boys," he introduced himself to the staid and respectable Player brothers, "I'm
Duke from New York come to buy your business."[24] Outraged,
his prospective victims set up their own combine, Imperial To-

bacco, which, after a bitter price and bonus war, forced "Buck"
Duke to concede defeat. American Tobacco agreed to stay out of
Britain if Imperial Tobacco kept away from the United States. A
joint company, British American Tobacco, would exploit sales in
the rest of the world.

These takeover battles of 1901–2 provoked a response of near
panic in Britain. The tobacco war in particular brought the "American peril" to the attention of the man in the street. Newspapers and
advertising billboards warned, in lurid terms, of enslavement by
American trusts and of the British workingman being kidnapped by
Uncle Sam. The journalist Frederick A. McKenzie, whose articles
in the *Daily Mail* had alerted Britain to the American invasion,
predicted the Americanization of every aspect of British society. "In
the domestic life," he wrote,

> we have almost got to this. The average citizen wakes in the morning
> at the sound of an American alarum clock; rises from his New En-
> gland sheets, and shaves with his New York soap, and a Yankee safety
> razor. He pulls on a pair of Boston boots over his socks from West
> Carolina [*sic*], fastens his Connecticut braces, slips his Waterbury
> watch into his pocket and sits down to breakfast. . . . Rising from his
> breakfast table the citizen rushes out, catches an electric tram made
> in New York, to Shepherds Bush, where he gets into a Yankee
> elevator, which takes him on to the American-fitted railway to the
> city. At his office of course everything is American. He sits on a
> Nebraskan swivel chair, before a Michigan roll-top desk, writes his
> letters on a Syracuse typewriter, signing them with a New York
> fountain pen, and drying them with a blotting sheet from New
> England. The letter copies are put away in files manufactured in
> Grand Rapids.[25]

It was a journalistic fantasy. American goods and capital were still
only a small proportion of the total British economy, but a general
debate on the economic problems of Britain had been opened up,
with the protagonists drawing indiscriminately on American evidence to support their theories. It was like the debate over American
democracy in the mid-nineteenth century. Some employers, with
the support of *The Times*, argued that "the English disease" was
caused by the restrictive practices of trade unions. Trade unionists
themselves, on the other hand, and industrial reformers visited the
United States and criticized the lack of incentives in Britain and the
inadequacies of the education system. Technologists urged more

mechanization. Conservatives argued for protective tariffs, pointing to the American duties on imports that averaged more than 50 percent. And the journalist W. T. Stead, who predicted in 1902 that the world would be Americanized in the twentieth century, argued that Britain's only hope was an Anglo-Saxon-race union. "Is there no Morgan," he pleaded, "who will undertake to bring about the greatest combination of all—a combination of the whole English-speaking race?"[26]

This theory was already being put into practice by the British upper classes, who had discovered that the new American wealth was not averse to trading its money for social status. The pre–World War I generation saw over a hundred dynastic marriages between British and American families, propping up a faltering British aristocracy in the style to which it was accustomed. Sometimes both sides went too far. Consuelo Vanderbilt, heiress to the shipping and railroad fortune, had to be dragged to the altar in 1895 to marry the Duke of Marlborough, and the match ended bitterly in separation and divorce. The Duke's uncle had made a more propitious mar-

A patriotic British advertisement during the Anglo-American tobacco war.

riage to the vivacious daughter of a New York financier, Jennie
Jerome. Their first child, born prematurely in November 1874,
survived to be christened Winston Leonard Spencer Churchill. A
later transatlantic marriage, that of a British publisher with the
daughter of Dr. Tarleton Belles of Spencer, Indiana, gave Britain
another Conservative prime minister in Harold Macmillan, who,
like Churchill, made much of his American ancestry. And Joseph
Chamberlain, the arch-proponent of Anglo-Saxon union, finally
practiced what he preached. His third wife was the daughter of
President Cleveland's secretary of war, Mary Endicott. The wealth
that inspired many of these marriages was prodigious, far exceeding
that of even the richest British families. By 1900 the Rockefellers,
the Fords, the Mellons were dollar billionaires, twelve times as rich
as British counterparts like the Duke of Westminster.[27]

There was an unsavory side to America's rapid rise to industrial
greatness. British newspapers began to report on political corruption, on violent strikes, and on the ruthlessness of moneymaking
tycoons like Morgan and Rockefeller. Radicals who in the previous
century had pointed admiringly to America's classless democracy
were shocked by the new development. "Plutocracy," rule by the
rich, seemed to be at odds with Democracy. The Chartists and their
fellow mid-nineteenth-century radicals had praised America as a
paradise for the workingman. By the 1900s the intellectuals and
trade unionists responsible for creating the Labour party saw a
different society, which seemed to embody the very worst features
of capitalism. William Clarke, a convert to socialism, wrote in the
mid-1890s:

> A quarter of a century ago the American Republic was the guiding
> star of advanced English political thought. It is not so now: candour
> compels me to say that. It is not merely a question of machine politics,
> of political corruption, of the omnipotent party boss. . . . Over and
> beyond this is the great fact of the division between rich and poor,
> millionaires at one end, tramps at the other, a growth of monopolies
> unparalleled, crises producing abject poverty just as in Europe.[28]

In future the United States would be held up no longer by Britian's
socialists as an example of the promised New World but as the
epitome of all that was wrong with the Old. For those disappointed
idealists the dawn of the twentieth century marked an era of aliena-
tion rather than of rapprochement in Anglo-American relations.

Across the ocean, however, America's elite welcomed the rapprochement. Alarmed that mass immigration was destroying the country's Anglo-Saxon character, it found previously unsuspected virtues in its English cousins. For at the turn of the century the United States was facing an influx of newcomers unprecedented both in number and background. Twenty-three million entered the country between 1880 and 1914, by which time over one in seven of America's 105 million population had been born abroad. In the past English-speaking immigrants had been in a majority, but by the 1900s only one in twenty came from England. Most were from Eastern or Southeastern Europe. They dressed, ate and spoke in unfamiliar ways and in the main were not Protestant but Roman Catholic, Orthodox or Jewish. They settled in large numbers in the big cities, so that by 1914 over one-third of the population of New York, Boston and Chicago was foreign-born. New York had more Germans than Hamburg, more Italians than Naples, twice the number of Irish in Dublin and a larger Jewish population than the whole of Western Europe.[29]

The WASP Americans—white, Anglo-Saxon Protestants—who had effectively run America, felt endangered. They were already disturbed by the growing political strength of the older immigrant groups from Germany and Ireland. The Irish, many of them emotionally involved in the cause of Irish independence, were bitterly opposed to the domination of American government by those of English origin. As they grew wealthier and more numerous their political influence began to be felt. They not only campaigned for their own interests, but also represented the recent immigrants, using the advantage of being English-speaking to mediate between the newcomers and the WASP elite. Even more alarming to the WASPS were the German Americans. They were fragmented by religion, dialect and politics, but nevertheless united on issues that affected their national identity. Encouraged by a German-language press that had adopted the Kaiser's views of Germany's innate superiority, many fought against assimilation and encouraged the growth of their culture in opposition to the English.

The WASP response was to draw instinctively closer to Britain and to campaign, in an attempt to maintain their supremacy, for restrictions on further immigration from Europe. Senator Henry Cabot Lodge of Massachusetts was a staunch American nationalist from a Boston family that traced its ancestry back to the era of the *Mayflower*. He had been brought up to be suspicious of Britain as

a great power despite having many British friends, among them
A. J. Balfour. In 1895 Lodge was arguing that Canada should be
seized from Britain if war broke out over the Venezuela crisis, but
by 1900 had changed his tune. He decided that Britain and America
must now stand together in the struggle to preserve Anglo-Saxon
supremacy in America and around the world. He wrote to Teddy
Roosevelt about America's stance on the Anglo-Boer war. "However much we sympathize with the Boers, the downfall of the British
Empire is something no rational American could regard as anything
but a misfortune to the United States."[30] Lodge became a leading
advocate of the restrictions on immigration.

"The one indispensable feature of our foreign policy," declared
John Hay, the American secretary of state (1898–1905), "should be
a friendly understanding with England." But this Yankee Republican, one of the principal architects of rapprochement, bridled when
accused, as he often was, of being an Anglophile. "All I have ever
done with England is to have wrung great concessions out of her
with no compensation. And yet, these idiots say I'm not an American because I don't say, 'To hell with the Queen,' at every breath."[31]
Anglo-American cooperation, in other words, did not mean American submission to Britain's interests. It was America's interests that
were being advanced. "As long as England succeeds in keeping 'the
balance of power' in Europe, not only in principle, but in reality,
well and good," Theodore Roosevelt observed in 1910. "Should she
however for some reason or other fail in doing so, the United States
would be obliged to step in at least temporarily, to restore the
balance. . . . In fact, we ourselves are becoming, owing to our
strength and geographical situation, more and more the balance of
power of the whole world."[32] America was to be tested more
quickly than he anticipated, for the balance of power in Europe was
soon upset again, and this time Britain was unable to restore it alone.

At the beginning of the twentieth century Britain faced two
principal rivals to her supremacy, Germany and the United States.
With both she was locked in industrial competition and in a series
of diplomatic disputes. Both were building fleets that threatened her
traditional supremacy at sea. But her response to these two disturbing new powers was very different. As we have seen, with the
United States she began to cultivate what would later be called a
"special relationship." With Germany she drifted into a deep antagonism that led to two world wars.

America's challenge to Britain was remote, being mainly concentrated in the Western Hemisphere. Germany, on the other hand, was much closer to home, a potential menace to the Low Countries, the North Sea and the English Channel. Concern for national security was reinforced by the alien nature of German society, dominated by a Prussian aristocracy that extolled militarist values and denied popular liberties. Compared with the liberalism of Britain's Anglo-Saxon cousins across the ocean, Germany seemed a far greater threat. Henry Adams—Bostonian, historian, descendant of two American presidents—described Germany as "the grizzly terror which in twenty years effected what Adamses had tried for two hundred in vain—frightened England into America's arms."[33]

The Kaiser saw no reason why Britain should be the world's supreme imperial power and was determined to win Germany a place in the sun. As the German Navy raced to outbuild Britain's, talk of war became commonplace. A crisis in the Balkans in 1914 brought the rivalry to a head. The assassination by Serbian nationalists of the heir to the Austro-Hungarian Empire, Germany's only ally, posed a fundamental threat to Germany's credibility. If nothing was done the empire might disintegrate and Germany could be encircled and reduced to impotence by the increasingly powerful Triple Entente of Russia, France and Britain. By August 1914 Russia and France were at war with Germany and Austria, and Britain joined in after the German invasion of Belgium, whose neutrality Britain was bound by treaty to protect. Belgium provided the immediate cause and the moral indignation to overcome the antiwar feelings of many British Liberals. But the underlying issue was Britain's survival as a great power. In the words of one senior British diplomat, to say "that England cannot engage in a big war means her abdication as an independent state."[34] The British lion now had to fight for its supremacy; it would be the survival of the fittest.

From Berlin to London, from Paris to the Russian capital of St. Petersburg, the mood in August 1914 was one of relief, even euphoria. War would purify the soul, release the pent-up tensions of industrial life, and offer a golden opportunity for valor, patriotism and glory.

And everyone knew it would all be over by Christmas.

CHAPTER 3

TO FIGHT OR NOT TO FIGHT?

1914–1917

From the beginning President Woodrow Wilson made clear that this was not America's war. "The United States must be neutral in fact as well as in name during these days that are to try men's souls," he told his fellow countrymen two weeks after hostilities began. "We must be impartial in thought as well as action, must put a curb upon our sentiments as well as upon every transaction that might be construed as a preference of one party to the struggle before another."[1]

This stance of strict neutrality was to be much misunderstood in Britain, castigated as vacillation, moral insensitivity or even rank cowardice. But Wilson, like most Americans, could see no reason of morality or of national interest for the United States to enter Europe's war. Instead, Wilson believed, America's growing power and the influence that would stem from neutrality should be used in what he called "the proper performance of our duty as the one great nation at peace, the one people holding itself ready to play a part of impartial mediation."[2] Already the President was turning over in his mind ideas for a postwar world in which conquest would be outlawed by "an association of nations, all bound together for the protection of the integrity of each."[3]

Wilson was a man of deep, often self-righteous moral conviction. He was a high-minded Christian, the son and grandson of Presbyte-

DON'T MIX IN A FAMILY QUARREL, UNCLE

Uncle Sam stands and watches while the Europeans—one big, happy royal family—fight it out.

rian ministers, and an academic who had previously been president of Princeton University. Personally his deepest instincts favored Britain. His ancestry was English. He loved the English countryside, and spent several bicycling holidays touring it in his forties. His whole political thought was steeped in the English liberal tradition, with Gladstone as his great hero, and his first book had suggested that America adopt the British Cabinet system instead of retaining its cumbersome separation of powers. But none of this blinded Wilson to the essential differences of values and interests between the two nations. Even in December 1914 he was sure that "Germany is not alone responsible for the war,"[4] and as the conflict dragged on, his conviction grew that America offered the only salvation for a war-torn world.

But political prudence as well as moral conviction dictated Wilson's stance. As he said in his neutrality message, "the people of the United States are drawn from many nations, and chiefly from the nations now at war." He warned that Americans "may become divided in camps of hostile opinion, hot against each other, involved in the war itself in impulse and opinion, if not in action."[5] Wilson feared that America, already racked by the cultural struggle between those of British stock and the rest, would now tear itself apart over the war.

German Americans were the most numerous group of recent immigrants. Over eight million of America's 105 million population in 1914 had been born in Germany or had at least one German parent. Some were indifferent to the war, others kept their heads down, but many eagerly championed the cause of the Fatherland. German-language papers celebrated the Kaiser's victories, while groups such as the National German-American Alliance, which boasted two million members in 1914, raised money for German war relief, bought the imperial government's war bonds and pressed the media to give the German case a fair hearing.

The Irish Americans, some 4.5 million at the start of the war, also hoped that Britain would be taught a lesson. One, a boy at the time, remembers his family's reaction: "They thought Britain was going to get whipped and they were happy about it. . . . It was time they got it."[6] In the small, mainly Irish mining town of Butte, Montana, the young men drilled secretly and learned to use weapons in readiness for the day when they would be called back to Ireland to take part in the revolution. Patriotic societies in Butte and in the big Irish communities of cities like Boston and New York raised money for the Irish cause, sometimes working hand in glove with German agents. To them any foe of Britain was necessarily Ireland's friend.

Groups like the German Americans and Irish Americans may have been vociferous and organized, but pro-British feeling remained strong in the United States. A majority of Americans still traced their ancestry back to British roots and many of these were inclined to the Allied cause even though they had no intention of fighting for it. British sympathizers were to be found in high places. They included Colonel Edward House, the Texan adviser of the President, and Teddy Roosevelt, one of Wilson's opponents for the presidency in 1912. Pro-British feeling was particularly strong in Wall Street, where J. P. Morgan, Jr., son of the great financier and heir to his vast banking empire, was an ardent Anglophile, who spent half of each year in Britain. It was to Morgan's that the British government turned in the early months of the war to handle its military purchases in the United States, to arrange contracts for rifles, shells and heavy guns, for food and vital raw materials, such as oil, cotton and copper.

The British government had not expected to need so much American assistance. Like most of the belligerents, it had assumed that the war would be over before Christmas. But by 1915 the conflict had become a war of attrition, bogged down in the trenches of northern France and Flanders where thousands of lives and millions of shells were being expended in futile offensives. Morgan's was ideally placed to act as the channel for Britain's purchases in America. It was well connected in London through its partner house, Morgan Grenfell, and it also had contacts throughout American industry. But, to begin with, J. P. Morgan moved cautiously. It seemed unwise to draw attention to Britain's growing dependence. Some of the companies he dealt with, his "war babies," never officially knew the ultimate destination of the goods they supplied to Morgan's. The president of the British Board of Trade, Walter Runciman, a friend of J. P. Morgan, attempted, for instance, to corner the market in American-produced electro-copper to deny supplies to Germany. He and Morgan agreed that twenty different agents should be put on to the job, each apparently buying for a different client, and succeeded in securing three-quarters of America's output for Britain without attracting comment.

Despite his call at the outbreak of war for strict neutrality, there was little Wilson could do, or perhaps wanted to do, to prevent American supplies from being shipped to Britain. It was traditional American policy to trade freely with belligerent countries in time of war. But the Allies benefited more than Germany and the Central Powers from this stance, thanks to Britain's dominance of the seas, her financial reserves and her close links with Wall Street. America's exports to Britain and France rose from $750 million in 1914 to $2.75 billion in 1916, while exports to Germany dwindled in the same period from $345 million to a mere $2 million.

American "neutrality" was clearly favoring the Allies. But to have restricted the war trade by law would have been a deliberate tilting of neutrality against the Allies in favor of Germany. Better, then, Wilson and his advisers believed, to let market forces take their course, especially when the war boom was helping pull America out of depression and opening up new markets around the world that Europeans were forced to abandon. The *New York American* gloated a few days after war broke out: "TWO THOUSAND MILLIONS in trade is the prize which world conditions have set before the American people. Europe's tragic extremity becomes . . . America's golden opportunity."[7] Few were as blunt, but the prediction was apt. As Thomas Jefferson had put it over a century before, "The new world will fatten on the follies of the old."[8]

There was, however, a price to be paid for sharing in this enviable feast. All the goods America manufactured and sold to Britain had to be shipped across the Atlantic. As a neutral the United States claimed the absolute right of freedom to the seas. But, as belligerents, neither Britain nor Germany conceded this right, especially with the war on land deadlocked, and it became essential for each side to try to strangle the other's economy. Each declared the waters around the other's coastline a war zone. Under international law, belligerents could search neutral ships and seize their cargoes if these were destined for the enemy war effort. This assumed the ability to stop a ship at sea, board it and examine the contents. The Royal Navy, with its superiority on the surface, had little difficulty in doing this and thus in conducting its ever-tightening blockade of Germany broadly within international law. The Germans relied on their new weapon, the U-boat, but this was extremely vulnerable once on the surface. Faced with Britain's policy of starving Germany into submission and America's growing trade with the Allies, the Kaiser's government abandoned the legal niceties of search and seizure and struck from under water. On February 4, 1915, it announced that all enemy merchant vessels encountered within the war zone would be destroyed on sight. To avoid attack Britain had authorized her merchant ships to fly neutral flags. Consequently, the German declaration added, "Neutral vessels cannot always be prevented from suffering from the attacks intended for enemy ships."[9]

At 2:10 P.M. GMT on May 7, 1915, the German submarine U 20 attacked the British Cunard liner *Lusitania* off the south coast of Ireland near the end of her voyage from New York. Only one torpedo was fired at the thirty-thousand-ton vessel, but the initial explosion was followed by a much louder one from within the hull. Fire spread rapidly, water flooded in, and within eighteen minutes the supposedly "unsinkable" *Lusitania* had vanished beneath the surface of the waves. Twelve hundred and one lives were lost, among them 94 children; 124 of those who died were American citizens.

Germany claimed that the *Lusitania* was a legitimate target because she was entering the war zone and had been carrying ammunition to Britain. Morgan's, it later emerged, had shipped a consignment of 1,248 cases of shells, six million rounds of ammunition and eighteen cases of percussion fuses for the British Army, and the second and fatal explosion had almost certainly been caused by the detonation of this secret cargo. But American opinion was not assuaged. All but a few extreme German Americans were consumed with horror and outrage. "Wholesale murder on the high seas," the action of "wild beasts," the New York *Nation* called it.[10] For Anglophiles, such as Teddy Roosevelt and Colonel House, the war was now clearly shown to be a moral contest between civilization and barbarism. Roosevelt redoubled his efforts to persuade Wilson that America should rearm and protect its neutral rights by force.

The President tried to calm the hysteria. Speaking in Philadelphia three days after the sinking, he insisted:

> The example of America must be a special example. The example of America must be the example not merely of peace because it will not fight, but of peace because peace is the healing and elevating influence of the world, and strife is not. There is such a thing as a man being too proud to fight. There is such a thing as a nation being so right that it does not need to convince others by force that it is right.[11]

In Britain the President's remarks were greeted with contempt. "Too proud to fight"? Or too scared? America's neutrality began to look more like cowardice than principle, moral blindness than visionary idealism. Music hall comedians mocked the President. In the trenches of France dud shells that failed to explode were nicknamed "Wilsons."

Despite his high-minded words, however, the President did not intend to turn the other cheek. Sitting at his typewriter, Wilson drafted a diplomatic note holding the German government "to a strict accountability" for any loss of American ships or lives within the war zone, and calling on it in the name of the "sacred principles of justice and humanity" to abandon its indiscriminate U-boat campaign.[12]

Secretary of State William Jennings Bryan was deeply unhappy. He wanted the President to avoid the growing risk of war by forbidding American citizens to enter the war zone defined by Germany and by banning them from sailing on passenger vessels belonging to belligerent countries, such as the British Cunard liners. That might have been a prudent policy, but Wilson refused and Bryan resigned. The public demanded a tough line, and Bryan's counsel seemed inconsistent with upholding America's honor and its rights as a neutral country. Wilson believed that he was standing up for all peace-loving countries, but in doing so he had made a fateful decision: if Germany did not back down, America might have to choose between peace and honor.

Thus began a yearlong war of words between the American and German governments, punctuated by further sinkings of passenger liners and further American casualties. In September 1915 the German ambassador to Washington publicly promised that "liners will not be sunk by our submarines without warning and without safety of the lives of non-combatants."[13] But enemy merchant vessels were still torpedoed on sight. After a Channel steamer, the *Sussex*, had been sunk in March 1916, with four Americans among the casualties, Wilson typed out a new note threatening to break off diplomatic relations unless *all* noncombatant ships, passenger or cargo, were given security against attack without warning. On May 4 the Kaiser's government reluctantly agreed. The so-called *Sussex* pledge was a major diplomatic victory for Wilson. It seemed that the typewriter had proved mightier than the sword.

While taking a tough line against the German U-boat, the Wilson administration found itself increasingly unable to control America's economic entanglements with Britain. By mid-1915 Morgan's was spending millions each week to pay for Britain's war needs, and despite large sales of British investments in the United States, reserves were running low and sterling was under strain, driven down more than twenty cents from the official rate of $4.86. In September 1915 the British government decided that a half-billion-dollar loan, raised through Morgan's, was the only way to keep financing Britain's vital American trade.

At the beginning of the war, Bryan, in line with his policy of strict neutrality, had announced with Wilson's consent that "in the judgment of this Government loans by American bankers to any foreign nation which is at war is inconsistent with the true spirit of neutrality."[14] But Bryan had resigned by September 1915 and Wilson's advisers insisted that such a policy was no longer tenable when the American economy was so dependent on the war trade with Britain. Robert Lansing, Bryan's Anglophile successor as secretary of state, warned that without loans Britain's trade would collapse, throwing the American economy into depression and distress. "Can we afford," he asked, "to let a declaration as to our conception of the 'true spirit of neutrality' made in the first days of the war stand in the way of our national interests which seem to be seriously threatened?"[15]

Reluctantly Wilson agreed that henceforth the administration would not discourage loans to belligerent governments. As with the war trade, so with finance: market forces would be left to dictate America's policy. Morgan's became Britain's fund-raiser as well as her purchasing agent.

By the early months of 1916 America's neutrality was in practice, therefore, increasingly tilted toward Britain. The tough line on German submarine warfare and the permissive attitude to British supplies and loans were pushing America into the Allied camp. Yet Wilson now felt increasingly alienated from the British cause. He was particularly angry at London's failure to cooperate in his efforts to end the war.

In February 1916 Wilson's adviser, Colonel Edward House, had reached an understanding with the British foreign secretary, Sir Edward Grey: when Britain and France judged the moment to be opportune, Wilson would propose a conference to end the war. Should Germany refuse to participate or should it reject terms that both the President and the Allies considered reasonable, then, according to the House-Grey memorandum, "the United States would probably enter the war against Germany."[16] For Wilson this was an important first step toward the peace table. But in London more cynical views prevailed. Like most of his colleagues, the prime minister, H. H. Asquith, considered the American proposal "humbug and a mere manoeuvre of American politics"[17] aimed at strengthening Wilson's chances of reelection in November. The past twenty months had only hardened British resolve. The U.S. ambassador in London, Walter Hines Page, told House in May: "The English do not see how there can be any mediation. . . . this German military caste caused all the trouble and there can be no security in Europe as long as it lives in authority. That's the English view. It raped nuns in Belgium. . . . it planned the destruction of the *Lusitania*. . . . It'll do anything."[18] Wilson's apparent indifference to the moral issues at stake seemed incredible and deeply offensive in London.

But the British failure to act on the House-Grey memorandum left Wilson equally angry and disillusioned. Britain seemed willing to pay any price for victory, a suspicion confirmed by the summer offensive on the Somme. On July 1, after seven days of artillery bombardment in which 1.5 million shells were fired, thirteen British divisions climbed out of their trenches to attack the German line.

Within two hours of their going over the top, twenty thousand were
dead. Even Ambassador Page in London, a staunch supporter of the
British cause, was sickened at the carnage. He compared it to

> certain horrible, catastrophic, universal-ruin passages in Revela-
> tion—monsters swallowing the universe, blood and fire and clouds
> and an eternal crash, rolling ruin enveloping all things—well, all
> that's come. There are, perhaps, ten million men dead of this war and,
> perhaps, one hundred million persons to whom death would be a
> blessing. Add to these many millions more whose views of life are
> so distorted that blank idiocy would be a better mental outlook, and
> you'll get a hint (and only a hint) of what the continent has already
> become—a bankrupt slaughter-house inhabited by unmated
> women.[19]

Britain's moral reputation in America suffered a further blow in
1916 from the brutal suppression of the Easter Rising in Dublin.
The leaders were summarily tried and shot, while Sir Roger Casement was hanged for treason, despite a plea of clemency from the
U.S. Senate. The British pleaded national security—Casement had
arrived in Ireland from Germany in a U-boat—but most Americans,
not just those of Irish extraction, were outraged. "I doubt if the
Germans have ever been as hopelessly stupid," wrote one of House's
correspondents. "Certainly everything for which British Liberalism
has stood, as contrasted to Prussian Junkerism, has been brushed
away."[20]

But the most dangerous crisis in Anglo-American relations occurred in 1916 over Britain's blockade of Germany. The British had
been able to enforce this by traditional methods, intercepting ships
and inspecting their cargoes, thereby avoiding the U-boats' indiscriminate attacks on shipping. The British blockade nonetheless was
seriously damaging to American commercial interests, and the State
Department had lodged repeated protests. The cotton trade, employing some four million people, had been particularly hard hit in
1915.

In the summer of 1916 matters came to a head. After the *Sussex*
pledge, which ended unrestricted submarine warfare, Germany's
blockade was much less emotive in America. At the same time the
British tightened their own blockade even further in a desperate
effort to starve Germany into surrender. American mail passing
through British ports was opened and inspected, and eighty-seven

U.S. firms figured on a new blacklist of companies suspected of trading with Germany, thus banning them from all commerce with Britain. The damage to American trade was infuriating, for the blacklist was a commercial death sentence throughout much of the world, but even unaffected Americans were incensed at the idea that they sold goods or sent letters only with the approval of John Bull. In late July, Wilson wrote to House, "I am, I must admit, about at the end of my patience with Great Britain and the Allies. This black list business is the last straw. . . . I am seriously considering asking Congress to authorize me to prohibit loans and restrict exports to the Allies."[21]

Wilson was now more determined than ever to bring about a peace settlement. In November, buttressed by a narrow presidential election victory on the slogan "He kept us out of war," he was ready to act. This time he decided not to approach London first: the failure of the House-Grey understanding had shown the folly of that. Instead, he would treat both sides impartially, as befitted a true neutral. Colonel House was distinctly unhappy. He warned Wilson that if Germany went along with a peace proposal and the Allies did not, America might drift into war with Britain. But the President was defiant, House recorded. "He went so far as to say that if the Allies wanted war with us we would not shrink from it."[22]

As Wilson argued with his advisers, producing one draft after another on his typewriter, an opportunity emerged to soften up the Allies for his new peace effort. Britain's perilous financial position provided the key. She was now spending $25 million on the war effort every day, of which $10 million had to be found in America. Of this, $4 million was currently being raised daily by American loans, but because of the drain on Britain's gold and American securities, the figure would soon be $8 million. In short, American loans would soon have to cover a third of Britain's war costs.

From the British Treasury, economist John Maynard Keynes warned the Cabinet bluntly of its dependence on the United States. It must not merely avoid irritating the Wilson administration, it must actively conciliate the American public, who was now being invited to lend their savings on a scale far larger than America's own national debt in order to keep Britain going. Keynes added: "Any feeling of irritation or lack of sympathy with this country or with its policy in the minds of the American public (and equally any lack of confidence in the military situation as interpreted by this public) would render it extremely difficult, if not impossible, to carry through financial operations on a scale adequate to our needs."[23] Grimly the Chancellor of the Exchequer, Reginald McKenna, summed up the implications of Britain's financial crisis. "If things go on as at present," he warned the Cabinet on October 24, 1916, "I venture to say with certainty that by next June or earlier the President of the American Republic will be in a position, if he wishes, to dictate his own terms to us."[24]

The following month Morgan's tried to ease Britain's financial crisis by selling up to a billion dollars in short-term British Treasury bonds on the American market, but on November 27 the Federal Reserve Board issued a public warning to America's banks. It had been checked first with Wilson, who had deliberately strengthened the wording. The board cautioned the banks that it did "not regard it in the interest of the country at this time that they invest in foreign Treasury bills of this character."[25] The effect was immediate. The price of Allied bonds fell precipitously, and the following day Morgan's spent some $20 million to support sterling. The British were soon aware that the warning had been issued on Wilson's authority. The ambassador in Washington, Sir Cecil Spring Rice, told the Foreign Office gravely that "the object of course is to force us to accept the President's mediation by cutting off supplies."[26]

Wilson's initiative followed swiftly. On December 18, 1916, the President dispatched identical notes to the governments of both sides. Under pressure from House and Lansing, Wilson had toned down his language. The notes stressed that "the President is not proposing peace; he is not even offering mediation." But Wilson did urge the belligerents to state their peace terms clearly and fully so that it would be possible to see whether there was common ground. For, he noted, "the objects which the statesmen of the belligerents on both sides have in mind in this war are virtually the same, as stated in general terms."[27] The British government was infuriated by Wilson's gratuitous insult, his equation of its war aims with those of Germany. It was said that the King wept when he read the note.

The following month, January 1917, Wilson spelled out in detail the new world order he envisaged once the war was over. It would center on a League of Nations, a "concert of power which will make it virtually impossible that such a catastrophe should ever overwhelm us again." America would play its part in keeping the peace, Wilson promised, but only if it was "a peace without victory." For "victory would mean peace forced upon the loser. . . . It would be accepted in humiliation, under duress, at an intolerable sacrifice, and would leave a sting, a resentment, a bitter memory upon which terms of peace would rest, not permanently, but only as upon quicksand. Only a peace between equals can last." Wilson went on to outline other principles of a just peace, including the freedom of the seas, the reduction of armaments and the right of national self-determination, all of which challenged British as well as German interests. "These," he proclaimed, "are American principles, American policies. . . . And they are also the principles and policies of forward looking men and women everywhere. . . . They are the principles of mankind and must prevail."[28]

Wilson's appeals met with no response in Europe. In December 1916 the Asquith government fell and a new coalition was formed under the energetic leadership of David Lloyd George. For two years he had chafed at the inadequacies of Britain's war effort, and he felt little sympathy for Grey's conciliatory attitude to the United States. To forestall a mediation attempt by Wilson in September 1916 he had insisted publicly that there could be no end to the war "until the Prussian military despotism is broken beyond repair. . . . It took England twenty years to defeat Napoleon," he reminded Americans, adding, "it will not take twenty years to win this war, but whatever time is required, it will be done. . . . The fight must be to a finish—to a knock-out."[29] Though less dismissive of Wilson's December note than the Germans, Lloyd George and his colleagues did not take it seriously. Nor were they enthusiastic about Wilson's talk of a League of Nations. The general British view was that planning for peace was irrelevant until "the lawless Hun" had been crushed. As Ambassador Spring Rice observed tartly from Washington: "The Good Samaritan did not pass by on the other side and then propose to the authorities at Jericho a bill for the better security of the highroads."[30]

Despite public bravado, the Allied position was now precarious. "We are going to lose this war," Lloyd George sighed in a moment of desperation.[31] The carnage of 1916 had been appalling and yet totally ineffectual. On the Somme 450,000 British casualties had been sustained, 540,000 Frenchmen had fallen in the defense of Verdun, while on the eastern front the Czar's armies had lost more than a million. Financially, Britain could not continue her American purchases much longer. Her gold was virtually exhausted, most of her American assets had been sold and the Federal Reserve was in effect blocking new loans. Admittedly, Wilson could not afford to

pull the financial strings too hard, for America was now almost as
dependent as Britain on the transatlantic trade. Exports were now
more than 11 percent of America's gross national product. Nor, for
all his irritation with Britain, would the President have wanted to
bring down the Allied cause if that meant an outright German
victory. But Wilson did not realize the full extent of Britain's financial crisis. He did not know, for instance, that by February 1917 the
British Treasury had only enough gold and securities to cover four
more weeks' purchases in the United States.

Fortunately for Britain, the Germans were even more ignorant
than Wilson about her financial predicament. On January 9, 1917,
the Supreme Command, led by Hindenburg and Ludendorff, persuaded the Kaiser to resume unrestricted submarine warfare at the
end of the month. All suspect shipping in the war zone around the
British Isles would be liable to attack, whether belligerent or neutral,
warship or merchantman. This broke all Germany's previous assurances to Wilson, including the *Sussex* pledge of May 1916, and made
it almost inevitable that America would declare war. Apparently
unaware that Britain might collapse from financial exhaustion
within weeks, a desperate German leadership gambled that by mid-
summer, long before America would be able to mobilize, the U-boat
blockade of Britain would have forced her to surrender.

In a speech in Milwaukee, a German American stronghold, the
previous year, Wilson had warned: "There may at any moment
come a time when I cannot preserve both the honor and the peace
of the United States. Do not exact of me an impossible and contra-
dictory thing."[32] On February 3, 1917, the President broke off
diplomatic relations with Germany. Many of his advisers now considered war unavoidable, but Wilson, like most of his countrymen,
was still looking for a way out. He hoped that a policy of arming
U.S. merchant vessels might suffice to protect American neutral
rights. "So he is not going to fight after all!" Lloyd George exclaimed contemptuously. "He is awaiting another insult before he
actually draws the sword!"[33]

Britain did her utmost to induce America to join her. On January
16 British naval intelligence intercepted a message from the German
foreign minister, Arthur Zimmermann, to the government of Mexico. In Room 40 of the Old Admiralty Building the message was
quickly decoded. Zimmermann had proposed that if America went
to war, an alliance should be forged between Germany, Mexico and
Japan. He promised "that Mexico is to reconquer the lost territory

in Texas, New Mexico and Arizona," which the United States had taken in the 1840s.[34] British intelligence was sure this telegram could secure America's entry into the war. A copy was given to the American ambassador, who communicated it to Wilson. The President's own attitude was not deeply affected, but when the telegram was published in the press on March 1 the public was at first incredulous and then incensed. Germany's atrocities in Belgium or even on the high seas were one thing; plotting, however ineptly, to conquer three American states was quite another.

The mood in America was hardening. The sinking of three American ships by German U-boats with the loss of fifteen crew finally forced Wilson to act. There could no longer be any doubt about German intentions. After a Cabinet meeting on March 20 an anguished Wilson decided to give up armed neutrality and take the final step.

On the evening of April 2, 1917, the President addressed a special session of the Congress and asked it formally to "accept the status of belligerent which has thus been thrust upon it." In words that must have brought sighs of relief in Whitehall he explained what war would mean. "It will involve the utmost practicable cooperation in counsel and action with the governments now at war with Germany, and . . . the extension to those governments of the most liberal financial credits, in order that our resources may so far as possible be added to theirs." But Wilson also made clear that America was still not identifying itself completely with the Allied cause. "We have no selfish ends to serve. We desire no conquest, no dominion." America would fight for the same goals that it had championed as a neutral, for "liberty," "peace" and "the rights of mankind." "The world must be made safe for democracy."[35] His wife, Edith, wrote in her diary: "Through cheering multitudes we drove home in silence. The step had been taken. We were both overwhelmed."[36]

Congress quickly approved the President's request, although six senators and fifty members of the House voted against. At 1:18 on the afternoon of Good Friday, April 6, 1917, the President signed the war resolution. No photographers were present: the occasion, Wilson felt, was far too solemn for that. After thirty-two months of uneasy neutrality, the United States was finally at war.

CHAPTER 4

VICTORY WITHOUT PEACE
1917–1920

Modern Britain was founded on liberal values. In nineteenth-century Britain there was no standing army, no military conscription. Economic life was left to the initiative of individual entrepreneurs. Freedom of speech and freedom of assembly were highly prized civil liberties. But by 1917 British liberalism was under siege. Conscription and tight censorship had been imposed, government controls applied to the economy, and a bitter hatred of Germany was fostered in the do-or-die war effort. The old Liberal party had been split beyond repair, and Lloyd George, once a passionate civil libertarian and antimilitarist, was now lusting for victory at all costs.

As Woodrow Wilson had feared, America found it equally hard to maintain liberal values in an atmosphere of total war. Whole industries, such as railroads and shipping, were brought under government control. Official boards in Washington directed key areas of the economy. The administration soon drew up its own blacklist of firms suspected of trading with the enemy, and in December 1917 the British ambassador reported wryly to London: "The blacklist is now published and is far more extensive than our own. The *New York Times* which railed against ours publishes the American list almost without comment."[1]

But the most marked antiliberal outburst was the backlash against everything German. In Pittsburgh Beethoven's music was banned, and the violinist Fritz Kreisler was ostracized from American concert halls. In scores of cities the German language was removed from school curricula. Hamburgers were renamed "liberty steaks," sauerkraut "liberty cabbage." One patriotic doctor in Massachusetts decided that even diseases were too good for Germans and insisted on diagnosing "liberty measles."

Many Americans of German stock were loyal or at least discreet. A few made dramatic gestures of patriotism: the Germania Club of Jacksonville, Florida, turned over its new hundred-thousand-dollar clubhouse to the American Red Cross free of charge. But parts of America came close to civil war. Even today older citizens of New Ulm, a small town in Minnesota, cannot forget the summer of 1917. Shortly after war was declared, Wilson introduced the draft. Fearing that they would be sent to fight their own people in Europe, the strong German American community in New Ulm organized a rally to contest the legality of the draft. On July 25, 1917, more than five thousand people marched to the City Hall, where they heard some speeches and then dispersed. It was hardly seditious, but within weeks the head of the new Public Safety Commission for Minnesota had removed the mayor and several other officials from their posts. There was talk of burning New Ulm down and some leading German Americans received death threats. Local banks, doing what they thought was their patriotic duty, insisted that their German American customers invest in U.S. government war loans, the Liberty Bonds, even if they had to borrow to do so. The names of those who refused to buy leaked out and the mob painted their farms and houses yellow.[2]

Even the President's mood hardened. During the summer of 1917 he denounced the "hyphenate" minority, those German Americans who, he claimed, were doing the Kaiser's bidding. He became more reticent about his peace aims and spoke out so vigorously against a negotiated peace that liberals in America and Britain feared he had deserted them. His aim was now peace *through* victory, not the "peace without victory" he had proclaimed only a few months before. But Wilson was still clear about the peace he eventually wanted to achieve.

America's declaration of war on Germany meant that it would cooperate with Britain but not that it would sign a treaty of alliance. Wilson explained to A. J. Balfour, Grey's successor as foreign secretary, in April 1917 that the United States would be an "associate" power, remaining independent of the Allies and able to make peace on its own terms when it chose. Although they were on the same side for the moment, Wilson was convinced that the United States and the Allies had fundamentally different war aims: America wanted a just peace and a new world order in which imperialism, arms races and military alliances were a thing of the past, whereas the Allies wanted territorial gain, vengeance and reparation for the damage they had suffered. But he thought he could bring the Allies to heel. He wrote in July 1917: "England and France *have not the same views with regard to peace that we have* by any means. When the war is over we can force them to our way of thinking, because by that time they will, among other things, be financially in our hands. . . ."[3]

But in 1917 the end of the war seemed a long way off. Just as the German Supreme Command had expected, the United States was slow to mobilize. In April 1917 the regular army numbered a mere 110,000, and the President's call for the draft was a major break with tradition and a further blow to American liberal values. "Good Lord!" exclaimed one senator. "You're not going to send soldiers over there, are you?"[4] Draft registration did not begin until June, and by the end of 1917 only 175,000 American troops had crossed the Atlantic.

But few who made that journey ever forgot it. Many of the troopships left from Hoboken pier, on the New Jersey shore opposite New York.

> We boarded the ship under cover of darkness and then pulled as unobtrusively as possible out into the roadstead. . . . I had never seen the Statue of Liberty and I got to a porthole and I remember the thrill that I had, that has always stayed with me, when I saw the Statue of Liberty and realized that maybe I might not see it again. We had fifteen hundred men on board. We were stacked in there like sardines and it took us fourteen days to get across, and we had about eight days of storm. Most of us were sick. Many men actually wanted somebody to shoot them, get them out of their misery.[5]

When news that a troop convoy was arriving spread through Liverpool, children ran down to the docks to greet the strangers in the big Boy Scout hats. "It was fantastic," recalls one of them, now in his seventies. "All you could see was Hershey bars getting thrown as far as they could. . . . We used to run alongside them asking for cents, or spearmints, anything at all. . . . I thought they were cow-boys. I really never thought they'd do any fighting."[6]

The American "doughboys" were bound for France. Most passed through Britain quickly, en route from Liverpool to Southampton. But those who did stay were intrigued by what they saw: buildings older than anything in the United States, children sometimes close to starvation because of the growing food shortages, a country ap-parently devoid of young men outside the military hospitals. And then there were the women. "We were absolutely stunned by the pure peaches-and-cream complexions of the English girls. We had never seen anything like that. We were used to girls with deep tans in the West. They gave us this impression that they were like porcelain dolls, they were so pretty."[7]

The private soldiers may have been enjoying themselves, but Britain's leaders wanted action. On both sea and land they were now desperate for support, yet the Americans seemed determined to fight the war in their own way and in their own good time.

Admiral William Benson, the U.S. chief of naval operations, wanted to keep his fleet in American waters as defense against U-boat attacks. It needed further training, and Benson also feared that Britain might be defeated, leaving America to fight Germany alone. He was deeply suspicious of the British. According to Admi-ral William Sims, who was sent to London in April 1917 to liaise with the British Admiralty, Benson's parting words were: "Don't let the British pull the wool over your eyes. It is none of our business pulling their chestnuts out of the fire. We would as soon fight the British as the Germans."[8] It took all Sims's powers of persuasion to convince Washington that the U-boat campaign was nearly starving Britain into submission, with shipping losses of six hundred thou-sand tons in March and nine hundred thousand in April. By July 1917 thirty-six of America's fifty-one operational destroyers had been moved to British ports. In an unprecedented gesture, Sims placed them under British command to combat the U-boat menace off the west coast of Britain and Ireland.

The American Army proved less cooperative. In the spring of 1918 the Germans mounted a series of massive new offensives on the western front. The previous November Lenin and the Bolsheviks had seized power in Russia. Within weeks they had pulled their country out of the war, freeing Germany to concentrate all its resources in a final onslaught against the British and French. On March 21 Ludendorff's armies ripped through the unprepared British front on the Somme. The British lost as much ground in that one day as they had gained in 140 days of suicidal fighting in the great Somme battles of 1916. In April and late May the Germans mounted further hammerblows. The first nearly drove a wedge between the British and French; the second brought the Germans within forty miles of Paris.

Where were the Americans? Stateside the bands were trumpeting out "The Yanks are Coming," but the British were getting impatient. One private in the 2nd Worcesters recalls the song: "We did a bit of laughing about this because we thought it was typically Yank, you know, boasting. We thought they were just a boastful lot." But the laughter was now grim: "We realized we were getting to the end of our manpower resources. . . . we knew there weren't many left in England to back us up."[9] After the March disaster a panic-stricken Cabinet started withdrawing men from essential industries, such as munitions and the mines. It even contemplated extending conscription to Ireland, only to be told by the chief secretary for Ireland that it "might as well recruit Germans."[10] Vehemently Lloyd George and the British commander in chief, Sir Douglas Haig, demanded that the United States send over as many combat troops as possible, for immediate amalgamation in hard-pressed British and French units.

But the commander of the American Expeditionary Force, General John J. Pershing, had no intention of using his troops as a replacement pool for the Allies. He interpreted his orders to mean that he should build up a separate American army in Europe, properly trained and supplied, to be used in action when American policy determined. Haig complained that Pershing "did not seem to realise the urgency of the situation. . . . He hankers after a *great self contained American Army*" but . . . it is ridiculous to think such an Army could function unaided in less than two years time."[11] Pershing, however, would not be rushed, nor diverted from his aim. By the time the fifth and last great German offensive of 1918 had petered out in the middle of July, 1.2 million American troops were in France but few of them had seen action.

Pershing's conduct was a graphic illustration of what America's "associate" status really meant. The United States would use its own power in its own way, not at the Allies' behest. And in January 1918 President Wilson had issued a new reminder of America's independent approach to world affairs when he set out his Fourteen Points for a just peace.

Upon seizing power in Russia, Lenin and the Bolsheviks had ransacked the Czar's files. They published secret treaties which confirmed that once Germany and the Central Powers were defeated, the Allies intended to divide up the spoils between them. France was to take parts of Germany and Italy pieces of Austria. The Turkish empire would be dismembered, with Britain a major beneficiary. In response, Wilson insisted that America was above such Old World duplicity. His first five points were a direct challenge to Britain's global power. They called for an end to secret diplomacy and its replacement by "open covenants of peace, openly arrived at"; for "absolute freedom of navigation upon the seas"; for "the removal, so far as possible, of all economic barriers"; for the maximum possible disarmament "consistent with domestic safety"; and for "a free, open-minded and absolutely impartial adjustment of all colonial claims" after weighing "the interests of the populations concerned" equally with the rights of the governing powers.[12] Clearly Wilson had not abandoned his aim of reshaping the Old World in the image of the New. And it appeared as 1918 wore on that Pershing's army would be his chosen instrument.

In mid-July the Allied counteroffensives began. For the first time Pershing's divisions, now formed into the First U.S. Army, saw action in large numbers, but the brunt of the fighting was still borne by the British and French. In London it seemed that the war would drag on into 1919 or 1920. The Cabinet was increasingly anxious that Britain would by then be exhausted and at the mercy of any terms that Wilson cared to impose. Some even used this as a renewed argument for a negotiated peace. General Jan Smuts warned Lloyd George in August 1918: "It may well be that, by the indefinite continuance of the war, we shall become a second or third-class Power, and the leadership, not only financially and militarily, but in every respect will have passed on to America and Japan."[13] Lloyd George was particularly angry that while Britain had provided half the shipping needed to transport Pershing's recalcitrant army to Europe, the American merchant fleet, now grown to 40 percent of Britain's, had captured a quarter of world trade.

Then, suddenly, it was all over. Germany's allies, Bulgaria, Turkey and Austria-Hungary, collapsed in the early autumn. Germany was left alone, its reserves exhausted, aware now that, with the strong, well-fed Americans coming into the line in their thousands, the Allies could not be beaten. Germany's morale snapped. At the beginning of October 1918 a new government assumed power under Prince Max of Baden, and as revolution smoldered in Germany an end to hostilities was agreed. But Prince Max was not negotiating with the Allies. He appealed over their heads to Wilson, asking for an armistice on the basis of the President's Fourteen Points. The Germans believed that these offered them much more generous terms than anything available from the embittered British and French.

Wilson negotiated an armistice with the Germans. He then sent House over to Paris to inform the Allies of what their "associate" had decided. The Allied leaders were furious, but House stopped them short. If the Fourteen Points were not accepted as the basis for negotiation, he warned, Wilson would go to Congress and ask whether America should continue to fight for countries that did not share its war aims. This ended most of the debate, but Britain still refused to accept Point Two dealing with the freedom of the seas. The Admiralty saw it as a challenge to Britain's sea power and her right of blockade, an attack on "the very source of our national life, the maintenance of which is an act of self-preservation."[14] House warned that if agreement could not be reached, there would ensue an all-out race to build the most powerful navy in the world. "The United States," he said, "had more resources, more men and more money than Great Britain and in a contest, Great Britain would lose." Lloyd George replied "that Great Britain would spend her last guinea to keep a navy superior to that of the United States or any other power, and that no Cabinet official could continue in the Government in England who took a different position."[15]

In the end Lloyd George won that point. He would not accept the principle of freedom of the seas in advance, but agreed to discuss the issue at the peace conference. He also secured another reservation allowing the Allies to demand reparations from Germany. He decided that the rest of the Fourteen Points were "wide enough to allow us to place our own interpretation upon them."[16] Despite their dependence on American money and manpower, the British clearly still had some leverage of their own. But there was no denying on Armistice Day, November 11, 1918, that President Wilson had ended the war virtually on his own terms. It remained to be seen whether he could write the peace treaty as well.

Wilson left New York on board the SS *George Washington* on December 4, 1918. In today's world of summits and shuttle diplomacy it is worth remembering that he was the first American president to travel to Europe while in office. It was a controversial, eventually a fateful, decision. For Wilson was staking his whole personal reputation on the peace conference, convinced that he alone could guide the world to a just and lasting peace.

After a few days in France the President reached Dover on December 26. As he disembarked schoolgirls strewed rose petals in his path. The King's train took him on to London amid scenes of rejoicing and celebration. There he and his wife, Edith, stood on the balcony of Buckingham Palace with King George V and Queen Mary, acknowledging the cheers of a crowd who chanted "We want Wilson." A young English girl, Edith Sowerbutts, was among those watching. "Everybody cheered and clapped. He spoke optimistically. The world was going to be safe for democracy and there would be no more wars, which pleased everybody. We were all very young and we believed all we were told."[17]

These were heady days for the President. During the war he had appealed to large sections of British radical opinion, Liberal and Labour, who were revolted by the slaughter and yearned for a new and better world. The ecstatic reception in Europe confirmed his belief that he alone spoke for "the silent mass of mankind." The economist John Maynard Keynes was one of the welcoming liberals. Wilson "enjoyed a prestige and a moral influence throughout the world unequalled in history," he wrote later. The President also controlled "the realities of power," with Europe dependent on America for manpower, food and finance. "Never," judged Keynes, "has a philosopher held such weapons wherewith to bind the princes of this world."[18]

The President's sense of his own virtue was dramatically illustrated at the state banquet held in his honor at Buckingham Palace on December 27. After the privations of wartime this was an opportunity for the leaders of triumphant Britain to celebrate in pomp and pageantry. Dr. Cary Grayson, Wilson's physician, was dazzled by the scene in the great dining room. "On the walls," he wrote in his diary, "are hundreds of pieces of solid gold decorations, plaques, shields and the like. . . . All of the table service is of solid gold, bearing the royal arms. The value of the gold dishes is said to be approximately $15,000,000."[19] The guests at the banquet represented all parts of Britain and her empire, resplendent in dress uniforms, medals, and jewelry. The display was all the more striking when one remembered that four rival imperial dynasties, the Romanovs, the Hapsburgs, the Hohenzollerns and the Ottomans, had recently disintegrated in bloody chaos. Left alone in battered but solitary splendor was the House of Saxe-Coburg-Gotha, prudently renamed the House of Windsor in 1917.

Yet the guest of honor at this pageant of princes cut a very different figure. Wilson was dressed in an ordinary black suit without medal or braid. His speech of thanks was clipped and formal, making not even passing reference to the contribution of the British Empire to the defeat of Germany. Those listening were chilled. "There was no glow of friendship or of gladness at meeting men who had been partners in a common enterprise," Lloyd George recalled.[20] It was as if Wilson had been fighting his own private war. Later the President warned the King:

> You must not speak of us who come over here as cousins, still less as brothers; we are neither. Neither must you think of us as Anglo-Saxons, for that term can no longer be rightly applied to the people of the United States. Nor must too much importance in this connection be attached to the fact that English is our common language. . . . No, there are only two things which can establish and maintain closer relations between your country and mine: they are community of ideals and of interests.[21]

In some ways British and American "ideals" were not so far apart as Wilson often implied. Many of his cherished convictions, such as disarmament, anti-imperialism and free trade, were not distinctively American. They were the traditions of nineteenth-century British liberalism in which the President was rooted, the ideals of Richard Cobden, John Bright and Wilson's great hero, Gladstone. Even the idea of a League of Nations was as much British as American. The term itself was popularized by a Cambridge don, Lowes Dickinson, who had helped found the League of Nations Society in Britain in 1915. Sir Edward Grey, the Liberal foreign secretary, had pressed the idea on Wilson in the early part of the war, and after Grey's fall Lord Robert Cecil had kept the idea alive in the British Cabinet. He and General Jan Smuts of South Africa prodded Whitehall into drawing up detailed proposals for a League during 1918. The British came to Paris better prepared on the issue than Wilson himself.

Nevertheless, Wilson was right to assert that he and the British were far apart. Lloyd George and his colleagues had deserted the old liberal traditions that Wilson still espoused. No one else in the Cabinet was as enthusiastic as Cecil about making the League of

Nations the centerpiece of a new system of international security. Britain had too much at stake in the old order to welcome the creation of a new, as the argument about the Fourteen Points had shown. And after a long and bloody war, in which 750,000 Britons had died, the demand for vengeance was overwhelming, voiced especially by Lloyd George's powerful Conservative partners in the coalition government. In the election campaign of November 1918 Lloyd George had started out promising that "we must relentlessly set our face against . . . squalid principles of either revenge or avarice." But under pressure from an enraged public, orchestrated by the *Daily Mail* and other Northcliffe newspapers who wanted Germany squeezed "until the pips squeak," he was soon calling for reparations from Germany "up to the limit of her capacity," a sum estimated by the Treasury at £25 billion.[22]

While liberalism was dying in Britain, Woodrow Wilson gave it a new lease on life. The United States, of course, was not completely disinterested. Freer trade, for instance, would obviously benefit the world's most powerful economy. But America, with no territorial claims and only about 130,000 dead, had far less at stake in the peace conference than any other belligerent. "Wilsonianism" was British liberalism transformed by America's crusading sense of mission and enforced by America's enormous new power. The values abandoned by the Old World were now being turned against it by the messiah from the New.

The peace conference formally opened in Paris on January 18, 1919. It was the most momentous international gathering since the Congress of Vienna a century before, which had determined the shape of Europe after Napoleon. But this was a far larger affair. Britain had fewer than twenty diplomats at Vienna, but in 1919 it required five hotels to accommodate her staff of over two hundred. The Americans had thirteen hundred in their delegation at its peak. There were also thirty other national delegations, each with a vested interest in the outcome of the conference, and a press corps of five hundred, including one hundred fifty Americans, all determined to make a reality of Wilson's call for "open diplomacy." Little wonder, then, that for many participants the conference seemed totally chaotic. The British diplomat Harold Nicolson compared it to a "riot in a parrot house."[23]

The first month of the conference was dominated by Wilson. His overriding aim was to keep the League of Nations at the top of the agenda until its foundations had been established. After intense debate a draft agreement was reached. For the first time in history there would be an international assembly, led by the great powers but open to all, which pledged itself to maintain peace and stability. If the territory of any state was endangered, or its independence threatened, the other League members would come to its aid by applying economic sanctions or direct military force.

Lloyd George doubted the wisdom of this last provision. It seemed dangerously utopian and, if observed to the letter, would place impossible obligations on great powers like Britain to intervene in every dispute. Personally he would have preferred a looser League based on the Allied Supreme War Council he had set up in 1917. This would expedite consultation between the powers, without making their response to aggression preordained. But Wilson believed that this automatic commitment, enshrined in Article Ten of the League's Covenant, was indispensable. Reluctantly the British Cabinet went along with his grand design. It seemed the price necessary to ensure the President's cooperation on issues they regarded as vital at the peace conference. As Australia's prime minister, Billy Hughes, put it: "Give him a League of Nations and he will give us all the rest."[24]

The President himself presented the Covenant to a full session of the conference on St. Valentine's Day, February 14, 1919, his triumph, as he thought, complete. Immediately afterward he left Paris for home to handle urgent domestic business. The outlines of the League had now been agreed, but the peace terms to be imposed on Germany still had to be decided.

Wilson's return to Washington showed clearly that he had misjudged the temper of Congress. Under the U.S. Constitution any international treaty has to be approved by two-thirds of the Senate, and in the midterm elections of November 1918 the Republicans had won a majority in both houses of Congress. This meant that Wilson's archenemy, Henry Cabot Lodge, would be chairman of the Senate Foreign Relations Committee, responsible for managing the hearings and the debate on the treaty.

Wilson had little time for members of Congress: he regarded them for the most part as small-minded and parochial. He had taken no Republican politicians with him to Paris, and assumed he could railroad the treaty through the Senate. But back in Washington in February he discovered the depths of the opposition. He was flouting the most hallowed precept of American diplomacy, dating back to George Washington, that America should avoid entangling al-

INTERRUPTING THE CEREMONY

McCUTCHEON, CHICAGO TRIBUNE—NEW YORK NEWS SYNDICATE, INC.

liances. He was apparently overriding the right of Congress to declare war by committing the country to automatic action whenever the League's Covenant was violated. It also seemed that the Covenant denied the Monroe Doctrine, the United States' claim that it could rightfully intervene if any outside power tried to establish itself on the American continent.

Wilson felt sure of his position. He reported to House, still in Paris, that "the people of the United States are undoubtedly in favor

of the League of Nations by an overwhelming majority. I can say
this with perfect confidence."[25] But the Senate remained unim-
pressed by his explanations of the League and of how it squared with
American rights and interests. "I feel as if I had been wandering
with 'Alice in Wonderland' and had had tea with the Mad Hatter,"
complained one frustrated senator.[26] Wilson's liberal international-
ism was not shared by the hardheaded nationalists in Congress.

When Wilson returned to Paris on March 14, he had lost the
initiative. Previously he had based his case for the League on a
position of purity and high-mindedness. He had argued that the
new world order should be free of all taint of imperialism and
"balance of power" politics. But now the Senate had insisted that
America's sphere of influence in Central and South America, as
defined by the Monroe Doctrine, should be admitted as an exception. Such special pleading was acutely embarrassing. Worse still,
it was tactically disastrous, for if America claimed a special right to
pursue its own self-interest the Allies would naturally do the same.

The French seized the opportunity to press their demand for
punitive reparations from Germany. They considered these essential to rebuild their ravaged country. They also wanted permanent
control of the Rhineland to ensure their security against renewed
German attack. Lloyd George's position was midway between that
of America and France. Under intense pressure at home, he was
forced to plead Britain's own case for reparations. But he had no
desire to build up French power in Europe and he opposed their
demands for the Rhineland. He feared that if Germany lost too
much of her homeland, that would sow the seeds of future war and
also accelerate the spread of Bolshevism. Unlike France, Britain's
main interests lay outside Europe. Britain wanted to destroy Germany as a world power: to strip her of her colonies, to take over her
navy and merchant fleet, and to safeguard the position of the British
Empire.

By April 1919 Wilson, Lloyd George and Clemenceau were
evenly matched. Britain and France depended much less on America now that the fighting was over and Wilson's leverage greatly
reduced. Lloyd George and Clemenceau were more in step than
Wilson with opinion back home, which made their negotiating
positions far stronger. The British premier, often nicknamed the
Wizard, was also tactically astute. He shifted discussions into a small
Council of Four, comprising the leaders of Britain, France, America
and Italy. There, without advisers and secretaries, business could be

accelerated in a way that benefited the Europeans, trained in the cut and thrust of parliamentary debate. Wilson's mind, though powerful, was slower, less subtle. In long, informal discussions in late March and early April 1919 the President's resistance was gradually worn down.

Compromise, after all, is the essence of diplomacy. And it was now imperative that agreement be reached and a peace treaty signed. For Europe seemed on the brink of anarchy and revolution. The defeated powers were in economic chaos, but a proper program of feeding and recovery could not be mounted until the war had formally come to an end. On March 22 Colonel House noted in his diary: "I am discouraged at the outlook. We are not moving as rapidly now. From the look of things the crisis will soon be here. Rumblings of discontent every day. The people want peace. Bolshevism is gaining ground everywhere. Hungary has just succumbed. We are sitting upon an open powder magazine and some day a spark may ignite it."[27] Lloyd George and Wilson shared these fears of Bolshevik revolution. Pressure mounted in Paris to reach a rapid agreement, and it was the exhausted President, for a while seriously ill from the influenza epidemic that was sweeping the world, who now made most of the concessions.

To satisfy Britain and France, Wilson agreed that greater reparations should be exacted from Germany than had first been proposed. After another row with Lloyd George he stopped pressing Britain on the freedom of the seas. And to placate Clemenceau, Wilson and Lloyd George agreed to a temporary occupation of the Rhineland for fifteen years. They also offered him an Anglo-American guarantee of French security. If Germany attempted to invade France, Britain and America would come to her assistance. This marked a historic departure from both countries' traditional policy of avoiding entangling alliances with continental Europe. But it also opened up a vast breach in the League's principle of global collective security. In return, the Allies accepted the Senate's modifications of the Covenant. The League could now start its work, which remained Wilson's overriding objective.

The final text of the treaty, some two hundred pages, was published on May 7, 1919. Liberals in the British and American delegations, who had been excluded from the intense top-level negotiations of the last few weeks, were horrified at what they read. The ideals of the Fourteen Points seemed to have been totally abandoned. John Maynard Keynes resigned from the British delegation in protest. "I've never been so miserable as for the last two or three weeks; the peace is outrageous and impossible," he wrote. "Certainly if I was in the Germans' place I'd rather die than sign such a peace."[28]

It nearly came to that. The German delegation had been kept waiting while the peace terms were worked out by America and the Allies. Now they too were aghast at what they read, rejecting the draft treaty as a travesty of the terms on which they had originally accepted the armistice. They had assumed that the Fourteen Points would be the basis of the eventual peace. Lloyd George, increasingly alarmed about the dangers of harsh terms, secured some minor changes, but Clemenceau was instransigent and an exhausted Wilson was in no mood for further alterations. Finally Germany was given twenty-four hours to accept the treaty or be invaded. On June 28, 1919, in Louis XIV's great Hall of Mirrors at Versailles, two quaking German delegates signed the treaty.

For the French, it was a moment to savor. Bismarck had imposed a humiliating peace treaty on them in the same place thirty-eight years before. Now the tables had been turned with a vengeance. Yet even those who had struck the deal had their doubts. After the signing Lloyd George commented: "We shall have to do the whole thing over again in twenty-five years time at three times the cost."[29] Germany was left weakened but not crushed. The treaty might well have been far harsher, given the grimness of the war, but it still left a legacy of deep and abiding bitterness. Before long an aggrieved Germany would once again demand the status of a world power, this time under a leadership of appalling depravity.

On June 29, 1919, the day after the Treaty of Versailles had been signed, Wilson set off for home. He had reached agreement with the Allies. Now he had to win over two-thirds of the U.S. Senate, in which the Republicans, under the hostile Lodge, had a majority. Looking ahead to the presidential election of 1920, they saw political capital to be made out of the League. But many senators were not isolationist, opposed to any American involvement in the affairs of Europe. Lodge himself favored the Anglo-American guarantee of France. Most senators in fact shared Lloyd George's outlook, welcoming a loose international organization but opposing the automatic, unlimited, global commitments proposed by Wilson. Eventually Lodge offered fourteen reservations to the proposed League that would give the United States the right to choose its own course of action on any issue of national importance. America would not be committed automatically to defend another country's territorial integrity, to implement economic sanctions or to accept the League's decisions on disarmament. The right of the Congress to determine America's foreign policy would be safeguarded.

Among the most ardent opponents of the League were Irish Americans. They had expected Wilson to put Irish freedom high on the agenda at Paris, and in March 1919 a resolution swept through the House of Representatives demanding that the peace conference, "in passing on the rights of various peoples, will favorably consider the claims of Ireland to the right of self-determination."[30] But Wilson had enough problems in Paris without adding Ireland to the list. The issue was hardly discussed, and angry Irish Americans, backed by over one million dollars from their Irish Victory Fund, campaigned against the League to get their own back on Wilson and the British. "If the League of Nations goes into effect as now presented," the *Philadelphia Irish Press* declared, "Americans will be found to assist England in crushing any insurrection that might occur in Ireland."[31]

Despite the mounting opposition, Wilson remained confident of his rightness. He tried to go over the Senate's head and appeal to public opinion. In 1919, just before the age of radio, long before the era of regular air travel, that meant a long speaking tour around the vast American heartland, journeying by special train. Wherever he went the President's message to the American people was clear: the treaty and the Covenant had taken months of negotiation and could not now be changed. "If we want a League of Nations," he insisted in Portland, Oregon, "we must take this League of Nations. . . . We must leave it or take it." In Sioux Falls, South Dakota, he declared that the whole world was waiting for America to join the League, because "America is the only idealistic Nation in the world. . . . If America goes back upon mankind, mankind has no other place to turn." And for those who "do not want me to be too altruistic," he told an audience in St. Louis, "let me be very practical. If we are partners, let me predict that we will be the senior partner. The financial leadership will be ours. The industrial primacy will be ours. The commercial advantage will be ours. The other countries of the world are looking to us for leadership and direction."[32]

In the first three weeks of September 1919 Wilson traveled eight thousand miles by train, giving nearly forty hour-long speeches, often without the help of any amplification, as well as holding innumerable informal conferences. Coming after months of travel

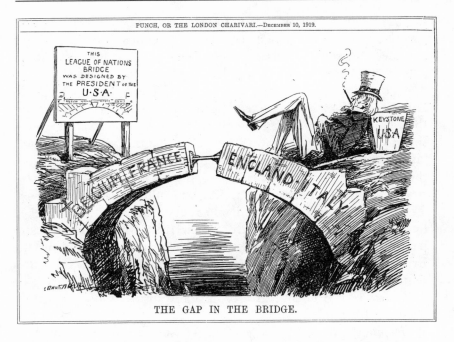

THE GAP IN THE BRIDGE.

The British magazine Punch *expresses British frustration at the Senate's rejection of the League.*

and argument, to and fro across the Atlantic, the strain was too much for the sixty-three-year-old President. On September 25, in a state of nervous and physical exhaustion, Wilson was forced to return to Washington. On October 2, he suffered a severe stroke. For two weeks he was close to death; for several months he lay virtually helpless, and his wife, Edith, ran the White House.

It was now clear that Lodge could deny the President his two-thirds majority. But illness clouded Wilson's judgment and hardened his will. He still refused to make any fundamental compromise, despite the urging of Senate Democrats and of his wife. On November 18, 1919, the day before the senators voted, he sent them a letter stating that to vote for Lodge's reservations would amount to "the nullification of the treaty."[33] Next day neither side could win the necessary two-thirds majority. Wilson's proposed League fell well short, but so did Lodge's League with reservations. In another vote in March 1920 an inflexible Wilson still retained the loyalty of enough Democrats to keep Lodge seven votes short. The United States would not be a member of the League of Nations, nor would it guarantee French security. One of the most momentous decisions that America had been asked to take was decided by stalemate.

Back in April 1917 Woodrow Wilson began a great crusade to make the world safe for democracy. American supplies sustained the Allied armies, its loans kept them fighting, its troops proved the last straw for the exhausted Germans. In October 1918 Wilson was able to dictate armistice terms to friend and foe alike. But once Germany had collapsed, much of his leverage over the Allies disappeared. He was forced to compromise extensively at Paris to win European support for his League. Liberals felt the President had betrayed their trust. Worse, Wilson could not then secure approval in Washington for what had been agreed at Versailles. The League itself was betrayed by the country whose president had been its architect. "America," said Lloyd George, "had been offered the leadership of the world, but the Senate had tossed the sceptre into the sea."[34]

CHAPTER 5

THE
BIG TWO
1921-1935

The United States did not join the League of Nations, but as Woodrow Wilson rightly pointed out, its place in the world had changed irrevocably. "By the sheer genius of this people and the growth of our power we have become a determining factor in the history of mankind," he declared in 1919, "and after you have become a determining factor you cannot remain isolated, whether you want to or not."[1] Although in the 1920s America maintained its cherished tradition of no entangling alliances with the Old World, the war had made it a major force in international affairs. Its fleet was nearly as large as the Royal Navy, it had the second biggest merchant marine in the world, and its vast loans to the Allies had transformed it from a debtor into a major creditor nation.

While the New World prospered, the Old World had destroyed itself. The Austro-Hungarian empire had disappeared, splintered into small chaotic rival states. Germany—defeated, disarmed and embittered—was now under a weak and unpopular republican regime. Russia had been torn apart by revolution and civil war, losing huge tracts of territory on its western frontier. And France, though a victor, had suffered 1.5 million killed, including over a tenth of its active male population. Seen from the vantage point of today, the Great War was a turning point in Europe's decline.

But one of the old European powers had come through the war

EUROPE AFTER WORLD WAR ONE

NORWAY

SWEDEN

FINLAND

• Petrograd

ESTONIA

• Pskov

LATVIA

LITHUANIA

U S S R

DENMARK

E PRUSSIA

• Minsk

HOLLAND

Berlin •

• Warsaw

POLAND

• Kiev

GERMANY

BELGIUM

• Paris

CZECHOSLOVAKIA

BESSARABIA

Vienna •

• Budapest

FRANCE

AUSTRIA

HUNGARY

ROUMANIA

SWITZERLAND

S TYROL

• Bucharest

ITALY

Belgrade •

YUGOSLAVIA

BULGARIA

• Rome

ALBANIA

• Salonika

TURKEY

GREECE

0			300
Miles

0			400
Km

INTERNATIONAL BOUNDARIES

TERRITORY LOST BY GERMANY

AUSTRO-HUNGARIAN EMPIRE
UNTIL 1918

TERRITORY LOST BY RUSSIA

much better than the rest. Great Britain had suffered 750,000 dead, the loss of 15 percent of her overseas assets and the collapse of many of her old industries. But she had not been invaded, and the main threat to British security, the German Navy, lay rusting at the bottom of Scapa Flow. On the ruin of the old Turkish empire she acquired vast mandates from the League of Nations in Palestine and Mesopotamia (later Iraq), making her the major power in the oil-rich Middle East. The British Empire was now larger than it had been at Queen Victoria's death. "England is the only real winner from this war," wrote the German historian Erich Marks in 1920, "England together with North America: one can see an Anglo-Saxon world dominion rising on the horizon."[2]

Marks was not alone. To many in Germany and France it seemed that the era of "the Anglo-Saxons" had dawned. Symbolically this could be seen in the language of the Paris peace conference, which, to the annoyance of France, had been conducted in English as much as in French, previously the lingua franca of diplomacy and culture. The Big Three—Wilson, Lloyd George and Clemenceau—used English almost exclusively for their crucial discussions in March and April 1919. The substance as well as the language of diplomacy had changed. The League of Nations, as drafted in Paris, was basically a compromise between Woodrow Wilson and Robert Cecil: it was an Anglo-American plan, thrust on the rest of the world. Britain and America were the strongest financial powers, possessed the largest navies, and were relatively secure, stable and satisfied. During the 1920s they were to shape the postwar world.

Nevertheless, Britain was disconcerted by America's dramatic entrance onto the world stage. Few had anticipated how rapidly American power and influence would grow as a result of the war. No one in government had enjoyed the humiliation of being, in the words of the British press baron Lord Northcliffe in 1917, "down on our knees to the Americans."[3] In the wake of the Great War many British leaders decided that it was vital to maintain the closest cooperation with the Americans in order to safeguard British inter-ests. As Cecil put it in 1917, "If America accepts our point of view . . . it will mean the dominance of that point of view in all interna-tional affairs." He was convinced that America could be guided by Britain, because it was new to the affairs of Europe and because, "though the American people are very largely foreign, both in origin and in modes of thought, their rulers are almost exclusively Anglo-Saxons, and share our political ideals."[4]

Henceforth the hope of a special relationship with America, the Old World discreetly managing the New, was to be at the center of British policy. But the war had already shown that the relationship would not be easy to manipulate in the way Britain wanted. The Senate vote on the League dramatically illustrated the fact that an American president had much less freedom of action in foreign affairs than a British prime minister. Congress could easily upset the best-laid plans of the diplomats. And, as Cecil's comments showed, British leaders were prone to exaggerate the "Englishness" of America, despite Wilson's emphatic warning to the King at Buckingham Palace that the United States was no longer "Anglo-Saxon."

The most serious obstacle to cooperation was the fact that the Big Two of the postwar world were rivals as much as collaborators. Whatever the French suspected, "Anglo-Saxon" unity was often only skin-deep. Sir William Wiseman, the British diplomat closest to Wilson and Colonel House, wrote at the time of the armistice about "the growing consciousness that after the war there will be only two great powers left—Great Britain and the United States. Which is going to be the greater, politically and commercially?"[5] Likewise, House, who visited London after the Treaty of Versailles had been signed, told Wilson:

> Almost as soon as I arrived in England, I sensed an antagonism to the United States. The English are quite as cordial and hospitable to the individual American as ever, but they dislike us collectively. ... While the British Empire vastly exceeds the United States in area and population and while their aggregate wealth is perhaps greater than ours, yet our position is much more favorable. It is because of this that the relations between the two countries are beginning to assume the same character as that between England and Germany before the war.[6]

At the heart of Anglo-American relations in the twenties were two issues: navies and finance. In these essential attributes of a great power Britain and America were in a class of their own. Together they set the framework within which lesser states would have to operate. But sea power and finance were also the issues around which their struggle for supremacy centered. Unlike the prewar rivalry between Britain and Germany, it was a peaceful struggle, but no less intense or important for that.

The strength of the rival navies was a continual source of hostility

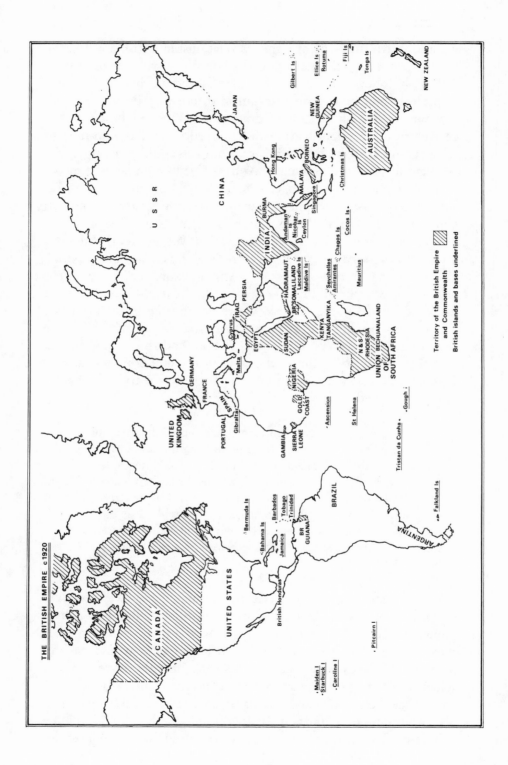

THE BRITISH EMPIRE c 1920

CANADA

UNITED STATES

British Honduras
Bahama Is
Bermuda Is
Jamaica
Barbados
Tobago
Trinidad
BR GUIANA

BRAZIL

ARGENTINA

Falkland Is

Pitcairn I

Maiden I
Starbuck I
Caroline I

UNITED KINGDOM
PORTUGAL
FRANCE
GERMANY
SPAIN
Gibraltar
Malta

USSR

Cyprus
IRAQ
PERSIA
EGYPT
SUDAN

GAMBIA
SIERRA LEONE
NIGERIA
GOLD COAST

Ascension
St Helena
Tristan da Cunha
Gough

HADRAMAUT
BR SOMALILAND
KENYA
TANGANYIKA
N & S RHODESIA
UNION OF SOUTH AFRICA
BECHUANALAND

Seychelles
Amirantes
Chagos Is
Mauritius

Laccadive Is
Maldive Is
Ceylon

INDIA
BURMA
Andaman Is
Nicobar Is

CHINA

JAPAN

Hong Kong
MALAYA
Singapore
BORNEO
Christmas Is

NEW GUINEA

Cocos Is

AUSTRALIA

Gilbert Is
Ellice Is
Rotuma
Fiji Is
Tonga Is

NEW ZEALAND

Territory of the British Empire and Commonwealth

British islands and bases underlined

and misunderstanding until the early thirties. The mutual distrust reached such a pitch that in July 1927 Winston Churchill, then Chancellor of the Exchequer, told his Cabinet colleagues that "no doubt it is quite right in the interests of peace to go on talking about war with the United States being 'unthinkable.'" But, warned Churchill,

> everyone knows that this is not true. However foolish and disastrous such a war would be . . . we do not wish to put ourselves in the power of the United States. We cannot tell what they might do if at some future date they were in a position to give us orders about our policy, say, in India, or Egypt, or Canada, or on any other great matter behind which their electioneering forces were marshalled.[7]

It was a remarkably frank statement, and coming from a British leader who was half American and a fervent apostle of Anglo-American friendship, it was a vivid demonstration of how low relations had sunk in this struggle over who should rule the waves.

The origins of the naval race are to be found in the First World War. America's wartime program of naval building had transformed it into a major sea power. Japan, too, had embarked on its own expansion, and Britain's supremacy was under threat. In 1919 the Royal Navy still had 42 capital ships (battleships and battle cruisers), compared with America's 16 and Japan's 14. But by 1924, if current building programs continued, Britain would have 43 capital ships, America 35 and Japan 22. The Admiralty was alarmed at the trend, but in 1921 Lloyd George, still premier of a now shaky coalition government, was convinced that Britain could not afford a naval race with America. The country was facing a severe postwar recession, and the government was desperately trying to reduce the national debt, vastly inflated by the war, and to cut public spending.

The direct naval rivalry between Britain and America was complicated by the existence of the Anglo-Japanese alliance. First signed in 1902 to help protect British interests in China against Russia, it was about to expire in 1922. Although policymakers in London were unhappy about Japanese encroachments into China during the war, most favored continuing the alliance in some form to retain influence in Tokyo and to avoid the need for large naval forces in the China Sea. But many Americans were becoming concerned about what was called the Yellow Peril, including Japanese migration into the United States. The U.S. Navy viewed Japan as its main potential enemy in the Pacific and feared that if war broke out between them, the Anglo-Japanese alliance could bring the Royal Navy in on the Japanese side. America and Britain had last been at war over a century earlier. Despite their bluster and their newfound power, American admirals like William Benson had no desire to repeat the experience.

America had the wealth to outbuild Britain in a naval race. The U.S. Navy was determined to achieve parity with Britain and to destroy the Anglo-Japanese alliance. But Congress and the American public were not anxious for confrontation. In America as in Britain, there were growing demands for economy in 1921 as the postwar boom faded. And a powerful peace movement emerged, under the leadership of Senator William E. Borah of Idaho. Borah's bogeymen were the British and also the East Coast industrial and financial interests, such as Morgan's, which, he believed, were starting the world on a new arms race. When Borah introduced a Senate resolution calling for an international conference to limit armaments, it passed through Congress with scant opposition. The new Republican administration of President Warren G. Harding, originally sympathetic to the "big Navy" lobby, felt obliged to follow suit. It invited Britain, Japan, France and other sea powers to participate in a conference in Washington to limit armaments.

On November 12, 1921, the Washington conference formally opened. The delegates settled back in their seats, expecting the high-flown but hollow peace rhetoric characteristic of such grand occasions. Instead the welcoming address by U.S. Secretary of State Charles Evans Hughes included a bombshell proposal for a ten-year holiday in naval building, including the abandonment of America's ambitious expansion programs. But in return Hughes wanted to establish a 5:5:3 ratio in capital ships between America, Britain and Japan. He went so far as to list the names of twenty-three ships that, he said, the Royal Navy must give up. The British delegation suddenly appreciated the gravity of what Hughes was saying. The reaction of an astounded Admiral Beatty, the First Sea Lord, was compared by one American journalist present to "a bulldog, sleeping on a sunny doorstep, who had been poked in the stomach by the impudent foot of an itinerant soap canvasser."[8]

Beatty and the Admiralty strenuously opposed the "holiday," with its damaging effects on the Royal Navy's modernization programs. But Lloyd George overruled them. The British government needed an agreement to stop a ruinous arms race. In Washington the British also agreed, in the face of American hostility, not to renew their alliance with Japan. It had not proved a successful conference for them. They had conceded equality at sea to the Americans, at least on paper, and they had terminated an important if shaky alliance, setting them on a path of growing confrontation with Japan. In 1921–22, however, none of this was considered disastrous. The ability of the great powers to prevent an arms race and resolve their differences peacefully seemed an encouraging improvement in international relations compared with the previous decade.

The Washington Treaty, signed in February 1922, covered only ships over ten thousand tons. It did not include cruisers, destroyers and submarines. In February 1927 President Calvin Coolidge, interested in controlling both armaments and defense budgets, invited the world's major sea powers to convene again, this time to discuss smaller ships. France and Italy, at loggerheads over the Mediterranean, refused, but Japan, Britain and the United States of America were again represented at the conference that opened in Geneva in June 1927. This time, however, Britain and America were openly at odds.

The U.S. Navy's General Board was still intent on acquiring a navy second to none. "Equality with Great Britain is the sole basis on which a just treaty limitation can be imposed," it stated categorically.[9] America's strategic planners were worried about the possibility of war against Japan, but Congress and the public were anxious to keep arms expenditure under control. Matching economy with strategy, the American delegation therefore demanded about thirty large cruisers, able to cruise at long range from base and with the heavy armament to deal with Japanese warships. The British, who were not particularly worried about Japan but were concerned about the protection of their global commerce, claimed the right to seventy cruisers, most of them smaller vessels suitable for protecting trade routes and patrolling Britain's sprawling empire. British and American interests differed fundamentally.

The chief American delegate described the talks at Geneva as not "negotiations at all, but merely a form of hostilities."[10] American shipbuilders lobbied intensively behind the scenes, helping create a hostile attitude toward arms control in the American press. The British delegation was increasingly overruled by anti-American sentiment in the Cabinet. Amid mutual recriminations the conference broke up in August. Such was the vehemence of American feeling that Prime Minister Stanley Baldwin canceled plans for an official visit to the United States.

The Anglo-American dispute was only part of the complex web of arms control negotiations in the 1920s, involving armies as well as navies. Deadlocked with America, Britain turned to France, the principal land power and also a major force at sea, seeking a bilateral Anglo-French agreement that could then be enlarged to include America and other interested powers. During the summer of 1928 a compromise was reached that would leave the French free to build up their army and the British to construct the number of small cruisers they wanted. When garbled reports of this were leaked in the American press, there was an outcry against the way wily John Bull was apparently trying to fix up a deal behind Uncle Sam's back. One senior congressman accused Britain of trying to "retain domination of the high seas by subversive diplomacy," while the *Manchester Guardian*, a leading British newspaper, declared in November 1928 that "not for many years have the Americans and the British been on terms as bad as they are now. There is ill-feeling, suspicion, misunderstanding and estrangement between the two nations."[11] A frustrated Coolidge cited Britain as the main obstacle to arms control and threw his support behind a bill then going through Congress for fifteen new cruisers. It seemed like the start of a new arms race.

The detailed haggling about the size and number of cruisers was part of a larger problem. Britain remained adamant that in any future war she must be able to command the seas and blockade her enemies. Equally the United States insisted on its right as a potential neutral to unimpeded trade and travel. This was the old issue of the "freedom of the seas" that had embittered relations in 1914–18. What gave the argument a new twist, the British Foreign Office believed, was the growth of the American Navy, now approaching equality with Britain. In future it might well be able to force the British to accept the freedom of the seas. In the words of Robert Vansittart, head of the Foreign Office's American Department, "America has in fact served notice on us that she will never again accept restrictions as existed between 1914 and 1917."[12]

The Foreign Office believed that Britain must back down. She should promise that in a future war she would modify her strategy and no longer enforce the blockade with her traditional ferocity. America, it was argued, would then be less intransigent about the size of its Navy. But after considerable debate in 1927–28 the Admiralty and the Cabinet refused to shift their position. They saw the blockade as a vital national interest and, convinced that America would not retaliate, were prepared to call its bluff. There was growing feeling that since 1919 Britain had appeased America too often for too little in return. Sir Maurice Hankey, the influential secretary to the cabinet, complained in October 1928: "We played up to America over the Covenant of the League, abandonment of the Japanese Alliance, Washington Treaties, debt settlement, Irish settlement . . . always making concessions and always being told that the next step would change their attitude. Yet they are, as the result, more overbearing and suspicious against us than anyone else."[13]

It took a change of government in both countries to break the deadlock. In March 1929 Herbert Hoover was sworn in as president, while Labour's Ramsay MacDonald became prime minister after elections in June. Unlike their predecessors, Coolidge and Baldwin, the new leaders took a keen, assertive interest in foreign affairs. In particular, they believed that disarmament was far too important to be left to the admirals. Geneva had shown the folly of that. Weeks of painstaking diplomacy that summer prepared the way for an eventual conference.

To improve relations, MacDonald himself paid a very successful visit to the United States in October 1929. It was the first time that a British prime minister had visited the United States while in office—further evidence of America's new importance in world affairs. Highlights of MacDonald's trip included a ticker-tape parade through New York, several days of informal talks with Hoover and a moving address to the U.S. Senate. The visit also helped improve Britain's image in the United States, for MacDonald did not fit the American stereotype of a British leader as aristocratic, languid and cunning. He was a Scot, a committed socialist and an outspoken opponent of the war in 1914, who convinced Americans of his sincere desire to end the arms race. The *New York Times* called the visit "an overpowering success . . . On divers strings he has sounded the one clear note of a passion to secure established peace on earth through every reasonable and honorable means."[14]

In January 1930 another naval conference opened in London. This time the ground had been properly prepared. Agreement was reached to extend what was sometimes called the "Rolls-Royce: Rolls-Royce: Ford" formula. The ratio of 5:5:3 agreed at Washington in 1922 for American, British and Japanese capital ships would now apply to cruisers as well. The agreement was flexible enough to allow America to build more big cruisers and Britain more smaller cruisers. The U.S. Navy had been forced by Hoover to reduce the total number of cruisers it was allowed, but the biggest concession was made by the British. Under intense pressure from MacDonald the Admiralty accepted a ceiling of fifty cruisers instead of the seventy it had demanded in 1927. The Labour government thus averted an Anglo-American arms race, but by making concessions to America of a kind deplored by many Tories. The U.S. Navy was still smaller than Britain's, but the British now acknowledged America's right, in theory at least, to a navy as large as their own.

But the London agreement of 1930 did not lead to real cooperation. Japan, the third member of the naval triumvirate, chafed at the restrictions imposed on her by the Big Two. She was anxious to become a great power in her own right. The easiest pickings lay in nearby China, a ruined empire fragmented by civil war, its economy dominated by foreign powers. In the winter of 1931–32 the Japanese army overran the Chinese province of Manchuria, in which it already had a foothold, and set up a puppet state. Manchuria's people and natural resources would strengthen the Japanese economy, and its vast spaces were attractive for colonization by Japan's expanding population.

At the height of the war, early in 1932, fighting spread to the great Chinese port of Shanghai. Under a treaty signed in Washington ten years earlier the United States and Great Britain were guarantors of China's integrity, but when the crisis came neither government was willing to become involved. America had too little at stake to risk war, and Britain far too much. Not only was she the largest foreign investor in China but she also kept close diplomatic and commercial links with Japan. Both Hoover and MacDonald therefore refused to countenance sanctions against the Japanese.

But Hoover's secretary of state, Henry Stimson, wanted to make a moral protest. He enunciated the Stimson Doctrine, withholding diplomatic recognition of Japan's conquests. In February 1932 he also pressed Britain's foreign secretary, Sir John Simon, for a joint condemnation of Japan under the 1922 treaty. But Simon was evasive. He was trying to negotiate Japan's peaceful withdrawal from Shanghai and saw little point in provoking her gratuitously. He also believed, from past experience, that no real assistance would be forthcoming from the Americans, even if they talked big. Recalling Wilson's notorious speech of 1915, he noted, "I am afraid America is 'too proud to' do anything." Stimson was piqued. Convinced that he had been betrayed by what he called the "soft and pudgy" members of the British Cabinet, he became increasingly bitter about the whole affair.[15]

British policy was not wholly inert. Simon later pushed the non-recognition doctrine through the League of Nations, but Stimson developed his own account of the Manchurian crisis in writings during the 1930s, and despite British efforts, it became the orthodox version. The whole episode became so overblown that in 1939, for example, the eminent Midwestern newspaperman William Allen White went so far as to claim that "Munich became inevitable when England refused to join Stimson in the protest against the Japanese invasion of continental Asia."[16] Stimson was an Anglophile and White an ardent anti-Nazi. For Britain's natural sympathizers to be so suspicious of her is an indication of the tenuousness of Big Two cooperation.

By the early 1930s, therefore, after British concessions, America and Britain had reached an official agreement on sea power, but it did not herald any real cooperation between the two governments. In finance, also, America's influence was increasingly apparent, and again the relations between the Big Two became severely strained.

In 1913 Britain had been the commercial and financial center of the world. The City of London managed international money, and sterling was used as the main trading currency. The exchange rate of sterling, like other currencies, did not float but was set at a fixed price in terms of gold. This system, known as the gold standard, was meant to provide economic stability automatically because countries that allowed high inflation would price themselves out of foreign markets, run up a balance of payments deficit, and then be forced back into line through a drain on their gold reserves. In fact, the system depended for its successful operation largely on the economic leadership of Britain.

The war had destroyed the old order. The volume of world trade in 1920 was only about half that of 1913. Britain, after spending millions of pounds defending her exchange rate, was forced to abandon the gold standard in 1919, with most other countries except the United States. To pay for the war the Allies and their enemies had run up huge domestic and foreign debts. Eighty percent of the war costs had been paid for by borrowing. The debts owed by the Allies to one another amounted to some $26.5 billion. In addition, under the Treaty of Versailles the Allies were entitled to demand

reparations from Germany. These were eventually adjudicated at
$33 billion. The consequence of this huge increase in national and
international debt was disastrous hyperinflation, above all in Germany.

Most bankers and politicians believed that a return to the gold
standard was essential, but the debts and inflation were major obsta-
cles in the way. In addition, Britain was no longer strong enough
to take the lead alone. To help finance the war effort she had sold
off most of her once vast American assets, and from 1916 the United
States had become the Allies' main banker. The effect on the United
States' international position was dramatic. In 1913 it had been a net
debtor to the tune of $3.7 billion. By 1919 it was a net creditor of
$3.7 billion. In the process New York had become a major world
money market, with houses like J. P. Morgan's and the National
City Bank developing expertise and influence as they mobilized
American funds for investment overseas. Re-creating the gold-stan-
dard economy could not therefore depend on the City of London
alone. It required the combined resources and skills of the British
and American financial communities.

At the center of the story was Montagu Norman, governor of the
Bank of England from 1920 to 1944. Norman was a fastidious,
secretive man, who cultivated an aura of mystery and power, going
to abnormal lengths to avoid publicity. To one French banker he
looked like someone "out of a Van Dyck canvas: the long face, the
pointed beard, the big hat . . ."[17] Norman's overriding goal was to
maintain London as a major money market, which, he believed,
could be achieved only through restoring Britain to gold. He realized this could not be done by Britain acting alone. He knew and
liked America, having spent three years there as a young banker in
the 1890s, and he developed a close relationship with his American
counterpart, Benjamin Strong, the governor of the Federal Reserve
Bank of New York. Strong was an Anglophile who shared Norman's dedication to getting the world back on gold. But America's
financial system, like its central government, was weaker than that
of Britain. Strong's powers were much less extensive than Norman's. So Norman worked with Strong but also relied on his ties
with the Wall Street banks, of which Morgan's was the most cooperative and important.

The war debts were the chief obstacle to financial reconstruction.
America had loaned $11.9 billion to the various Allied countries, of
which $4.7 billion was owed by Britain alone. But the British had

also lent a similar amount to their allies, some $11.1 billion. The British government proposed that *all* war debts should simply be canceled. To the Americans they argued that the proper equation was not dollars against dollars, but dollars against lives. British war deaths had been 750,000, America's 130,000. Some American policymakers were sympathetic, but Congress and the American public took a different view. The money had been lent, not given, and if repayment was not made, the whole burden would fall on the American taxpayer. The United States government, it was pointed out, had spent more during the war years than in the whole of its previous history since 1789. A third of this had been loaned to the Allies, and they had a duty to repay it. America's insistence was not popular in Britain. Uncle Sam gained the nickname Uncle Shylock. It "made the average Englishman think that the Americans are dirty swine," complained a senior Foreign Office man.[18]

Wilson's belief that Britain's financial dependence on America would give him carte blanche to determine the future of Europe had proved an illusion at the Paris peace conference, but the United States was still in a powerful position. Sir Auckland Geddes, the ambassador in Washington, argued in 1921 that if the American Congress was adamant about repayment of the loans, Britain must comply or risk being treated "as a vassal State as long as the debt remains unpaid."[19] Montagu Norman also believed that foreign confidence in London as a financial center would collapse if Britain tried to avoid her obligations. In January 1923 he and Stanley Baldwin, the Conservative Chancellor of the Exchequer, spent ten days of tough negotiation in Washington. They eventually secured a package whereby Britain would repay in installments, ten years at $161 million, then fifty years at $187 million. On that schedule Britain would be reimbursing America for its help during World War I until 1984.

The agreement was unpopular in Britain, but it did relieve transatlantic tension and restored Britain's international credit. An Englishman's word, it seemed, was still his bond. It also opened the way to deal with the vexed problem of German reparations to the Allies. Germany, in the throes of hyperinflation, had stopped its payments to France. In January 1923 French troops entered the Ruhr, as they were entitled to do under the Treaty of Versailles if Germany defaulted. Some in the French government saw the occupation as a way of gaining permanent control over the vital Rhineland: taking by force what the "Anglo-Saxons" had denied them at the peace

conference. The German government responded by subsidizing a
campaign of passive resistance, which exacerbated its already spiral-
ing inflation. By the time the campaign ended, with the German
economy in ruins, France had gained only a hollow victory. For
Germany was now in no position to repay anything. Without British and American help there would be no reparations and no recovery.

France having tried and failed to enforce the Treaty of Versailles,
Britain and America combined to impose a new settlement on their
terms. In April 1924 two committees of experts, chaired by the
American and British bankers Charles Dawes and Reginald
McKenna, recommended a reduction of Germany's reparations
burden and a $200 million loan to support the German central bank.
The City of London floated only a quarter of the loan, and half of
it came from New York, a further indication of how financial power
was shifting across the Atlantic.

The Dawes Plan boosted international confidence and encouraged the return of gold and foreign investment into Europe. The
sterling-dollar exchange rate began to drift up toward the prewar
parity of $4.86 to the pound, and Strong and Norman assisted the
process in 1924–25 by informal cooperation in monetary policy:
Strong relaxing U.S. interest rates while Norman kept British rates
high. By now most of Britain's trading partners were ready to
return to the gold standard regardless of Britain. The new British
Chancellor of the Exchequer, Winston Churchill, announced on
April 28, 1925, that Britain would also return to gold. "If we had
not taken this action," he confessed later, "the whole of the rest of
the British Empire would have taken it without us, and it would
have come to a gold standard, not on the basis of the pound sterling,
but of the dollar."[20]

For a time in the mid-1920s the international economy seemed to
be back on an even keel, with the leading roles now shared by Great
Britain and the United States. But appearances were deceptive. By
1931, in the worldwide depression, America's economy collapsed
and Britain was once again forced off the gold standard—a crisis that
highlighted the widening gulf between the two great powers.

In the 1920s U.S. trade with the rest of the world had surged.
America had become the world's largest exporter and, second only
to Britain, its largest importer as well. Britain still had larger total
foreign investments, but America had now become the world's
principal source of *new* investment, lending $6.4 billion abroad

between 1924 and 1929. This was nearly double Britain's contribution. Roughly half of America's new investment was in Europe, particularly Germany, where it helped pay for reparations and for the funding of the Weimar Republic's welfare state. But most of it was lent short-term by private investors looking for new outlets for their surplus capital. The collapse of Wall Street from October 1929 and the deepening recession in America meant that many of the loans were withdrawn by investors who were being called upon to meet their obligations in the United States. The money had lubricated Europe's economy. Without it the system began to grind to a halt.

In May 1931 the Credit Anstalt, Austria's leading bank, collapsed. By June the crisis had spread to Germany, and in an attempt to stem the run on the Reichsmark, President Hoover called for a one-year moratorium on all debts and reparations payments. His action failed to stabilize the situation, and in early July the German government imposed exchange controls. That shifted the crisis to Britain, whose foreign lending was three or four times the size of her gold reserves. Investors in huge numbers sold sterling, and the Bank of England was forced to spend large sums to support the $4.86 exchange rate for the pound. As in 1915, it turned to J. P. Morgan for help, but this time the situation, and the answer, were very different. The crisis that followed marked the end of Britain's postwar pretensions to match America's economic strength.

The Labour government had done its best to counter the effects of the slump in Britain. It had kept interest rates low and welfare payments high, but the result was a mounting budget deficit of over £100 million. An official committee, headed by Sir George May, recommended that the budget must be balanced, mainly by a 20 percent cut in unemployment insurance. Montagu Norman and the City agreed, convinced that only this would revive foreign confidence. When asked about the chances of raising loans from American investors, Morgan said "that before they could safely borrow in the USA, the Government would have to show at least some plan of restoration of financial stability and should at least have expressed the intention to reduce the expenditures to come within their means."[21]

The Labour Cabinet wrestled with its dilemma during July and August as the sterling crisis worsened. Which was more important—Britain's position as a financial power or the well-being of its citizens? Norman believed that the latter depended on the former, but many in MacDonald's Cabinet were not so sure. By Friday August 21 the Treasury warned that without help from New York and Paris Britain's reserves would last only four more days. Over the weekend Cabinet members debated a compromise austerity package, including only a 10 percent cut in unemployment insurance, while awaiting a reply from New York. Eventually they were reduced to walking around the garden of 10 Downing Street for over an hour on the Sunday evening until the message arrived. Morgan's put the ball back in the British court. "Are we right in assuming that the program under consideration will have the sincere approval and support of the Bank of England and the City generally and thus go a long way towards restoring internal confidence in Great Britain." They also warned that "of course our ability to do anything depends on the response of public opinion particularly in Great Britain to the Government's announcement of the program" and on the willingness of the French to help as well.[22]

An anguished MacDonald admitted to his colleagues "that the proposals as a whole represented the negation of everything that the Labour party stood for, and yet he was absolutely satisfied that it was necessary in the national interests to implement them if the country was to be secured."[23] But nearly half his Cabinet disagreed, and the Labour government resigned on August 24. MacDonald was persuaded by the King to form a National Government including Tories and Liberals. The new Cabinet adopted the cuts, and loans to support sterling were raised in America and France. But these failed to check the outflow of funds. Further requests were made to New York, but Morgan's had found the first loan hard enough to place at a time when America was sliding into Depression, and despite a direct appeal to the White House a U.S. government loan was out of the question. On September 21, 1931, the National Government gave up the struggle and Great Britain renounced the gold standard.

It was easy to blame the Americans for what had happened, and many in the Labour movement did so. The day after the Labour government resigned the *Daily Herald* denounced the "virtual ultimatum from New York bankers" and claimed that they had been allowed "to dictate, as the condition for a further credit to the Bank of England, the policy to be pursued in relation to unemployment benefit."[24] But in reality Morgan and his colleagues were only echoing the judgment of the City and of financiers in Paris. Ultimately

A VICTIM OF CHANGING WORLD CONDITIONS

John T. McCutcheon, veteran cartoonist of the Anglophobe Chicago Tribune, *depicts John Bull giving up his world power. (October 29, 1931.)*

blame lay with British leaders of all parties for failing to come to terms with the harsh realities of the postwar world.

In the early 1920s the government and the City had been determined to rebuild London as a financial center, and they had returned to the gold standard at the prewar rate. This decision was supported by all three political parties and nearly all economists. Yet it was an act of faith, even nostalgia, taken on the basis of only the most rudimentary economic analysis. As a result sterling was overvalued, probably by 10 percent, helping make British exports uncompetitive in world markets compared with those of America and of France, who undervalued the franc. By the late 1920s both these countries had much larger gold reserves than Britain and yet much smaller foreign obligations. The British were still trying to run the world financial system but without the resources they had before 1914. September 1931 made this clear. Douglas Dillon, a future U.S. treasury secretary, started his career as a Wall Street banker the week Britain went off gold. He recalled later: "We'd looked to the pound for years—everything I'd been brought up with—so when I started it was with the realization that we were coming into a new era and a new world. . . . England was no longer commanding the world financial markets. They were just another player in the game."[25]

But if Britain was unable to play her part in ensuring economic stability, America, the one country that could have helped limit the effects of the worldwide depression, also failed to act. Most Americans had not yet grasped their new dominant position and the responsibilities that came with it. The American investment in Europe was private capital, not government loans. The Hoover administration could do nothing in 1930–31 as American investors withdrew funds from Europe just when the money was most needed to shore up the financial system. In other ways, too, America acted at odds with its new international role. Congress insisted on repayment of war debts, despite the burden this placed on Europe's already grave balance of payments, and the administration encouraged the growth of protectionism. In 1930 American tariff rates on imports were raised to new heights, shutting out foreign goods and raw materials from the vast American market and thereby intensifying the world depression.

America's new protectionism helped push Britain into a major shift in her own policy. Since the middle of the nineteenth century she had been a free-trade nation, encouraging world trade by minimizing her tariffs against foreign imports. As the dominant economy of the Victorian era she could afford to do that. By the 1930s, however, she was increasingly challenged by industrial competitors who had grown strong behind tariff walls, and as the depression deepened, the pressure to strike back became uncontrollable. In 1932 Britain imposed tariffs on roughly three-quarters of her imports. But at the Ottawa conference that summer she also agreed to keep tariff rates lower for countries within the British Empire. This was the system known as Imperial Preference. These advantages were later extended to more than a score of Britain's other trading partners, particularly in South America, who relied heavily on sterling and the City for financing their trade. An informal Sterling Area began to emerge.

Protectionism was another sign of British weakness. Like the end of naval supremacy and the abandonment of the gold standard, it was further evidence of Britain's decline from a position of unchallenged dominance. Imperial Preference and the embryonic Sterling Area were conceived in part as a way of fighting off the challenge from America, by providing a secure base from which Britain could compete. The press baron Lord Beaverbrook, owner of the *Daily Express*, was a notable exponent of this policy. And the United States was particularly vulnerable because Britain was the largest customer for its exports. Imperial Preference became one of the most rancorous issues dividing Britain and America over the next two decades.

By 1932 Britain had left the gold standard and was starting to consolidate her own economic bloc. The world economic system she had shaped and led was falling apart. In 1933 she also defaulted on the repayment of her war debts to the United States, arguing that America had made repayment virtually impossible at a time of depression by accumulating much of the world's gold reserves and imposing ever-higher tariffs against British goods. Americans, nevertheless, were bitter at what they considered Britain's lack of good faith.

In the summer of 1933 a world economic conference was held in London to try to sort out the mess. The prospects of success were never good: every country was now putting its short-term national interest first and adopting stringent protectionist measures. But the new American president, Franklin Roosevelt, brought discussions to an end by suddenly announcing in July 1933 that the United States would not support any permanent stabilization of world currencies until the American economy was back on its feet. His bombshell message strengthened British frustrations about the United States. Neville Chamberlain, Chancellor of the Exchequer, grumbled: "I should think there has never been a case of a conference so completely smashed by one of the participants."[26]

The rivalry of the Big Two and the conflict of their economic aims meant that the world had no effective leadership during its most acute economic crisis of the century. Britain was now too weak to stabilize the world economy unaided. Yet the United States was not ready to accept new responsibilities. Under a political system of "checks and balances" the administration lacked the power to override a nationalist Congress. Furthermore, American trade and foreign investment, though vital to the outside world, was of relatively little importance to the American economy itself, whose health still depended on the huge domestic market. America did not share Britain's self-interest in world prosperity. The economic historian Charles Kindleberger sums up the crisis of leadership starkly:

> The world economic system was unstable unless some country stabilized it, as Britain had done in the nineteenth century and up to 1913. In 1929, the British couldn't and the United States wouldn't. When every country turned to protect its national interest the world public interest went down the drain, and with it the private interests of all.[27]

By the early 1930s relations between America and Britain were marked by bitterness and recrimination. They had fought on the same side in one war and they were soon to fight in another, but in the years between, without a clear common enemy and in the throes of world depression, their own rivalry became intense. In the process long-standing suspicions of each other's society came to the surface.

At the end of the war British leaders had entertained extravagant hopes of a close relationship. Lloyd George asserted confidently in 1921: "The people who govern America are our people. They are our kith and kin. The other breeds are not on top."[28] By the time of the naval row in 1927 the Foreign Office had modified this Anglo-Saxonist theory, warning that "we have treated them too much as blood relations, not sufficiently as a foreign country."[29] And after the ravages of the depression most British leaders were almost totally alienated. One crisis after another, from the League fiasco in 1919 to the London Economic Conference in 1933, had shown, they believed, that no faith could be placed in the United States, particularly when its presidents had so little control over Congress.

In 1932 Baldwin summed up British conventional wisdom: "You will get nothing from Americans but words, big words but only words." In October 1933 this usually mild-mannered politician refused to dine with one of President Roosevelt's sons because he "says he has got to loathe the Americans so much that he hates meeting them."[30] Sir Robert Vansittart, now the top official at the Foreign Office and himself married to an American, had been preaching the appeasement of America in the naval crisis of 1927, but by 1934 he believed that "we have been too tender, not to say subservient, with the US for a long time past. It is we who have made all the advances, and received nothing in return. It is still necessary, and I desire as much as ever, that we should get on well with this untrustworthy race. But," he added, "we shall never get very far; they will always let us down."[31] This was the view of most British leaders in the 1930s.

Feelings were mutual. Across the Atlantic, Americans were alienated not merely from Britain but from Europe as a whole. It was customary to blame the depression on the failure of Britain and others to repay their war debts. There was a growing conviction that American involvement in the war had been a great mistake. By 1934 many argued that they had been sucked into war in 1917 by the so-called merchants of death, the big businessmen and financiers like J. P. Morgan. A Senate committee chaired by the Republican Gerald P. Nye examined their activities in a long-running inquiry from September 1934 to February 1936. Morgan and his partners were interrogated at length amid intense publicity about the firm's wartime activities as Britain's banker and arms buyer.

Nye's committee came up with little hard evidence to justify claims that Wall Street and the munitions manufacturers had dragged America into war, but their highly publicized hearings left a general impression that there was no smoke without fire. The influential American radio commentator Raymond Gram Swing claimed in May 1935 that "it is almost a truism that the United States went into the World War in part to save from ruin the bankers who had strained themselves to the utmost to supply Great Britain and France with munitions and credits."[32]

These ideas gained hold in 1935, just as Europe seemed on the brink of renewed war with the invasion of the African kingdom of Ethiopia by the Italian dictator, Benito Mussolini. In August Congress hastily passed a Neutrality Act, which banned the export of arms to any belligerent country in time of war. It also gave the president powers to warn Americans against traveling on belligerent passenger vessels. In 1936 Congress added a ban on loans to belligerents. These were the kind of measures Secretary of State William Jennings Bryan had sought, in vain, in 1915. Next time, Congress was saying, there must be no *Lusitania*, no Morgan loans, to involve America emotionally and economically in Europe's war.

The Neutrality Acts symbolized a sharp reversal of U.S. policies toward Europe. In the 1920s, although America had rejected political entanglements like the League, it had used its new economic strength to control the naval race and to help reconstruct Europe. But in the 1930s, disillusioned by the depression and the dictators, America tried to insulate itself from any future conflict. The Neutrality Acts signaled that the United States would not exert its naval and economic power to save Europe from its follies for fear of being dragged in itself. This was a far cry from the days of Woodrow Wilson. Novelist Ernest Hemingway captured the prevailing mood in 1935: "Of the hell broth that is brewing in Europe we have no need to drink. Europe has always fought: the intervals of peace are only armistices. We were fools to be sucked in once in a European war, and we shall never be sucked in again."[33]

CHAPTER 6

AMERICANIZATION
BUSINESS AND SOCIETY
BETWEEN THE WORLD WARS

America in the 1920s seized the imagination of a new generation in Britain. For a decade, until the depression of the 1930s, everything American seemed alluring, offering the prospect of escape from life in Britain, which was drab by comparison. America was modern. America was rich. America was The Future.

The message was received in different ways. For some it was the new products that came on the market to end domestic drudgery: the vacuum cleaner, the refrigerator, the electric toaster. For others it was the style of America that excited, the patent leather shoes worth queueing for in Oxford Street, the makeup advertised as "Used by the Stars of Hollywood," and, of course, the new music of the Jazz Age. But for most people the cinema was the Great Enchanter. Before television the main family outing for millions of people was the weekly visit to the movies. As the lights dimmed and the pictures flickered onto the screen the humdrum was swept away. A new, bright carefree world beckoned. It was, quite simply, what everyone longed for.

The impact of America was deplored by many of those who felt responsibility for the health of British society—teachers and politicians in particular. "All America is Niagara," moaned one Cambridge don. "Force without direction, noise without significance, speed without accomplishment."[1] But there was little critics could

do to counter the effect. British people found the vigor, the original-
ity and the verve of America appealing. These were not qualities
acquired by chance. They sprang naturally from the innate strength
and resources of the United States that had been demonstrated
during World War I and were now free to exert themselves.

The United States came out of the war into a boom, quickly
followed by a brief slump in 1920–21. But recovery was fast. From
1922 until the end of the decade unemployment was usually below
5 percent and manufacturing output increased by nearly a third. It
was a period of astonishing prosperity. America expanded into overseas markets, many of which Britain considered her own. The
United States' share of world exports rose to 16 percent by 1929 as
Britain's fell to 12 percent. The British were no longer the world's
largest exporters. All this was achieved by a country that sold abroad
only a twentieth of what it produced, unlike Britain, who, with her
smaller population, needed to export a quarter of her national production to survive. For America, foreign trade was the icing on the
cake; for Britain, a matter of economic survival.

When Britain's brief postwar boom burst in 1921, her economy
went into a recession from which it was slow to recover. Throughout the twenties unemployment averaged 10 to 12 percent and
demand was depressed. The root problem lay in the structure of
British industry. She still relied on the old staple businesses—mining coal, making iron and steel, building ships and weaving cloth.
Where America was revolutionizing business methods, mechaniz-
ing her factories and investing in research and development, much
of Britain carried on as if nothing had changed. America developed
new growth industries for the new world markets, based not on the
use of coal and steam but on electricity and oil. The motorcar and
gadgets for the office and the home driven by electricity lent themselves to efficient production, with standardized parts, assembly
lines and aggressive marketing to produce enormous profits.

In much of the world during the 1920s the United States was able
to erode Britain's dominance. In Japan and China, America replaced
Britain as the main trading partner. In South America, where before
the war the two had each sold a quarter of all the goods imported,
America was better able to meet the new demand for cars, trucks,
machinery and electrical goods, and by the end of the decade its
share of the region's imports had risen to 38 percent while Britain's
fell to 16 percent. By the end of the 1920s America had also sur-

passed Britain as the leading foreign investor in Canada and Latin America.

This natural rivalry was exacerbated by the American belief that Britain used unfair methods to protect her position. The British Empire at the start of the 1920s covered a quarter of the globe, and these possessions, whose subject status many Americans thought morally wrong, allowed Britain access to much of the world's supplies of raw materials, such as rubber, tin and oil. Although her indigenous wealth was limited, she was able to control a far larger proportion of essential materials than America, and after the economic losses of the war, which had cost 15 percent of her overseas wealth, she was determined to exploit her advantage to the full. British policy aroused intense hostility in the United States. In 1926 the U.S. ambassador in London warned Washington: "Just as England built up a new prosperity after the Napoleonic Wars by using iron and coal, so, I think, she is planning to rebuild her fortunes and to obtain world leadership again by making use of her raw materials to be found in her tropical and sub-tropical possessions."[2] Battling to break down Britain's monopoly, American businessmen called for an "open door" policy of equal access to the world's markets and raw materials. In 1929 Prime Minister Stanley Baldwin warned his successor: "The American money power is trying to get control of some of the natural resources of the Empire. They are working like beavers."[3]

The battle over rubber was particularly acrimonious, since its price directly affected the cost of automobile tires and thus hit a growing number of Americans where it hurt most—in their pockets. Harvey Firestone was angrier than anyone. He had begun his business life working for his uncle's Columbus Buggy Company. He suggested that these horse-drawn carts would ride more comfortably over the rough country roads if they were fitted with rubber tires, but the idea was rejected. Firestone left to set up on his own and soon established a successful tire company. Then, in his son's words, he met "a man called Henry Ford, and he was starting some kind of a newfangled vehicle that would run without horses."[4] Ford and Firestone agreed that pneumatic tires should be produced to give the motorcar a smooth ride, and Ford ordered two thousand sets. Firestone, with a factory in Akron, Ohio, soon became one of America's biggest tire manufacturers, meeting a demand that increased every year as car production rose from under 2 million vehicles a year in 1920 to nearly 4.5 million by 1929. By then one American in five had a car, compared with one Briton in fifty.

The automobile boom meant that America had become the world's leading importer of rubber, consuming over two-thirds of total production. And Britain, with plantations in Malaya and Ceylon, controlled about three-quarters of world supplies. She seemed to have a stranglehold on America. But the price of rubber started to fall in the early 1920s. Too much was being produced, and the costs, British rubber planters claimed, were no longer covered by the market price. The British government set up an inquiry that resulted in the adoption in 1922 of the Stevenson Plan to reduce production to 60 percent of its 1920 level. The inquiry found that while rubber cost 22¢ a pound to produce, it had sold in New York during 1921 for an average of 16.3¢, and at times as low as 12¢. Only by cutting output could the producers survive. But the effect of the cut was devastating for the United States. By 1925 the price of a pound of rubber, which had been intended to rise to about 30¢, had soared to $1.21.

The American secretary of commerce for most of the 1920s was Herbert Hoover, the future Republican president. In 1925, encouraged by Firestone, he mounted a vigorous campaign against the Stevenson Plan, denouncing the price-fixing as a violation of "open door" principles. In the war of words the British soon hit back, pointing out that America was prone to do exactly the same thing with cotton, manipulating output to keep prices up. One British diplomat commented: "Anything that increases the price of the American cotton crop reacts at once upon the prosperity of our Lancashire textile districts."[5]

The British also liked to remind Americans that although they might talk about the open door with its equal opportunity in foreign markets, the United States had the highest tariffs in the world. A third of American imports were liable for duty, and on these the average rate was 40 percent. Certain staple British exports, such as steel, china and textiles, it was pointed out, were simply unsellable in the United States. Hoover would not listen. While denouncing the tariff barriers of other nations, he insisted on keeping American tariffs high, failing to see that eventually American trade would suffer because others would not be able to sell their goods and thus afford to buy from the United States. "There is no practical force in the contention that we cannot have a protective tariff and a growing foreign trade. We have both today," he asserted flatly in 1928, just before the boom collapsed.[6]

In the battle over rubber, conducted in the atmosphere of chauvinism and self-righteousness that pervades all trade wars, Hoover appealed to the gut American emotion of Anglophobia. He promoted a rubber conservation campaign with the emotive slogan "1776—1925." He toured the country agitating against Britain and encouraging the development of synthetic substitutes. In the end, however, market forces proved even more effective. American rubber manufacturers gradually shifted to Dutch suppliers in the East Indies, who had not joined the Stevenson scheme, and Britain's price and sales declined. By 1928 British planters controlled only about half of the world's rubber supply and the Stevenson Plan was abandoned, much to the relief of the British ambassador in Washington, "since it removes a source of misunderstanding and continual bickering between the United States and ourselves."[7] But in the process America had begun to adopt policies that it reviled when they were used by Britain, policies that in one case came uncomfortably close to setting up America's own colonial empire.

Harvey Firestone was the empire builder. Encouraged by Hoover, he sent his experts around the world looking for suitable sites for rubber planting to break the British monopoly. He found an ideal spot in West Africa, in the state of Liberia, which had been founded in the mid-nineteenth century as a homeland for black slaves emancipated from the United States. Another American had also been interested in that land: Marcus Garvey, the militant black leader, who saw Liberia as an ideal base for his Back to Africa movement. In the early 1920s the Liberian government had encouraged his plans for settlement by American blacks. But they withdrew the offer in 1924 on learning of Garvey's secret intention to overthrow it because, as one Garvey adviser put it, the Americo-Liberian ruling elite was "the most despicable element in Liberia. . . . using the natives as slaves."[8] It was land that Garvey had been planning to settle that Firestone's scouts chose as the ideal site for rubber planting.

Protracted negotiations followed. Liberia was in desperate need of new investment and of financial support for its shaky economy. Firestone offered both: a lease to develop one million acres as rubber plantations and a $5 million loan to stabilize the country's finances. But the terms of the loan would leave Firestone virtually in control of Liberia's treasury, under an American "financial adviser" and his staff. The Liberian government protested vehemently to the State Department at this challenge to its sovereignty. Officially the American government claimed that it had nothing to do with economic negotiations by private American citizens, but behind the scenes informal pressure was applied. The secretary of state warned his Liberian counterpart that "obviously . . . it would be impossible to raise any loan in the United States on security which could be offered by Liberia unless there is to be the extensive development contemplated in the Firestone contracts. . . . It is also clear that American bankers would insist on some supervision of the finances."[9]

The battle dragged on for much of 1925 and 1926. To satisfy the Liberian desire for independence, Firestone allowed them to borrow the $5 million from "The Finance Corporation of America." But as one American commentator of the time pointed out, "while the Liberians may have believed that this is an independent organization, it is apparently an institution which Mr. Firestone established and financed for the purpose of making this loan."[10] The Liberians also tried to reduce the number and powers of American "advisers" and to keep control of their fiscal policy. But eventually, with Harvey Firestone threatening to call the whole deal off, they signed an agreement largely on his terms.

Such tactics were hardly a novelty in the history of international business. The British government had connived in this kind of commercial blackmail on numerous occasions in the past in Africa, South America and the Middle East. But America had always professed to be better than the Old World imperialists. As one of Marcus Garvey's followers ruefully comments: "America did not and does not want the physical expansion of an Empire, as England, but they would close their eyes to industrial, commercial empires. . . . wherever the American money is, there goes the flag."[11] Or, as one American commentator on the trade war put it: "We shall not make Britain's mistake. Too wise to govern the world, we shall merely own it."[12]

In its search for bigger markets it was inevitable that American business would turn, as it had before the world war, to Britain. Here the flag could not follow, but the advantages of a common language, a stable government and a people who admired things American, even if their ruling class was dubious, made it a good risk. A new reason for investing in Britain was the need to get around British tariff barriers. It was not until the Ottawa Conference of 1932 that general tariffs were imposed in the surge of protectionism during the depression, but vulnerable industries were already protected throughout the British Empire. Imported automobiles, for instance, attracted a 33⅓ percent tax. Setting up in Britain meant not only that an American company could avoid the tariff barriers protecting the British market, but that it could take advantage of tariff-free exports to all the countries of the British Empire.

American car manufacturers found such a move essential. In 1920 Henry Ford's Model T took two-thirds of the British car market, but within a few years its lead had disappeared. To avoid the 33⅓ percent duty Ford decided to set up a full-scale British operation. In 1928 he bought land at Dagenham, on the banks of the Thames east of London, and there built his largest plant outside the United States. Soon Dagenham was using the mass production methods pioneered in Detroit and was producing cars for Britain, the British Empire and much of continental Europe. America's General Motors, likewise anxious to avoid the tariff, bought the Vauxhall car firm in 1927, and the big tire companies, Goodrich, Goodyear and Firestone, also established British factories.

By 1929 there was nearly half a billion dollars of direct American investment in Britain. Only Canada, Cuba and Mexico had more. Many of the companies that arrived in Britain did so openly. Others, alarmed by the new wave of anti-Americanism that U.S. investment was arousing, came surreptitiously. General Electric of America went to great lengths to disguise its ambition to buy up the whole British electrical manufacturing industry. GE already owned a subsidiary in Britain—British Thomson Houston, or BTH, which made everything from giant turbines to light bulbs. But GE's president, Gerard Swope, had his eyes on his main competitor in Britain, Metropolitan Vickers. In February 1928 he bought a controlling interest in Metrovick for £1.6 million. Once acquired, the shares were immediately transferred into the hands of a millionaire British industrialist, Dudley Docker, who had a reputation as a staunch defender of the principle that British industry should be in British hands. Officially he now owned Metropolitan Vickers. Swope gave Docker £50,000 in Metrovick shares, calling it "a very inadequate compensation for all the assistance you have been."[13] Privately Docker believed that cooperation with General Electric was now inevitable because everywhere "the Americans were first in the field."[14]

Despite Swope's subterfuge, rumors soon spread that the real purchaser of Metropolitan Vickers had been American, and to end the speculation an announcement was made. At the annual general meeting of Metropolitan Vickers on March 29, 1928, the chairman, Sir Philip Nash, stated: "Messrs Vickers Ltd sold the control of this Company to the International General Electric Company. It was at this stage that Mr F. Dudley Docker came into the transaction and the control now lies in his hands."[15] Originally the statement was to say that Docker held "voting control." Since Swope owned 80 percent of Metrovick voting shares, that would have been a bare-faced lie, and Docker insisted on the change. But even to say Docker had "control" was to be economical with the truth. As the records of the company make clear, Swope was in full control. Docker was simply a convenient front.

Swope's ambitions did not stop with Metropolitan Vickers. He also acquired two other British electrical companies, but his real target was GE's British namesake and one remaining major European rival, British General Electric. He started to buy into this company, and in September 1928 its chairman, Sir Hugo Hirst, took the extraordinary step of having all foreign shareholders disfranchised. But the Americans continued to buy, amassing 60 percent of the stock by March 1929. Hirst then announced that new shares would be issued only to British citizens. Gerard Swope reacted with what the *New York Times* described as "virtually an ultimatum in this financial war."[16] If Hirst went ahead, he warned, American investors would boycott Britain. The point was not lost on the City of London and the British financial press, who condemned Hirst's "Bolshevistic" actions. He was forced to drop the proposed new British-only share issue, but the American shareholders remained disfranchised. Hirst made no apology for his "100 percent British" campaign and drew public attention to the need to fight off the American invasion. Swope had to be satisfied with setting up the biggest electrical company in Britain comprising virtually everything but General Electric. In 1929 his four major companies were merged into Associated Electrical Industries (AEI).

American interests were also buying their way into the British electrical supply industry, at this time in the hands of a plethora of private generating companies. Two American entrepreneurs, Samuel Insull and Harley Clarke, began to acquire British power stations. By 1930 Clarke's Greater London and Counties Trust controlled fifty-four power companies from Oxfordshire to East

Once America entered the war in 1917 a propaganda campaign was mounted against all things German. *Imperial War Museum, London*

American patriotic song sheet of 1918.
Peter Newark's Western Americana

The Old World welcomes the New: President Wilson at Dover, December 26, 1918. *BBC Hulton Picture Library*

President Wilson is driven through London's Trafalgar Square (December 1918). *BBC Hulton Picture Library*

Versailles, June 28, 1919: the Big Three—Georges Clemenceau, Woodrow Wilson and David Lloyd George. *BBC Hulton Picture Library*

Allied officers try to see the signing of the peace treaty with Germany in the Hall of Mirrors. *BBC Hulton Picture Library*

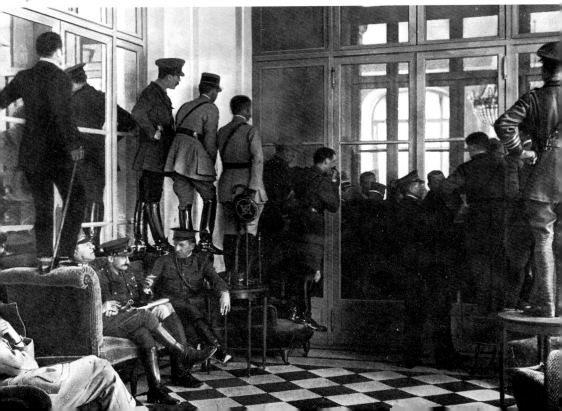

Montagu Norman, Stanley Baldwin and Sir Auckland Geddes in Washington to negotiate a settlement of Britain's war debt to the United States (January 1923). *BBC Hulton Picture Library*

Confrontation between Senator Gerald P. Nye and J. P. Morgan during Senate hearings on the munitions industry (February 1936). *Associated Press*

A Firestone rubber plantation in Liberia. *Firestone*

The Hoover factory on London's Western Avenue at Perivale, built in 1931. *Photo Source*

The British image of America: Edward G. Robinson in the gangster movie *Little Caesar* (1930). *Kobal Collection*

The American image of Britain: Robert Taylor in *A Yank at Oxford* (1938). *Kobal Collection*

Edward VIII and Mrs. Simpson, sightseeing in Yugoslavia in the summer of 1936. *Popperfoto*

Pro-Nazi rally in New York's Madison Square Garden in 1934. *BBC Hulton Picture Library*

King George VI and President Franklin D. Roosevelt outside the president's church at Hyde Park, New York (June 1939) *Popperfoto*

Anglia. Its American ownership could not be kept secret. When it became known, Clarke appointed the distinguished British lawyer and politician Lord Birkenhead, a former Lord Chancellor, as chairman. Birkenhead announced, disingenuously, that "the organisation with which I have decided to associate myself is British, although it is associated with the Clarke interests in the United States."[17] The pretense that the trust was simply making use of American capital while being under British control fooled no one, but no action was taken against it until 1936. By then its American ownership had become a liability. Profits from Britain were being siphoned back to America to support the ailing parent company. With government approval the Americans were bought out and the trust became wholly British-owned.

It would be wrong to suggest that there was universal hostility to America's investment in Britain. When the British Cabinet discussed the electrical supply industry in May 1928, most ministers concluded that restrictions on foreign investment were "undesirable and impossible."[18] It was also clear that Britain had much to learn from American management, production methods and sales techniques. When Hoover, the vacuum cleaner manufacturers,* set up in Britain, they sent some British sales managers to America to learn the extraordinary Hoover selling methods. Salesmen were taught to sing the Hoover songs, including the Hoover "Field Artillery March": "All the dirt, all the grit,/Hoover gets it, every bit,/For it beats, as it sweeps, as it cleans." Salesmen were sent to conferences at British seaside holiday camps, dressed in a uniform of blazers and flannels with different colored ties to represent the region of the country they came from. At the end of the course they were marched past a saluting stand and gave an "Eyes right" to the senior executives on the podium. Aggressive selling was required and the techniques used are legendary. The first hurdle was to get into the house to give a demonstration and then to find some way of wangling a down payment from the housewife. One American salesman, according to legend, persuaded a widow to pawn the headstone from her husband's grave.

The main beneficiary of all this activity was the consumer. In 1923 there were only 5,000 electric cookers in service in Britain; in 1930 alone 120,000 were installed. It was the vested interests who

---

*Founded by the Ohio industrialist Herbert William Hoover, no relation of President Herbert Clark Hoover.

All the dirt, all the grit

5

Tune : BYE, BYE BLACKBIRD

When the Hoover meets the foe,
This we know—one must go—
Bye, Bye, Bojack.
When the agitator acts
How it backs—all the facts !·
Bye, Bye, Bojack.
No one ever beat out agitation,
Cleanest cleaning known in all creation
Demonstrate without a doubt
Lay 'em out, every bout
Bo-jack, Bye, Bye.

* * * *

4   Tune : FIELD ARTILLERY MARCH

All the dirt, all the grit,
Hoover gets it, every bit,
For it beats, as it sweeps, as it cleans,
 It deserves all its fame.
As it backs up every claim,
 For it beats, as it sweeps, as it cleans.
O it's hi ! hi ! hee !
 The kinds of dirt are three
We'll tell the world just what it means,
 BING ! BING ! BING !
Spring or fall, the Hoover gets them all.
 For it beats, as it sweeps, as it cleans.

6

Tune : LET ME CALL YOU
       SWEETHEART

Let me take a Hoover,
To your home at two.
Let me do some cleaning,—
Make your rugs like new.
All the dirt surrenders,
And the germs go too.
Not another cleaner
Does what it can do.

* * * *

A page from a Hoover songbook of the early 1930s.

complained. Big business felt threatened by takeover and worried that Britain would become, in the words of one observer, "an appendage to the United States" unless she "Americanized" her methods.[19] Less powerful interests were hostile too. By 1929 Woolworth's had 350 stores in all Britain's major towns and cities, with nothing priced above sixpence. Local traders were peeved and vented their anger on everything American. Winifred Davis's father owned a hardware shop in Sheffield. Woolworth's came to the town and began undercutting Davis's prices. A tin bath, which cost two shillings and elevenpence in the family store was sold by Woolworth's for only sixpence. She remembers the day her father took her to the British Empire Exhibition at Wembley in 1924 and complained about the American stand, with its simulation of Niagara Falls and the latest line in Kewpie dolls. "They shouldn't be here," he fumed. "This is the *British Empire* Exhibition."[20]

American culture, as well as American goods, was invading Britain. Jazz began to catch on among the fashionable in the 1920s. Black regimental bands, such as the Seventy Black Devils, had toured France with great success in 1918, playing rag and march tunes, and in 1919 a white group, the Original Dixieland Jazz Band, performed to wild acclaim in Britain. Other white bands followed. Gradually a market for American records developed and British dance bands began to give their music "American" touches, with greater syncopation and the addition of drums, banjos and eventually saxophones. The Prince of Wales's well-known enthusiasm, particularly for drumming, helped give jazz a seal of approval. In nightclubs he often joined the band and beat time on the drums, although, when asked what he thought of the Prince's abilities, virtuoso drummer Dave Tough replied discreetly that "he might make a good King."[21]

Businessmen grumbled at the American commercial invasion. Guardians of morality frowned disapprovingly on the values of the Jazz Age. But these expressions of hostility to "Americanization" were as nothing compared with the reactions aroused by American domination of the film industry. In the television age it is difficult to imagine the impact the cinema had, first the silent films and then the talkies. By the late 1930s more than twenty million admission tickets on average were sold every week, and what moviegoers saw were almost always American films. The memory of one woman must have been the common experience of thousands. "I lived in a mining village, a very dull dark sort of place. . . . [In the cinema] you were in complete darkness, then all the screen would light up and you'd see all these marvelous film stars. Everything was bright. I just wanted to go there and be like them."[22] Children in the street imitated American slang: "O.K., kid" and "What are you doing tonight, babe?" It infuriated their parents and their teachers. By 1941 the Board of Education was mounting a campaign in schools "to make children realize that Hollywood, hot music and slang are not the most important features of the life of the U.S.A."[23]

The girls imitated the looks of the stars by putting flour on their cheeks and soot on their eyelashes. Instead of lipstick, they dabbed their mouths with red tissue paper moistened with water. Their childhood longing to look like their movie idols led to the mass production of makeup for the first time. Until then it had been worn only in fashionable circles. Ordinary people did not use it. But the American makeup artist Max Factor discovered that the actresses he made up for the screen wanted to look the same when they were out in public as they did in their films. He invented pancake powder and soon realized its potential not just for the stars but for the fans who wanted to imitate them. He set up factories in Britain and America and sold "The Make-Up of the Stars" to the women who had daubed flour on their cheeks as children.

The popular newspaper the *Daily Express* complained in 1927 that the bulk of picturegoers were being Americanized. "They talk America, think America, and dream America. We have several million people, mostly women, who, to all intent and purpose, are temporary American citizens."[24] The newspaper was not alone. Teachers, politicians and clergymen all complained that the films, apart from setting a bad example by showing a life either of crime or of luxury, instilled too many American ideas. One Tory MP protested that the cinemas were "booked up with masses of American rubbish forced on them by the monopoly of American interests."[25]

In 1927 and again in 1937 Acts of Parliament were passed to try to limit the impact of the American movie industry on Britain. "I want the world," said the president of the Board of Trade in 1937, "to be able to see British films true to British life, accepting British standards and spreading British ideals."[26] In 1927, when the first Cinematograph Films Act was passed, only 5 percent of films shown in Britain and throughout the empire were British-made. Britain's diplomats abroad complained that the flood of American movies was creating a demand for American rather than British products. The British press shared their alarm. "The film is to America what the flag was once to Britain," warned the *Morning Post*. "By its means Uncle Sam may hope someday, if he be not checked in time, to Americanize the world."[27]

The Films Acts were intended to protect the British film industry by requiring cinemas to show a quota of British films, to reach 20 percent by 1936. In fact, by 1934 28 percent of films shown in Britain were of British origin, but many of them were shoddy, cheap products, made solely to fulfill the quota. Quota Quickies, as they were contemptuously called, were often shot at night using sets that had been built for other films shot during the day. The actors and actresses arrived exhausted from productions on the West End stage and went through their lines in a perfunctory manner. To satisfy the law, the final product was sometimes seen only by the cinema's cleaning staff as they cleared up in the morning. No British audience would have paid to watch them.

In 1937 a new attempt was made to improve standards. This time the quotas were raised and a minimum financial outlay imposed. Hollywood, which depended on its overseas sales for its profits, was outraged by the British legislation. A third of its foreign income came from Britain. The State Department and Hollywood's trade organization protested indignantly to the British government. The State Department's standard line was: "This government has adopted no restrictive regulations similar in any way to those enforced in certain foreign countries."[28] That was strictly true, but then there was no need. In films as in commerce, the Americans demanded the open door abroad while keeping it tightly shut at home. By the late 1920s the Big Five American movie companies dominated the whole film industry in the United States. Because they made many of the major films, controlled the distribution network and owned most of the big movie theaters, even good British films had virtually no chance. Unable to remove the British quotas, the American giants, particularly MGM, adopted the same policy as Ford or Firestone toward British tariffs. They simply bought up British film companies and produced their own films in Britain.

It became clear that government action could not change public tastes. American films succeeded because they were slick and exciting, had high technical standards and good acting. No law could diminish their popularity. One cinema manager in the East End of London summed it all up. His audiences, he said, were very particular. "They like good pictures, good American pictures, pictures of movement and action. They won't stand British pictures here at any price. When we have one in the Programme, many of our patrons come in late or early to avoid seeing the British picture."[29]

The hostility and snobbery of Britain's elite were typified by the popular philosopher C.E.M. Joad. America, he wrote, was the epitome of "modern civilization." It perverted the traditional pursuit of Truth, Beauty and Goodness. Instead of Truth there was the worship of the machine and "the glorification of size, hustle and efficiency." Films, slang and advertisements were all America could manage to take the place of great literature. Morality was reduced to the "belief that all Americans are good and that all is therefore well with America." God, sneered Joad, was seen "as a glorified good American, receiving worship in return for His guaranteed support of all American enterprises."[30]

The intelligentsia might carp at what author Harold Nicolson liked to call "the eternal superficiality of the American race."[31] But to millions of Britons the picture of America they saw in the cinema was a source of hope and encouragement. "The skies were always blue, blue all the time, with a few white clouds. . . . this wonderful dream of a land of unlimited opportunity where we could really become something different and better from what we were."[32]

And America's intellectuals had no doubt that they were the wave of the future. "God damn the continent of Europe," exploded the novelist F. Scott Fitzgerald during a visit to London in 1921. "It is of merely antiquarian interest." Within twenty-five years, he predicted, New York would be the world's "capital of culture" because "culture follows money. . . . We will be the Romans of the next generations as the English are now."[33]

Britain was not alone in her love-hate reaction to the United States. In the 1920s ordinary people throughout much of Europe flocked to see American movies and buy American products. Many European governments imposed restrictions on American films and tried to prevent American takeovers of their companies. But there was general agreement that the business methods of Americans such as Henry Ford were the key to survival in the modern age. Even in introverted Russia *Fordizatsia* was all the rage. The new Soviet leaders, desperately trying to industrialize their backward economy, recognized the need for Western skills and technology, especially from the United States. Once Russia had acquired them, Trotsky predicted, then "Americanized Bolshevism will defeat and crush imperialist Americanism." For "Bolshevism has no enemy more fundamental and irreconcilable than American capitalism." He called them "the two basic and antagonistic forces of our age."[34]

Many Americans mirrored Trotsky's world view, regarding Bolshevik communism as the lurking enemy. The fears of Colonel House at Paris in 1919 were shared in America itself, where the wartime backlash against foreigners and political radicals mushroomed into a full-scale "Red scare." Alarmed by a few anarchist bombings, Attorney General A. Mitchell Palmer hounded and imprisoned the political left. He warned that "the blaze of revolution was sweeping over every American institution of law and order . . . licking at the altars of the churches . . . crawling into the sacred corners of American homes . . . burning up the foundations of society."[35]

The war and the Red scare broke America's Socialist movement, which had won nearly a million votes in the presidential election of 1912. From now on the United States would be unique among Western nations in having no viable socialist or left-of-center political party. In 1924 the British Labour party, backed by the trade unions, formed a government for the first time and quickly opened diplomatic relations with the Soviet Union. America did not recognize Communist Russia until 1933. The U.S. union movement, far weaker than Britain's, was staunchly apolitical. In 1931 Secretary of State Henry Stimson called it "our chief barrier against communism."[36] American workers saw little attraction in socialism, let alone communism. For most of them, particularly the immigrants from Europe, American capitalism seemed to work. They and their children were far better off than in the Old World. In the rueful words of one socialist commentator: "On the reefs of roast beef and apple pie socialistic Utopias of every sort are sent to their doom."[37]

America's boom in the 1920s was therefore more than simply an advertisement for its business methods. For Americans, and for many in Europe, it was a vindication of the whole American way of life. Capitalism, not Bolshevism, seemed the ideology for the modern world. "Americanization" was the dream and the coming reality.

But in October 1929 the dream ended and the nightmare began. For more than a year American investors had been borrowing feverishly to buy shares as Wall Street's "big bull market" climbed upward. General Motors shares, for instance, had more than doubled in value in three years. But then the market broke. At times on October 24, 1929, there were stocks on sale that no one would buy at any price. Experts thought the fall might be temporary, and bankers, led by J. P. Morgan, bought heavily to try to hold the market steady. But on Black Tuesday, October 29, sixteen million shares changed hands, and within a month the stocks listed on Wall Street had fallen 40 percent in value.

The Great Crash of 1929 heralded the longest and deepest recession in American history. The market for cars, houses and consumer goods was saturated. Farmers were hit by the worldwide collapse of prices. Banks, which had lent too much against the now useless security of share values, were forced to call in loans to protect their liquidity. The American banking system, with hundreds of small independent banks set up with inadequate assets, was used to seeing banks fail even in normal years. Now they closed in unprecedented numbers, six thousand between 1929 and 1932.

It took two years for the full effect to be felt. By 1932 the value of shares, and therefore of many people's savings, had fallen to one-tenth of their value at the peak of 1929. Starved of cash, businesses laid off workers. Unemployment rose from 3 percent to 25 percent by 1933. Output fell by a third. The effect was devastating. Laid-off coal miners shivered in tents through a West Virginia winter; below Riverside Drive in New York an encampment of destitute squatters lined the banks of the Hudson River for forty blocks; and between one and two million young people "rode the rails" in search of work. "There is not a garbage dump in Chicago," the writer Edmund Wilson reported in 1933, "which is not diligently harvested by the hungry . . . falling on the heap of refuse as soon as the truck had pulled out and digging in it with sticks and hands."[38]

America had lost confidence in itself. In March 1929 Herbert Hoover had been inaugurated president, proclaiming a New Era and assuring Americans, "I have no fears for the future of our country. It is bright with hope."[39] By 1932 Hoover, once the epitome of technocratic America, had become a synonym for disaster. The shantytowns of squatters that sprang up all over the country were nicknamed Hoovervilles. America, so recently the envy of the world, now attracted mostly pity. Some natives in the Cameroons, an impoverished French colony in Africa, had a collection and sent the city of New York $3.77. It was, they explained, relief for the "starving."[40]

America's next president, Franklin Roosevelt, tried to rekindle faith in the great American dream. "First of all," he said in his inaugural address of March 1933, "let me assert my firm belief that the only thing we have to fear is fear itself—nameless, unreasoning, unjustified terror."[41] Almost by force of personality Roosevelt restored confidence in the banking system. His New Deal gave American unions new rights and set up a basic framework of Social Security. Vast programs of "public works," funded by the federal government, kept many in employment and gave American cities new parks, highways and airports. But even the jaunty Roosevelt could not end the depression. In 1938 unemployment was still nearly 20 percent and the level of investment was half that of 1929. America no longer seemed to be the example for the world.

Many people in Britain also suffered in the depression. Old industries like coal and shipbuilding continued to decline, and parts of Tyneside and South Wales saw 20 percent unemployment. But Britain had grown used to such figures in the 1920s: they did not come out of the blue as in the United States. And the Midlands and Southeast recovered quickly from the slump of 1929–32 as they experienced the demand for houses, cars and consumer goods that had fueled the American economy in the twenties. New British factories were built, living standards in the South improved, and Britain's industrial growth rate in the 1930s was one of the highest in the world.

The exaggerated fears of "Americanization" receded as the flow of U.S. investment in Britain slowed down. Some American firms, in trouble at home, pulled out completely. In 1931 Woolworth's sold almost half their English holdings, and in 1933 Boots, the leading British drugstores, was returned by United Drugs to British shareholders. Between 1933 and 1940 the total U.S. overseas investment fell, while Britain, despite her rival's rapid expansion in the newer industries around the world, remained the world's largest overseas investor.[42]

Some salutary lessons were learned by British industry from the American example. Henry Ford's Model T, which dominated the British motorcar market in 1920, had been overtaken by smaller British products. The motor manufacturer William Morris urged patriotic drivers to buy British with such success that by 1929 he controlled 35 percent of the market. Another British company, Austin, was second with 25 percent, and Ford trailed with only 4 percent, partly because of its reluctance to find a modern replacement for the Model T that could challenge British products like the Austin Seven and the Morris Oxford. "We have been defeated and licked in England," groaned a top Ford executive in Detroit.[43] Partly recovering in the 1930s, with new models to break into the small-car market, Ford nevertheless remained in third place in 1938.

In other industries successful attempts were made to fight off the challenge of the American and German conglomerates. In chemicals the British Imperial Chemical Industries (ICI) was formed in 1926, followed in 1929 by the Anglo-Dutch Unilever, making soap and fats. One company, Courtaulds, a family textile firm from Essex, broke into the American market with particular success through its subsidiary the American Viscose Corporation. In 1928 this produced 60 percent of U.S. rayon and contributed half of Courtaulds' gross income. *Fortune* magazine described it as "a phenomenon comparable to Standard Oil or the automobile empire of Henry Ford."[44]

British ideas as well as British business seemed to be having an effect on thirties America. Some of Roosevelt's New Deal reforms borrowed from British precedents. The Securities Act of 1933, to tighten up the regulation of Wall Street and prevent another crash, was modeled on the British Companies Act. The Guffey Coal Act of 1935 was influenced by the British Coal Mines Act of 1930, which, in the words of one congressman, "had saved the British coal industry."[45] Roosevelt himself told an English friend that Social Security was the most important part of his domestic program and "said that he was really following in the pre-war footsteps of the Liberal party in that respect."[46]

A few British economists and political reformers believed that the New Deal could teach Britain some lessons in return. The Next Five Years Group, including the young Tory MP Harold Macmillan, announced in its 1934 manifesto that "dire poverty in the midst of plenty presents the sort of challenge to capacity for national organization which President Roosevelt has accepted, but our own Government has declined."[47] The following year Lloyd George, still bidding for a political comeback, called for a British New Deal with a massive program of public works. Piecemeal responses to the slump were not enough, he warned. "You have to think out your problem anew exactly as they are doing in America."[48]

But these were isolated voices. The British left, arguing that the depression proved the bankruptcy of American capitalism, looked to the Soviet Union as their example. And Whitehall regained its habitual condescending tone about America. Roosevelt's New Deal was seen as a confused and belated attempt to bring America's

economic and political institutions out of the age of liberal individualism into the twentieth century. The British embassy in Washington frequently referred to the "obsolescence of American
institutions."[49] In 1938 a Foreign Office report circulated to the
Cabinet claimed that "the glad, confident, boastful America has
passed away; in its place is left a country—we cannot yet say a
nation—that has lost its old landmarks, and seems to be staggering
forward, leaderless, into an uncertain future."[50]

The problem was that most British people had little informed
knowledge of the United States against which to judge the sporadic
reports in the media. Virtually no American history or literature
was taught in British schools, and the press paid little attention to
serious American news. Even in the quality papers, one survey
estimated in 1936–37, the United States rarely received more than
a sixth of the space devoted to foreign news, and of this more than
a third was given over to sensation, sex and crime.[51] There was,
then, little to correct the stereotypes of America seen on the movie
screen: cowboys out on the range, girls in satin negligées lounging
in luxurious Manhattan apartments, drunks in the doorways of the
Bowery, and fedora-hatted crooks with submachine guns tucked
under their arms. American politics was corrupt, violence paid, and
sex was a commodity. When Joseph Kennedy arrived as ambassador
to Britain in 1938, he was horrified at the way Britons seemed to
believe that America "was typified by motion pictures." In vain he
called for better press coverage of the United States "so that people
would believe that something happened there besides gangster
shootings, rapes and kidnappings."[52]

The American media paid greater attention to Britain. America's
major newspapers contained far more serious news about British
politics than the British press carried about America, and in 1922 it
was reckoned that nearly one in eight American pupils had a year
of English history at some time during their high school careers. But
the history they were taught, no less than the American films shown
in Britain, often projected a distorted, unflattering image. For
American history teaching was intensely nationalistic, a way of
fusing a disparate collection of ethnic groups into a proud nation.
Britain, particularly the Britain of the American Revolution, served
as a convenient whipping boy. One concerned U.S. historian asserted that "Americans are taught from childhood to hate Britishers
by the study of American history."[53]

These impressions of Britain as a repressive, class-dominated, imperialist society were reinforced by Hollywood's own portrayals of the British. The 1930s saw a rash of American films based on books by Dickens and Kipling. Some were enormous box-office successes, such as *The Lives of a Bengal Lancer*, starring Gary Cooper. Other money-makers in America, like a *A Yank at Oxford* and *Goodbye, Mr. Chips* (both made by MGM in Britain to get around the quota) gave stereotyped portraits of the English university and public school. But the British monarchy was the biggest hit in America. One of the few British films of the 1930s to succeed there, grossing more than $2.5 million, was *The Private Life of Henry VIII*, starring Charles Laughton as England's most notorious king.

For Americans, the monarchy also provided the most fascinating real-life British story of the decade—King Edward VIII's liaison with the American divorcée Mrs. Wallis Simpson. American press cuttings about the affair ran to half a million items, and it was one of the top three American news stories of the decade. The handsome young prince had long been a trendsetter in Anglo-American relations. His taste in clothes had set fashions in New York after his visit there in 1924, gray flannel trousers and blue shirts with soft collars becoming all the rage. And in Britain he took a particular liking to things American, such as jazz, perhaps in reaction to the stuffy atmosphere of his father's court. When he succeeded George V in January 1936, his affair with Mrs. Simpson became a matter of intense interest in the United States. Newspapers that summer were full of pictures of them cruising in the Mediterranean.

In Britain, however, the press kept a remarkable silence, in deference to the King's wishes, even though the affair was common gossip in London society. American interest reached fever pitch when Mrs. Simpson secured a divorce at the end of October 1936. To minimize London publicity the case was heard in Ipswich, by unhappy coincidence the birthplace of Cardinal Wolsey, who had managed Henry VIII's momentous divorce four hundred years before. KING'S MOLL RENO'D IN WOLSEY'S HOME TOWN, ran the most ingenious of the American headlines.[54] The way now seemed clear for a royal wedding, just before the coronation. One of William Randolph Hearst's newspapers stated categorically, KING WILL WED WALLY. It claimed that Edward VIII believed that "the most important thing for the peace and welfare of world is an intimate understanding and relationship between England and America, and that his marriage with this very gifted lady may help to bring about that beneficial co-operation between English-speaking nations."[55]

At last Prime Minister Stanley Baldwin stepped in. The American press speculation was now felt to be seriously damaging Britain's image abroad, particularly in the British Dominions, where, as Baldwin put it later, the Crown was "the last link of Empire that is left."[56] Backed by most leading politicans except Churchill, he insisted that if the King made this match, no political party would form a government to support him. In December Edward VIII was asked to choose. He could have his throne or his wife, but not both. He chose the woman he loved.

Despite London society gibes about "Queen Wallis" and some protests in the U.S. press, Mrs. Simpson's "Americanness" was not the basic objection, nor even her status, or lack of it, as a "commoner." At issue was the fitness of a twice-divorced woman, with both husbands still alive, to be the spouse of a king pledged as Defender of the Faith in a Church which still insisted that the sacrament of marriage was indissoluble. Mrs. Simpson's American background prevented her appreciating what most English women would have known instinctively. Contrary to her movie-world image of royalty, the king of England could not have his way in everything.

It was a love story perfectly designed to satisfy America's fascination with monarchy while vindicating its pride in republican institutions. Not even Hollywood's "dream factory" could have done better. Except, that is, for the ending. Despite William Randolph Hearst's predictions, no royal marriage consummated a new Anglo-American alliance. It would take the worst crisis in either country's modern history to bridge the gulf caused by isolationism, rivalry and misperception and bring Britain and America closer than ever before, or ever again.

CHAPTER 7

BRITAIN ALONE

1935–1941

It is a commonplace that if Britain and America had stood up to the dictators in the 1930s the Second World War would never have happened. Winston Churchill dubbed it "the unnecessary war," and the first volume of his war memoirs took as its theme "how the English-speaking peoples, through their unwisdom, carelessness and good nature, allowed the wicked to rearm."[1] With hindsight it is easy to castigate the leaders of both countries for their blindness to the dangers that threatened them and for a complacency that at times seems almost supine. It is harder to step back, to see the threats as they saw them at the time, and to understand the constraints that made effective Anglo-American cooperation so difficult.

By the early 1930s the world economy had collapsed into depression, and threats to peace were already apparent. In 1931 an expansionist Japan had taken Manchuria on the Asian mainland from China, with only ineffectual protest from the League of Nations. After Hitler came to power in January 1933, he rapidly rearmed Germany and planned a vast Aryan empire in Europe and beyond. The Italian dictator Mussolini, emboldened by Hitler's success, invaded Ethiopia virtually unchallenged in 1935, and from 1936 both dictators intervened on the side of Franco and the fascists in the Spanish Civil War.

Britain and America watched these events from the sidelines.

Both countries were preoccupied with recovery from the depression. Both were inhibited by a popular backlash against the slaughter of the Great War. They both shared a suspicion of the motives of the armaments industry and a reluctance to become entangled again in the continent of Europe. Rearmament was therefore slow, diplomacy hesitant and indecisive.

President Franklin D. Roosevelt, who succeeded Herbert Hoover in 1933, wanted to break the isolationist mold. Although he had lost faith in the League of Nations, which he had originally supported when a junior member of the Wilson administration, Roosevelt still believed that the United States should use its influence in the cause of world peace. That was not only a moral duty, he believed, but also a matter of self-interest. In 1937 he compared war to an infectious disease whose spread could be prevented only by putting the aggressors in "quarantine" through diplomatic isolation or economic sanctions.

Practical politics, however, made it difficult to implement any such remedies. The Congress was isolationist by conviction, not wanting to involve America in another war or even to take action entailing the risk of war. The Neutrality Act of 1935 was designed to prevent the economic entanglements of trade and loans that had helped drag America into the Great War. Roosevelt himself shared these anxieties. "I have seen war. . . . I hate war," he insisted in 1936.[2] He was also acutely sensitive to political realities, having watched the disintegration of Wilson's policies in the confrontation with the Senate in 1919. For Roosevelt, diplomacy had to be tailored to the public mood. His political posture was cruelly caricatured by Congresswoman Clare Boothe Luce as an index finger wetted and held up in the air.[3]

In the 1930s it was understandable for Americans to display little interest in world affairs. Three thousand miles of Atlantic Ocean seemed ample protection against Hitler's Germany, and the expansion of Italy or Japan was of limited concern to a country with few overseas possessions and little dependence on foreign trade. Britain, however, could not afford to take such a detached view. The English Channel, her moat in the past, was no barrier to the growing German air force, and British power and wealth depended on the survival of the empire and the protection of vulnerable trade routes. The First Sea Lord Admiral Chatfield summed up British thinking in 1934: "We are in the remarkable position of not wanting to quarrel with anybody because we have got most of the world al-

ready, or the best parts of it, and we only want to keep what we have
got and prevent others from taking it away from us."[4]

Britain therefore had to maintain a delicate balance. Her interests
lay in preventing not just renewed war but also the further erosion
of her power. She wanted peace, but not at any price. The problem
was that she lacked the means for a firm policy that would deter
worldwide aggression. Rearmament was not popular with the British electorate, nor with the Treasury, which feared that it would
damage economic recovery and so undermine foreign confidence in
sterling. In particular Britain's Navy, the main instrument for protecting her trade and empire, was inadequate for her responsibilities,
after the reductions of the 1920s and successive arms control agreements.

By the mid-thirties Britain could no longer respond to a crisis in
one part of the world while retaining sufficient ships to deal with
a threat elsewhere. If the Royal Navy was needed in the Far East,
the Mediterranean Fleet would have to sail for Singapore, denuding
the Suez Canal and the Middle East. In 1934 the Treasury opposed
a firm line against Japan, using this weakness as justification. In
1935–36 the Cabinet rejected oil sanctions against Mussolini over
Ethiopia on the grounds that the possibility of war with Japan made
tough action against Italy imprudent.

Since a policy of deterrence seemed impossible, British leaders
adopted a policy of appeasement. The attempt to buy off potential
foes, often denigrated as shortsighted and even cowardly, was really
a calculated gamble by Britain to negotiate her way out of danger.
The aim was to reduce the number of enemies by satisfying their
grievances in return for guarantees of peace and disarmament. Appeasement was the policy of the Tory-dominated National Government throughout the 1930s, but it was adopted with particular
enthusiasm by Neville Chamberlain, who became prime minister in
May 1937.

Chamberlain effectively seized control of foreign policy, trying to
reach personal agreements with Hitler and Mussolini. He and most
of his colleagues underestimated Hitler's long-term ambitions and
exaggerated Germany's immediate military strength. Fearful of
being plunged into a war on three fronts simultaneously, they were
unwilling to risk calling Germany's bluff, or Italy's or Japan's.
Chamberlain was also pessimistic about the chances of significant
help. The British Dominions were isolationist, France was in turmoil, and Russia was engulfed in Stalin's bloody purges. Like most

of his colleagues, Chamberlain was particularly skeptical about the United States after the bitter experiences of the 1920s and early 1930s. "It is always best and safest," he once observed, "to count on *nothing* from the Americans except words."[5]

As the crisis worsened Roosevelt wanted to reinforce Britain's efforts to reduce international tension, but his plans were often frustrated by rifts between the two governments.

Trade was a major issue. America was becoming increasingly irritated by British discrimination against U.S. products. In 1937, 16 percent of all the goods America exported went to Britain, making her America's most valuable trading partner, but their importance to Britain, who was expanding her trade with the empire, was declining. By 1937 only 11 percent of British imports came from America, whereas 39 percent came from the empire.[6] Roosevelt's secretary of state, Cordell Hull, was alarmed at the effects of this trend on American farmers and manufacturers. He put the blame on Britain's policy of Imperial Preference, which imposed lower tariffs on imports from the empire than on those from other nations. Hull felt the discrimination was unfair and was convinced that trade barriers and economic nationalism were the root causes of war. The British took a different view. Building up the empire's trade seemed the best way out of the depression, and they were not willing to reduce Imperial Preferences until America offered drastic cuts in its own tariffs. Negotiations on lowering trade barriers between the two dragged on from 1934 to 1938.

The political damage of this stalemate was considerable. It became a State Department axiom that there could be no cooperation on other matters with Britain until a trade agreement had been reached. "At present," a senior U.S. diplomat complained in 1936, "she [Britain] thinks she can count on our help politically and yet hit us below the belt commercially all over the world."[7]

The lack of cooperation was particularly apparent in East Asia. In 1937 Japan, encouraged by the lack of any effective reaction to her invasion of Manchuria, once again attacked China in violation of the 1922 treaty. Instead of coordinating their actions against Japan, Britain and America acted independently and ineffectually.

President Roosevelt restated the sanctity of the treaties Japan had signed and refused to approve her infringements on Chinese territory, but he took no real action. Verbal protests and a gradual rebuilding of America's naval strength to the size allowed by the treaties was the limit of the White House response. Britain was equally hesitant. From 1902 until 1922 she had been an ally of Japan, but, as mentioned earlier, in that year, under American pressure, she had failed to renew the treaty. Her interests in China were now under threat, but she felt that her resources would allow her to act only in concert with the United States. For a brief moment in December 1937, after a Japanese attack on British and American vessels in the Yangtze River, it seemed possible that Roosevelt would agree to a blockade of Japan, but before it could be considered, Japan had apologized for the incident and the crisis receded.

Early in 1938 Roosevelt turned his attention to the ominous situation in Europe. He put forward a proposal suggested by his under secretary of state, Sumner Welles, for a peace conference to be held under the auspices of the United States. He hoped it would establish basic principles for the conduct of international relations, reduce the level of armaments and open up world trade. Roosevelt secretly asked for Chamberlain's support, urging him to reply within a week, but the prime minister was not impressed. "The plan appeared to me fantastic," he wrote in his diary, "and likely to excite the derision of Germany and Italy. They might even use it to postpone conversations with us."[8]

Without consulting his foreign secretary, Anthony Eden, who was on a brief holiday in France, Chamberlain sent Roosevelt a cool reply, outlining his own plans for talks with Mussolini and Hitler and asking the President to hold off for the moment. Lord Home, then Chamberlain's parliamentary private secretary, now thinks the reply was a mistake: "It was the first indication that America was beginning to take some interest in the terrible situation that was developing in Germany. Chamberlain ought not to have turned it down."[9]

On hearing the news Eden was furious. He disliked Chamberlain's personal diplomacy and wanted to encourage closer cooperation between Britain and the United States. "What we have to choose between," he argued, "is Anglo-American co-operation in an attempt to ensure world peace and a piecemeal settlement approached by way of a problematical agreement with Mussolini."[10] However naive an American initiative might seem, he was sure it should be encouraged, not rebuffed. Hurrying back to London, he persuaded the Cabinet to react positively to Roosevelt's suggestion, and Chamberlain duly proposed that the President continue to explore his plan for an international conference while Britain tried direct negotiation with the dictators. But it was too late. By now

Roosevelt's enthusiasm for the idea had cooled, and he was willing to let Chamberlain act alone.

"The loss of the last frail chance to save the world from tyranny otherwise than by war" was Churchill's description of the failure of the Roosevelt initiative.[11] In fact it hardly seemed to deserve such a portentous epitaph. Roosevelt's ideas were vague and utopian, standing even less chance of success than Chamberlain's own policy of appeasement. Perhaps the sad story is better seen as yet one more episode in the chronicle of misunderstandings between Britain and America in the 1930s.

For the rest of 1938 and 1939, until the outbreak of war with Germany, Chamberlain conducted increasingly fruitless negotiations with Hitler and Mussolini. Such sympathy as there had been in Britain for Germany's expansion had now abated. When Hitler entered the Rhineland in 1936, Lord Lothian had commented that the Germans were simply walking into "their own back garden."[12] He was not alone in thinking that Germany had been treated vindictively at Versailles and was entitled to some redress. But during 1938 Hitler invaded Austria and then threatened Czechoslovakia. By September war seemed inevitable. In London air raid sirens were tested, trenches were dug in the parks, and millions of anti-gas masks were made ready for distribution. In a last effort to maintain the peace Chamberlain flew to Munich and made an agreement that gave Hitler half of Czechoslovakia in exchange for pledges that he would make no further territorial demands and that Britain and Germany would never fight each other again.

Roosevelt, who had been watching from the sidelines since the failure of his peace initiative, was relieved that war had been averted and hopeful of a lasting peace. After Munich he cabled Chamberlain: "I fully share your hope and belief that there exists today the greatest opportunity in years for a new order based on justice and law."[13] Privately, however, he became increasingly doubtful during the winter that any agreement with Hitler would stick, and began pressing for American rearmament. Yet he still believed it was the responsibility of the democracies in Western Europe to mount their own defense. America would back them up but not take the lead. "What the British need today," he wrote in February 1939, "is a good stiff grog, inducing not only the desire to save civilization but the continued belief that they can do it. In such an event they will have a lot more support from their American cousins. . . ."[14]

Relations between the two governments improved during 1939.

Uncle Sam entangled in isolationism. Clifford Berryman's 1938 version of the famous Greek sculpture.

The British were encouraged by Roosevelt's plans for rearmament and his condemnation of totalitarianism. The Americans applauded Britain's decision to end appeasement after Hitler took the remainder of Czechoslovakia in March 1939. A historic event that summer symbolized the new cordiality. King George VI became the first reigning British sovereign to set foot on the soil of the former colony. It was a brief visit, a four-day whirlwind tour that took the King and Queen Elizabeth, as guests of the President, to Washington, New York, and to the Roosevelt family home at Hyde Park on the Hudson River north of New York.

Everywhere the royal couple went they were greeted by enthusiastic crowds. Instead of a pompous, stuffy visit, the American press and newsreels showed a friendly and informal pair who lunched at Hyde Park not on caviar and champagne but on beer and hot dogs. The King discussed the signs of impending war with Roosevelt and gained the impression that the President would do everything in his power to help. The Foreign Office was delighted at the discreet courtship conducted during the royal tour, but it was hardheaded enough to know that while the visit had warmed American hearts, only events would change American policy.

On the night of August 31, 1939, Hitler invaded Poland, ignoring Britain's ultimatum, and three days later Britain and France declared war. Unlike Wilson in 1914, Roosevelt at once made clear that American sympathies lay with the Allies. In a "fireside chat" radio broadcast he said, "I cannot ask that every American remain neutral in thought. Even a neutral cannot be asked to close his mind or conscience."[15]

But neutrality was still America's official policy. The Neutrality Act had been amended in 1937 to permit Americans to trade with belligerent nations, except in armaments. To avoid the country being dragged into war by attacks on its ships and by foreign loans, as had happened in World War I, all these goods had to be collected by the buyer and paid for at the time of purchase, a system called Cash and Carry. Within two months of the outbreak of war Roosevelt persuaded Congress to modify the Act further. Britain needed supplies of armaments, which she had been ordering in increasing quantities from America as war loomed, but at the outbreak of hostilities, in keeping with the Neutrality Act, these supplies had been halted. American munitions factories fell idle. By early November, arguing that it was in America's own economic interest to supply Britain, Roosevelt secured the repeal of the arms embargo. Britain could now buy whatever she wanted, as long as she paid cash and arranged delivery.

For the British the revised Neutrality Act was a welcome improvement. As in the Great War, they could now draw on the vast industrial resources of the United States. But the ban on loans was worrying, and the inconvenient "carry" clauses drove the two countries to subterfuge. Airplanes, for instance, could not be flown directly from factories in America to Canada and then on to Britain. Some were dismantled and shipped in crates by sea. Lockheed in California, a small company that was expanding with orders from Britain, found an original solution that kept strictly within the terms of the Neutrality Act. The company bought a stretch of flat land in the far north of North Dakota on the Canadian border. Lockheed pilots flew the planes to the grass airstrip. The engines were turned off and the pilots disembarked. A local farmer hitched a team of

THINK — AMERICANS — THINK

"Against the insidious wiles of foreign influence, I conjure you to believe me, fellow citizens, the jealousy of a free people ought to be constantly awake; since history and experience prove that foreign influence is one of the most baneful foes of Republican Government. 'Tis our true policy to steer clear of permanent alliances with any portion of the foreign world."
(George Washington)

TODAY:

The King and Queen of England, are on our Border; en route to the United States.

WHY ARE THEY COMIMG?
WHAT IS THE MOTIVE?

Is this a vacation tour? OR purely a propaganda mission?

THINK — AMERICANS — THINK

As the result of English propaganda we were involved in a world war. No one questions this.

Why should America officially extend the hand of welcome to England's crowned heads, when Americans groan under the burden of billions of dollars of defaulted payments on loans. Loans made as the result of propaganda during that war.

A DEBT THEY NEVER INTEND TO PAY

Have you read "England expects every American to do his duty" by Quincy Howe. You Should.

Are we to again pull English chestnuts out of the fire — "On Tick" — Why cater to welchers.

THINK — AMERICANS — THINK

(Sponsored and distributed by a committee of Americans who believe in a revival of the spirit of "76")

60

Warnings printed for an Irish American club and dropped by aircraft over Detroit when King George VI was just across the Canadian border (June 1939).

horses to the front undercarriage and drew the machines a few yards across the border into Canada, thus ensuring that the planes had not left the United States under their own power. British or Canadian pilots then went aboard, restarted the engines and took off for Britain.

For seven months after war was declared there was little fighting. Poland was swiftly dismembered by Germany and Russia, with whom Hitler had signed a nonaggression pact. There then followed the period of inactivity known as the phony war. During it a last attempt was made by Roosevelt to explore the chances of peace. Sumner Welles was sent to Europe on a special mission. Chamberlain wrote scathingly of the intervention: "Heaven knows I don't want the Americans to fight for us—we should have to pay too dearly for that if they had a right to be in on the peace terms—but if they are so sympathetic they might at least refrain from hampering our efforts and comforting our foes."[16]

In April 1940 the phony war came to an abrupt end. Germany invaded Scandinavia. A British expeditionary force arrived in Norway too late and was soon forced to withdraw. On May 10 the German army invaded the Netherlands, Belgium, Luxembourg and northern France. The Allied forces were soon in headlong retreat. At six o'clock that night the British prime minister resigned, having lost a vote of confidence over Norway in the House of Commons. His successor was Winston Churchill.

Although a diehard Tory, Churchill had been out of office for most of the 1930s, when he had been an outspoken advocate of rearmament and a frequent critic of appeasement. Ed Murrow, head of CBS operations in Europe, reported to American radio listeners that evening that Churchill "enters office with the tremendous advantage of being the man who was right. . . . Mr. Churchill can inspire confidence. And he can preach a doctrine of hate that is acceptable to the majority of this country."[17] Unlike Chamberlain, Churchill was also an ardent champion of cooperation among what he liked to call "the English-speaking peoples." He had an American mother, knew the United States well and, on his appointment as First Lord of the Admiralty in September 1939, had responded eagerly to Roosevelt's secret request for regular information on naval matters. After his appointment as prime minister their correspondence was to develop into the most important channel of communication between the two governments. Between May 1940 and April 1945 Churchill sent Roosevelt a message, on average, once every thirty-six hours. "No lover," he said after the war, "ever studied the whims of his mistress as I did those of President Roosevelt."[18]

But all this was in the future in May 1940. When Churchill assumed office there were many in Washington who were wary. His belligerent stance on naval disarmament in the 1920s had not been forgotten. He was also suspected of erratic judgment and an excessive fondness for alcohol. When news of his appointment reached Washington, Roosevelt commented dryly that he "supposed Churchill was the best man that England had, even if he was drunk half of his time."[19]

It was the disastrous course of the war itself as much as the change of leaders that transformed Anglo-American relations. Within two weeks of Churchill's assumption of office the German Army had reached the Channel coast. Three hundred and thirty thousand British and French troops, miraculously evacuated from Dunkirk, reached Britain bedraggled and without most of their weapons and equipment. By the middle of June France had surrendered. Britain stood alone with an army wholly inadequate for the task of defending her shores from the attack that seemed imminent. In the House of Commons Churchill rallied his countrymen. "We shall never surrender; and even if, which I do not for a moment believe, this Island or a large part of it were subjugated and starving, then our Empire beyond the seas, armed and guarded by the British Fleet, would carry on the struggle until, in God's good time, the New World, with all its power and might, steps forth to the rescue and the liberation of the Old."[20]

As Churchill's rhetoric acknowledged, Britain now had nowhere to turn but to America. Doubts about American reliability still lingered. Chamberlain and others had not forgotten World War I and the price extracted then for American military help. But under Churchill's guidance the British government came to accept that without the United States Britain was lost. Disregarding the dangerously low level of her gold and dollar reserves, which could not, as in World War I, be covered by U.S. loans, Britain placed huge orders for munitions. When the money ran out, the government hoped that supplies would continue to flow. But new orders could not meet the current crisis. Ships and planes would take months to build, and by then Britain might have been overrun. Churchill begged Roosevelt for immediate practical help. On the East Coast of the United States were fifty Great War destroyers, "mothballed" in their dockyards. If these could be recommissioned and lent to Britain, they could be used to help repel a German invasion and to protect the sea-lanes, with their vital supplies of food, from German submarines.

"Not a day should be lost," Churchill cabled Roosevelt, emphasizing the urgency of his request. Roosevelt's reply, one that Churchill would become used to receiving, was that he wanted to help but that Congress was unlikely to allow it. Again Churchill cabled: "We must ask . . . as a matter of life or death to be reinforced with these destroyers." Roosevelt did not reply, and for two months after the fall of France sent no messages at all. Finally, in desperation, Churchill cabled on July 31: "Mr President, with great respect I must tell you that in the long history of the world, this is a thing to do now."[21]

Roosevelt's reluctance to meet Churchill's appeal was partly political. Cautious as ever, he was unwilling to abandon formal neutrality before Congress was ready. But there was also the fear fostered, among others, by the American ambassador in London, Joseph Kennedy, that Britain was on the verge of collapse. "If we had to fight to protect our own lives," Kennedy advised, "we would do better fighting in our own backyard."[22] Roosevelt himself assessed Britain's chances of survival in early July 1940 as no better than one in three. Offering destroyers, which America itself would need if Britain fell, could be a futile, even suicidal, gesture.

The President's military advisers were particularly reluctant to see too much given away. Although America was an industrial giant, its military strength was puny. In April 1940 the United States ranked twentieth among the world's military powers. The Dutch were nineteenth.[23] A country with an army of 250,000 men with outdated equipment and a navy only adequate to defend either the Pacific or the Atlantic, not both, simply did not have resources to spare. After Dunkirk five hundred thousand U.S. rifles were sold cheaply to the British Army, but this was still a commercial arrangement, paid for from Britain's dwindling foreign exchange. Lending fifty destroyers was a very different matter.

By the middle of August, however, Roosevelt felt able to act. Intelligence reports reaching Washington suggested that Britain might, after all, survive into 1941. Equally important was legal advice to the President that he need not go to Congress for special legislation but could act independently, under his authority as commander in chief. At last Roosevelt put a proposal to Churchill. Britain could have the destroyers, but she would have to offer something in return. The President wanted ninety-nine-year leases on eight British possessions in the Americas, stretching from Newfoundland to the Caribbean, on which the United States could build air and naval bases to strengthen its own defenses. Roosevelt also requested a pledge from Churchill that if Britain fell the Royal Navy would not be surrendered but would carry on the fight from ports in the British Empire. The bases and the promises, Roosevelt explained, were "molasses" to sweeten the pill in America.

When the British Cabinet received the proposal, its first reaction was to refuse. The secret War Cabinet minutes read: "The view of the War Cabinet was that a formal bargain on the lines proposed was out of the question."[24] Even Churchill was against giving what he called "a blank cheque on the whole of our transatlantic possessions."[25] But Britain no longer called the tune: she had little choice but to accept aid on whatever terms America proposed. Eventually a compromise was reached: two of the leases were designated a "gift" from the British government; the rest were made part of the formal deal that Roosevelt needed in order to persuade Americans that they were not, once again, being taken as suckers by the wily British. Even at a moment of world crisis, old suspicions died hard.

On September 2, 1940, the "destroyers for bases" deal was signed. It was of symbolic as well as practical importance. The United States was formally neutral, and yet, with this unneutral act, it had effectively pledged support for Britain as America's own front line of defense. When the destroyers finally arrived in Britain, they came with a moving display of American sympathy. Immense care had been taken in fitting them out. There were bars of soap and clean towels, cocktail cabinets fully stocked, toys left for the children of the sailors who would take them over, and everywhere messages of encouragement scrawled on the walls and bulkheads: "Sock 'em Hell" and "Kill the Bastards."[26]

Roosevelt's caution during this early part of the war, though unwelcome to Britain, was understandable. The presidential election was due in November 1940. Roosevelt had decided to run for a third term of office, an unprecedented and controversial decision. He had secured the endorsement of the Democratic party in July but did not want to do anything during the campaign that would give credence to Republican charges that he was a "war-monger."

The President was, however, encouraged by the growing public support for Britain in the United States. In May 1940 a Committee to Defend America by Aiding the Allies had been formed by a Kansas newspaper editor, William Allen White. The White committee soon established chapters across the country that agitated for every help to be given to Britain, short of declaring war. One of its leading members was the film star Douglas Fairbanks, Jr., who

joined to warn America of the dangers of isolationism. He recalls
Roosevelt telling him that as president he "had to be like the captain
in front of his troops. If he got too far ahead in expressing his own
sympathies and opinion, then he would lose the people behind. He
could only be a little ahead . . . and it was *our* job to push public
opinion."[27]

At times it took some pushing. Only two days after the "destroyers for bases" agreement there was a sharp backlash. A new committee was formed to keep America out of the war. America First was

WAKE UP! WAKE UP, UNCLE!

BISHOP, *ST. LOUIS STAR-TIMES*

*Pro-intervention: the Lilliputians tie down the sleeping Uncle Sam as the
Nazi monster wades across the Atlantic.*

a direct rival of the White committee, and drew its strongest support
from the Midwest, particularly around Chicago. This area had particularly large German populations, although opposition to entering
the war did not come from just them or from the Italians, or from
Britain's traditional opponents the Irish. Among supporters of
America First were many pacifists, those who did not believe the
war was America's concern, and mothers who simply wanted to
prevent their sons being sent as cannon fodder to Europe. By December 1941 the organization had 850,000 members. Its basic policy
was to build up America's own defenses and not to get entangled
in Britain's war.

The figurehead of America First, who was always in demand at
their rallies, was the aviator Charles Lindbergh, whom some suspected of fascist sympathies. Having toured German aircraft factories, he reported back to America the scale of German superiority
to Britain in the air and warned about the folly of believing that
Britain could win. Another supporter was the young Kingman
Brewster, in later years to be president of Yale University and
American ambassador to Britain. He believes the movement reflected a broadly based sentiment in the country. There were many
who feared that total war could mean the destruction of American
institutions, perhaps even of democracy itself. In particular, America Firsters disputed the claim that Britain was the United States'
front line. "There was a feeling that Hitler could not invade us and
we could not invade him. The Atlantic was just too big. . . ."
Looking back now, Brewster concedes that for America to have
followed the isolationists' cause "would have been a disaster. . . . But
it wasn't because we thought Europe ought to go hang. It was
because we didn't think America should hang in order to prevent
that."[28]

Roosevelt and those who believed America must do everything
possible to help Britain had powerful allies among the American war
correspondents stationed in London. During August and September the Battle of Britain was being fought out in the skies over
southern England. Day after day the Luftwaffe came to attack Britain's airfields and bomb her cities, to meet with a daring and effective
defense from Britain's fighter squadrons. It was a dramatic battle for
survival, watched and reported back each evening to America by
radio.

Before the war began, the Foreign Office had explored ways of
persuading America to help Britain in the event of war. The British

embassy in Washington had advised that "if America ever comes into an European war it will be some violent emotional impulse which will provide the last and decisive thrust. Nothing would be so effective as the bombing of London, translated by air to the homes of America."[29] It was a shrewd prediction. The most distinguished of the American radio correspondents in London was Ed Murrow, CBS's bureau chief, who in the autumn of 1940 broadcast daily reports of the massive Luftwaffe onslaughts on the capital. "The air raid is still on" he whispered to American listeners on September 11. "I shall speak rather softly, because three or four people are sleeping on mattresses on the floor of this studio."[30] On September 24 his quiet, tense voice was heard in America against the background sound of wailing air-raid sirens, the crump of bombs and the clatter of antiaircraft fire. The impact on Americans living in safety three thousand miles away was immeasurable. "You burnt the city of London in our homes, and we felt the flames," wrote the American poet Archibald MacLeish.[31]

By the autumn of 1940, with the presidential election only weeks away, the argument over America's response to the war was becoming bitter and sometimes violent. Fairbanks remembers abuse from the isolationist press, his films being banned or boycotted, his wife and children threatened with violence and kidnapping. He went to speak to a huge rally in Chicago. "We were scared to death. My knees were cracking together like biscuits on the platform, but I got through it all right."[32]

Roosevelt's opponent for the presidency was the Republican Wendell Willkie, a New York attorney and businessman with Midwestern roots. Willkie sympathized with Britain and personally supported Roosevelt's policy of aid short of war, but as the campaign developed he began to slip behind in the polls and succumbed to pressure to attack Roosevelt on the war issue. He implied that the President had made secret commitments to the Allies and warned "if you re-elect him you may expect war in April 1941." With two weeks of the campaign to go, Willkie was recovering and Roosevelt was forced to fight back. In Boston he gave a pledge for which he was later much criticized: "Your boys are not going to be sent into any foreign wars." Willkie fumed, "That hypocritical son of a bitch! This is going to beat me!"[33] On November 5, 1940, Roosevelt was reelected for a third term with 449 electoral votes to Willkie's 82, a massive vote of confidence that gave the President more freedom of maneuver to conduct foreign policy.

A DEADLY PARALLEL

When Woodrow Wilson was running for re-election in 1916.

When Franklin Roosevelt is running for a third election in 1940.

Anti-intervention: McCutcheon reminds Americans of what happened the last time a U.S. president campaigned on an antiwar platform (Chicago Tribune, October 30, 1940).

The election over, Roosevelt went for a rest in the Caribbean. There, early in December 1940, he received a message from Churchill that was timed to catch him in a relaxed, responsive mood. Churchill later called this letter "one of the most important I ever wrote."[34] He followed the advice of the British ambassador in Washington, Lord Lothian, by explaining Britain's predicament in detail. It was an alarming analysis. Britain urgently needed deliveries of munitions and aircraft. The worsening Battle of the Atlantic was threatening to strangle her lifelines and starve her into surrender. Every ton of merchant shipping surplus to American requirements, Churchill argued, should be put at Britain's disposal, as should American naval escorts to accompany cargoes across the Atlantic. He also reminded the President that "the moment approaches when we shall no longer be able to pay cash for shipping and other supplies." The letter ended with a moving request that Roosevelt "regard this letter not as an appeal for aid, but as a statement of the minimum action necessary to the achievement of our common purpose."[35]

Roosevelt's reaction, unlike his response to the request for fifty destroyers earlier in the year, was swift and imaginative. On his return from his Caribbean holiday he gave a press conference in which he warned of Britain's imminent dollar crisis. "The best immediate defense of the United States is the success of Great Britain in defending itself," he insisted, and put forward a proposal not, as in World War I, for financial loans to be repaid after the war but for America to lend Britain the goods she needed, leaving repayment or the return of the goods to be arranged later.

Roosevelt described his plan in terms that everyone could understand. "Suppose my neighbor's home catches fire, and I have a length of garden hose four or five hundred feet away. . . . Now what do I do? I don't say to him . . . 'Neighbor, my garden hose cost me fifteen dollars; you have to pay me fifteen dollars for it.' . . . I don't want fifteen dollars—I want my garden hose back after the fire is over." And, added Roosevelt, if "it gets smashed up—holes in it— during the fire," then the neighbor says " 'All right, I will replace it.' "[36]

On January 10, 1941, the Lend-Lease bill was introduced into Congress and ran the gauntlet of committee hearings by both houses, at which members of the administration and other witnesses were cross-examined in open session and with maximum publicity. The hearings provided a new forum for the debate about America's proper relationship with Britain.

Opponents of the scheme, the anti-interventionists like Congressman Hamilton Fish and Charles Lindbergh, concentrated their attack on two points: that the bill would give the President far too much power, making him a virtual dictator, and that it would suck America into war. The counterargument, put by Senator Claude Pepper and others, was that the proponents of Lend-Lease were the true America Firsters, since helping Britain was the only realistic way of defending America. The bill itself was shrewdly entitled "An Act to Promote the Defense of the United States."

The debate was acrimonious. Pepper had long supported more help for the Allies, and had spoken on the subject all over the country. For his pains he was hanged in effigy outside the Senate by a group of women protesting that he was trying to murder their sons. "I was trying to explain to everyone that this was the only way we could stay out of the war. We could not afford to let Hitler become the master of Europe and then maybe a master of a large part of the world. We would have to fight him all over the world by ourselves."[37]

The debate was not simply about the best means of defending America. It also reflected the deep-rooted American suspicions about Britain. The bill's opponents claimed that America was once more being taken for a ride by Britain, that cunning John Bull was inveigling a generous Uncle Sam into paying for a war that was not yet beyond his means. Many Americans found it hard to believe that Britain was short of cash when, as they saw it, she still owned a vast empire.

Roosevelt expected Churchill to make some gestures to help him with these political problems. These included releasing gold held in South Africa and selling one of Britain's major companies in the United States, American Viscose, a highly successful subsidiary of the textile giant Courtaulds. An American destroyer was sent to Cape Town to collect $50 million of gold, and American Viscose was compulsorily sold, only to be resold immediately at a much higher price by the consortium of American bankers who bought it—a profit that did not come back to Britain.

"Certain things were done," Churchill wrote after the war, "which seemed harsh and painful to us."[38] At the time he drafted a message of complaint to Roosevelt. "It is not fitting that any nation should put itself wholly in the hands of another, least of all a nation which is fighting under increasingly severe conditions for what is proclaimed to be a cause of general concern."[39] But Churchill controlled his anger and the message was never sent. As with the destroyers deal, Britain was in no position to dictate the terms of American help.

It took Roosevelt two months to push Lend-Lease through Congress. On March 11, 1941, after votes that split on party lines—Democrats mainly for, Republicans mainly against—the bill was signed into law. The businessman Averell Harriman was dispatched across the Atlantic to run the London end of Lend-Lease. His instructions from Roosevelt were blunt: "Recommend everything that we can do, short of war, to keep the British Isles afloat."[40]

Churchill later described Lend-Lease as "the most unsordid act in the history of any nation."[41] It came as essential relief to a hard-pressed government and, compared with the arrangements for lending funds in World War I, it was a generous and farsighted gesture. Roosevelt was determined to avoid another disastrous row over war debts. Lend-Lease was not, however, pure altruism. Supporting Britain was seen as a way of defending America by keeping it out of the war. Claude Pepper admits that he saw Britain as "a sort of mercenary" doing America's fighting for her.[42] Nor was Lend-Lease a gift. The terms had not been agreed upon, but repayment in some form was expected.

Churchill's overriding aim was still to persuade America to join forces with Britain. In 1917 President Wilson had finally declared war against Germany because of attacks on American shipping in the North Atlantic. In 1941 it seemed possible that this would happen again. German sinkings of merchant ships had reached new heights: 530,000 tons in March, 668,000 tons in April. At this rate, even allowing for new construction, Britain would have lost a quarter of her merchant fleet in a single year. Roosevelt issued secret orders that the American Navy should be ready to escort Allied convoys across the North Atlantic beginning in April, but at the last moment drew back in response to a renewed America First campaign against "convoying." Instead, to Churchill's dismay, he moved cautiously, extending U.S. patrols to the mid-Atlantic at the end of April, and in July taking over the garrisoning of Iceland from Britain.

The weary Prime Minister needed more than this. His government was demoralized by setbacks in Greece and North Africa. There were fears that once Hitler had achieved total dominance in the eastern Mediterranean he would turn once again to the invasion of Britain. For the first time since the desperate days of June 1940 Churchill now pleaded with Roosevelt to enter the war. On May 4 he cabled: "Mr. President, I am sure that you will not misunderstand me if I speak to you exactly what is in my mind. The one decisive

counterweight I can see . . . would be if the United States were
immediately to range herself with us as a belligerent power. . . . In
this war every post is a winning post and how many more are we
going to lose?"⁴³ In Washington many of Roosevelt's advisers
agreed with Churchill's analysis, but the President balked at leading
his people into war, convinced that this would only be possible
when Hitler affronted American interests or honor in such a way
that national unity would be guaranteed.

The two leaders had now been corresponding as heads of governments for over a year, but they had not yet met, except briefly in
1918. In the summer of 1941, however, the moment was opportune.
Hitler's surprise attack on Russia in June 1941 and Russia's stout
defense meant that the main thrust of the war was for the moment
being pursued on the Eastern European front, giving Churchill a
breathing space. He took advantage of it by accepting Roosevelt's
invitation to a full-scale conference to be held in Placentia Bay,
Newfoundland, in August. Churchill arrived aboard the battleship
HMS *Prince of Wales*. He had rested on the voyage, taking exercise,
striding the decks, and watching films in the wardroom at night. He
was in high spirits, hopeful, like many in London, that Roosevelt
now meant to call for a declaration of war. "I do not think," he had
told the Queen before his departure, "that our friend would have
asked me to go so far for what must be a meeting of world-wide
importance, unless he had in mind some further forward step."⁴⁴

The four-day meeting confirmed the friendship between the two
leaders and created new links among their advisers. The emotional
bonds between the two countries were symbolized by a service on
the quarterdeck of the *Prince of Wales*. Churchill himself chose the
hymns: "For those in Peril on the Sea," "Onward Christian Soldiers" and "Oh God, Our Help in Ages Past." The Union Jack and
the Stars and Stripes were draped on the pulpit, and the senior staffs
of both governments, with the crews of the American and British
ships, shared hymnbooks and sang together. It was an inspiring
occasion for all who took part.

The substance of the meetings was perhaps less to Churchill's
taste, though he put on a bold front. Roosevelt resisted Churchill's
call for a declaration of war. Instead he proposed a statement of joint
war aims, which, while they confirmed America's determination to
see Hitler defeated, exacted a price from Britain in the form of
pledges that could imperil the continuance of her empire after the
war.

It was not just opponents of Lend-Lease who suspected Britain's long-term motives. Elliott Roosevelt, the President's son, who was present at the conference, remembers his father also having doubts about Churchill. "He felt that in the period following the war . . . Churchill believed that Great Britain would have a bigger empire and greater influence, that he would take advantage of the help given by America, and that we would still be in a secondary role."[45]

It was the same fear that Woodrow Wilson had expressed on America's entry into World War I. Wilson had put forward his Fourteen Points to establish that America's aims were not the same as the Allies'. Roosevelt used the Atlantic Charter, the agreement signed at the end of the Placentia Bay conference, to try to bind Britain and America in common war aims that would satisfy the American people and embody America's distinctive vision of the postwar world.

Clause Three of the charter stated that both countries "respect the right of all peoples to choose the form of government under which they will live; and they wish to see sovereign rights and self-government restored to those who have been forcibly deprived of them." Although these words were mainly aimed at the subject peoples of Hitler's Europe, they were soon seized on by politicians in Britain's empire and by American anticolonialists to justify demands for independence. Clause Four of the charter was also significant. It pledged both governments "to further the enjoyment of all States, great or small, victor or vanquished, of access, on equal terms, to the trade and to the raw materials of the world." This latest American attempt to break down Britain's Imperial Preference system was weakened by the saving condition, inserted at British insistence, of "due respect for their existing obligations."[46] Nevertheless the Atlantic Charter served as a warning that the United States would use its leverage to try to force Britain to adopt policies in keeping with its own plans for the postwar world.

What mattered to Churchill, though, in the heat of war, was not the future import of Clauses Three or Four, but how to identify America firmly with Britain's cause. From that perspective the joint statement of war aims was invaluable. And although he failed to secure the American declaration of war he had hoped for, Churchill did obtain further promises of American naval help in the North Atlantic. The President had promised, he told the Cabinet on his return, to "become more and more provocative" in the Atlantic.

"Everything was to be done to force an 'incident' . . . which would justify him in opening hostilities."[47]

On September 4 such an incident occurred. A U-boat attacked the U.S. destroyer *Greer*, and Roosevelt used the opportunity to announce a state of virtual, though still undeclared, naval war. American warships now began escorting British and Canadian convoys, laden with vital military supplies and food, through "American defensive waters," which ran up to longitude 10 degrees west, or roughly three-quarters of the way across the Atlantic. The relief for Britain was immense. German vessels were warned that they would enter the area at their peril. In November these "Shoot on sight" orders were strengthened by the repeal of further sections of the Neutrality Act. Roosevelt could now arm American merchant ships and send them direct to Britain. He could also use the U.S. Navy to escort convoys all the way to British ports. But he did not rush to do so, aware of the strength of antiwar feeling in the country and in Congress. According to a Gallup poll on October 22, for instance, only 17 percent of the American people favored a declaration of war on Germany.[48]

The incident Roosevelt was waiting for, the affront that would unite the people behind him, was finally delivered not by Germany but by Japan. Germany's surprise attack on Russia removed Japanese fears that Stalin would be able to resist Japan's expansion in Asia. Britain was unable to spare large forces for Singapore and Malaya or capital ships to patrol the China Sea. Only the Americans with their main fleet at Pearl Harbor, Hawaii, offered any deterrent.

In July 1941 Japan overran the remainder of Indochina. The Americans reacted by imposing an oil embargo and strengthening their forces in the Philippines. By December it was expected that Japan would mount an attack on British and Dutch possessions in Southeast Asia. The attack on Pearl Harbor took everyone by surprise. On the morning of Sunday December 7 Japanese planes bombed the American base, sinking or immobilizing eight American battleships and leaving 2,400 dead. It was the most humiliating military disaster in American history.

The shock was palpable. An English visitor arrived by train in Chicago later the same day. "We got out at the Union Terminal . . . a huge concourse of glass and iron and steel, silent as the grave, silent as a cathedral in the middle of the night, everybody not speaking, silent. Even the people sitting at the eating places, the restaurants, not speaking to each other and looking into the dim distance, absolutely stunned. It was like visiting a drugged nation."[49]

At first some members of America First thought the news was a hoax, or some clever trick of Roosevelt's. But when the appalling truth dawned, they abandoned their campaign and joined forces behind the President. On the eve of Pearl Harbor the chairman of the New York chapter of America First had sent a long critical letter to Roosevelt. The Monday following the attack he wrote again: "Please consider the contents of our letter, dated December 6, 1941, null and void."[50]

America declared war on Japan, and Hitler, in turn, declared war on America. Roosevelt cabled Churchill, "Today all of us are in the same boat with you and the people of the Empire, and it is a ship which will not and can not be sunk."[51] The Prime Minister was jubilant. After nineteen months of lonely leadership Britain was now assured of survival and victory. On the night of Pearl Harbor, he recalled later, "I went to bed and slept the sleep of the saved and thankful."[52]

CHAPTER 8

MIXED UP
TOGETHER
1941-1945

The day after America's entry into the war one of the British Chiefs of Staff questioned the forthright language being used in a request to the United States and urged that a more deferential tone be adopted. Winston Churchill replied with a wicked leer: "Oh! that is the way we talked to her while we were wooing her; now that she is in the harem, we talk to her quite differently."[1]

Churchill's first reaction to Pearl Harbor was relief that he now had a powerful ally on Britain's side. His next thought was to go immediately to Washington. He was worried lest America, in its fury with Japan, abandon the priority confirmed at the Atlantic conference in 1941, of defeating Germany first. The attack on Pearl Harbor was only the prelude to successful Japanese assaults on the Philippines, Malaya, Singapore, Burma and the Dutch East Indies—victories that tipped the balance of power in the Pacific as profoundly as Hitler's blitzkrieg had done in Europe in 1940. Powerful voices, particularly in the American Navy, urged Roosevelt to concentrate on the Pacific and leave the Atlantic to Britain. Throughout the war these tensions persisted. Even today the British instinctively think of the Second World War as primarily a European war, with the Pacific as a sideshow, while the Americans give more weight to MacArthur's and Nimitz's battles against the Japanese. The Russians, for their part, single out their defeat of Hitler on the eastern front as the event that won the war.

Churchill arrived in Washington in time for Christmas, 1941, appearing with Roosevelt on the steps of the White House to turn on the Christmas lights. He stayed there for three weeks, often closeted with Roosevelt for hours on end, and his capacity for drinking and talking into the early hours of the morning worried Eleanor Roosevelt, who feared her husband would be exhausted. Although the two leaders had engaged in an intense correspondence, their wartime meetings had so far consisted only of the four days aboard ship in Placentia Bay which had led to the Atlantic Charter. At Arcadia, the code name given to this second wartime meeting, acquaintance ripened into genuine friendship. Harry Hopkins, Roosevelt's special adviser, liked to tell of FDR being wheeled one day into his guest's room only to find the Prime Minister emerging wet, glowing and completely naked from the bath. Apologizing, Roosevelt began to withdraw, but Churchill beckoned him back. "The Prime Minister of Great Britain," he announced, "has nothing to conceal from the President of the United States."[2]

During 1942 the Churchill-Roosevelt "special relationship" was at its closest. "Trust me to the bitter end"[3] were Roosevelt's parting words at the end of Arcadia, and after he had received cordial birthday greetings from the Prime Minister in late January, he cabled back: "It is fun to be in the same decade with you."[4] Warm private messages like this mingle with weighty strategic memoranda and quick-fire diplomatic salvos in their remarkable correspondence. Churchill recalled later in his memoirs: "My relations with the President gradually became so close that the chief business between our two countries was virtually conducted by these personal exchanges between him and me."[5] He told Foreign Secretary Anthony Eden in November 1942: "My whole system is based upon partnership with Roosevelt."[6]

The intimacy of the two leaders was reinforced by other friendships. Harry Hopkins, nicknamed Lord Root of the Matter by Churchill, and Averell Harriman, both trusted Roosevelt advisers, had already earned British confidence and served as mediators between the two governments. In Washington General George C. Marshall, the U.S. Army Chief of Staff, was a close friend of Field Marshal Sir John Dill, head of the British Joint Staff Mission. Their mutual trust helped resolve numerous disputes between the two governments over strategy. When Dill died in November 1944 Marshall wrote to his widow: "Officially the United States has suffered a heavy loss, and I personally have lost a dear friend, unique in my lifetime, and never to be out of my mind."[7]

At all levels of the British and U.S. bureaucracies personal contact made Anglo-American cooperation easier. In 1939 the British embassy in Washington had fewer than twenty diplomats. During the war the official British presence in Washington swelled to a peak of nine thousand, as almost every ministry from Whitehall established its own staff in the city. The same happened in London, with the old U.S. embassy at 1 Grosvenor Square soon proving inadequate and the Americans taking over much of Mayfair, including part of a famous Oxford Street department store, Selfridge's.

In the First World War America had refused to merge its war effort with Britain and France, jealously preserving its independence as an "associate" power. But at the Arcadia conference Marshall, who had witnessed the earlier squabbles at first hand as a member of Pershing's staff, successfully pressed for an unprecedented unified command. In each theater of operations there was to be a single commander for all British and American forces—air, sea and ground. Thus General Alexander, a Briton, was later to command in Italy and General Eisenhower, an American, in France. At the top the Combined Chiefs of Staff would resolve problems of strategy and logistics under the direction of the President and the Prime Minister.

Other combined bodies were created to handle the assignment of munitions, shipping, raw materials, food and production. A full exchange of intelligence information was also agreed upon, ranging from evidence about the Axis troop movements to information on the enemy's economy and morale. Back in August 1940 Churchill had predicted with cautious understatement that Britain and America would become "somewhat mixed up together in some of their affairs for mutual and general advantage."[8] What ensued far exceeded even his most optimistic expectations. The alliance of World War II was a far cry from the arms-length "association" of 1917–18, let alone the aloof suspicion of the 1930s. As Marshall said later, it was "the most complete unification of military effort ever achieved by two Allied nations."[9]

Churchill returned to Britain in January 1942 well pleased with his achievements at Arcadia. The conference reaffirmed that "notwithstanding the entry of Japan into the War, our view remains that

Germany is still the prime enemy and her defeat is the key to victory. Once Germany is defeated, the collapse of Italy and the defeat of Japan must follow."[10] A decision on where to commit American troops to battle had not yet been taken, but Roosevelt, to stress his commitment, dispatched the first GIs to the British Isles within weeks. Churchill told the King on his return from Washington that after months of "walking out" together, Britain and America were now "married."[11]

But the new warmth of the relationship could not disguise basic differences of interest. Throughout the war there was a fundamental disagreement between Britain and America over the best strategy for defeating Hitler. To the Americans, and to Stalin, Churchill seemed unduly cautious about getting back onto the continent of Europe. They were suspicious of his motives, believing his aim was not simply to beat Hitler, but to do so in a manner that allowed the British Empire to remain intact, with Britain still controlling the main sea routes and the world's resources.

The American Joint Chiefs of Staff were impatient for a cross-Channel invasion at the first opportunity. In April 1942 General Marshall arrived in London secretly with their plans. They envisaged a massive buildup of Allied troops in Britain, including an American Army of one million by April 1943, backed by airfields, supply depots and other support facilities. The aim was a full-scale Anglo-American invasion of France the following summer (code-named Round-up). Marshall also wanted cross-Channel raids throughout 1942 and entertained the possibility of an emergency invasion that year (Sledgehammer) if either Russia or Germany seemed on the verge of collapse. The Americans insisted that this was the crucial theater in Europe. "In no other area can we attain the overwhelming air superiority vital to successful land attack; while here and here only can the bulk of the British air and ground forces be employed. In this area the United States can concentrate and maintain a larger force than it can in any other." Marshall's message was clear: "Through France passes our shortest route to the heart of Germany."[12]

Churchill and the British Chiefs of Staff pored over Marshall's plans. Sir Alan Brooke, Chief of the Imperial General Staff, told the Americans "that we were all completely in agreement as regards 1943 but if we were forced this year to undertake an operation on the Continent it could only be on a small scale."[13] The United States had virtually no battle-ready troops, and British forces, who would therefore have to bear the brunt of any fighting, were already tied down in North Africa and the Far East. Privately Brooke, a veteran of Dunkirk, was even more skeptical about Marshall's "castles in the air."[14] The Americans seemed to have little idea of the immense logistical problems of the buildup or the difficulties of any breakout from the beachhead.

Brooke nonetheless agreed with Churchill that they could not afford an outright row with the Americans at such a desperate moment in the war. In a personal letter Roosevelt had made clear to the Prime Minister that Marshall's plan "has my heart and *mind* in it." Brooke's doubts were therefore swept under the carpet and Churchill cabled the President: "I am in entire agreement in principle with all you propose, and so are the Chiefs of Staff."[15] But General Marshall was not deceived. In the flying boat on the way back to Washington he turned to his senior Army planner, Colonel Albert Wedemeyer, and said, "I think the British have bought your plan, but I think they did so with their tongues in their cheek."[16]

By June 1942, confirming Marshall's suspicions, Churchill was back in Washington to persuade Roosevelt that no cross-Channel assault could be mounted that year. The British Chiefs of Staff had now studied the implications and "unanimously agreed that operation 'Sledgehammer' offered no hope of success and would merely ruin all prospects of 'Round-up' in 1943."[17] But Roosevelt, like Churchill, felt it essential to open a second front somewhere in Europe during 1942. He had promised as much to the hard-pressed Russians, and he was also concerned that without action across the Atlantic the American public would demand an all-out effort in the Pacific. Opinion polls indicated that most Americans wanted revenge on Japan for Pearl Harbor, but up to 30 percent favored a compromise peace with Germany. "I can see why we are fighting the Japanese," commented one respondent to a Gallup poll, "but I can't see why we are fighting the Germans."[18]

Determined to give Americans the will to fight in Europe, Roosevelt went along with Churchill's plan for an invasion of Algeria and Tunisia (operation Torch). British troops had their backs to the wall in Egypt; Torch would relieve the pressure and give the Allies their first taste of victory. General Marshall was appalled. He was sure that if the Allies diverted their resources to the Mediterranean it would make it impossible to invade France in 1943. But Roosevelt overruled his own Joint Chiefs of Staff. Torch would be mounted that autumn. Bitterly Wedemeyer told Marshall that British plans "have been designed to maintain the integrity of the British empire" and would lead to the Allies' total defeat in Europe and Asia.[19] General Dwight D. Eisenhower, recently arrived in England to prepare for the invasion of France, predicted that it could well be the "blackest day in history."[20]

A fundamental divide in strategy was now opening up between the two allies. Churchill, prompted by Brooke, inclined toward a step-by-step approach to defeating Germany. After victory in North Africa, the Allies should strike at Italy, the "soft underbelly" of the Axis. This would weaken Hitler and make him vulnerable to a subsequent invasion of France, mounted only when the chances of success were high. The Pentagon became convinced that Churchill's principal purpose was to keep the Suez Canal secure for Britain and maintain her traditional influence in the Middle East. The U.S. secretary of war, Henry Stimson, agreed: "The British . . . are straining every nerve to lay a foundation throughout the Mediterranean area for their own empire once the war is over."[21]

That Churchill was obsessed with the empire is beyond doubt, but there is scant evidence to suggest that he put its protection before the defeat of Hitler. It was a major consideration, but not an overriding one. The British were also influenced by their memories of the slaughter in World War I, of the Somme and Passchendaele, and by two years of defeats in the present conflict. They knew, from Dunkirk, the peril of an army perched precariously with one foot on the continent of Europe. They knew that the English Channel, with its fierce tides and sudden storms, could not be treated with the disdain that its mere twenty-mile width might suggest. It had, after all, defended Britain from invasion many times and would, as dispassionately, act as a protector of the German Army on the French coast.

The British preference was to "close the ring" on Germany, picking off its allies and bombing its cities into ruin, before the final assault on Hitler's Fortress Europe was mounted. Many in Washington became convinced that the British would invade the Continent only when there was no resistance left, when they could march in "behind a Scotch bagpipe band," as Admiral Ernest King put it scathingly.[22]

What also irked the Pentagon in 1942 and 1943 was the ability of the British to get their own way. This was partly because Britain could call the strategic tune as long as her forces were doing most of the fighting in Europe. But the Americans were also at a disad-

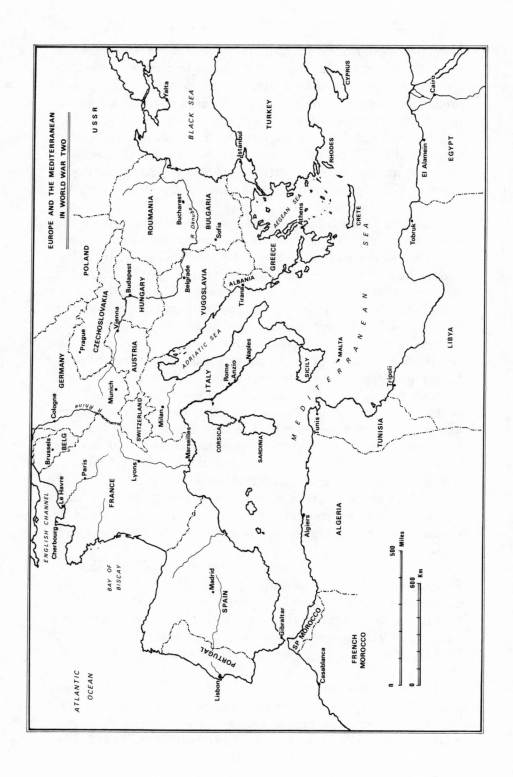

EUROPE AND THE MEDITERRANEAN
IN WORLD WAR TWO

vantage because of poor administrative coordination. The British by
now had a tightly run strategic machine. Brooke and his colleagues
often fumed at Churchill's "midnight follies," and the Army, Navy
and RAF had their own deep-rooted differences, but agreement was
always thrashed out in committee meetings and the British arrived
at conferences with the Americans having concerted their position
in advance. By contrast, American methods in 1942 were haphazard.
Roosevelt frequently failed to consult his Joint Chiefs, and the latter
were sometimes unable to resolve their own differences and argued
openly before the British.

The most vivid example was the Pacific strategy. Admiral King
and the U.S. Navy saw little scope for themselves in Europe,
whereas the war in the Pacific would be won or lost by command
of the seas. They pressed repeatedly for supplies to be diverted to
that theater, and when the decision for Torch showed that there
would be no invasion of France in 1942 or probably 1943, a bitter
Marshall was unable to resist their demands. Planes, shipping and
landing craft were moved to the Pacific. In London Churchill was
peeved. "Just because the Americans can't have a massacre in France
this year, they want to sulk and bathe in the Pacific," he complained
privately.[23] But, having had his own way over the Mediterranean,
he was in no position to resist.

By January 1943, when Churchill, Roosevelt and their staffs met
at Casablanca, they had to face the full implications of their previous
strategic decisions. Fighting a truly world war, against Germany,
Italy and Japan, with major fronts already operating in the Pacific
and the Mediterranean, they simply did not have enough men,
supplies and, above all, ships to open up a new front across the
English Channel. In the circumstances the Americans had little
alternative but to accept British strategy to capitalize on their victories in North Africa and use them as a springboard into Sicily and
then Italy.

Even so, the conduct of the negotiations at Casablanca further
confirmed Britain's reputation for cunning. With Marshall and
King now openly at odds over the "Germany first" strategy, Roosevelt warned that the British would come with a plan and stick to it.
He was right. Once again the Americans arrived with divided counsel, and paid dearly for it. They were outnumbered and outmaneuv-
ered. Wedemeyer, assisting Marshall with the presentation of the
American proposals, found the British armed with a host of statistics
and logistical projections to show that the American invasion plans

would fail. "The British descended on me like locusts," Wedemeyer cabled back to Washington, and at the end of the conference, admitting defeat, he summed up: "We came, we saw, we were conquered."[24]

The plans for an invasion of Northern Europe were shelved for another year, to the relief of Churchill's staff. "I said at the end of the Casablanca Conference," recalls Sir Ian Jacob, then military assistant secretary to the British War Cabinet, "that if I had written the report I had wanted beforehand, it would have been the one I wrote at the end."[25]

On his way to Casablanca President Roosevelt's plane had to refuel in the Gambia, a British colony on the west coast of Africa. Driving through the streets, the President was appalled at what he saw. "The natives were just getting to work. In rags . . . glum-looking." He was told that the prevailing wage was the equivalent of fifty cents a day, plus half a cup of rice. He asked about the average life expectancy and was told twenty-six years. "Those people are treated worse than the live-stock," he exploded to his son. "Their cattle live longer."[26] It was said by the British at the conference that this visit confirmed his worst suspicions. Here was clear evidence of a poor country sucked dry by colonialism. The President wanted the British, French and Dutch to hold their empires as "trusteeships" of the United Nations and to set firm timetables for independence.

Many Americans shared his deep hostility to European imperialism. That, after all, was part of their heritage, dating back to 1776. *Life* magazine, one of America's most widely read weeklies, published an "open letter" addressed to "the People of England" in October 1942. Americans might disagree among themselves on war aims, it said, but "one thing we are sure we are *not* fighting for is to hold the British Empire together. We don't like to put the matter so bluntly, but we don't want you to have any illusions. If your strategists are planning a war to hold the British Empire together they will sooner or later find themselves strategizing all alone."[27] Churchill's reply a month later was equally frank: "We mean to hold our own. I have not become the King's First Minister in order to preside over the liquidation of the British Empire."[28]

These disagreements had come to a head over India, the largest part of Britain's empire and by 1942 the last bastion against Japanese expansion westward. By March the whole of Southeast Asia, including the British colonies of Malaya, Singapore and Hong Kong and the American-dominated Philippines had fallen to Japan. Australia and India were now the Allied front line in the Pacific war, and the Roosevelt administration was concerned that Britain's repressive behavior in India would undermine the Indian war effort.

In 1939 the British viceroy had declared war on India's behalf, and put almost two million of her men under arms, without consulting India's political leaders. It led to a campaign of civil disobedience that disrupted the war effort. Roosevelt urged Churchill to announce that India would be given independence and to set up an interim government. "Why should India defend a freedom she hasn't got?" asked one State Department official.[29] Many of the British Cabinet agreed that concessions were essential. Reluctantly, Churchill sent a Labour member of his government, Sir Stafford Cripps, to negotiate with the leaders of the Indian Congress party about independence within the British Commonwealth once the war was over. To Churchill's intense irritation, Roosevelt dispatched an American envoy, Louis Johnson, to use his good offices.

Cripps's mission was not successful. Gandhi, for Congress, believed too little was being offered too late, and objected to the proposal to allow Muslims a state of their own. The talks broke down. Roosevelt was not satisfied and urged Churchill to reopen negotiations, arguing that American public opinion would blame Britain for their failure. Churchill usually did his best to fall in with Roosevelt's wishes, since he considered cooperation with the United States to be the cornerstone of British policy. But the empire was not negotiable. He told Harry Hopkins, then in London, that if Roosevelt pushed the issue he would resign. According to Hopkins's vivid account, "the string of cuss words lasted for two hours in the middle of the night."[30] Roosevelt got the message. He never urged Indian independence again.

But the debate about imperialism would not go away. It particularly bedeviled the Anglo-American war effort in Southeast Asia. Divergent strategies stemmed from divergent interests. In 1943 Britain wanted to drive south through Burma to recover her lost colonial territories in Malaya and Singapore. The Americans wanted to go northeast along the Ledo Road to assist China, whom they were trying to cultivate as a new ally. The American deputy commander of Southeast Asia Command (SEAC), General "Vinegar Joe" Stilwell was scathing about his British superior, Lord Louis Mountbatten. In his diaries he referred to him as "childish Louis," the "Glamour Boy," who was intent on "playing the 'Empah'

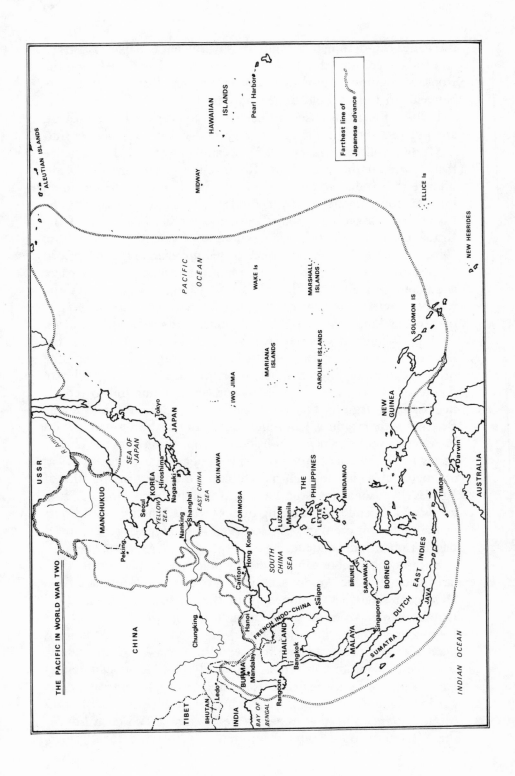

THE PACIFIC IN WORLD WAR TWO

Farthest line of
Japanese advance

Game." The Americans soon nicknamed SEAC "Save England's Asiatic Colonies," and the deteriorating relationship was summed up in a ditty: "The Limeys make policy,/Yank fights the Jap,/And one gets its Empire, and one takes the rap."[31] The British were furious. They were providing most of the troops in SEAC, and there was particular resentment in 1944, when the Allied victories in Burma were represented by the U.S. media as almost an American show, with barely a reference to General Sir William Slim's "forgotten" Fourteenth Army.

In these disputes it was easy for America to pose as the disinterested idealist. Unlike Britain, still nominally ruling nearly a quarter of the globe, the United States had few colonies, and its major one, the Philippines, was slated for independence once the war had ended. But anti-imperialism was also a matter of self-interest. American businessmen wanted access to markets protected by Imperial Preference. The American military cast covetous eyes on Japanese islands in the mid-Pacific, such as the Marshalls and Carolines, which they wanted for naval and air bases after the war. And Roosevelt's insistence that Chiang Kai-shek's corrupt regime in China must be regarded as one of the great powers, a claim regarded by Churchill as "an absolute farce,"[32] was largely intended to ensure support for U.S. aims in the wartime conferences. In short, American professions of pure idealism were disingenuous. General Eisenhower summed up the position fairly: "Britishers instinctively approach every military problem from the viewpoint of the Empire, just as we approach them from the viewpoint of American interests."[33]

It was therefore with some satisfaction that the British were able to take America to task for its treatment of blacks in the United States. The American Army was still segregated during the Second World War, with the black regiments doing the more menial tasks, such as cooking and truck driving, rather than fighting in the front line. In deference to black pressure groups, however, the Pentagon agreed that some black troops would be sent overseas, and by D-Day over one hundred thousand were in Britain. In general, they were given a good reception by the British public, many of whom had never seen a nonwhite before. Black GIs were liked for their humor and courtesy (which often compared favorably with the brashness of white GIs), and their musical skill, especially in choirs and jazz bands, was much in demand. Joseph Curtis, a black schoolteacher from Washington, D.C., was pleasantly surprised to discover that the English were not the "stiff-necked racists" he had expected. While in Cornwall in 1944 he became close friends with the Barnes family of Chacewater, considering "Mom" and "Pop" Barnes his second parents. He recalls with pleasure the little birthday cake they baked for him from their meager rations, covered with icing but made without sugar.[34]

Unlike the American Deep South, where many of the blacks lived, Britain was not a segregated country. Blacks could enter pubs, shops, dance halls and other public facilities. But the U.S. Army authorities in Britain were sure that this would lead to trouble. White GIs were used to traveling, drinking and dating girls without coming into contact with blacks. The Army therefore practiced its own form of discreet segregation by giving black and white units leave passes on different days of the week. Towns near American bases were "black" one night and "white" the next, and American military police (generally white) were heavy-handed with troublemakers.

Officially the British government turned a blind eye to these practices. If the U.S. Army wanted to adopt them, British policemen were told, that was its own concern. But behind the scenes the British authorities went further. Despite the welcome shown by many Britons to the black GIs, the British attitude was often patronizing, and contact between the blacks and white women was frowned upon. The British War Office went so far as to propose a special campaign among British troops to "educate them to adopt towards the U.S.A. coloured troops the attitude of the U.S.A. Army authorities."[35] The Colonial Office warned that this would cause an uproar in the British Empire, and the War Office moderated its line. After debate, the Cabinet agreed in the autumn of 1942 that British troops should only be told to "respect" the white American attitude and to avoid arguments about race relations. But some specific guidelines were laid down: "For a white woman to go about in the company of a Negro American is likely to lead to controversy and ill-feeling," and while it was acceptable to offer "friendly hospitality" to the GIs, "care should be taken not to invite white and coloured American troops at the same time."[36]

In general, trouble was confined to fights between black and white GIs, which the British, if they were wise, avoided. John Wilson, an English aircrewman, was traveling by train from Cardiff to York. "The train was crowded but there was room next to me for another one. There was a colored soldier outside [in the corri-

GI JOE

Cartoon from Stars and Stripes, *the U.S. servicemen's newspaper.*

dor]. I opened the door and said, 'Hey, Jack, there's a seat here.' The others in the compartment, except two of us, were all American soldiers. As soon as this colored man sat down this other big chap got up and said 'Get out, you goddamn nigger.' I told him to belt up, and he came for me. My teeth were knocked right through my tongue."[37]

The high commands on both sides of the Atlantic were keen to foster a good relationship between the GIs and British troops and civilians. Unlike World War I, when most of the U.S. troops had passed quickly through Britain en route to France, World War II witnessed the greatest single encounter between ordinary Americans and ordinary Britons, as hundreds of thousands of GIs trained in Britain in readiness for D-Day or manned the airbases used to bomb Hitler's Europe. By June 1944 one and three-quarter million Americans were in Britain. The Foreign Office pointed out that they would "return to the United States with an impression of this country which will be an important, possibly the most important, factor in colouring, for many years to come, American opinion of us and our ways."[38] Good relations between the GIs and the British people could help cement the alliance at the bottom as well as the top.

In general the relationship did work well, despite the prejudices of the history books and the fantasies of countless Hollywood feature films, which led some Americans to expect a country populated by stuffy aristocrats in cold country mansions, and some British to expect all Americans to be cowboys with the looks of Gregory Peck or gangsters in the mold of Al Capone. The authorities tried to overcome such misconceptions by commissioning a special film to be shown to all GIs arriving in Britain. *A Welcome to Britain*, made in 1943, starred American actor Burgess Meredith in the role of an ordinary GI. He took his fellow soldiers through the strange customs of the host country, teaching them how to avoid offending the natives. His advice was direct: Don't laugh at them, don't tease the Scots about their kilts, don't flirt with barmaids, and if you are invited into their homes, don't eat them out of house and home. One good American meal might clean them out of a week's rations. Above all, remember that these people have had a rough time in the war, and they, unlike us, have been fighting since 1939. Don't just come in and flash your money around and expect everyone to welcome you as a conquering hero.

These were timely warnings. It was easy for the young GIs, many of whom had never left America before, to have their heads turned by their reception in Britain. They were paid, on average, three times as much as British soldiers, they had superior rations, and they were admired by the local girls for their smart uniforms and dashing manners. Margaret Whiting, an English teenager in Cambridge, remembers the stir they caused. "To go to one of their bases was absolutely fantastic because there was no shortage of anything. Each base was a little America, with plenty of food and drink and fantastic great iced cakes. Every night you could, you were out. All the girls were doing it. It was a lovely atmosphere. At the dances they were really friendly. They'd just come up and say: 'Cut a rug.' "[39]

William Stock, who was a GI from Milwaukee, admits, "We were cocky. We were Yankee. We took pride in that. A lot of the English girls thought the Yankees came from Hollywood. I told them I was from California. Did I know Clark Gable? Lived next door. It was foolish, but everybody was doing it." British soldiers were resentful, often violent, at the GIs' success with the girls, but as airman John Wilson sadly admits: "They could have looked like Quasimodo and it would have made no difference, as long as they were American."[40] About seventy thousand British girls did their bit to put the Anglo-American alliance on a permanent footing by marrying GIs. Most settled in the United States.

As the numbers of American troops in Britain mounted, the Combined Chiefs of Staff were planning the next stage of the war. The conference of Roosevelt, Stalin and Churchill, held in Tehran in November 1943, marked a turning point in the relationship be-

tween Britain and America.⁴¹ Until now Britain had been the dominant partner, through her greater experience and her superior
forces. At Casablanca, as in the conferences of 1942, it was Churchill's and Brooke's Mediterranean strategy that had held sway over
the divided Americans. But during 1943 the U.S. Joint Chiefs sorted
out their differences, improved their coordination and secured the
full support of the President. America's superior strength was now
beginning to tell within the alliance. Britain still had more troops
in action than the United States, but they were dependent on the
continued flow of American supplies. Influenced by American
pledges to continue Lend-Lease aid after Germany had been defeated, Churchill had finally agreed in August 1943 to invade France
the following summer. At Tehran the Americans were determined
to hold him to his promise. They now had the organization and the
muscle to do so.

The political relationship had also changed. Roosevelt had
watched Russia's courageous stand against Hitler's invasion and her
survival when collapse had been predicted. He recognized in Stalin
not just a war leader who had played a major role in defeating Hitler,
but a politician who would dominate the postwar world. The lesson
was clear. America must come to terms with Russia on her own and
not allow Britain to claim an equal role. Back in 1942 he told
Churchill: "I think I can personally handle Stalin better than either
your Foreign Office or my State Department. Stalin hates the guts
of all your top people. He thinks he likes me better, and I hope he
will continue to do so."⁴² At this, the first meeting of the Big Three,
Roosevelt was determined to prove his point.

At Tehran Roosevelt went out of his way to demonstrate to Stalin
that Britain and America were not ganging up on the Russians. He
refused to meet Churchill in private either before or after the conference, and at various times during the meetings and at dinner publicly teased and baited him. At one point Stalin had to persuade
Churchill not to leave the room in a huff. Roosevelt, Averell Harriman observed, "always enjoyed other people's discomfort. I think
it fair to say that it never bothered him very much when other
people were unhappy."⁴³ Elliott Roosevelt, the President's son, de-
fends FDR's conduct. "It was most important for Father not to
appear to have a close relationship with Churchill. It would have
made Stalin furious that there was a gang-up between Churchill and
Roosevelt against him and that he was fighting a lone battle. He
[Roosevelt] wasn't able to say 'Look, Winston, I have to do this,'

because Winston would have smirked and acted as though he was in on the joke."[44]

At Tehran Roosevelt in fact generally sided with Stalin, not Churchill, when there were disagreements. The decisions reached there bore the hallmarks of the new Russo-American axis. There would be tough treatment for Germany after the war, a minor role for France and sympathy for Russian demands for territory in East Asia and Poland. Above all, on grand strategy, Churchill was outvoted by Roosevelt and Stalin. "Overlord," the invasion of France, would now be the military priority, with a date fixed for the summer and an American supreme commander appointed.

Tehran left Churchill drained and despondent. A heavy cold turned to pneumonia, and he had to stay in North Africa for a month to recuperate. There he reflected gloomily on how the Anglo-American marriage of 1942 had become part of an eternal triangle. Like Roosevelt, he was anxious to forge a good relationship with Russia, which he could clearly see would be the greatest land power in the world after the defeat of Germany and Japan. But he believed that a lasting alliance between Britain and America was the key to world peace. He wrote: "It is my deepest conviction that unless Britain and the United States are joined together in a special relationship, including the Combined Staff organisation and a wide measure of reciprocity in the use of bases—all within the ambit of a world organisation—another destructive war will come to pass."[45]

His military assistant secretary, Ian Jacob, who had exulted at the British triumph at Casablanca, recalls the very different mood after Tehran. "Our strength was declining and the Russians were rising. Roosevelt wanted to be in a position where he could deal with Stalin by himself, not tied to anyone else. So he was going to keep the British at arm's length. Increasingly, as the war went on, the Americans paid no attention to anything we said, unless it happened to coincide with something that they wanted to do."[46]

This shifting balance of power within the alliance was most dramatically revealed by the story of the development of the atomic bomb. The outbreak of war in 1939 coincided with the discovery of nuclear fission. At that stage theory and practice were far apart. Few physicists thought that the discovery could be transformed into a weapon of war in time for it to be used in the conflict. But in 1940 two refugee physicists working at Birmingham University in England demonstrated that it was practicable. The Frisch-Peierls memorandum was studied intensively by a British government committee, and on their recommendation, in September 1941, Churchill gave approval for work on the development of an atomic bomb to proceed with urgency. The committee's findings were also made available by Britain to the United States, where work on an atomic bomb had been desultory and poorly funded. Roosevelt was now convinced that America should follow suit and the U.S. program began in earnest.

At this early stage Roosevelt asked Churchill to set up a joint Anglo-American project. There were cogent arguments in favor. If Britain's theoretical lead could be harnessed to America's resources and skills, it might be possible to produce an atomic bomb ahead of Germany, who was presumed to be conducting her own research. There were practical arguments too. Britain was now under daily aerial bombardment, and the laboratories used for the atomic research were constantly at risk. Churchill, however, demurred, suggesting that it was sufficient for the two countries to exchange information, rather than work together. British ministers were reluctant to give up a lead that could give her a disproportionate influence during and after the war. There was also an understandable reluctance to share such a potent weapon with a country that was still neutral.

The two programs therefore went ahead independently, under their code names: "Tube Alloys" in Britain, and the "Manhattan Project" in the United States. It did not take long for the British team to discover that, once decided on a course of action, Americans pursued it with prodigious energy and determination. By mid-1942 it was obvious that they were pulling ahead, and it was Britain's turn to extol the advantages of cooperation. Sir John Anderson, the minister responsible for Tube Alloys, reported to Churchill that "the Americans have been applying themselves with enthusiasm and a lavish expenditure, which we cannot rival. . . . We must . . . face the fact that the pioneer work done in this country is a dwindling asset and that, unless we capitalise it quickly, we shall be rapidly outstripped. We now have a real contribution to make to a 'merger.' Soon we shall have little or none."[47]

In the summer of 1942 Churchill believed he had secured Roosevelt's agreement for full cooperation. But those involved with the American program stonewalled, resorting to the same arguments used against it by Britain the previous year. If America was ahead, why should it share what it knew and so relinquish the influence its exclusive possession of the weapon would confer? As in Britain, the argument for self-interest was supported by a suspicion that all-important security was best guaranteed by going it alone. There were also fears that what Britain really wanted was the industrial benefits of nuclear energy once the war was over, an ambition America saw no reason to advance, especially when, as Secretary of War Henry Stimson put it in October 1942, "We were doing nine-tenths of the work."[48]

These views were held particularly strongly by the director of the Manhattan Project, General Leslie Groves. Suspicious of British motives, he became a fierce guardian of America's discoveries. By early 1943 the flow of information to Britain had virtually dried up, with collaboration limited to specific aspects of the project where British research was of use to the Americans. No overall picture of what America was doing was allowed to emerge. Visiting British scientists were excluded from key research areas that did not directly concern them. Churchill badgered Roosevelt and Hopkins for seven months to renew full cooperation, writing plaintively, "My whole understanding was that everything was on the basis of fully sharing the results as equal partners."[49]

It was not until the two leaders met at Quebec in August 1943 that partnership was resumed. The agreement reached there called for "full and effective collaboration between the two countries in bringing the project to fruition."[50] Churchill, however, had to disclaim any interest in the industrial and commercial aspects of nuclear energy and agreed to leave it to Roosevelt to decide what information of this kind should be given to Britain.

With this top-level authorization, the British team left for America to work at Los Alamos and the other research laboratories. On a personal level their leader, Professor James Chadwick, worked extremely well with Groves, but the Americans continued to deny the British access to information Groves thought they did not need. "The salad," observed a report from the British embassy, "is heaped in a bowl permanently smeared with the garlic of suspicion."[51]

The Americans spent over $2 billion on developing the atomic bomb. Compared with their vast manpower and resources, in Groves's words, "the contribution of the British was helpful but not vital. Their work at Los Alamos was of high quality but their numbers were too small to enable them to play a major role." Nevertheless, Groves admitted that the initial British impetus in 1941 had been essential to get the American program going and commented that "Churchill was probably the best friend that the Manhattan

Project ever had" because of his constant interest and support. The Americans could have developed the bomb themselves, but without the British it might not have been developed in time. "I cannot escape the feeling," wrote Groves, "that without active and continuing British interest there probably would have been no atomic bomb to drop on Hiroshima."[52]

But that contribution did not prevent Britain being treated as the junior partner in the enterprise once the Americans had established their lead. When the war was over, even the limited cooperation came to an abrupt halt, to the fury of the British government and British scientists.

June 6, 1944, D-Day, began the last act of the war in Europe. Right up to the first landings some British leaders, including Churchill and Brooke, feared that the invasion might be premature and that Hitler would slaughter the Allied troops or pin them down for months on the beachhead, as had happened at Anzio in Italy earlier in the year. As he waited edgily on the eve of D-Day Brooke wrote in his diary: "I am very uneasy about the whole operation. . . . it may well be the most ghastly disaster of the whole war."[53]

Despite the carnage on Omaha Beach and the slowness of the breakout, Brooke's grimmest fears were not realized. Eisenhower's armies were soon sweeping across northern Europe, and for some weeks that summer there was heady talk of victory by Christmas. But what also preyed on Brooke's spirits, and those of Churchill, was the recognition that henceforward this would be America's show. Italy was a theater under overall British command in which British forces had dominated and American units had been employed at Britain's behest. But once fronts were opened up in northern and southern France, the Americans diverted their shipping and divisions from Italy. Churchill begged Roosevelt to relent. But the President, stiffened by his Joint Chiefs, was adamant: "My interest and hopes center on defeating the Germans in front of Eisenhower and driving on into Germany, rather than limiting this action for the purpose of staging a full major effort in Italy."[54] It was galling to the British, denied the chance of further advances toward the Alps and into Austria. But having dictated strategy in the early part of the alliance, they had to accept that America now called the tune.

After D-Day the United States for the first time had more troops in combat than the British, and the GIs kept on coming. Britain and the Commonwealth had mobilized all their available manpower, but in America thousands of young men were starting basic training to

fight for Uncle Sam. America's Army was now second only to
Russia, its Navy three times the size of Britain's, while its industry,
spurred on by the demand for war matériel and secure from Hitler's
bombs, was producing three times the output of 1939. Churchill was
acutely aware of Britain's waning influence. "Our armies are only
one-half the size of the American and will soon be little more than
one-third," he lamented in December 1944. "It is not so easy as it
used to be for me to get things done."[55]

Churchill and his colleagues were particularly afraid that their
relative weakness within the alliance would have serious diplomatic
consequences in the long term. The head of British publicity in
America had warned back in 1942 that if Americans "regard our
contribution to victory as having been secondary, and second rate,
they will consider our views on the peace settlement as of secondary
importance."[56] A British publicity campaign was mounted in the
United States to demonstrate that Lend-Lease had not been the
one-way street that many Americans believed. Although Britain had
received $27 billion of aid, she put the cost of "reverse Lend-Lease,"
including supplies and services to the American troops training in
Britain, at $6 billion, and, as a proportion of national income, each
country's aid to the other was about the same, at around 5 percent.
In June 1944 Whitehall mounted another campaign to explain the
scale of Britain's involvement in D-Day. The Joint Staff Mission in
Washington had announced somberly that "OVERLORD is the last
chance we shall have to put across to the American public the
magnitude of the British military effort."[57]

But there was little that publicity could do to redress the overwhelming impression in America that this was now America's war.
In August 1944 the Anglophobe *Chicago Tribune*, which had earlier
been a vociferous supporter of the America First campaign, spelled
out its view of what was happening. "We Americans are winning
this war. We are doing all of the fighting in the Pacific and have
made virtually all the advances in France. . . . This is an American-
made victory and the peace must be an American peace."[58]

But Churchill was not deterred from attempting to play a full role
in peacemaking. Increasingly his thoughts centered on Russia. After
Tehran he had been alarmed and depressed at the apparent scale of
Stalin's territorial ambitions. But his moods were erratic. In January
1944 he wrote to Anthony Eden of "the deep-seated changes which
have taken place in the character of the Russian State and Government" in recent years, and of "the new confidence which has grown

in our hearts towards Stalin."⁵⁹ By the summer of 1944, however, as the Red Army swept through Poland and south into the Balkans, his fears welled up anew. "The Russians are drunk with victory," he warned Eden, "and there is no length they may not go."⁶⁰ If Stalin could not now be stopped, perhaps his ambitions could be channeled? Despite Roosevelt's disapproval, Churchill flew to Moscow in October for a private meeting with the Soviet leader at which they determined the relative influence of Britain and Russia in southeast Europe. Under their "percentages agreement" Russia was to be the dominant foreign power in Rumania and Bulgaria, while Britain was accorded similar status in Greece. Stalin did not dispute Churchill's insistence that "Britain must be the leading Mediterranean Power."⁶¹

Publicly the Americans condemned such agreements as Old World power politics. American opinion was particularly critical of the British military intervention in the Greek civil war. But at their last Big Three conference, at Yalta in the Crimea in February 1945, Roosevelt, despite again keeping his distance from Churchill, actually followed much the same line. The Red Army now controlled Poland and most of the Balkans, and was driving on toward Berlin. The President privately acknowledged that "the Russians had the power in Eastern Europe, that it was obviously impossible to have a break with them and that, therefore, the only practicable course was to use what influence we had to ameliorate the situation."⁶² At times in early 1945 Churchill was even more fatalistic. "Make no mistake," he told his private secretary two weeks before Yalta, "all the Balkans, except Greece, are going to be Bolshevized; and there is nothing I can do to prevent it. There is nothing I can do for Poland either."⁶³

Top priority for Roosevelt, and even for the skeptical Churchill, was to keep the Big Three together. Only this, they believed, could ensure the defeat of Germany and Japan and guarantee international peace once the war was over. At Yalta the best they felt they could do for Poland was to secure a pledge from Stalin for a new government, broadening out the existing Moscow-backed Communist regime, and for "free and unfettered elections as soon as possible."⁶⁴

These agreements depended on mutual trust. Most of the British and American participants left the conference hopeful that this had been achieved. Later Harry Hopkins recalled the mood: "The Russians had proved that they could be reasonable and far-seeing and there wasn't any doubt in the minds of the President or any of us that we could live with them and get along with them peacefully for as far into the future as any of us could imagine."[65] Even Churchill came back optimistic. He reported to his ministers on February 23: "Poor Nevil[l]e Chamberlain believed he could trust Hitler. He was wrong. But I don't think I'm wrong about Stalin."[66]

Churchill's optimism was short-lived. Over the treatment of Russia's old enemies, Poland, Rumania and Bulgaria, Stalin would brook no interference, and the hopes of free elections for Poland were quickly dashed. Churchill was soon urging tough Anglo-American diplomacy to hold the Russians to the Yalta agreements. Then, on April 12, Roosevelt died suddenly from a cerebral hemorrhage. Churchill's own anguish was heartfelt. He cabled Mrs. Roosevelt: "I have lost a dear and cherished friendship which was forged in the fire of war." He told the House of Commons that "in Franklin Roosevelt there died the greatest friend we have ever known, and the greatest champion of freedom who has ever brought help and comfort from the New World to the Old."[67]

Yet Churchill's grief and his foreboding about Russia could not sour the sweet taste of victory. On May 7 news broke of the German surrender. Next day was a national holiday in Britain, with festivities, services of thanksgiving and, at night, a fairyland of lights to celebrate the end of years of blackout. In Whitehall Churchill was mobbed by ecstatic Londoners. "It is you who have led, uplifted and inspired us through the worst days," wrote Anthony Eden, one of his closest colleagues. "Without you this day could not have been."[68]

But the war was not yet over. Japan remained unconquered, and for many Americans this was the only war that mattered. From 1942 the main Pacific theater had been an American command, with General Douglas MacArthur grimly struggling back to the Philippines from Australia while Admiral Chester Nimitz's task forces worked their way across the Pacific islands from Pearl Harbor. The British had little say in this campaign. They even found it hard to hold on to the white parts of their empire in Australasia.

The crisis in the Pacific in 1941–42 had loosened Australia's ties with Britain. Traditionally reliant on the Royal Navy for their defense, Australians suddenly found themselves facing a possible Japanese onslaught with no British fleet anywhere near the Pacific. In a dramatic message at the end of December 1941 the Labour premier, John Curtin, declared that "Australia looks to America, free of any pangs as to our traditional links or kinship with the

"I don't care if the war is nearly over—I'm not selling my cab for a fiver for a souvenir."

One of British cartoonist Giles's many digs at the rich Yanks and the cantankerous British.

United Kingdom."[69] The Americans obliged, and soon Australia became a major American base for the Pacific conflict. As the war progressed Australians began to chafe at American direction, and by 1945 Commonwealth sentiment was reasserting itself. But although the war did not mean a total break with Britain, it did start a new trend. Henceforth Australasia would look increasingly for its security to the United States, now unquestionably the major Western power in the Pacific. For Australia and New Zealand, like Canada a decade or so before, the war was dissolving even the strongest bonds of Britain's empire.

During 1944 U.S. forces drove the Japanese at great cost from the Solomon Islands and New Guinea. The following winter MacArthur honored his vow to return to the Philippines. Now America's B-29 bombers could pound Japan's cities with high explosives and incendiaries. Yet the Japanese fought on with ruthless ferocity, often employing suicidal kamikaze pilots against American warships. The Pentagon contemplated an invasion of Japan without relish. It might take another year after the defeat of Germany and cost up to one million American casualties. Staff officers in Tokyo urged that "all able-bodied Japanese, regardless of sex, should be called upon to engage in battle. . . . Each citizen was to be prepared to sacrifice his life in suicide attacks on enemy armored forces."[70]

Little wonder that at Yalta Roosevelt was almost more concerned about the Pacific than about Europe. He was determined to ensure Russian entry into the war against Japan within three months of victory in Europe. In return he agreed to Russia's territorial demands in China. For General Marshall, Russia's pledge to declare war on Japan made it worth spending two weeks away from Washington. Even Yalta's bedbugs and cold water seemed endurable. "For what we have gained here I would gladly have stayed a whole month," he confessed afterward.[71] In all these arrangements Britain had little say. Her day as the leading foreign power in East Asia had now passed.

Russia duly declared war on Japan on August 8, 1945, and thus helped force the Japanese to surrender. But the real "winning weapon" proved to be the atomic bomb, dropped first on Hiroshima on August 6 and then on Nagasaki three days later. Under the terms of the Quebec agreement British approval to use the bomb was required. Churchill had readily agreed. But it was only a formality. The United States alone controlled the world's newest and most appalling weapon of mass destruction. On August 14 Japan surrendered. That night an estimated two million people thronged the area around Times Square in New York, cheering, dancing and drinking. Next day some five thousand tons of ticker tape, confetti and wastepaper were cleared from the streets of Manhattan. "Ours is the supreme position," exulted the *New York Herald Tribune*. "The Great Republic has come into its own; it stands first among the peoples of the earth."[72]

Victory had been won. The wartime alliance was over, and the GIs were soon on their way home. Often it had been a tempestuous affair, with bitter arguments and mutual jealousy. But, as Churchill frequently observed, "there is only one thing worse than fighting with allies, and that is fighting without them!"[73] Between 1941 and 1945 the two countries had indeed become "somewhat mixed up together . . . for mutual and general advantage." It was the closest wartime alliance in modern history, and it had helped destroy one of the most barbarous dictatorships the world had ever seen. Wartime memories would not be forgotten, but, as events were soon to show, the relationship would never be as close again.

CHAPTER 9

UNITING AGAINST RUSSIA
1945-1949

The troopship glided into New York harbor early in the morning as the first rays of sun glinted on the Statue of Liberty. Donald Worby was on deck with hundreds of others straining for a glimpse of the Manhattan skyline. "There was a lot of big tough guys there, and boy, we all had a lump in our throat as big as our fist."

On the voyage back across the Atlantic, memories of war had given way to thoughts of home. Worby knew he was coming back to an America that had become richer as a result of the war, where people expected as a right luxuries that were unimaginable in Europe. He admired the way the British had put up with hardship, no "whining or complaining," and wondered whether "the folks back home" would have accepted it as gracefully. Homecoming was not easy. It took time to adjust to a country that was largely un-scathed. One day, shortly after his return, he overheard a woman in a bakery explaining to another customer how sorry she was that the war was over. If only it had lasted another year she and her husband could have paid off the loans on the four properties they had bought with their wartime earnings. "The other lady," Worby recalls, "had a son in the Marines who had been killed. She was very upset and angry. She slid a banana cream pie off the counter and went over to this woman and smashed it right into her face and said, 'That's for my boy who got killed in World War Two.' " Worby reached in his pocket and said, "I'd sure like to pay for that pie!"[1]

The wartime boom laid the foundations for American prosperity for the next quarter of a century. As the arsenal of democracy the United States was producing 40 percent of the world's armaments by 1944. There had been little rationing, few shortages, no bombing, and, as a result, incomes and consumption had soared. The contrast with Britain was most vivid not for returning GIs but for the seventy thousand British girls they brought home with them. Barbara Markus, one of these war brides, felt she had dropped into another world. There was an abundance of everything, "a light airy feeling," whereas Britain seemed "quite somber, quite stark." On her wedding day she went to a steak restaurant. "We had filet mignon. It was a good seven years since I had seen a piece of meat this size. I was the first one served, as I was the bride. I thought the steak was to be shared between everybody. It was quite a surprise when I found we got one each."[2]

Britain had come out of the war exhausted by her efforts. Over four hundred thousand had died, more than in America, a country with three times her population. She had been fighting longer than any of the Allies and had borne the brunt of German bombing. The centers of many of her major cities were piles of rubble. Everything was scarce, clothing as well as food. With manpower concentrating on the war effort and overseas markets hard to reach, her export trade by 1944 was running at only a third of its prewar level. She had lost a quarter of her national wealth. It was apparent that recovery would be slow and painful.

At this moment in her history, instead of returning to the prewar free enterprise system to revive her fortunes, Britain embarked on a wide-ranging program of social and political reform. In 1942 a plan had been drawn up for the postwar years to provide everyone with a minimum standard of living, free health care, and better support when unemployed or retired. To implement the Beveridge Plan the electorate rejected Winston Churchill, a traditional Tory, as prime minister and chose instead Clement Attlee, leader of the Labour party, who was elected in July 1945. Churchill had won the war, but he did not seem the man to win the peace. When the results were declared, Churchill's wife tried to console him. "It may well be a blessing in disguise," she said. Churchill grunted: "At the moment it seems quite effectively disguised."[3]

The Labour government initiated a program that included nationalization of major industries, strict central control of resources and the construction of a welfare state. Taken on its own, this was a heavy financial burden for an impoverished country, and one senior British diplomat feared "a weak foreign policy, a private revolution at home and the reduction of England to a 2nd-class power."[4] But Attlee and his colleagues, while intent on social change, did not propose to give up Britain's place at the top table. Under the leadership of Ernest Bevin, the bluff former union leader who was now foreign secretary, they still acted on the assumption that Britain was "one of the Powers most vital to the peace of the world," one of the "Big 3 (or 2½!)."[5] Lord Keynes, an economic adviser to the Treasury, sounded the alarm: "The gay and successful fashion in which we undertake liabilities all over the world and slop money out to the importunate represents an over-playing of our hand." He warned the Cabinet that it could lead to a "financial Dunkirk."[6]

The crisis came almost at once. Eight days after the war ended with Japan's surrender, President Truman canceled Lend-Lease, the provision of food and weapons on credit. The British Food Mission, dispatching tons of supplies from the United States, learned about it only when one of their ships was refused permission to sail. Next day the official announcement was made.

The speed with which the decision was taken shocked the British. It was as though a close friend who had seen her through a crisis turned away without saying good-bye. Claude Pepper, the liberal Democratic congressman, who had been hanged in effigy for supporting Lend-Lease in 1941, understood Britain's sense of grievance: "You don't suddenly stop when the horse passed the mark, but let it canter to the end."[7] But Congress had authorized Lend-Lease strictly as a wartime measure, and America's instinct was now to put the war behind it as fast as possible. "Bring Daddy Home" clubs were formed in towns and cities across America to put pressure on the President to demobilize. Marion T. Bennett, a congressman of the 1940s, recalls the instinctive American reaction to the war: "We'd given our allies everything they asked for and more, and now people were sick and tired of it and didn't want to hear any more about it."[8]

The British government immediately sent Lord Keynes to Washington to explain the damage that cancellation of Lend-Lease would do and to ask for a grant to help Britain out of her crisis. On arrival he was told that a free gift was out of the question and that at best

Britain might get an interest-bearing loan. Over the next three months there were complex and often heated negotiations, about both the loan and the method of repayment for Lend-Lease. The eventual terms for the latter, when compared with the arrangements for settling the World War I debts, were generous. Some $27 billion had been borrowed, but Britain had spent about $6 billion in "reverse Lend-Lease" aid to America. Of the outstanding balance of about $21 billion, Britain was asked to repay only $650 million (or £162 million).

The generosity of the terms for the repayment of Lend-Lease was obscured by the resentment felt in Britain when the credit terms for the loan were announced. The sum of $3.75 billion was to be lent at 2 percent interest, repayable over fifty years from the end of 1951. To Britain, used to the easy credit of Lend-Lease, any interest payments seemed unduly harsh, given the circumstances in which she now found herself and the sacrifices she had made in 1939–41, while America was still neutral. In the United States, however, a less sentimental approach was adopted. Returning GIs were paying more than 2 percent for their home loans. Why should Britain be offered better terms? One leading American businessman told the State Department that the easy terms were justified: "If you succeed in doing away with the Empire preference and opening up the Empire to United States commerce, it may well be that we can afford to pay a couple of billion dollars for the privilege."[9] That accorded with the prevailing mood in Washington. The real price for the loan and the generous settlement of Lend-Lease was to be Britain's endorsement of the agreements on a new world economy concluded at the New Hampshire mountain resort of Bretton Woods in July 1944.

Throughout the war, economists on both sides of the Atlantic had been working on ways of creating a stable and prosperous postwar world. During the depression of the 1930s the international economy had disintegrated into separate blocs, tied to the leading currencies—sterling, the dollar, the franc and the mark. Trade had been mainly within these areas rather than through the world at large. British and American leaders both wanted to see a new, open world economy, but they found it hard to agree on the appropriate means. The State Department favored making currencies freely convertible, one into another, and eliminating discriminatory tariff barriers, particularly Britain's Imperial Preference. That would benefit American trade and would also, U.S. leaders believed, promote world peace. "Nations which act as enemies in the marketplace cannot long be friends at the council table," warned Will Clayton of the State Department.[10] But the British were unwilling to surrender protection for Britain's weakened trade and currency until they were sure that America would assume the burdens it had rejected during the depression for sustaining the world economy. Churchill was emphatic: "No abandonment of Imperial Preference unless or until we are in presence of a vast scheme of reducing trade barriers in which the United States is taking the lead."[11]

The crucial negotiations dealt with a new international monetary system. They were conducted for the British by Keynes and for the Americans by Harry Dexter White. Both were men of outstanding intellect, but with very different styles: Keynes, witty, arrogant, with a mind like quicksilver; White, blunt, more defensive and perhaps less deft in argument. But it was White, in the end, who won the day.

Keynes had wanted to put the onus of the new monetary system on the United States, the world's strongest economy. He proposed that America's payments surpluses and stocks of gold should provide much of the capital needed for helping poorer nations whose currencies were in difficulty. Generous overdrafts would be made available to them from an international fund of over $25 billion, much of which would be provided by the United States. But, as in most of the wartime negotiations, he who paid the piper called the tune. It was Harry White's plan that became the basis of the agreement reached in July 1944 at Bretton Woods. This was for a more modest fund of $8.8 billion, of which the United States would contribute only $3.2 billion. Countries in difficulties would receive help, but on a smaller scale than Keynes had envisaged and with tough conditions about putting their own economies in order. Also contrary to Keynes's wishes, the new system would be denominated in gold or dollars, the one being freely convertible into the other. The dollar was now the world's leading currency. Henry Morgenthau, secretary of the U.S. treasury, confessed that his aim in office had been "to move the financial center of the world from London and Wall Street to the United States Treasury."[12] Bretton Woods marked the achievement of that aim.

In Britain, however, there was little enthusiasm, and the government dragged its feet on the Bretton Woods agreements throughout 1944 and 1945. As a further condition of the loan in the autumn of 1945, the U.S. government therefore insisted that Britain must ratify the agreements before the end of December and agree to make sterling freely exchangeable within a year. Attlee hastily placed the loan agreement, the settlement of Lend-Lease and the Bretton Woods arrangements before an unprepared Parliament.

In the Commons the mood was shocked and angry. Critics on the Conservative benches objected to the provisions for freer trade, calling them a sellout of the British Empire, "an economic Munich." On the left it was feared that the government had surrendered its power to direct the economy and ensure full employment. One Labour MP described the agreements as "niggardly, barbaric, antediluvian."[13] Underlying the economic issues was a sense of national humiliation. Once again, it seemed, Britain was begging for American aid and being told the terms. The British weekly *The Economist*, usually well disposed to the United States, was particularly bitter: "It is aggravating to find that the reward for losing a quarter of our national wealth in the common cause is to pay tribute for half a century to those who have been enriched by the war."[14] In the end the government won its majority, but 100 MPs voted against the loan agreement and 169 abstained, including Churchill and most of the Tories. Having imposed terms on others for two centuries, the British were discovering what it was like to be on the receiving end.

After all the difficulties in Britain were resolved, the loan agreement became bogged down in the U.S. Congress. Americans were concerned about problems at home—strikes, inflation, high taxes. Why should the United States again have to bail out a decaying empire? Britain should sell the Crown jewels or some of her vast imperial real estate. To these familiar complaints about empire and monarchy was added a new one—maybe American money would be used by the new Labour government to turn Britain into virtually a communist state. One congressman summed it up. The loan, he said, would "promote too damned much Socialism at home and too much damned Imperialism abroad."[15] For many months in 1946 Britain's desperately needed loan was held up in congressional committee.

The row over the loan was not the only sign that the relationship between Britain and America was changing. Another casualty of America's new nationalism was the atomic partnership. Throughout the war, as we have seen, it had been a checkered affair, with suspicion on both sides, but in September 1944 Roosevelt and Churchill signed a new agreement at the President's home at Hyde

WHAT. NO HOOVES ? NO TAIL ?

*British cartoonist David Low uses Attlee's visit to Washington to mock America's phobia about socialism. (*Evening Standard, *November 15, 1945.)*

Park, New York. Using the British code name Tube Alloys, this affirmed that "full collaboration between the United States and the British Government in developing tube alloys for military and commercial purposes should continue after the defeat of Japan unless and until terminated by joint agreement."[16] The American copy of the memo was lost in Roosevelt's papers, wrongly filed by his naval aide among documents dealing with submarine torpedo tubes. But Churchill sent Truman a photocopy in July 1945. The following November the new president signed another secret understanding "for full and effective co-operation in the field of atomic energy between the United States, the United Kingdom and Canada."[17]

These two agreements seemed to promise continued Anglo-American partnership in developing the weapon that was seen as the basis of postwar security. But during 1946 Truman had second thoughts. Despite much talk at the end of the war about international control of atomic energy, there was a growing feeling in Congress that America should keep something so valuable and dangerous to itself. In February 1946 that conviction was strengthened when news broke of a Soviet spy ring in Ottawa, implicating British atomic scientists. In August the President approved the McMahon Act, which terminated virtually all communication with foreign states about atomic energy. Congressmen were unaware of the agreements made with Britain in 1944 and 1945, and the administration made no effort to enlighten them.* Truman concluded that to carry out the agreements in the frenzied atmosphere of 1946, with Washington seething with rumors about atomic spies, "would blow the Administration out of the water," in Dean Acheson's words.[19] A bitter Labour Cabinet, cut off by the United States, decided in January 1947 that for reasons of security and prestige Britain must start work on its own atomic bomb. As Bevin observed with typical pungency: "We have got to have this thing over here whatever it costs. . . . We've got to have the bloody Union Jack flying on top of it."[20]

There were other indications that the wartime alliance had broken down. The two governments were publicly at odds over Palestine because of Truman's support for increased Jewish immigration into Britain's strife-torn mandate. Bevin added fuel to the flames by suggesting that the President did so because Americans "did not want too many Jews in New York."[21] The President had also ordered abolition of all the combined committees by which the two countries had run the war effort, and it was only with great difficulty that the British kept the Combined Chiefs of Staff in existence.

Most disturbing of all for the British in 1945–46 was the American attitude toward the Soviet Union. Germany's defeat had brought Russia deeper into Europe than at any time since 1814. Losses of perhaps twenty million people had left her paranoid about future security and alert for opportunities to expand farther at little cost. The Yalta agreements of February 1945 were not honored as Churchill and Roosevelt had hoped. In Poland, Rumania and Bulgaria, states regarded by Russia as buffers against renewed German aggression, pro-Soviet regimes were quickly installed with the backing of the Red Army. Stalin's insistence on vast reparations from Germany was a major obstacle to Allied agreement on a peace treaty. Pressure was applied on Turkey to secure access for the Soviet fleet through the Dardanelles, and in Iran the Soviets failed

---

*The principal author of the Act, Senator Brien McMahon, admitted to the British in 1949 "that, if he had been given all the information for which he asked the American authorities on the history of the co-operation with the United Kingdom and Canada, there would probably have been no need for his Act to have been passed or, at any rate, not on such restrictive lines."[18]

to withdraw their troops, as agreed, in early 1946. All these Soviet actions were regarded with growing alarm in Whitehall. By September 1945 Bevin was complaining that "our relations with the Russians about the whole European problem were drifting into the same condition as that in which we had found ourselves with Hitler."[22]

Bevin, like Churchill, wanted a firm Anglo-American front against Soviet expansion, but the Truman administration would have none of it. When Britain had come to the aid of the royalists in Greece in their civil war against Communist forces at the end of 1944, the State Department had been openly critical. Many Americans viewed the Greek and Turkish problems not as examples of Soviet expansion but as part of the traditional Anglo-Russian rivalry that had afflicted the eastern Mediterranean for more than a century. Over Eastern Europe the State Department protested strenuously about Soviet behavior, but it would do nothing in concert with the British, and eventually Truman's secretary of state, James Byrnes, recognized the new governments with only cosmetic changes. All this time U.S. troops were being withdrawn from Europe, the total falling from 3.5 million in June 1945 to two hundred thousand two years later.

Within months of victory, therefore, Britain seemed in a desperate position. The Big Three, regarded at Yalta as the basis of postwar security, was in ruins. Disowned by America, browbeaten by Russia, Britain seemed at the mercy of the superpowers—to quote the head of the Foreign Office like "Lepidus in the triumvirate with Mark Antony and Augustus."[23]* Another British diplomat observed: "This is the opportunity for a power on the make to grab territory and stake out interests beyond the limits of war-time conquests. . . . The Russians see that the war has left us financially and economically weak and dependent upon the United States. They also know the American phobia about the British Empire and calculate that we cannot count fully on American support when defending our Imperial interests."[24]

Winston Churchill, now out of office, was deeply disturbed at America's inertia in the face of what he saw as a clear Soviet threat to Europe. In Harry Truman he found a supporter who, by January

---

*A reference to Shakespeare's *Julius Caesar*, Act IV, Scene 1, where Antony describes Lepidus as ". . . a slight unmeritable man,/ Meet to be sent on errands: is it fit,/ The threefold world divided, he should stand/ One of the three to share it?"

1946, was also uneasy about the policy the State Department was pursuing. "I'm tired [of] babying the Soviets," the President complained.[25] In March, while on a private visit to America, Churchill traveled with him to Westminster College, in Fulton, Missouri, Truman's home state. The President had read Churchill's speech on the train, pronouncing it "admirable . . . It would do nothing but good," he said, "though it would make a stir."[26] Churchill's message was stark: "From Stettin in the Baltic to Trieste in the Adriatic, an iron curtain has descended across the Continent." He did "not believe that Soviet Russia desires another war" but was "convinced that there is nothing they admire so much as strength." In other words, the extent of Soviet expansion would depend on the West's response. Churchill called for "a special relationship between the United States and the British Commonwealth," which would mean combined military staffs, shared bases, resources and weapons, and eventually, perhaps, common citizenship. This "fraternal association of the English-speaking peoples" was, he insisted, the only hope for a "haggard" world, in which all countries, except America and the British Commonwealth, were now confronted by the peril of communism.[27]

As Truman predicted, Churchill's speech did indeed "make a stir." His warnings about Soviet conduct were echoed in Washington. On February 22 George Kennan, U.S. chargé d'affaires in Moscow, had sent Washington an immensely influential analysis summing up Soviet conduct on lines similar to Churchill's. Although Russia, he argued, was "committed fanatically to the belief that with the U.S. there can be no permanent *modus vivendi*," the Soviets were "still by far the weaker force," and they could be contained "without recourse to any general military conflict" provided the United States ensured "the cohesion, firmness and vigor" of the West.[28] In March the Joint Chiefs of Staff warned privately that "the defeat or disintegration of the British Empire would eliminate from Eurasia the last bulwark of resistance between the United States and Soviet expansion. . . . Militarily, our present position as a world power is of necessity closely interwoven with that of Great Britain."[29]

But popular reaction to Churchill's speech was less enthusiastic. Although a poll in March 1946 indicated that 70 percent of Americans disapproved of Soviet foreign policy, the idea of a "fraternal association" with Britain had few public supporters. Americans had only recently been converted to the idea of a United Nations Organization to maintain world peace, and many feared that a special Anglo-American relationship would undermine its foundations. "Winnie, Winnie, go away. UNO is here to stay," chanted protesters in New York.[30] The *Wall Street Journal* commented that "the country's reaction to Mr. Churchill's Fulton speech must be convincing proof that the United States wants no alliance or anything that resembles an alliance with any other nation."[31]

It was only gradually that opinions altered. The Soviet failure to withdraw from northern Iran hardened American attitudes. So too did the growth of Communist parties in France and Italy. Mounting anxiety about Europe helped passage of the British loan through Congress in the summer of 1946. Joseph Kennedy, fainthearted American ambassador to Britain in 1940, was among its supporters. "The British people and their way of life," he said, "form the last barrier in Europe against Communism; and we must help them hold that line."[32] But there was little readiness in Congress or the country to do more, and no enthusiasm for the kind of special relationship Churchill believed essential. It was not until the following year that events on the continent of Europe led Americans to reconsider the transatlantic relationship and take urgent steps to rebuild the alliance they had precipitately abandoned in 1945.

In Britain the winter of early 1947 was the worst since 1881. For weeks villages were cut off by snowdrifts as the country shivered in blizzards and sub-zero temperatures. Coal stocks ran down so fast that electricity had to be rationed. Factories closed, production plummeted, and British industry, vital to the country's recovery, ground to a virtual halt. The fuel shortage was exacerbated by a shortage of coal miners, the result of Britain's slow demobilization of her forces. Her commitments overseas were so heavy that in October 1946 conscription had been reintroduced, the first time that this had happened when Britain was at peace.

Pressed by the Treasury, the Cabinet accepted that the country was overstretched and in February 1947 decided to cut back on Britain's obligations. This would release manpower for industry and reduce Britain's overseas spending, which was draining her reserves and using up the American loan at what the Treasury called "a reckless, and ever-accelerating, speed."[33] The Palestine mandate would be handed back to the UN. Britain would pull out of India by June 1948. And by the end of March 1947 she would end financial aid to Greece and Turkey. The last decision was of particular importance for Anglo-American relations. On February 21 the British embassy delivered to the State Department notes explaining the new policy and stressing the vital importance of Greece and Turkey in the deepening cold war. With Britain pulling out, "His Majesty's Government trust that the United States Government may find it possible to afford financial assistance."[34]

Britain's decision was not unexpected. The Truman administration knew the situation in Greece and the state of British finances, and the State Department warned the President independently that only "urgent and immediate support" for Greece would prevent a Communist victory and the probable "loss of the whole Near and Middle East."[35] But the speed of Britain's withdrawal and the short notice were a shock. Truman's Democratic administration had to mobilize public support rapidly at a time when Congress was under Republican control.

Truman summoned senior congressmen to a meeting in the White House. They were unhappy both about the cost and about having to bail Britain out yet again. But Dean Acheson, an under secretary of state, warned that a collapse in Greece would carry the Communist "infection," like "apples in a barrel infected by one rotten one," through Africa and Europe, with Italy and France the next victims.[36] The congressmen were impressed by Acheson's grim appraisal. Senator Arthur Vandenberg advised Truman that to get public support he had to take this sort of line in "a personal appearance before Congress and scare hell out of the country."[37]

On March 12, 1947, the President duly addressed a joint session of Congress, setting out what became known as the Truman Doctrine. He first explained the problems of Greece and Turkey, the one racked by civil war and facing a Communist takeover, the other needing economic support to resist Russian pressure. But they were only part of a larger issue, for the world as a whole faced a choice between "freedom" and "totalitarianism." Totalitarian regimes imposed on free peoples undermined "the foundations of international peace and hence the security of the United States," Truman stated. It must therefore be "the policy of the United States to support free people who are resisting attempted subjugation by armed minorities or by outside pressures."[38]

Truman had couched the appeal for what he admitted was "little more than one-tenth of one per cent" of America's investment in World War II in deliberately apocalyptic terms to overcome resistance in Congress. His speech, which persuaded legislators to approve $400 million in aid for Greece and Turkey, was to redefine

American foreign policy. Its object was now expressed in global terms as the defense of all free peoples threatened by totalitarianism. A threat to any one of them was seen as a threat to America itself. Britain, in abdicating responsibility for Greece and Turkey, had acted as the catalyst for this change. Her inability, similarly, to cope with the growing problems of Western Europe was to draw America fully into the new cold war.

THE TRUMAN LINE

The British magazine Punch, *May 28, 1947.*

The state of Europe in 1947 was desperate. After a tour of Europe, U.S. Under Secretary of State Will Clayton reported in May that "it is now obvious that we grossly underestimated the destruction to the European economy by the war. . . . Europe is steadily deteriorating," he warned. "Millions of people in the cities are slowly starving," and the European governments, including Britain, would run out of reserves to pay for essential imports before the end of the year. "Without further prompt and substantial aid from the United States, economic, social and political disintegration will overwhelm Europe." And, unlike previous UN aid projects, he emphasized, *the United States must run this show.*"[39]

The State Department was already concerned about the problem and Acheson had spoken publicly about it, but his speech made little impact. On June 5, 1947, however, Secretary of State George C. Marshall was due to speak at the graduation ceremony at Harvard University. He made the European crisis his central theme. Marshall spelled out the breakdown in Europe and the need for a coordinated recovery plan. Aware of Congress's resistance to foreign aid, he insisted that America would help only those who helped themselves. "It would be neither fitting nor efficacious for this government to undertake to draw up unilaterally a program designed to place Europe on its feet economically. This is the business of the Europeans. The initiative, I think, must come from Europe."[40]

The State Department had made sure that the British had been alerted in advance about Marshall's ideas. On hearing reports of Marshall's speech over the radio, Bevin moved fast. It was, he said later, "like a life-line to sinking men,"[41] and he grasped it with both hands. He quickly arranged a meeting with the French foreign minister, Georges Bidault, and together they approached the Russians to help draw up a European recovery program. But, on discovering that membership would mean revealing Russia's own industrial strategy and allowing her new East European satellites to trade freely with the West, the Soviet Union withdrew, leaving the relieved Bevin and Bidault free to proceed. In July 1947, with Bevin in the chair, sixteen countries began work in Paris to list their needs. Throughout, American officials shared in the discussions, but, as one of them admitted, the Marshall Plan was still rather like "a flying saucer—nobody knows what it looks like, how big it is, in what direction it is moving, or whether it really exists."[42] Bevin played a leading part in bringing it down to earth.

The urgency of their work was dramatized by Britain's sterling crisis. On July 15, 1947, reluctantly honoring the terms of the 1946 American loan, Britain ended exchange controls and made sterling freely convertible. Holders of sterling seized the chance to convert into dollars, forcing the British government to suspend convertibility within five weeks. By then Britain had lost nearly $900 million and had been forced to draw on another $450 million of the loan, which was now almost exhausted. The "dollar gap" had to be bridged before Europe could recover.

In late September the committee in Paris completed its work and put its proposals to Truman for American loans totaling $29 billion. The President cut that to $17 billion, spread over four years, and sent it to Congress. The administration prepared the ground well. Congressmen had been taken to Europe to see the devastation for themselves. They had been told that Marshall aid would protect Europe from communism, revive America's economy, save spending more on armaments—in short, anything they wished to hear. The bill was eventually approved by Congress in March 1948. But it took more than Truman's propaganda to get it past the tightfisted Republican majority. It needed nothing less than fears that World War III was imminent.

In February 1948 the Communists seized power in Czechoslovakia and Foreign Minister Jan Masaryk, well known in America, was found dead in suspicious circumstances. There were reports of mounting Soviet pressure on Finland and Norway to sign "security" pacts. Rumors were rife that Italy would go Communist in the April elections. A crisis atmosphere pervaded Washington. Truman scribbled a note to Marshall on March 5: "Will Russia move first? Who pulls the trigger? Then where do we go?" The same day General Lucius Clay, U.S. commander in Germany, reported a subtle change in Soviet attitudes and warned that war "may come with dramatic suddenness."[43] After a direct appeal from the President, Congress approved both Marshall aid and restoration of the draft.

Bevin did not believe that the Soviets wanted to fight, but he too was deeply alarmed at their "war of nerves" and the growing influence of Communism in Europe, Asia and the Middle East. In March 1948 he told the Cabinet: "It has really become a matter of the defence of western civilisation, or everything will be swamped by this Soviet method of infiltration."[44] Economic aid was no longer enough. That same month Britain, France, Belgium, Luxembourg and the Netherlands concluded the Brussels Defense Pact. Bevin, again, was its principal architect, but he knew that only American backing could ensure Western Europe's defense. In the crisis atmosphere of March 1948 Washington was ready to respond. "Please inform Mr. Bevin," Marshall told the British ambassador on March 12, "that . . . we are prepared to proceed at once in the joint discussions on the establishment of an Atlantic security system."[45] Their talks were soon being swept along by the momentum of a new crisis.

At the center of the deepening cold war was Germany. In 1945 it had been divided into four zones—Russian, American, British and French—with all four powers occupying parts of the city of Berlin, which lay in the Russian zone. They were supposed to draw up a peace treaty, set up a new democratic government and then withdraw. But the four powers could not agree on Germany's future. Russia wanted massive reparations. She and France, both of whom had suffered most from Germany in the past, wanted German economic recovery to be carefully controlled. But the British were using up scarce resources, including their American loan, to feed a starving German population. By 1947 they agreed with the Americans that Germany must be made self-sufficient again. And as the cold war intensified in 1948 and France came around to the Anglo-American view, these three powers prepared to create a new West German state out of their zones of occupation. The alternative, the State Department argued, would have been to "accept stalemate without action and thus permit Germany to sink deeper into political and economic chaos, with the attendant threat to the general welfare and security."[46]

Russia opposed any new German state until Soviet security was guaranteed. In June 1948 the Western Allies introduced a new currency in their zones, a step toward economic stability as well as political unity. In response, on June 24, the Russians imposed a total blockade of all routes into Berlin.

Washington was initially indecisive. "No one was sure, as yet, how the Russian move could be countered or whether it could successfully be countered at all," recalled George Kennan later.[47] Truman considered various options, including forcing a way through with tanks or with an armored train. But Bevin successfully urged a subtler riposte, one less fraught with the risk of war: an Anglo-American airlift of supplies from western Germany into the Allied sectors of Berlin. On June 30 both Bevin and Marshall proclaimed their determination to stay in Berlin and to keep it supplied.

Over the next year more than two million tons were flown into the beleaguered city, some in ramshackle aircraft manned by private entrepreneurs.

The crisis over Berlin found America militarily unprepared. Its air power, like its army, had been demobilized after the war. The U.S. wartime bases in Britain had also been closed down, though a secret understanding had been reached between leading airmen in 1946 that some should be available again in an emergency. In June 1948 Marshall asked Bevin to allow U.S. bombers to use British bases, and a Cabinet committee gave rapid approval.

General Leon Johnson was stationed at Colorado Springs when he received an urgent summons to Washington. Arriving at the Pentagon, he was told: "We want you in England on a permanent change of station." "How soon?" Johnson asked. "Yesterday." Johnson grinned: "I don't think I can make it that quickly, but I'll make it rather soon."[48]

On July 18 two B-29 bomber groups, sixty planes in all, flew into Britain. Their arrival was given wide publicity. A third group followed in August. The B-29s were known as "atomic bombers" because they had dropped the first nuclear weapons on Japan, and it was officially hinted that the aircraft arriving in Britain were armed with nuclear weapons. Facing the possibility of war over Berlin, the Labour government was relieved to see them, and no hard questions were asked about the terms of the new American military presence. In June 1949 General Johnson commented: "Never before in history has one first-class Power gone into another first-class Power's country without an agreement. We were just told to come over and 'we shall be pleased to have you.' "[49] By the time the British government tried to establish a clear agreement, the U.S. Air Force had an unshakable foothold on British soil. Secretary of Defense James Forrestal noted in his diary in July 1948 that the bombers' presence "would accustom the British to the necessary habits and routines that go in the accommodation of an alien, even though an allied, power." He added that "once sent they would become somewhat of an accepted fixture, whereas a deterioration of the situation in Europe might lead to a condition of mind under which the British would be compelled to reverse their present attitude."[50]

Ironically, a few months before the B-29s arrived, the British government had surrendered its veto over the American use of the atomic bomb, a right secured by Churchill in the Quebec agreement of August 1943. Given America's dominance of the atomic bomb program, the power was largely nominal, and Churchill had quickly given his consent in July 1945 when asked to approve the use of the atomic bomb on Japan. But U.S. senators were appalled when they learned privately of the veto in April 1947. Vandenberg called it "astounding" and "unthinkable," while Senator Bourke Hickenlooper warned Marshall that he "would be unable to support American economic aid to Britain unless the situation was rectified at once."[51] Pressed by the administration, the British agreed in the so-called Modus Vivendi of January 1948 to surrender their veto power in return for promises of a new exchange of technical information on atomic energy. These promises were largely unfulfilled. Even the official historian of the British atomic energy program found it surprising that "in view of the potential issues of life and death that were involved, neither officials nor Ministers showed any concern or interest in the surrender of Britain's veto, or right to consultation on the use of the bomb."[52] By the time the B-29s arrived the British government had no control over their use.

None of this was seen to matter, however, in the crisis atmosphere of mid-1948, when Europe seemed close to war. The Berlin blockade gave added urgency to the talks about an Atlantic security pact, which was now gaining support in Congress as well the administration. Some favored a unilateral American pledge, akin to the Monroe Doctrine or Truman Doctrine, stating that an attack on Western Europe would be regarded as an attack on the United States. But, as Bevin observed, that would leave people in Britain "very doubtful as to whether they had incurred any reciprocal obligation,"[53] and the Pentagon was determined to secure access to European bases in return for the offer of American support. So the negotiators worked on a mutual defense pact, in which each of the twelve signatories would regard an attack on one as an attack on all.

A draft was ready by late 1948, but it was toned down by leading senators who feared that the United States "was rushing into some kind of automatic commitment" to defend Europe in any crisis.[54] When the treaty was signed, on April 4, 1949, America agreed only to assist its allies by taking "such action as it deems necessary, including the use of armed force, to restore and maintain the security of the North Atlantic area."[55] Thirty years on from 1919, the U.S. Senate was still wary about excessive entanglements. But the North Atlantic Treaty was the first peacetime alliance the United

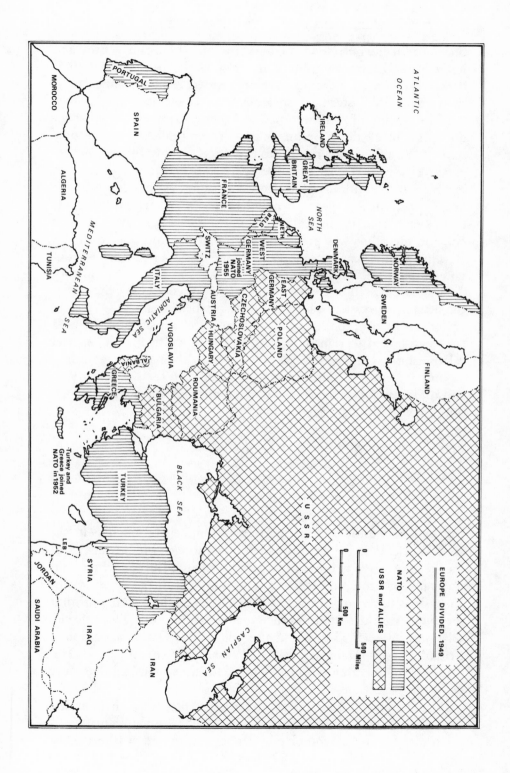

EUROPE DIVIDED, 1949

NATO

USSR and ALLIES

0   500 Miles

0   500 Km

ATLANTIC OCEAN

MOROCCO

PORTUGAL

SPAIN

ALGERIA

TUNISIA

MEDITERRANEAN SEA

FRANCE

IRELAND

GREAT BRITAIN

NORTH SEA

BELG.

NETH.

WEST GERMANY

SWITZ

joined NATO 1955

ITALY

ADRIATIC SEA

AUSTRIA

YUGOSLAVIA

HUNGARY

CZECHOSLOVAKIA

ALBANIA

GREECE

BULGARIA

ROUMANIA

DENMARK

EAST GERMANY

POLAND

NORWAY

SWEDEN

FINLAND

U S S R

Turkey and Greece joined NATO in 1952

TURKEY

BLACK SEA

CASPIAN SEA

LEB.

SYRIA

JORDAN

SAUDI ARABIA

IRAQ

IRAN

States had made outside its own hemisphere. If Donald Worby and
his fellow GIs returning home in 1946 had been told that within
three years America would have committed itself permanently to
the security of Western Europe, they would have been incredulous.

In the spring of 1949 international tension relaxed. Stalin abandoned his blockade of Berlin, acknowledging defeat, and the new
state of West Germany came into existence. During July the Senate
approved the North Atlantic Treaty by an overwhelming majority.
Truman and his advisers felt deep satisfaction as they looked back
on the previous four years. A new Europe had risen from the ruins
of the old: even if one half was impoverished and under Soviet
control, the other was prospering and allied to the United States.
Recalling American isolationism in the past, Truman was convinced that the North Atlantic Treaty was "a milestone in history
. . . if it had existed in 1914 and in 1939 . . . it would have prevented
the acts of aggression which led to two world wars."[56]

For the British, too, there seemed cause for satisfaction. In 1945
they had hoped to remain a great power by cultivating a "special
relationship" with the United States, seeing themselves as guiding
a powerful but still immature young giant with their superior skill
and diplomatic experience. As one anonymous verse writer put it
during the 1945 loan negotiations:

> *In Washington Lord Halifax*
> *Once whispered to Lord Keynes:*
> *"It's true they have the money bags*
> *But we have all the brains."*[57]

But in 1945–46 the wartime partnership broke up, much as it had
after World War I. Britain was left alone to face the Soviets, until
the crises of 1947–49 brought America back into Europe with an aid
program for economic recovery and a revolutionary Atlantic alliance. Britain, through Ernest Bevin, had taken the lead in enlisting
the New World to redress the balance of the Old. The "special
relationship" seemed to work, after all. As the U.S. ambassador to
Britain, Lewis Douglas, cabled Washington in August 1948,
"Anglo-American unity today is more firmly established than ever
before in peacetime."

But Douglas also noted an underlying problem: "Britain has
never before been in [a] position where her national security and
economic fate are so completely dependent on and at [the] mercy

of another country's decisions. Almost every day brings new evidence of her weakness and dependence on [the] US. This is a bitter pill for a country accustomed to full control of her national destiny."[58] Over the next few years the truth of this contention was amply demonstrated.

CHAPTER 10

GLOBAL COLD WAR
1949–1954

On June 24, 1950, President Truman was enjoying a brief respite from the burdens of office in his hometown of Independence, Missouri. Just after he finished dinner with his wife and daughter the telephone rang. It was a tense Dean Acheson, the secretary of state, on the line from Washington. "Mr. President, I have very serious news. The North Koreans have invaded South Korea."[1] The conflict that followed shifted the cold war from a European into a global arena and brought Anglo-American relations, so recently restored, to a state of acrimony unmatched since the naval rivalry of the 1920s.

Asia, unlike Europe, did not often make the headlines in the late 1940s. Yet vast changes were taking place beneath the surface of events. The United States had assumed control in Japan, leaving its allies with only a token say in the fate of their former enemy. Under General Douglas MacArthur's authoritarian leadership the Americans tried to reconstruct Japan as a democracy in America's image. On the mainland of Asia, communism was on the march, challenging the French in Vietnam and the British in Malaya. Korea had been occupied by America and Russia in 1945, but, as in Germany, the two superpowers could not agree on the terms for a peace settlement. By 1948 two separate Korean states had emerged—the North tied to Moscow, the South to Washington—each bitterly hostile to the other and claiming authority over the whole country.

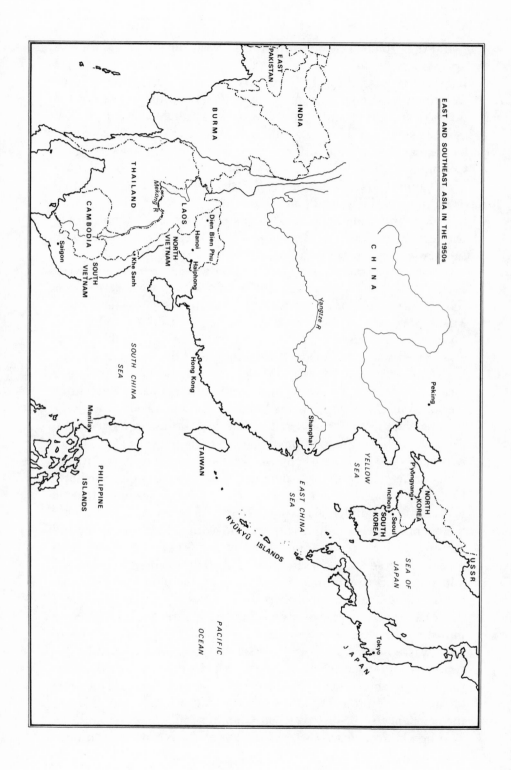

EAST AND SOUTHEAST ASIA IN THE 1950s

EAST
PAKISTAN

INDIA

BURMA

THAILAND

Mekong R.

CAMBODIA

LAOS

NORTH
VIETNAM

Dien Bien Phu

Hanoi

Haiphong

Khe Sanh

SOUTH
VIETNAM

Saigon

Hong Kong

SOUTH CHINA
SEA

CHINA

Yangtze R.

Shanghai

Peking

YELLOW
SEA

EAST CHINA
SEA

TAIWAN

PHILIPPINE
ISLANDS

Manila

RYUKYU ISLANDS

PACIFIC
OCEAN

Pyôngyang

NORTH
KOREA

Inchon

Seoul

SOUTH
KOREA

SEA OF
JAPAN

USSR

Tokyo

JAPAN

But the principal Asian battleground was China, where the 1940s saw American influence replaced almost completely by that of Russia. For the Chinese the Second World War was only an episode in a thirty-year civil war in which millions had died. The United States continued to support the Nationalists under Chiang Kai-shek, as it had since 1937. But $3.5 billion of American aid was insufficient to prevent the collapse of his corrupt regime. In October 1949 the Communist leader, Mao Tse-tung, proclaimed the People's Republic of China. Chiang withdrew to the island of Taiwan, still claiming to be the rightful ruler of all China.

Britain and America parted company over their reaction to the Chinese revolution. The British needed to keep on good terms with the new regime to safeguard Hong Kong and to protect their still-substantial investments in China. Commonwealth countries, particularly India, were also anxious for Britain to normalize relations as soon as possible. So in January 1950 Britain therefore recognized Mao's government. But the Truman administration intended to "wait until the dust settled,"[2] for America was now in the grip of a new Red scare that made 1919 seem trivial by comparison.

In Congress a powerful group of pro-Chiang Republicans blamed Truman for letting China fall into Communist hands. Congressman Karl Mundt claimed that while building dikes in Europe the President had let the "red waters rush unchecked through the flood plain of Asia."[3] Others jumped on the anti-Communist bandwagon. In February 1950 Senator Joseph McCarthy of Wisconsin, seeking an issue for his reelection campaign, denounced Acheson for shielding Communists in the State Department. McCarthy claimed that he had a list of 205 diplomats "known to the Secretary of State as being members of the Communist party and who are still working and shaping policy in the State Department."[4] His charges, though unsubstantiated, caused a sensation, and other dissident Republicans joined the anti-Communist crusade, among them prospective presidential candidate Senator Robert Taft. It was also in February 1950 that Mao signed a treaty of friendship with Stalin. To anyone versed in history, the idea of a permanent alliance between their two countries was absurd: China and Russia had been bitter enemies for centuries. But given America's mood in 1950, it was a further reason for Truman and Acheson to move very cautiously over recognition of the new Communist regime. They could not afford to give further evidence of being "soft" on Communism.

When he received Acheson's call about the North Korean inva-

sion of the South in June 1950, Truman therefore responded deci-
sively. This was barefaced aggression, sanctioned, he presumed, by
Stalin, and it seemed vital to reassure Americans and the world that
the defender of democracy would stand firm. Acheson told the
British government: "Centrally directed Communist Imperialism
has passed beyond subversion in seeking to conquer independent
nations and is now resorting to armed aggression and war."[5] With
the Russians boycotting the UN Security Council because of Mao's
exclusion, America was able to secure a resolution condemning
North Korean aggression and committing a UN force to counter it.

Most of the UN troops were American, under the command of
General MacArthur, recalled to active duty from his governorship
in Japan. MacArthur stemmed the South Korean rout in September
by his brilliant landing at the port of Inchon, two hundred miles
behind enemy lines. Now the North Koreans were in full retreat,
and a jubilant Truman administration proclaimed that its goal was
the reunification of the whole country under a democratic government. The Chinese warned that an American-dominated Korea, on
their doorstep, would be unacceptable, but the administration believed they were bluffing and allowed the rampaging MacArthur to
press on to the Chinese border. On the night of November 25–26
some three hundred thousand Chinese troops attacked, driving the
Americans in headlong retreat out of North Korea. MacArthur was
blamed for his impetuosity, but Truman had approved his drive
north, and it was Truman who soon caused an even greater ferment.

On November 30, just after the Chinese invasion, the President
gave a press conference. Convinced that a new world war was very
close unless America demonstrated its resolve, he insisted that the
United States would take "whatever steps are necessary" in Korea.
"Will that include the atomic bomb?" asked one reporter. "That
includes every weapon we have," the President replied. "Does that
mean that there is active consideration of the use of the atomic
bomb?" "There has always been consideration of its use." Pressed
about possible targets, Truman added: "It's a matter that the military
people will have to decide."[6]

Paul Nitze, director of policy planning at the State Department,
heard the news in his fifth-floor office. "For goodness sakes, Paul,
get over here right away," an agitated Truman aide told him. "The
President has just suggested in answer to a question that MacArthur
had the authority to use atomic weapons if he determined they were

necessary. What do we do about it?" Nitze raced over to the White
House and suggested that they simply "change the record" of the
news conference "to say that General MacArthur did not have the
authority to do it." But he was too late. "All the press of the world
had it. It was already out on the wires, so it couldn't be taken back."[7]

In Britain Truman's ill-judged remarks caused consternation. In
July 1950 the Cabinet, pressed hard by Washington, had agreed to
send British troops to Korea. But there was growing concern about
Washington's failure to consult with its allies and also alarm at the
cost of the war, which had inflated world commodity prices and
thus weakened the British economy. One senior member of the
Foreign Office even warned that "the American attitude may pre-
cipitate a general war in the Far East and thus World War."[8] When
news of Truman's press conference came through, Churchill and
other Conservatives expressed their alarm and one hundred Labour
MPs signed a motion of criticism. Attlee was determined to reassure
British opinion and to demonstrate to America and the world that
this was a UN operation, not a purely American affair. When he
told the Commons that he proposed to go immediately to Washington for talks with Truman, the House rang with cheers. It seemed
like a dramatic reassertion of Britain's great-power status and her
special relationship with the United States.

Attlee knew that the press had blown Truman's remarks out of
proportion, but his underlying concern was well founded. Whitehall was waking up to the fact that Britain had become, in George
Orwell's words, America's "Airstrip One."[9] When the B-29s arrived during the Berlin crisis of 1948, they had used RAF bases in
East Anglia. But in 1949 the U.S. Air Force had asked to develop
four airfields of its own in the Oxford area. This was a different
issue. The Berlin crisis was over and Russia now had an atomic
bomb, together with aircraft of sufficient range to drop it on Britain.
The Ministry of Defence acknowledged that in all probability "acceptance of the American proposals will involve the United States
Air Force remaining in this country indefinitely."[10] Bevin reminded
the U.S. ambassador: "What we had done was to allow the B.29
groups to be brought here as a protection during the difficult time
arising out of the Berlin blockade. But there had never been a
decision taken by the Cabinet regarding the permanent location of
American bombers in this country; neither had we ever reported the
question to Parliament."[11]

Parliament was never consulted. Whitehall departments examined the matter secretly. The Foreign Office listed possible objections, including the effect on the local population of the base personnel with their high standard of living, the opportunity given Russian propaganda to suggest that Britain had become "an occupied territory," and the fact that "in allowing this island to become a forward base for American strategic bombing we increase the likelihood of becoming a primary target for any Russian atomic attack." Despite these "substantial objections," the Foreign Office believed that "the arguments on the other side appear, however, overwhelming. The primary aim of our Foreign Policy must be to keep the United States firmly committed in Europe. The presence of American troops in Germany is, of course, the main anchor which at present holds them, but . . . the establishment of secure air bases in this country . . . would certainly constitute an important additional tie. . . . We must face the fact that this island is strategically well placed as an advanced air base and that we must accept this role."[12]

The Cabinet's Defence Committee decided to open negotiations with the United States, and in April 1950 agreement was reached on the development of four airfields at Fairford, Upper Heyford, Brize Norton and Greenham Common, with costs shared between the two governments. But these plans were soon superseded by the onset of the Korean War. With real fears of a Russian attack in Europe, additional air bases in Britain were required and the Pentagon now wanted to have the components of atomic weapons stockpiled there ready for any emergency. With Truman's approval, planes were flown to Los Alamos and parked over a pit, where they were loaded in secret. The crews were never told exactly what they were carrying. When the bombers arrived in England, they were taken out of the hands of the aircrew and moved to a classified area where a shroud was stretched around the fuselage to protect it from prying eyes. David Rolain, who flew on one of these B-29 "Silverplates," recalls that the British "were strictly in the dark all the way round on this, but I think the RAF probably knew because we worked hand and foot with them."[13]

Informally the British government had given the nod, but they could not be consulted officially because the passing of atomic information to any foreign power was still forbidden under the McMahon Act of 1946. For the same reason the British were given few details about U.S. war plans like "Offtackle," which envisaged Britain as America's major base in any European war. The chief of the Air Staff, Sir John Slessor, complained privately in July 1950 as the

atomic bombs were brought to Britain: "We know little about the
United States Strategic Air Plan with reference to the part to be
played by aircraft based in this country. . . . In a matter like this,
which was of life and death for the country and Western Europe,
we were entitled not only to know the details of the plan but also
to be consulted about them."[14]

Little wonder that in December 1950, with Truman apparently
threatening to use the bomb and Britain in the front line of Soviet
retaliation, Attlee wanted, belatedly, to safeguard his country's position. He nearly succeeded. He was a shrewd politician, belying the
mild manner that led Churchill to remark that "there is less there
than meets the eye."* Attlee quietly took Truman aside during their
White House meeting of December 7 to talk about the use of the
atomic bomb. Returning to the conference table, Truman informed
his aides he had told Attlee "that the Governments of the United
Kingdom and the United States had always been partners in this
matter and that he would not consider the use of the bomb without
consulting with the United Kingdom." Attlee "asked whether this
agreement should be put in writing, and the President replied no
that it would not be in writing, that if a man's word wasn't any good
it wasn't made any better by writing it down."[16]

As Attlee, smiling quietly, expressed his thanks, Truman's advisers sat in horrified silence. Then Dean Acheson spoke. "Let's ad-
journ the meeting for a few minutes, Mr. President, we have
something to talk to you about." Gordon Arneson, Acheson's special assistant on atomic energy, went with them into a private room.
He recalls that Truman "was told in no uncertain terms, 'You can't
do that, Mr. President. We can't do it. It's unconstitutional.' "[17]
Under the U.S. Constitution, Acheson insisted, the president, as
commander in chief, must be totally free to take actions he deemed
necessary to defend the United States. Truman's promise was duly
deleted from the official American record of the conference, and the
British were obliged to accept a much weaker passage in the final
communiqué. This read: "The President stated that it was his hope
that world conditions would never call for the use of the atomic
bomb. The President told the Prime Minister that it was also his
desire to keep the Prime Minister at all times informed of develop-
ments which might bring about a change in the situation."[18]

---

*To Truman, en route to Fulton in March 1946. The President defended Attlee: "He seemed
like a modest sort of fellow." "Yes," muttered Churchill, "he's got a lot to be modest about."[15]

Keeping allies informed was not the same as joint consultation on the use of the bomb. A few months later, when Acheson was asked by Senator McMahon "if any commitment had been made to any other nation which might serve to delay the employment of U.S. atomic weapons after the President had decided in his own mind that he wished to use them," he replied that "no such commitment exists."[19] Even the promise to keep Britain informed "always has to be qualified by events," comments Lucius Battle, one of Acheson's key advisers at the time. He supports his interpretation with a telling example. During Attlee's visit of December 1950 a morning meeting was arranged at the White House. Just before it was due to begin, Dean Acheson was called by the number two at the Pentagon, Robert Lovett, and told that radar reports suggested that planes were attacking in strength from the north. Lovett said he would have to "deal with it from an operational point of view." Acheson explained that he was on his way to see Attlee. "What shall I do? What shall I tell him?" Lovett replied: "Explain it to him, but there's no way you can consult or ask him what to do." After thirty minutes of panic at the State

David Low, Daily Herald, January 12, 1951.

Department, the radar reflections proved to be not incoming Russian bombers but a flight of migrating geese.[20]

Attlee's visit to Washington exposed disagreements between the Allies not just on the Bomb but over other issues too: the danger of America getting too involved in Asia; the degree to which China was a Soviet satellite; and the chances of an acceptable cease-fire and negotiated settlement in Korea. The final communiqué merely patched over the differences, and the following month the British government was appalled when the United States proposed a UN resolution to brand China as the aggressor and impose punitive sanctions. On January 25, 1951, a majority of the Cabinet decided to vote against the U.S. resolution, and only when the Americans watered it down was a public rift avoided.

Bevin was worried about the growing anti-American feeling in Britain. He reminded Attlee of the rationale of the "special relationship": quiet persuasion, not public confrontation, was the way to change objectionable American policies. The British Commonwealth and Western Europe, he wrote, were simply not "strong enough, either economically or militarily, to hold out against the forces actively opposing them. The full participation of the United States is essential. . . . Now is the time to build up the strength of the free world, morally, economically and militarily with the United States, and at the same time to exert sufficient control over the policy of the well-intentioned but inexperienced colossus on whose cooperation our safety depends. . . . It can only be done by influencing the United States Government and people, not by opposing or discouraging them."[21]

Bevin believed that British acquiescence in Asia was the price that had to be paid for American support in Europe. It was widely assumed that the Korean attack could be the prelude to a Russian offensive in Germany. The War Office advised the Cabinet in February 1951: "War possible in 1951, probable in 1952."[22] Previously the North Atlantic Treaty, for all its symbolic importance, had amounted to little more than a mutual defense pact. But in the crisis atmosphere of 1950–51 Washington began to "put the 'O' in NATO," to quote Averell Harriman, turning it from a paper commitment into an organized military alliance.[23] A proper command structure was established under the leadership of General Eisenhower, and four new American combat divisions were sent to Europe, the first troop reinforcements since 1945. In return, Britain and France were persuaded to accept the principle of German rearmament and to boost their own defense spending. As America's main European partner, Britain increased the proportion of gross national product spent on defense from 8 to 14 percent, second only to the United States.

The costs of rearmament provoked a sharp left-wing backlash against the American alliance. In 1945–47 the Labour left had called for an independent socialist foreign policy, denouncing the idea of Britain as "a pensioner of America . . . a junior partner in an American security system,"[24] but they were silenced by the speed and generosity of Marshall aid. Richard Crossman, a vociferous left-wing member of Parliament, admitted in January 1948 that "my own views about America have changed a great deal in the last six months. Many Members have had a similar experience."[25] But dissent revived in April 1951, when a rearmament budget was introduced proposing Health Service charges for spectacles and dentures. Aneurin Bevan, the fiery Welsh ex-miner who had been the architect of the National Health Service, resigned from the Cabinet in protest, warning that the massive rearmament program prompted by the Americans would undermine the economy. "We have allowed ourselves to be dragged too far behind the wheels of American diplomacy," he told the Commons.[26] According to Bevan, the Soviet threat had been exaggerated, China was being driven into Stalin's hands by American conduct, and Britain's security and prosperity required a more independent line from the United States. One Conservative newspaper mocked that "he would leave Britain confronting a perilous world, armed with false teeth."[27]

Bevan did not have many followers in Parliament, but he caught the growing anti-American mood. In mid-1952 the Labour politician Hugh Gaitskell noted that "hostility to America is fairly widespread in Britain today and has certainly increased since the outbreak of the Korean war." The two main causes, he judged, were "resentment at her wealth and power" and "fear that she will involve us in war . . . The truth is that we have a dilemma. We do not like to admit our relative weakness, because we should then look much too like a satellite. But if we try and live up to a military standard we cannot afford, that means economic trouble. A poor relation who is driven to live beyond his means by his rich cousins will not feel well disposed to them."[28]

By the time Gaitskell was writing, Labour was out of power. A new Conservative government was elected in October 1951, headed

America cannot win, says Cummings, Daily Express, *June 17, 1952: condemned for deserting Europe, abused when coming to her aid.*

by Winston Churchill, with Anthony Eden at the Foreign Office. This was the old wartime team that had managed the Grand Alliance of 1941–45. Churchill deprecated the growing friction between Britain and America and was determined to restore relations to the intimacy he had enjoyed with Roosevelt. But times had changed, though Churchill, nearing eighty, found that hard to accept. Evelyn Shuckburgh, Eden's private secretary, attended a meeting between Churchill and Truman in January 1952 at which the Prime Minister "suddenly made an impassioned plea for Anglo-American co-operation in this great tradition we had had. And Truman said, 'Thank you, Mr. Prime Minister, we might pass that on to our advisers for further consideration.' We felt very distressed by that," Shuckburgh recalls.[29] Nor did Churchill enjoy greater success with Truman's Republican successor, Dwight D. Eisenhower. "Ike" held his wartime leader in great esteem, but when they met in January 1953, soon after the President's inauguration, he concluded that "Winston is trying to relive the days of World War II" and that he "had developed an almost childlike faith that all of the answers are to be found merely in British-American partnership."[30]

The limits of Churchill's influence became clear over the question of the atomic bomb. He had been furious at the way, in his view, Labour had surrendered his wartime agreements with Roosevelt for atomic partnership and joint use of the bomb, at the time when "by creating the American atomic base in East Anglia we have made ourselves the target, and perhaps the bull's eye of a Soviet attack."[31] But in October 1951, just before the election, British diplomats had finally secured a formula from the Americans to cover the use of the bases in Britain. Privately Gordon Arneson of the State Department considered it "quite thin" from the British point of view. But "since the UK is prepared to accept it," he told the secretary of state, "it would seem desirable to us to agree on the text as promptly as possible. If Churchill is returned to head the Government he will doubtless want to get a greater commitment from us. We would be in a better position to withstand his onslaught if this statement had already been agreed upon."[32]

Arneson was right. On his visit to America in January 1952 Churchill had little choice but to accept the draft already agreed covering the U.S. bases in Britain. The formula that he and Truman confirmed read: "The use of these bases in an emergency would be a matter for joint decision by His Majesty's Government and the United States government in the light of the circumstances prevailing at the time."[33] Each side was able to interpret this "understanding" in its own way in public, Washington playing down any possible limitation on presidential power while Whitehall insisted that British interests were fully safeguarded. The words themselves seemed vague, but privately the British position on the bases was that "there is naturally no question of their use in an emergency without our consent." It seems from the available evidence that the Americans privately accepted this, although they urged the British to avoid saying so in public.[34] This Truman-Churchill "understanding," backed by the secret interpretations, has remained the basis of the American presence in Britain ever since.

Despite this limited British success, the early 1950s had seen a marked shift in the tone of Anglo-American relations. Facing the threat of Soviet-backed Communism in Europe in the 1940s, the two countries had taken the lead in creating a unique Atlantic alliance. But, outside of Europe, Britain and America had taken a very different view of the Chinese revolution, with the Americans becoming committed to an obsessive crusade against "Red China." By the end of 1950 the cold war was global, and many, thinking back to the 1930s, feared that the sequence of crises would soon escalate into full-scale hostilities. The British government had recovered some control over the use of U.S. bases in Britain, but it had no other say on American use of the atomic bomb, which, Truman and Eisenhower had both hinted, might be used to settle the Korean War.

The handling of the cold war in Asia was not the only issue dividing the two allies. Equally contentious was their attitude to colonialism, which now assumed major importance as Britain tried to hold on to her position as a world power in the face of mounting anti-Western nationalism. In the past America's denunciations of imperialism had seemed to the British a way of picking up the spoils of empire for itself. Nowhere was the problem more acute than in the oil-rich Middle East, where the 1950s saw the last act of a drama that had been played out since World War I.

In the early twentieth century oil replaced coal as the essential fuel for modern industrial economies and for the navies and later the air forces of the world. America was blessed with large indigenous reserves, which satisfied most of its needs until the Second World War, but Britain produced no oil of her own at this stage and, even before the First World War, had used her dominant position in the Middle East to secure essential supplies. This was a costly business. Apart from the expense of exploitation, it was essential to protect pipelines and refineries and to agree with the rulers of the desert, under whose land the oil lay, the terms on which drilling should take place and how the profits should be shared. So important was oil to Britain that the government took a majority shareholding in the Anglo-Persian Oil Company (forerunner of British Petroleum). Anglo-Persian, and Royal-Dutch Shell, in which British capital had a 40 percent share, were the major companies outside the United States.

Until the 1920s American oil companies concentrated almost entirely on exploiting domestic reserves, in states like Texas and Oklahoma. Unlike Anglo-Persian, they were private corporations with no government ownership, but the vital importance of oil meant that the U.S. government offered informal support for their activities. In the 1920s, motivated by the growing anxiety about America's access to raw materials, U.S. companies started moving abroad, particularly in Latin American countries like Venezuela, but also into the Middle East, which had previously been a British domain. In Persia British and American companies agreed to develop some concessions jointly: Standard Oil of New Jersey needed Anglo-Persian's transport and finance, while the British decided that the American presence helped prevent Russian expansion. "Better Americans than Bolsheviks," sniffed the head of the Foreign Office in 1921.[35] But despite these agreements and a growing American presence in Saudi Arabia, Britain remained the predominant oil producer in the Middle East. In 1938 only about 10 percent of production in the region came from American-owned wells.

In oil, as in so many aspects of the relationship, the Second World War marked a turning point. The conflict placed huge demands on American oil resources. Of the seven billion barrels produced for Allied use between December 1941 and August 1945, six billion

To void breaching America's Neutrality Act, U.S.-made bombers are dragged across the Canadian border by horse, en route to Britain (winter 1939–40).

King George VI inspects one of the Hudson aircraft built by Lockheed for the RAF. *Office of Public Information, Lockheed, California*

American, British and Canadian radio commentators plan a joint outside broadcast, "Round London After Dark," during the blitz (August 1940). Ed Murrow is to the left of the lamp. *BBC*

The Atlantic conference, August 1941. The British and American delegations worship on board HMS *Prince of Wales*. *Imperial War Museum, London.*

Roosevelt and Churchill after the service, with General George C. Marshall behind them. Left of Roosevelt, standing with heads bowed, are Harry Hopkins and Averell Harriman. *Imperial War Museum, London*

U.S. aid to Britain: the first flotilla of old U.S. destroyers arrives at Devonport (September 28, 1940).
Imperial War Museum, London

U.S. aid to Britain: GIs bear the Stars and Stripes through Trafalgar Square (March 30, 1944).
BBC Hulton Picture Library

In Southeast Asia the Allies' Deputy Commander, General "Vinegar Joe" Stilwell, and his British superior, Admiral Lord Louis Mountbatten, did not always see eye to eye. *Imperial War Museum, London*

Inside the American servicemen's club Rainbow Corner, on Shaftesbury Avenue, near London's Piccadilly (January 27, 1945). *BBC Hulton Picture Library*

Two hundred London children are guests of American servicemen for Thanksgiving. *Imperial War Museum, London*

How not to behave in Britain: (above) do not make fun of the money or (below) insult a Scotsman's kilt. Scenes from *A Welcome to Britain* (1943). *Imperial War Museum, London*

Planning the invasion of France: (left to right) Bradley, Ramsay, Tedder, Eisenhower, Montgomery, Leigh-Mallory and Bedell Smith (February 1944). *Popperfoto*

Yalta (February 1945). Behind Churchill, Roosevelt and Stalin are their foreign ministers: Eden, Stettinius and Molotov. *Popperfoto*

The Iron Curtain speech. Churchill at Westminster College, Fulton, Missouri, with President Truman behind him (March 5, 1946). *Popperfoto*

George C. Marshall and Ernest Bevin at a Thanksgiving luncheon in London (November 27, 1947). *Popperfoto*

An American aircraft transporting supplies into the blockaded city of Berlin in 1948. *BBC Hulton Picture Library / UPI / Bettmann Newsphotos*

Inspection at a U.S. air force base in Britain in 1952. *BBC Hulton Picture Library*

President Truman greets the British prime minister, Clement Attlee, in Washington on December 4, 1950.
Associated Press

John Foster Dulles is welcomed by Anthony Eden on arrival in London on April 11, 1954. *Popperfoto*

Advice from Secretary of State John Foster Dulles to President Dwight D. Eisenhower (April 1954). *Popperfoto*

British paratroops soon after landing in Port Said (November 1956). *Popperfoto*

A Thor missile being raised into the firing position at Feltwell, Norfolk (November 1958). *Popperfoto*

Balmoral Castle (August 29, 1959). Prince Philip, Princess Anne, President Eisenhower, Queen Elizabeth, Prince Charles, John Eisenhower. *Popperfoto*

John F. Kennedy and Harold Macmillan at Birch Grove, Macmillan's Sussex home (June 30, 1963). *Popperfoto*

The Polaris-equipped submarine USS *Patrick Henry* and its support ship, the *Proteus*, in Holy Loch on the Clyde (March 8, 1961). *Associated Press*
Inset: an antinuclear protester perched on the tail fin of the *Patrick Henry* (March 27, 1961). *Popperfoto*

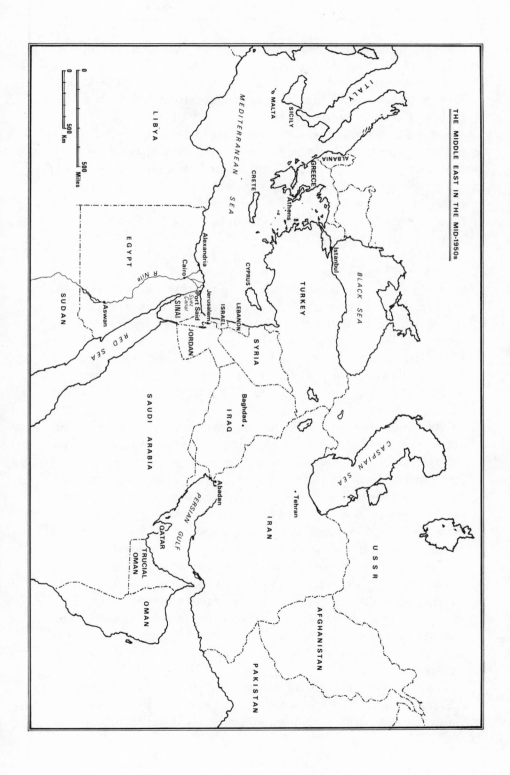

THE MIDDLE EAST IN THE MID-1950s

came from the United States.[36] By 1943 the Roosevelt administration could see that America's own reserves were no longer adequate and was determined to break Britain's stranglehold on the Middle East. Soon both governments were assiduously bribing local rulers, such as Ibn Saud of Saudi Arabia, to keep them friendly and to secure oil concessions, while at the same time sending each other fulsome pledges of their good intentions. "Please do accept my assurances," Roosevelt cabled a suspicious Churchill in March 1944, "that we are not making sheep's eyes at your oil fields in Iraq or Iran." "Let me reciprocate," Churchill replied, "by giving you the fullest assurance that we have no thought of trying to horn in upon your interests or property in Saudi Arabia."[37]

It was not always a story of rivalry and suspicion. British and American oil companies often made common cause against consumers and local rulers. But the underlying trend was clear. Gradually the British were being obliged to relinquish the dominant position in the Middle East that they had acquired, often by force, when there were few competitors and little local opposition. After World War II they were fighting a losing battle against American and Russian oil expansion and against the mounting nationalist reaction to the hated foreign oil companies. The final struggle came in Iran (the new name for Persia).

The Anglo-Iranian Oil Company, as it was now known, had become a symbol of imperialist exploitation for the Iranians. Nationalization of the oil fields and refineries became an increasingly popular demand, finally enacted by the Iranian prime minister, Dr. Mohammed Mossadeq, in April 1951. The Labour government was furious, despite its own record of nationalization. By 1951 Iran was Britain's only non-dollar source of oil and a vital bastion against Soviet expansion. Mossadeq's action was also a humiliation. The foreign secretary, Herbert Morrison, was among those advocating force to recover Anglo-Iranian's property, but it soon became apparent that Britain lacked the money and men to mount such a hazardous operation. Above all, the United States was opposed. The Cabinet agreed on September 27 that the American attitude was decisive. "We could not afford to break with the United States on an issue of this kind."[38]

The Truman administration saw the matter in a fundamentally different light from that adopted by the governments of Attlee and Churchill. The British regarded Mossadeq with contempt as a bald, runny-nosed little man, dressed in pajamas and prone to fainting in public. The British ambassador in Tehran regularly referred to him as a "lunatic."[39] The Americans, by contrast, considered Mossadeq to be a histrionic but rational nationalist who was trying to recover for his own countrymen what decades of imperialist exploitation had denied them. Acheson believed that the crisis could have been averted if Anglo-Iranian had made timely concessions, instead of living in the nineteenth century, when natives were seen and not heard. "Never," commented Acheson, "had so few lost so much so stupidly and so fast."[40] He held up as a model for the future the deal recently concluded by Aramco, the American oil giant, for a fifty-fifty profit-sharing arrangement with the Saudis. This, the Americans claimed, was the way to do business in a profitable but enlightened way.

Truman and Acheson did their best to mediate, pressing the British to accept nationalization with adequate compensation. They were unsuccessful. Instead, British oil personnel were withdrawn from Iran, production was halted, and other major oil companies were persuaded not to buy Iranian oil until the dispute had been settled. Stalemate ensued, but gradually the Iranian economy was crumbling and with it the stability of the Shah's regime.

The new Republican administration in January 1953 shifted American policy. Like Truman and Acheson, Eisenhower and his secretary of state, John Foster Dulles, feared that the economic crisis might drive Mossadeq into Communist hands. Unlike their predecessors, they were prepared to act ruthlessly to prevent this. British intelligence judged that there was sufficient opposition to Mossadeq to mount a coup against him. Eden passed on the information to Washington, and the British and American secret services concocted plan Ajax to topple Mossadeq. "So this is how we get rid of that madman," Dulles chuckled when he was given a copy.[41] Led by Kim Roosevelt, Teddy's grandson and a cousin of FDR, the Central Intelligence Agency orchestrated anti-Mossadeq demonstrations and an army revolt in August 1953. The Shah, who had briefly fled the country, was restored and Mossadeq tried and imprisoned.

This was the first major "covert operation" by the CIA, precursor of things to come—Guatemala in 1954 and Cuba in 1961. Eisenhower was much readier than Truman to use the CIA to achieve American ends in situations where public intervention would be impolitic. It was another sign that America was having to compromise its pristine moral principles when assuming the messy burdens of world power.

In Iran the oil crisis was settled with the new government. After tough bargaining a deal was arranged in 1954 that brought the British substantial compensation but broke their oil monopoly for good. Anglo-Iranian's share dropped to 40 percent and a consortium of American companies secured another 40 percent, leaving Dutch and French companies with the rest. As a result of the settlement, America's share of total Middle Eastern oil rose from 44 percent to 58 percent, while Britain's dropped from 53 percent to 24 percent.[42]

The Americans always denied that they had used the crisis to muscle in on British interests. George McGhee of the State Department, himself a former oilman, says, "In Iran we came in your support, at your request. So I wouldn't call it flexing power."[43] But the British were skeptical. The ambassador in Washington, Sir Roger Makins, pointed out in 1954 that the United States was "now firmly established as the paramount foreign influence in Turkey and in Saudi Arabia. They are gaining a similar ascendancy in Persia, and it now seems that Pakistan may to some extent be drawn into their orbit. . . . Are the Americans," he asked, "consciously trying to substitute their influence for ours in the Middle East?"[44]

In the early 1950s the global cold war and the mounting opposition to colonialism saw America becoming a major influence in parts of the world it had previously ignored, while Britain found it ever harder to hold on to her great-power position. But it would be wrong to imply that Britain no longer mattered in the world. She was still the third strongest power. Much of her empire remained intact, she had substantial armed forces because she still retained conscription, and her industrial output vastly exceeded that of France or West Germany, let alone Japan. In 1952 she was the third country to test an atomic bomb, becoming the only other nuclear power apart from America and Russia.

Britain was therefore still America's most important ally in the struggle to contain the spread of Communism around the world. British bases from Gibraltar to Singapore, from Alexandria to Simonstown, were invaluable supports for American ships and planes. Long-standing British contacts with native rulers could help shore up unstable governments teetering on the brink of revolution. Behind the scenes a secret worldwide alliance in the monitoring of signals intelligence had developed between America, Britain, Canada, Australia and New Zealand. Despite the Anglo-American rivalries and disagreement, therefore, the two had much in common, even in the depths of the cold war. Privately American policymakers like Paul Nitze used Churchill's phrase "a special relationship" to describe the alliance,[45] even though such language was eschewed in public because of the continued Anglophobe feeling in the United States and the jealousy of America's other allies.*

Despite Britain's debacle in Iran, the reality of her influence was displayed clearly during 1954 on the other side of the world, in Vietnam. When Mossadeq nationalized the Iranian oil fields in 1951, it was the Americans who restrained the British, discouraging the use of force and urging on them a negotiated settlement. In the Vietnam crisis in the spring of 1954, the boot was on the other foot, with Britain dissuading America from armed intervention and forcing through a negotiated settlement, which, had it lasted, might have saved America from the quagmire of the 1960s.

In 1954 Vietnam, with Laos and Cambodia, was still part of France's crumbling empire in Indochina. For eight years the French, dominant in the south of Vietnam, had struggled against the Vietminh forces of the Communist leader Ho Chi Minh. By March 1954 twelve thousand of France's crack troops were trapped in Dien Bien Phu, a remote northern village, surrounded by hills packed with Vietminh insurgents. Like human ants the Vietminh carried up the steep slopes the parts of heavy artillery pieces with which, reassembled, they knocked out the French airfield, making resupply impossible. If Dien Bien Phu fell, it was unlikely that the French public would be willing to carry on the unwinnable war.

The United States had welcomed the tide of decolonization in Asia in the 1940s, even threatening the Dutch with termination of Marshall aid if they did not pull out of Indonesia in 1949. But their tune began to change after the Chinese revolution, when it seemed that Communist forces were exploiting the growing nationalist revolt to extend the influence of Moscow and Peking. At the end of 1949 the National Security Council warned Truman that the loss of Southeast Asia to Communism would be "a major political rout the repercussions of which will be felt throughout the rest of the world."[47] During the Korean War both America and China pro-

---

*In May 1950 Secretary of State Dean Acheson discovered a memo written by his subordinates discussing the special relationship. He ordered all copies to be burned. Acheson did not dispute "the genuineness of the special relationship," but "in the hands of troublemakers," he argued, the memo "could stir no end of a hullabaloo, both domestic and international."[46]

vided increasing support to the two sides in Vietnam, and by 1954 the United States was bearing nearly half the cost of the French war effort. Obsessed with the menace from "Red China" the Americans had to decide in March 1954 whether to let Dien Bien Phu fall, and with it the French position in Vietnam, or to enter the war themselves. "My God, we must not lose Asia," Eisenhower exclaimed, "we've got to look the thing right in the face."[48]

Admiral Arthur Radford, chairman of the Joint Chiefs of Staff, favored an air strike to relieve the French and even talked about using atomic weapons, but his colleagues, together with Dulles and Eisenhower, believed that this would lead to full-scale American intervention. Congressional leaders made it clear that they wanted "no more Koreas," with America supplying most of the manpower, and they insisted that any American involvement, even air strikes, must be conditional on the support of America's allies, particularly Britain. Dulles set to work to build a common front in Southeast Asia.

On April 5, 1954, Eisenhower sent an urgent appeal to Churchill. He asked for "united action" to contain China, and played on their common wartime experience: "we failed to halt Hirohito, Mussolini and Hitler by not acting in unity and in time. . . . May it not be that our nations have learned something from that lesson?"[49] In March the British had agreed to talks about united action, but fearful of the trend of American policy, Eden backtracked, much to Dulles's anger. The Foreign Secretary insisted that Britain would have nothing to do with military action or the American proposal for a Southeast Asian equivalent of NATO until the chances of a negotiated settlement had been fully explored. The British believed that the French were finished in Vietnam, but they did not think this was disastrous, dismissing as grossly exaggerated Dulles's warnings that Indochina was like the first in a row of dominoes whose fall would have "a vital effect on Thailand, Malaya, and Indonesia" and could eventually "lead to the loss of Japan."[50] As in December 1950, the British feared that the Americans were bringing the world close to the brink of war by their visceral hatred of Mao's China.

American officials privately denounced the British as deceitful and "weak-kneed,"[51] but London's response proved decisive. The Eisenhower administration sent no military support to the French; Dien Bien Phu fell and with it France's will to fight; and in the summer of 1954 the big powers convened in Geneva to negotiate—

America, Britain, France, Russia, and, for the first time in a major conference, Communist China.

Relations between Eden and Dulles were now close to the breaking point. Eden fumed to his officials "that all the Americans want to do is replace the French and run Indo-China themselves." He went on: "They want to replace us in Egypt too. They want to run the world."[52] Without consulting Dulles, he unveiled his own peace plan for Indochina, which involved independence for Cambodia and Laos and the partition of Vietnam, with the Communists dominant in the north. For Dulles, the idea of the United States and Red China negotiating an apparent sellout to Communism was abhorrent. At Geneva he "conducted himself with the pinched distaste of a puritan in a house of ill repute,"[53] staying only briefly before turning matters over to his subordinates and publicly refusing to shake hands with Chou En-lai, a snub the Chinese never forgot. Dulles's principal expert on East Asia, Walter Robertson, insisted that they would have no dealings with the Chinese, official or social. "You do not take a drink, when the court rises, with the criminal at the bar."[54]

With the Americans sulking on the sidelines at Geneva, the initiative fell to Britain and Russia, who both wanted a settlement. Even so, nothing would have been achieved without the French, whose new government was bent on ending the war. But Eden kept the negotiations going, and his partition plan formed the basis of the final settlement in July 1954. Vietnam would be divided in two, but unlike Korea and Germany, it was intended that free elections in 1956 would pave the way for reunification of the country. The British privately had little doubt that Ho would win those elections, but they did not believe that this would be fatal for the West. The Americans, however, disagreed. They compared Eden's conduct at Geneva to Chamberlain's at Munich and refused to accept the accords. It took an indefatigable Ho twenty years to achieve his aim, and in the process America experienced the worst defeat in its history. Whether the United States would have been better advised to have accepted the inevitable in 1954, much as Britain, with more at stake, had to do over Iran, is an intriguing conjecture.

In Britain Eden was widely praised for the Geneva settlement and credited with saving the world from war. After several years of resentment about American power, the British press relished the feeling that Britain was an independent actor on the world stage once more, and there was ill-disguised satisfaction at what the left-wing *New Statesman* called America's "unmitigated defeat at Geneva."[55] It seemed to confirm that the Anglo-American relationship was not a one-way street: Britain consoled herself that she still had the brains to manage the sometimes irrational American brawn.

Eden enjoyed another diplomatic success in the autumn of 1954 over the vexed issue of German rearmament. Ever since the Korean War began the Americans had been pressing for this, arguing that Western Europe would not otherwise be able to defend itself against Soviet attack. But it took several years to find a solution acceptable to the French, who still feared German aggression. In August 1954 the French Assembly finally vetoed the idea of a European Defense Community, which would have included a rearmed Germany. It did so in the face of a warning from Dulles that rejection "would compel an agonizing reappraisal of basic United States policy."[56]

Eden and his officials were alarmed. They feared that America, now embroiled in McCarthyism and preoccupied with Asia, might pull out of Europe and thus unravel the Atlantic alliance on which all British foreign policy was based. Eden himself toured European capitals to find a solution, arguing that "this was a moment when Europe had to take the initiative to sort this essentially European problem out."[57] Eden's approach indicated his desire for a more independent, though cooperative, relationship with the United States. At a conference in London in the autumn of 1954 he presented his proposals. Germany would rearm and join NATO but under suitable restrictions, including a pledge never to have nuclear weapons. Eden also made an unprecedented offer. For years the British had refused to commit troops permanently on the Continent, despite intense French efforts before both world wars. But on September 30 Eden told the conference that the British would keep four divisions and a tactical air force in Germany for as long as her allies desired. The conference was deeply moved. The French ambassador wept openly, saying that "for fifty years . . . French public opinion has waited for this announcement."[58] With this new British commitment to reassure the French, the conference reached agreement and West Germany joined NATO in May 1955.

By the end of 1954 Britain could feel that she had redressed the balance of the Anglo-American alliance, which had seemed to have tipped so markedly against her in 1950–51. The British government could claim credit for major diplomatic agreements over Vietnam and Germany. In the first she had restrained America, and in the second led Western Europe into a creative solution to its dilemma over German rearmament. Even over Iran, where Britain had been forced to share its oil monopoly with America, the Mossadeq regime had been toppled by Anglo-American action, and it was tempting to assume that in any future Middle Eastern crises America could eventually be brought around to the British position.

Few would have guessed at the end of 1954 that in less than two years not only the Anglo-American alliance but also Britain's position as a great power would be in ruins.

CHAPTER 11

THE EMPIRE'S LAST GASP
1955–1956

The Suez crisis of 1956 saw the worst rift of the twentieth century between Britain and America. It reflected their contrasting attitudes to communism and colonialism, the different stake each had in the Middle East, and the growing disparity in power between the two countries. But Suez was also a tragedy of personalities, dramatically demonstrating how common language and even personal friendship could not prevent complete misunderstanding. Three main figures were involved: Prime Minister Anthony Eden, President Dwight D. Eisenhower and Secretary of State John Foster Dulles. But lurking behind Eden was Winston Churchill, from whose shadow Eden had been trying to escape for most of his political life and whose approach to Anglo-American relations was often at odds with his own.

Churchill was prime minister from October 1951 to April 1955. By this time he was a pale reflection of the war leader who had galvanized Whitehall and led his country through the darkest hours of her history. The old appetite for work had gone, he was often querulous and indecisive, and he found it hard to maintain concentration, particularly on unfamiliar problems. "I have lived seventy-eight years without hearing of bloody places like Cambodia," he complained in 1953.[1] But despite a serious stroke in June 1953, Churchill soldiered on, unable to contemplate political oblivion, but tantalizing Eden, his heir apparent, with repeated hints that he would soon resign.

Churchill reserved much of his limited energy for one foreign policy issue—the search for a great-power summit to control nuclear weapons. There is some irony in the cold warrior of Fulton becoming a leading apostle of détente, but Churchill was convinced that the vastly greater power of the hydrogen bomb (tested by America in 1952 and Russia in 1953) had transformed everything. He told his private secretary, Jock Colville, "we're now as far from the atomic bomb as the atomic bomb was from the bow and arrow."[2] He felt that it was his duty to guide the United States into "world easement." "America is very powerful," he remarked, "but very clumsy."[3]

In May 1953, after Stalin's death, the moment seemed propitious and Churchill called publicly for an informal great-power summit, which, at the very least, he said, could help convince the participants "that they might do something better than tear the human race, including themselves, into bits."[4] But the Prime Minister's stroke dashed his hopes of a visit to Moscow, and his subsequent efforts to revive the project were frustrated by Eisenhower and Eden, who both regarded it as rash and premature. They did not share Churchill's belief that his wartime meetings with Roosevelt and Stalin demonstrated the wisdom of personal summitry.

With Churchill ailing, much of British diplomacy was left in the hands of his foreign secretary, Anthony Eden. Eden was a handsome, elegant man, who had made his name as a determined opponent of appeasement in the 1930s. His diplomatic experience was immense, having headed the Foreign Office in 1935–38 and 1940–45. Yet Eden was in some ways an undiplomatic personality: capable of great charm, but volatile in mood and often petulantly angry with events and people. He lacked Churchill's resilience of character, and his insecure vanity was legendary in Whitehall. "He is like a sea anemone," noted Evelyn Shuckburgh, his private secretary, "covered with sensitive tentacles all recording currents of opinion around him. He quivers with sensitivity to opinion in the House [of Commons], the [Conservative] party, the newspapers."[5]

Eden was very different from his American counterpart. John Foster Dulles evoked memories of his Princeton professor Woodrow Wilson. Although more heavily built, there was the same gravity of manner, the same severe, bespectacled face. And despite the fact that Dulles was a Republican, not a Democrat, there was also

a similar ideological approach to foreign affairs, grounded in Calvin-
ist Christianity, and, in Dulles's case, animated by a burning hatred
of Communism. In the 1952 election campaign Dulles had achieved
notoriety by his rhetoric about "rolling back" Communism and
"liberating" Russia's subject peoples. "Why should we assume that
what Soviet Communism can *do* in China, we cannot *undo*?" he
asked a New Jersey audience in October 1952.[6] Much of the rhetoric
was for domestic political consumption, to prove his credentials to
a McCarthyite Republican party. But he so alarmed the British that
Eden and Churchill had even lobbied discreetly against Dulles's
appointment as secretary of state. They failed, but after seeing Eisenhower in Washington on November 20, 1952, Eden cabled
Churchill: "The new Secretary of State would not have been my
choice. Ike was almost apologetic. We must do the best we can with
him."[7]

In private Dulles could be congenial company. But to most people he seemed ponderous and legalistic ("Dull, Duller, Dulles," in
the words of one Washington joke). Trained as an international
lawyer, he often found Eden vague and imprecise, and Eden's languid habit of addressing colleagues as "dear" was particularly disqui-
eting. More important still, Dulles's legal ties had been with French
and German leaders. He had no experience of the wartime partnership with Britain, which had shaped the outlook of other American
policymakers of the postwar period, such as Marshall, Acheson and
Eisenhower. At times Eden and Dulles worked well together, but
the American never fully forgave Eden for his conduct over Vietnam in 1954 and relations between them were rarely good thereafter.

Eden's rifts with Dulles were, however, attributable to more than
temperamental differences. Unlike Churchill, Eden was not convinced that cooperation with America should be the overriding
priority of British policy. The half-American Churchill believed in
the special relationship with almost religious fervor. "My hope for
the future," he told Eisenhower in 1953, "is founded on the increasing unity of the English-speaking world. If that holds all holds. If
that fails no one can be sure of what will happen."[8] Eden had no
doubt that Anglo-American cooperation was important: that had
been a major reason for his break with Neville Chamberlain in 1938.
But he believed that Britain need not subordinate her foreign policy
to every whim of Washington. His successes over Vietnam and
Germany in 1954 strengthened these convictions, and when he

finally became prime minister in April 1955 he was not willing to defer to the Americans if British interests seemed to dictate an independent line.

The search for disarmament was a striking example. In the spring of 1955 Eden suddenly saw great merits in the idea of a summit conference. Churchill commented with a sly smile, "It is wonderful what difference it makes to your views about a top-level meeting when you get to the top."[9] Although the Foreign Office still wished to concert policy on disarmament with the United States, Eden told his Cabinet that "we should be unwise to wait too long upon the Americans in this matter: it might be some considerable time before they produced any views of their own. We should not hesitate to go forward with our own enquiries . . . and to bring forward suggestions of our own as soon as we were ready."[10] When the summit conference, the first in ten years, was convened in Geneva in July 1955, Eden confidently expected to be the star, as he had been over Indochina the previous year.

This comfortable assumption of continued European superiority was illustrated for the British by the conference cuisine. One day the Americans hosted lunch. According to Harold Macmillan, then Eden's foreign secretary, it was "a disgusting meal, of large meat slices, hacked out . . . and served . . . with marmalade and jam." When the French reciprocated, their guests were treated to "a long series of exquisite courses with wines of equal distinction." It was, Macmillan mused contentedly, "a demonstration of the refinements of the Old World against the barbarism of the New, whether in East or West."[11]

But the center of attention at Geneva in 1955 was not Eden but Eisenhower, a man whom the British were prone to underestimate. Their recollections of him as Allied supreme commander in Europe during World War II were pleasant but unflattering. "In the war," said Churchill in July 1953, "he had a very genuine gift for friendship and for keeping the peace. But I decided in the States six months ago that he was really a Brigadier." By the end of the year Churchill had concluded that "everything is left to Dulles. It appears that the President is no more than a ventriloquist's doll."[12] This was a common judgment in London: Sir Philip de Zulueta, Eden's private secretary at the time, feels that Eden never quite came to terms with Eisenhower's elevation from army officer to head of state.[13]

The British were therefore ill prepared for the President's performance at the 1955 summit. Unlike at the Geneva conference a year before, the Americans were serious participants, and Ike surprised everyone, including the British, with his radical proposal on arms control. The President recognized that the central obstacle was verification, the need for each side, in the absence of mutual trust, to have an agreed method for reassuring itself that the other was not cheating. He therefore suggested an Open Skies policy under which East and West would exchange maps showing the location of their military installations and would permit aerial photographic reconnaissance over their territory. Just as he finished his dramatic proposal there was a tremendous clap of thunder and all the lights in the conference hall went out. "Well," said Eisenhower, "I expected to make a hit but not that much of one."[14]

The President's plan did not, however, make a hit with the Russians, who rejected it as licensed espionage. But Open Skies captured the headlines and was an indication of Ike's true role. Despite his easygoing manner, his verbal slips and the wide latitude he gave his subordinates, Eisenhower was the man who ultimately decided American foreign policy. Dulles understood that; the British did not—until it was too late.

Despite the shock to British pretensions at Geneva, Eden and his colleagues remained confident of their ability to play an independent role in the world. During 1955 the British made crucial decisions that left them outside the European Common Market when it came into being in 1958. It was a fateful step, taken against American advice, which would require a quarter-century fully to correct, but which, at the time, seemed both right and inevitable.

The British had always been reluctant to throw in their lot with the countries across the English Channel, often using the word "Europe" to exclude Britain and signify only the Continent. Back in 1930 Churchill had insisted: "We are with Europe, but not of it. We are linked, but not compromised. We are interested and associated, but not absorbed. . . . We belong to no single continent, but to all."[15] Two world wars had modified that attitude but had not fundamentally altered it. In 1947–48, at a time when America seemed isolationist and Russia malevolent, Bevin talked of Western European Union and instigated greater cooperation with France, Belgium, Holland and Luxembourg. But the British only favored cooperation between governments; they did not intend to surrender national sovereignty to form a European federation. Nor would they accept the more limited idea, proposed by the French in 1950, for a European coal and steel community in which the industries of participating countries would be subject to a "higher authority."

Insofar as proposals like the coal and steel community brought France and Germany together after years of strife, they were welcomed in London. But that did not mean Britain joining in. "I meant it for them, not us," remarked Churchill about the idea of a European army.[16] For Britain, still a world power, relations with continental Europe were not the top priority. France, West Germany and their neighbors were still struggling to recover from the defeat and devastation of the war. They hardly seemed fit allies for the victorious British, whose empire, investments and commerce still girdled the globe. Ties of kinship were also important. Eden used to say "that if you were to open the personal mail arriving from overseas in any post office in England you would find that 90 percent of it came from beyond Europe, from Australia, Canada, India, Africa, anywhere, indeed, where British soldiers and administrators had served or British families settled."[17] These countries meant much more to British people than France, Germany or Italy. Eden therefore spoke for Conservatives and Labour alike in 1952 when he called the suggestion that Britain should join

> a federation on the continent of Europe . . . something which we know, in our bones, we cannot do. . . . For Britain's story and her interests lie far beyond the continent of Europe. Our thoughts move across the seas to the many communities in which our people play their part, in every corner of the world. These are our family ties. That is our life: without it we should be no more than some millions of people living on an island off the coast of Europe, in which nobody wants to take any particular interest.[18]

Britain's instinctive feeling that she was not really European was incomprehensible to most Americans. During the years of the Marshall Plan the Truman administration had encouraged the British government to accept the goal of a united, and ultimately federal, Western Europe, which would help reduce the burdens on the United States. As the Marshall aid administrator, Paul Hoffman, observed, the aim was "to get Europe on her feet and off our backs."[19] Leadership of the "new Europe" by Britain, America's closest ally, could ensure that it developed in a way that furthered American objectives. And, unlike the British, Americans were used to a continent-wide common market and a federal system of government. They believed that these had helped make America great and, if implemented across the Atlantic, would finally convert the mad, bad Old World from its obsessive rivalries and bloodshed. But constant American pressure on Britain was unavailing. The British were resentful that even close friends, such as Averell Harriman, entertained "besetting fallacies . . . that Britain is a part of a Continental Europe that can be run as a single economic unit."[20] They remained immune to American advice, and eventually the two governments agreed to differ on this fundamental issue.

When, in the summer of 1955, the six members of the European Coal and Steel Community—France, West Germany, Italy, Belgium, the Netherlands and Luxembourg—met to plan a full-scale common market, the British government sent only observers. They regarded the meeting as likely to create an inward-looking, protectionist organization, at odds with Britain's trading interests around the world. Unable to steer the negotiations in the direction they desired, the British left the Six to develop the Common Market without them. Nor were they interested in plans for a European atomic energy project. As the only country apart from the superpowers to hold nuclear weapons, Britain, it was felt, "would have much to give but little to gain."[21]

Within eighteen months, however, Britain's complacency was shattered. She was reduced to a point where the Foreign Office seriously considered abandoning its relationship with America and throwing in its lot with the Six.

The setting was Egypt. Since its construction by the British and French in 1869 the Suez Canal had been the main artery of the British Empire, connecting Britain with India and the Pacific. After India became independent in 1947 that function became less important, but in the days before supertankers it was still the route by which two-thirds of the oil produced in the Persian Gulf was shipped to the West, and therefore a sea-lane of immense strategic importance.

Britain had dominated Egypt since the 1880s, and the Canal Zone was the center of her military presence in the eastern Mediterranean. This was a vast area of garrisons, airfields, supply depots and training grounds stretching from the canal almost to Cairo. It was as if the heart of England, from London to Birmingham, was under foreign military rule. For the Egyptians the Canal Zone was a visible reminder of the hated British occupation, and, after a military coup in 1952 that toppled the plump, sybaritic King Farouk, efforts to evict Britain were intensified. British personnel were attacked, mobs burned British property and Egyptians boycotted British employment, making it increasingly difficult to operate the Canal Zone.

Churchill and Eden, prime minister and foreign secretary, disagreed about the correct response. Both were determined to maintain Britain's position as a Middle Eastern power, but Eden argued that she had to adopt new methods in view of her diminished power and the growth of anticolonial nationalism. He believed Britain should bow to the inevitable and evacuate the Canal Zone, while retaining the right of reentry in an emergency. Churchill disliked what he called "this policy of scuttle in Egypt,"[22] and much of the Conservative party agreed. Eden had to battle hard for many months. "What we are trying to do in Egypt," he told one critic, "is not to run away from a regime which often says crude and hostile things, but rather to lay the foundations of security in the Middle East in the new and changed circumstances that now prevail there. . . . It is a case of 'new times, new methods.' "[23] Gradually Eden won through, particularly when the beginning of the H-bomb age convinced Churchill and many of the military that sprawling conventional bases were now redundant. In 1954 the British agreed to withdraw all their troops from the Canal Zone by June 1956. The canal itself would continue to be operated by the Anglo-French company that owned it.

Eden hoped that the agreement had cleared the decks for a new relationship with Egypt, where Colonel Gamal Abdel Nasser had now emerged as leader. And once the British presence had been terminated, the Americans were willing to step in with aid for Egypt. In late 1955 Britain and America agreed to provide Nasser with a loan of $70 million toward the Aswan High Dam, which would provide Egypt with electric power and better irrigation. But Nasser's ambition was not only the economic modernization of his own country but the political resurrection of the whole Arab world. His brand of socialist nationalism was not just anticolonial but opposed to the exploitation of the Middle East by all the great powers. He set out to exploit the exploiters.

While accepting the loan from Britain and America, Nasser also ordered arms from the Soviet Union by way of Czechoslovakia. He tried to undermine the British-led Baghdad Pact, which Eden had hoped would be a Middle Eastern equivalent of NATO, and he dismissed the Anglo-American plan for a peace treaty with Israel. Eden "compared Nasser with Mussolini and said his object was to be a Caesar from the Gulf to the Atlantic, and to kick us out of all

of it."[24] By March 1956 both the British and American governments
had had enough. With the successful coup against Mossadeq in
mind, the British prepared plans for covert operations against
Egypt. Eden "was quite emphatic that Nasser must be got rid of,"
Shuckburgh recorded on March 12, 1956. "It is either him or us,
don't forget that," the Prime Minister said.[25]

The Americans were not yet ready to go that far, but the CIA
started making contingency plans, and Dulles subjected the dam
project to renewed scrutiny. In Congress the Israeli and cotton
lobbies were against it, and Nasser's recognition of Communist
China was a slap in the face for Dulles. On July 19 the secretary of
state summoned the Egyptian ambassador, told him that the loan
had been canceled and issued a humiliating statement to the press
casting doubt on Egypt's "readiness and ability to concentrate its
economic resources upon this vast construction program."[26] The
British were taken aback by the abruptness of Dulles's action, expecting the offer to be allowed simply "to wither on the vine,"[27] and
Eisenhower also expressed disquiet at the way the Egyptians had
been handled. Even Dulles had second thoughts. He normally
walked straight out of his office with his hat on about seven-thirty
each evening. But after work on July 19 he unexpectedly stopped
and slumped down in a chair by the desk of one of his aides, William
Macomber. "Well," he said, "I hope we did the right thing." Macomber tried to reassure him: "I'm sure we did, sir." "Well," said
Dulles, "I hope we did." Then he put on his hat and walked out.[28]

The cancellation of the Aswan loan was the kind of dramatic
gesture Nasser understood. A week later he more than matched it.
On July 26, 1956, in a three-hour diatribe against the imperialists,
he announced to an astonished world that he had nationalized the
Suez Canal. In future it would be run by Egypt and the revenue
would be used to finance the Aswan Dam. "We shall build the High
Dam," Nasser proclaimed, "on the skulls of 120,000 Egyptian work-
men who died in building the Suez Canal."[29] Eden was beside
himself with rage. Fundamental British interests seemed in jeopardy, because a third of the ships using the canal were British, and
Britain had oil reserves for only six weeks. Eden's fury was fueled
by his sense of betrayal. He had gone out on a limb in 1954, arguing
against strong Tory opposition that it was time to build a new, more
trusting relationship with Egypt. Now his many critics were claiming that they had been totally vindicated.

Although the British started by imposing economic and political sanctions on Egypt, Eden was ready to use force. The Egypt Committee, set up by the British Cabinet to handle the crisis, noted on July 30: "While our ultimate purpose was to place the Canal under international control, our immediate objective was to bring about the down fall of the present Egyptian Government."[30] Eden also made his attitude clear to Eisenhower. The day after nationalization he cabled the President that although currently exploring diplomatic measures, "my colleagues and I are convinced that we must be ready, in the last resort, to use force to bring Nasser to his senses."[31] A few days later he told Eisenhower again that "the removal of Nasser and the installation in Egypt of a regime less hostile to the West" were major objectives, and he argued that "I have never thought Nasser a Hitler. . . . But the parallel with Mussolini is close. Neither of us can forget the lives and treasure he cost us before he was finally dealt with."[32] At the height of the Dien Bien Phu crisis in Vietnam in 1954 Eisenhower had invoked the lessons of World War II when he appealed to the British for help. Eden was trying the same tactic in reverse.

But Eisenhower was as unreceptive in 1956 as the British had been in 1954. His own Joint Chiefs of Staff favored military action, but the President believed the British were "out of date in thinking of this as a mode of action."[33] It smacked of old-fashioned gunboat diplomacy, which would array the whole developing world against America. It would also outrage American anti-imperial sensitivities.* Eisenhower was not indifferent to what had happened. He shared the growing alarm at Nasser's ambitions, and the Suez nationalization had disturbing implications for America's control of the Panama Canal. But Suez was not a vital interest for America, as it was for Britain, and Eisenhower believed that the best way to react was through diplomacy. He sent Dulles to London at the beginning of August to persuade Eden to call a conference of those nations that used the canal. Eden was reluctant but finally agreed on the grounds that the delay while military action was prepared could be fruitfully used to harden international opinion against Nasser.

During August 1956 Britain mobilized her forces and called up some reservists. Parts of southern England looked as they had in the

---

*Back in December 1953 Eisenhower had got into an argument about colonialism with Jock Colville, Churchill's private secretary, who insisted hotly that "India had been better governed by the Viceroy of India and the British Government of India than at present." Eisenhower replied "that as a matter of fact he thought so himself, but that to Americans liberty was more precious than good government."[34]

Second World War, with long convoys of trucks and tanks, newly
painted in brown-and-black desert camouflage, grinding through
the country lanes on their way to the ports. The popular mood was
bellicose, with shouts of "Give 'em Hell" sending the troops on their
way to the Mediterranean.

Officially all this was a precaution, for diplomacy was still being
tried. The Canal Users' Conference met in mid-August and proposed that an international body working under the United Nations
should operate the canal. Nasser said no. Dulles then suggested that
the users would operate the canal themselves. Eden went along with
that, on, he believed, the clear understanding that the United States
would back the scheme by force if Egypt resisted. But then in
mid-September Dulles told a news conference that the United States
would not shoot its way through the canal. On October 2 he confessed to the press that the Users' Association had "no teeth" and
explained that the United States wished to promote the peaceful
transition from colonialism to independence "without identifying
itself 100 per cent either with the so-called colonial Powers or with
the Powers which are primarily and uniquely concerned with the
problem of getting their independence as rapidly as possible." Suez,
he added for good measure, was an area outside America's obligations to her allies under the North Atlantic Treaty.[35]

Eden received news of Dulles's remarks while sitting in the Cabinet Room at 10 Downing Street. He was arguing with Anthony
Nutting, a Foreign Office minister who opposed the use of force and
was urging Eden to conciliate American opinion. Eden read the
report, then threw it across the Cabinet table at Nutting, demanding
contemptuously, "Now what can you say for your American
friends?"[36]

These were grim months for Anthony Eden. Sick from the recur-
rence of fevers caused by a badly executed gall bladder operation,
he faced an impossible dilemma. Two months had passed since
Nasser's seizure of the canal, and during that time world opinion
had clearly shown itself to be against the use of force, as had the
Labour opposition at home. Worse still, the Egyptians were proving
capable managers of the waterway and there was no disruption of
shipping. Nevertheless Eden's convictions about Nasser had not
changed, and he was under intense pressure from his own party to
recover the canal. He needed a pretext for reviving a crisis that was
in danger of running down.

Salvation came from across the Channel. The French, co-owners of the canal, believed that escalating border raids in Sinai between Egypt and Israel signaled that another Arab-Israeli war was imminent. They were determined to exploit the opportunity. On October 16 Eden and his foreign secretary, Selwyn Lloyd, traveled secretly to Paris. The French proposed that Israel should be encouraged to invade Egypt and threaten the canal, thereby giving Britain and France a pretext for intervening to safeguard the waterway, their own property. Eden quickly agreed, and at a further meeting on October 24 British diplomats confirmed the details in writing. The following day the British Cabinet was asked to approve contingency plans for a British response, should Israel attack Egypt, without being told of the collusion. The United States government was told nothing at all.

Eden's neglect of America was consistent with his view that Britain could, if necessary, act on her own, without the assistance of the United States. Back in October 1955 he had told the Cabinet:

> Our interests in the Middle East were greater than those of the United States because of our dependence on Middle East oil, and our experience in the area was greater than theirs. We should not therefore allow ourselves to be restricted overmuch by reluctance to act without full American concurrence and support. We should frame our own policy in the light of our interests in the area and get the Americans to support it to the extent we could induce them to do so.[37]

In planning the attack on Egypt, Eden seems to have decided that the Americans, though unhappy in principle, would go along with the operation or at least offer no serious opposition. That was certainly the view of the British Treasury as it prepared plans for the war. It was operating quite explicitly on only "two hypotheses": "full U.S., and general U.N. and Commonwealth support" or "Go it alone with France—with only limited U.S., Commonwealth and other support."[38] No one seems to have expected outright American hostility.

Yet that is what Britain soon faced. On October 29 the Israelis began their offensive into Sinai, with the agreed feint toward the canal. The following day London and Paris gave the belligerents twelve hours to pull back from the canal and allow British and French forces to occupy it. Israel accepted the ultimatum; the Egyptians rejected it, not surprisingly, since it would have meant that they retreated and the Israelis advanced about one hundred miles. On the thirty-first British bombers went into action against Egyptian airfields, another action of dubious propriety, since the two countries were not at war and Britain was claiming only to be trying to separate the Israeli and Egyptian forces.

Eisenhower's initial reaction was astonishment, then anger that the British should have reverted to gunboat diplomacy accompanied by glaring deception of their closest ally. "I've just never seen great powers make such a complete *mess* and *botch* of things," he exploded. "Of course, there's just nobody, in a war, I'd rather have fighting alongside me than the British. . . . But—*this* thing! My God!"[39] He telephoned Downing Street. The call was intercepted by Eden's press secretary, William Clark. "Is that you, Anthony?" the angry voice inquired. "Well, this is President Eisenhower, and I can only presume you have gone out of your mind."[40]

There was more than a touch of hypocrisy in the American position. Eisenhower had no doubt about the threat posed by Nasser. On October 6, less than a month before the Suez operation, he vetoed a CIA plan to "topple Nasser" on the lines of the plot against Mossadeq, but he did so on grounds not of principle but of prudence. According to notes of the meeting, "The President said that an action of this kind could not be taken when there is as much active hostility as at present. For a thing like this to be done without inflaming the Arab world, a time free from heated stress holding the world's attention as at present would have to be chosen."[41] Eisenhower differed with Eden not on the goal of getting rid of Nasser but on the appropriate issue and the method. The canal seemed a remnant of dated imperialism, and overt action to recover it would simply outrage the international community. As he told Eden in a letter on September 3, "American public opinion flatly rejects the thought of using force" to recover the canal. Likewise America's "friends in the Middle East," though eager to "see Nasser's deflation," were "unanimous in feeling that Suez is not the issue on which to attempt to do this by force."[42]

What made Britain's action even worse for Eisenhower was its timing. America's presidential election would take place on November 6. Ike, the leader whose reputation rested on his ability to handle the world's diplomatic and military crises, could not afford at this juncture to be humiliated by his closest allies. His anger, and that of Dulles, were compounded by events in Eastern Europe. In Hungary a new liberalizing regime had briefly come to power, defying the Soviet Union and announcing the country's withdrawal from the Warsaw Pact. At the moment when Britain and France were bombing Egypt, Russian tanks rumbled into Budapest and the brutal suppression of the uprising began.

Despite Dulles's campaign rhetoric about "liberating" oppressed peoples, Washington had no intention of providing military assistance to the Hungarian rebels. But it hoped at least to present a united NATO front, deploring Russia's use of force and demonstrating to the Third World the West's moral superiority. The Suez operation tore that policy to shreds. Dulles told the National Security Council that if America wished to condemn "Soviet colonialism in Eastern Europe" it would have to break with "Anglo-French colonialism." Otherwise "all the independent countries will turn from us to the USSR. We will be looked upon as forever tied to British and French colonialist policies."[43] Eisenhower was determined to go straight to the United Nations and ask for a resolution calling for a cease-fire and requiring all UN members to refrain from the use of force. He told a British diplomat: "We plan to get there first thing in the morning—when the doors open—before the USSR gets there."[44]

The Americans introduced their resolution in the Security Council on October 30, where it was vetoed by Britain and France. On November 1 it was reintroduced by Dulles himself in the General Assembly. That same evening Eisenhower made his last speech of the election campaign in Philadelphia. Referring to the crisis, he declared: "We cannot subscribe to one law for the weak, another for the strong; one law for those opposing us, another for those allied with us. There can be only one law—or there shall be no peace."[45]

America's unprecedented public stand against its closest allies won it unaccustomed acclaim from Asian and African nations. Even cleaners and typists at the UN Building went out of their way to congratulate American diplomats. The resolution was passed on November 2 by sixty-four votes to five. Only Australia and New Zealand sided with Britain, France and Israel. Canada was among the abstainers. In the 1980s denunciations of the West by the Third World in the United Nations were commonplace. In the 1950s they were rare. Britain, an architect of the UN, accustomed to instructing others about international morality, was now facing intense criticism from almost all the world, orchestrated by her principal ally. The shock was almost physical.

What followed was the humiliating collapse of the conspiracy, undermined by opposition at home and America's actions in the UN. At the time of the Assembly resolution the Anglo-French invasion force had not even reached the canal. Britain's nearest deepwater base to Egypt was Malta, almost a thousand miles away. To preserve the pretext that the force was acting in response to a threat to the canal, it could not set out from Malta until October 31, after the Israelis had attacked and the Anglo-French ultimatum had been issued. By November 4 both Egypt and the Israelis, who had achieved their objectives in Sinai, were ready to accept a cease-fire, but the invasion force was still a day's sailing away. On November 5 British and French paratroops were finally dropped around Port Said. But by this time the Soviets were threatening to intervene, Parliament and the country were bitterly divided, and there was serious talk of UN sanctions against Egypt's attackers. The operation had also lost every shred of credibility. Eden and his Cabinet colleagues were exhausted from days of unrelenting criticism. On November 6, according to the minutes, "there was general agreement in the Cabinet that, in order to regain the initiative and to re-establish relations with those members of the United Nations who were fundamentally in sympathy with our aims, we should agree, subject to the concurrence of the French Government, to stop further military operations."[46] Later that day Eden informed the French that Britain was accepting a cease-fire, just as the combined invasion force finally landed.

Even the Americans, who wanted a cease-fire, professed to be astonished at the timing of Eden's decision. Dulles asked Foreign Secretary Selwyn Lloyd on November 17 why, having started, the British did not "go through with it and get Nasser down?"[47] But Eisenhower's principal reaction was relief that the conflict had ended before Russia had a chance to intervene. The cease-fire also coincided with news of his election victory. So when Eden phoned first thing on November 7, Ike was in a buoyant and forgiving mood. He agreed that Eden should come to Washington, adding that the affair had been "like a family spat."[48]

Eden was delighted. He wanted to repair the breach and exploit Britain's position, with forces astride the canal, to ensure a satisfactory settlement. But Eisenhower's aides warned the President that an invitation to Eden would look as if America was conniving with Britain behind the back of the UN. So Eisenhower called back to say that the meeting was off. Subsequent telegrams from the President made it clear that there would be no contact until Britain and

"Freezing to Death Isn't So Good Either"

Eisenhower douses America's irresponsible European allies.
(*Herblock*, Washington Post, *November 29, 1956.*)

France had completely withdrawn their troops from Egypt and a
UN peacekeeping force had been installed. "Once these things are
done," Eisenhower told Eden, "the ground will be favorable for our
meeting."[49]

Cold-shouldering the British was not Eisenhower's only weapon
to evict them from Egypt. The crisis had started a heavy run on
sterling, and the Bank of England was digging deep into the reserves

to preserve the value of the pound, a symbol of Britain's status in the world. Further loans from the United States became essential. The British Treasury had originally assumed that America would be cooperative or at least acquiescent during the Suez operation. Chancellor of the Exchequer Harold Macmillan returned home from a visit to Washington in late September convinced "that the American Government, while publicly deploring our action, would be privately sympathetic, and thus content themselves with formal protests."[50] But on November 8 the British ambassador, Sir Harold Caccia, reported an alarming meeting with U.S. Treasury Secretary George Humphrey, a vehement critic of Britain's conduct. Humphrey's line, Caccia warned London, was that "for the United States to offer financial aid to the United Kingdom and France in the light of our actions in the last ten days would be totally unacceptable politically for some considerable time."[51]

Britain's efforts to shift the Americans were unavailing. All would depend, they made it clear, on Britain showing that she was "conforming to rather than defying the United Nations."[52] The sterling crisis continued, and during November Britain lost nearly $280 million, 15 percent of her reserves. On November 28, Macmillan impressed on the Cabinet that to avoid financial disaster "the good will of the United States Government was necessary; and it was evident that this good will could not be obtained without an immediate and unconditional undertaking to withdraw the Anglo-French force."[53] Eden, now a sick man, was recuperating in Jamaica. In his absence the Cabinet capitulated, and the last British troops were out of Port Said by Christmas.

As so often, Winston Churchill went to the heart of the matter. Pondering the debacle later, he admitted that it was hard to know how he would have behaved had he still been prime minister. But he was clear on two points. "I cannot understand why our troops were halted. To go so far and not go on was madness." He was also "certain" that he "wouldn't have done anything without consulting the Americans."[54] There in essence lay his differences with Eden.

The Suez crisis destroyed many of Britain's cherished illusions about the "special relationship"—about the community of interests between the two countries and the ability of Britain to manipulate American policy. Relations had been strained in the previous decade, of course, over China, Korea and Iran. But the disputes had generally been in private, and in the last analysis, British leaders believed, America could be induced to follow their lead. Suez exploded these assumptions: the divisions were fundamental, the row was public, and the Americans were unremitting in their opposition. Immediately afterward there was an angry backlash against the United States, with some 120 Conservatives signing a Commons motion accusing America of "gravely endangering the Atlantic Alliance."[55]

Anti-American feeling was understandable, but what brought Eden down was not an American stab in the back: Britain's crisis was in reality self-induced. Until 1956 it remained the assumption in Britain, particularly among the general public, that the country was still a great power. India had been lost, but most of the other colonies and territories remained part of the British Empire, or the Commonwealth, as it was now named, and British influence continued to pervade Asia, Africa and the Middle East. Suez exposed the extent of Britain's pretensions. Eden had tried to take an independent line in the Middle East, only to discover that Britain lacked the means to do so. Her armed forces were ill prepared, she antagonized world opinion by her spurious cover story, she lacked the bases and air transports needed for a swift operation, and her economy was vulnerable to American pressure. The outcome was the worst humiliation in Britain's twentieth-century history, beginning a long period of self-analysis and doubt as the country tried to assimilate the lessons and rethink its role in the world.

Some members of the Foreign Office seized on the feelings of impotence and resentment in a memorandum submitted to the Cabinet in January 1957. "Two great Powers, America and Russia, now immeasurably outstrip all the others," the memo began bleakly. Britain had tried to keep up with them, but now, in the age of the hydrogen bomb, "if we try to do so we shall bankrupt ourselves." Instead, the Foreign Office advised, "we should pool our resources with our European allies so that Western Europe as a whole might become a third nuclear power comparable with the United States and the Soviet Union."[56]

Even at this grim moment the Cabinet was not willing to surrender Britain's status as an independent nuclear power. But there was general agreement that in non-nuclear matters a closer relationship with Western Europe was desirable:

> the Suez crisis had made it plain that there must be some change in the basis of Anglo-American relations. It was doubtful whether the United States would now be willing to accord to us alone the special

position which we had held as their principal ally during the war. We might therefore be better able to influence them if we were part of an association of Powers which had greater political, economic and military strength than we alone could command.[57]

For a decade Britain had kept her distance from the continent of Europe, sure that she remained a world power, confident of her special relationship with the United States. Suez seemed to have shattered both assumptions and opened up a new view of Britain's future role.

CHAPTER 12

DEPENDENCE
AND DETERRENCE
1957–1963

The Cabinet discussed Britain's relations with America and Europe on January 8, 1957. The following day Anthony Eden announced his resignation as prime minister on grounds of ill health. The man chosen by the Conservative leadership to succeed him was Harold Macmillan, formerly Chancellor of the Exchequer. In foreign policy Macmillan wanted the best of both worlds: to bring Britain into a closer European partnership while restoring relations with the United States. His six and a half years as prime minister would show whether the two policies were compatible.

Macmillan's appointment was in some ways an ironic choice, for he shared much of the blame for the Suez debacle. In the early days of the crisis he had been a leading hawk in the Cabinet, pressing Eden for military action and urging collusion with Israel. In the autumn of 1956 his advice that "Ike would lie doggo"[1] had helped lull his colleagues into unjustified complacency. By November, alarmed at the prospect of American economic sanctions, he had reversed his position to become a leading dove, urging the Cabinet to withdraw the troops and trying to open up private contacts with Eisenhower.

Of all the possible leaders of the Conservative party Macmillan was the best suited to heal the transatlantic breach. Like Churchill, he was the offspring of one of the Anglo-American marriages at the turn of the century and felt close ties with his mother's homeland. He had established a warm relationship with Eisenhower during the war as the British minister resident in Eisenhower's Mediterranean Allied Force Headquarters in 1943–44. Grappling with the political complexities of dealing with the Allies, Eisenhower had come to trust Macmillan's "skill, his insight, his intelligence, his ability to handle complex issues and advise on them in a way in which Eisenhower had great confidence."[2]

The attempt to resume normal relations, which both countries wanted, began awkwardly. The new British ambassador, Sir Harold Caccia, was warned by Dulles not to visit the State Department too often but to come instead to see him at his home in Washington on weekends to avoid attracting attention. But a formal invitation was soon issued to Macmillan to meet Eisenhower in March. Tactfully the President proposed Bermuda, British territory, rather than Washington as the venue, to save Macmillan from appearing to come begging to America. The atmosphere at the conference was frank, with blunt exchanges on Suez. Macmillan told Eisenhower that "our Government and many of our people think that you were too hard on us—and rather let us down," a comment the President took up "rather sharply," Macmillan recorded in his diary.[3] But the exchanges helped clear the air. The two leaders reestablished top-level contacts between their governments, agreeing to write to each other regularly and informally as Roosevelt and Churchill had done during the war.

Evidence of the new rapport was an agreement reached at Bermuda that confounded Foreign Office skeptics about the Atlantic alliance and laid the basis of an Anglo-American nuclear relationship that has endured to the present day.

The British had never forgiven the Americans for reneging on the agreements reached in 1943–45 to develop nuclear weapons in partnership. The McMahon Act, which ruled out the exchange of nuclear secrets, rankled particularly with Churchill, leaving him, according to Sir Roger Makins, a senior diplomat of the period, in "a bitter frame of mind."[4] Denied access to American research, Britain had gone ahead with her own atomic program, successfully testing an atomic device in October 1952 and a hydrogen bomb in May 1957. With America and Russia, she was one of the world's three nuclear powers, but she had not yet devised a method for reliable delivery of the weapon apart from dropping them from increasingly vulnerable bombers.

Eisenhower felt that Britain had been treated "unfairly and unjustly."[5] He wanted to see her sharing with the United States in the nuclear deterrence strategy evolving within NATO. He told Churchill in 1953 that "he had, in 1945 and 1946, used all his influence to prevent the McMahon Act and urged that good faith between the Allies, not the legal interpretations of documents, was required." Shown a copy of Churchill's 1944 agreement with Roosevelt, "he seemed deeply impressed," Churchill noted. "He had never seen it before."[6] In 1954 Eisenhower had managed to achieve some minor amendments to the McMahon Act, despite a hostile Congress.

At Bermuda in March 1957 he went one step further. Agreement was reached there for sixty Thor missiles to be based in Britain. Thor was an intermediate-range missile, fitted with a nuclear warhead and capable of traveling 1,500 miles. The U.S. government wanted to deploy it within range of the Soviet Union, and Britain was the obvious place, given the long-standing arrangements for American bases. In 1952 Churchill and Truman had agreed that "the use of these bases in an emergency would be a matter for joint decision,"[7] but the Thor agreement replaced "joint decision" with joint control. Macmillan informed the Commons that "the rockets cannot be fired by any except British personnel, but the warhead will be in the control of the United States."[8] This "dual-key" system meant that each side held a veto over the use of the weapon, and each benefited from the deal. America had missiles within reach of Russia, and Britain shared in a missile deterrent long before she could develop her own. Bermuda, Eisenhower said, was "by far the most successful international conference that I had attended since the close of World War II."[9]

The nuclear relationship was further strengthened a few months later, this time as the direct result of a Soviet threat. On October 4, 1957, the Soviet Union launched the first man-made satellite, Sputnik, which circled the earth, passing across the United States as it did so. It came as little surprise to American experts who were preparing a similar satellite launch, but the reaction of the American public and press bordered on the hysterical, once the scale of the achievement had sunk in. Communist Russia, supposedly their technological inferior, had beaten them into space with a satellite reportedly eight times the weight of America's—a success followed within weeks by an even larger satellite carrying a live dog.

The military implications were alarming. In the past America, protected by vast oceans to the east and west, had felt almost invulnerable to direct attack. The air age and even the development of the atomic bomb did not seem to threaten the United States directly in the way it did countries in Europe. Russia had been slow to develop an intercontinental bomber with a range equivalent to that of the American B-52. But with the launch of Sputnik the Soviet Union proved it had a missile powerful enough to reach the United States in only thirty minutes. The Pentagon would not be ready to deploy its first Inter-Continental Ballistic Missiles (ICBMs), able to strike Russia directly from the United States, until the early 1960s. The Soviet leader Nikita Khrushchev crowed that the American B-52 belonged in a museum. Edward Teller, father of the U.S. H-bomb project, called Sputnik a greater defeat for the United States than Pearl Harbor.[10]

Eisenhower rode out the storm. He used his authority as a former military supreme commander to ward off demands to put the country on a panic alert. Instead he seized the opportunity to further strengthen the nuclear relationship with Britain. It was no longer just because he wanted to right a perceived wrong, but because he needed allies as never before and only Britain had a nuclear capability. Within three weeks of the launch of Sputnik Macmillan was invited to Washington, and on October 24, 1957, the British saw restored to them the nuclear cooperation they had been denied for so long. Special Anglo-American committees were set up to handle collaboration on nuclear weapons, and Eisenhower promised to fight for further amendments to the McMahon Act in Congress. In July 1958 those revisions duly became law, and the British and U.S. governments signed a new agreement permitting a much fuller exchange of nuclear information, plant and materials. A further accord the following May allowed Britain to acquire nuclear weapons or nuclear weapon parts from the United States and to exchange nuclear fuels: British plutonium for American uranium. What Britain saw as the wrongs of 1945 had at last been righted.

The rapprochement between Britain and the United States was reinforced in the Middle East. Eisenhower was anxious to limit the damage caused to Western interests by Suez. He told congressional leaders in January 1957 that "the existing vacuum in the Middle East must be filled by the United States before it is filled by Russia."[11] He later spelled out the Eisenhower Doctrine, which called for economic and military aid to nations in the area that were threatened by "International Communism." But it was Arab nationalism, rather than Khrushchev's maneuvering, that was the real threat. Early in 1958 Egypt and Syria merged to form the United Arab Republic. In July, as enthusiasm for Nasser swept the Arab world, the Iraqi monarchy and its government, led by Nuri Said, Britain's leading ally in the region, were toppled in a bloody coup and Nuri's body was dragged naked through the streets of Baghdad to the delight of the mob. Fearful of a similar fate, the government of Lebanon, racked by internal strife, called on America for help, and King Hussein of Jordan, who had been obliged to expel British forces from his country in 1956, appealed to Britain to come back and give assistance.

Eisenhower acted swiftly. He told Macmillan that U.S. marines were going into Lebanon. "You are doing a Suez on me," Macmillan protested.[12] Supported by the Sixth Fleet, ten thousand U.S. marines landed in Lebanon, to a friendly welcome from sunbathers on the beaches. Eisenhower did not want to give the impression of collusion between Britain and America, but when British paratroops flew into Jordan, American transports ferried in supplies while the Royal Navy made available its bases in Cyprus for U.S. ships supporting the Lebanon operation. Khrushchev protested vociferously, doing his best to discredit the interventions in the United Nations. What mattered more to Britain was that Nasser had been rebuffed, and less than two years after Suez she and America were again collaborating closely in the Middle East. At the end of the operation Eisenhower told Macmillan that they could "take special satisfaction in the complete understanding and special co-operation which was evident between our two governments in these undertakings." The Prime Minister replied that "so long as your country and mine continue to act together in spirit and in deed, as we have over the last months, I am sure we can deal successfully with any eventuality."[13]

The restoration of the relationship with America could not disguise the fact that Britain was now a poor relation, in straitened circumstances. It was most strikingly revealed in her inability to keep up with the superpowers in the arms race. Like the United States, she had adopted nuclear deterrence as the main plank of national defense, but, unlike America, she had no effective modern method of delivering the bomb. The Americans relied on their B-52 bomber force, which, in spite of Khrushchev's scorn, remained unrivaled. Britain's much smaller V-bomber force was only coming into service in 1957–58, just as the dawn of the missile age made airborne deterrence obsolescent. Britain's reaction was to try to develop a nuclear missile of her own, Blue Streak.

Blue Streak was not as independent as was claimed. It relied on American technology for its rocket engine and guidance system, but even so, by 1960 it had become clear that the missile was inadequate. The rocket was propelled by liquid fuel and took thirty minutes to prepare for launching. It operated from fixed sites and would therefore be vulnerable, like Thor, to a Soviet first strike. In February 1960 the British Cabinet's Defence Committee decided in principle that, rather than spend another £600 million on top of the £65 million already spent, it would scrap the missile. However, the final verdict would depend on whether the United States offered to help Britain acquire an alternative.

In Washington at the end of March 1960 Macmillan and Eisenhower agreed on a substitute, the new U.S. Skybolt missile. Skybolt, which was still in the development stage, was an aircraft-launched missile and therefore particularly attractive to Britain because it could prolong the life of the V-bomber force. A jubilant Macmillan noted in his diary: "This allows us to abandon Blue Streak . . . without damage to our prospects of maintaining—in the late 60s and early 70s—our *independent* nuclear deterrent."[14] The terms agreed were generous. Only the cost of the missiles she ordered would have to be met by Britain, with no contribution being made toward the research and development costs of the whole project. But there was a quid pro quo. In return for Skybolt Macmillan secretly agreed that U.S. submarines, armed with the new Polaris missiles, would be offered the use of Holy Loch on the Clyde in Scotland as their forward base. Like the Thor deal, Holy Loch would allow the United States to strike at the Soviet Union from close range. Unlike Thor, however, these missiles were to be solely under U.S. control, and when, in November, Macmillan announced details of the Polaris base he ran into a storm of criticism.

During 1960 the "ban the bomb" movement had taken a firm hold on the British Labour party. The marches of the Campaign for Nuclear Disarmament (CND), Britain's abandonment of Blue Streak and then the decision to buy Skybolt from America provoked a passionate debate about whether Britain should stay in the nuclear "club." In April 1960 polls indicated that a third of the country favored unilateral disarmament—in other words, that Britain should abandon the Bomb. Macmillan's talk of an "independent nuclear deterrent" seemed fanciful in view of Britain's reliance on American missiles. Labour MP Denis Healey called nuclear independence "the virility symbol of the atomic age . . . Britain and France both clutched at it in the shock of having their military impotence exposed at Suez."[15]

When on November 1, 1960, Macmillan announced in the Commons that the Americans would be given a base in Britain for the world's most advanced nuclear weapon, the protests from disarmers and Scottish nationalists were strident. John Rankin, a Labour MP from Glasgow, claimed that "we are not really an ally of the United States; we are a satellite. We live on an expendable American base."[16] Macmillan insisted that Holy Loch would be covered by an extension of the basing agreement reached in 1951–52 between Churchill and Truman. To avoid embarrassing the Americans, however, Macmillan was careful to speak only of

> my understanding of the position reached. This is that we can be satisfied that the United States Government will not use these missiles anywhere in the world without the fullest possible previous consultation with us and our allies. I use the words "fullest possible" consultation because consultation might obviously be impossible in circumstances of a sudden, surprise attack upon the West. We would, indeed, not wish to insist on prior consultation in such circumstances, because it is the absolute certainty of retaliation which deters aggression.[17]

The Skybolt–Holy Loch arrangement was inspired by the same mixture of sentiment and self-interest as the wartime "destroyers for bases" deal of 1940. It cemented the nuclear relationship that Eisenhower and Macmillan had created, one enjoyed by no other ally of the United States. Britain, unable to afford to remain a member of the nuclear club on her own account, had persuaded America to pay the subscription for her. Macmillan argued that this strengthened deterrence; his critics claimed that he was keeping Britain in the bull's-eye of a Soviet attack.

Britain's three Conservative prime ministers in the 1950s all believed profoundly in the American alliance as the foundation of Britain's security, but each adopted a different approach toward it. Churchill, nostalgic for his wartime partnership with Roosevelt, tended to exaggerate Anglo-American harmony. Eden overestimated Britain's independent power and paid the price at Suez. Macmillan sought the middle ground. Unlike Eden, he was assiduous in consulting the Americans, but he was still ready to take an independent line when British interests dictated. Macmillan, no less than Eden, refused to be a lackey of Washington, but believed the lesson of Suez was clear: British initiatives had to be based on transatlantic trust. With trust restored, Macmillan tried, like his two predecessors, to use British influence to thaw the cold war.

The urgency of the task was apparent. Late in 1958 a new crisis had blown up between the superpowers over the status of Berlin, a divided and occupied city since the end of World War II. Khrushchev, in effect, was insisting that Berlin be incorporated into East Germany, a demand that Eisenhower was determined to reject. Macmillan agreed, anxious to show solidarity with the United States, but he feared that the crisis could escalate into uncontrollable confrontation. He decided to accept a long-standing Russian invitation to visit Moscow. Eisenhower, according to his staff secretary general, Andrew Goodpaster, was "concerned that Macmillan might be led into suggesting . . . concessions that went beyond what we were prepared to agree to."[18]

In February 1959, theatrically adorned with a white fur hat, Macmillan arrived in Moscow, the first Western head of government to go there since the end of the war. The panache with which Macmillan conducted himself helped to create worldwide interest, as did his appearance on Russian television and photographs of him arm in arm with Russian milkmaids. The talks were tough, and at one point Khrushchev snubbed Macmillan publicly by saying he could not accompany the British visitors to Kiev because he was having a tooth filled. Nevertheless, Macmillan persuaded the Russians to show some flexibility. Khrushchev had set a six-month deadline for settling the Berlin crisis. This he now soft-pedaled, accepting instead a meeting of foreign ministers as the precursor to a full-dress summit. Eisenhower was reluctant to take part in a summit meeting until the ground had been thoroughly prepared, but Macmillan kept up the pressure and in July the President agreed with Khrushchev to a joint exchange of visits to Washington and Moscow. At Camp David in September 1959 the two superpower leaders agreed in a private talk that if Khrushchev would publicly drop the deadline for an agreement on Berlin, Eisenhower would consent to a Big Four summit in Paris in May 1960 involving America, Russia, Britain and France.

Fifteen days before the Paris summit was due to begin an American high-altitude U-2 reconnaissance plane was shot down over

Russia. Since July 1956 there had been regular spy flights, each approved by the President. When Gary Powers's U-2 was shot down, the Eisenhower administration at first issued a prepared cover story about a weather research aircraft that had gone astray. To its embarrassment the Soviet authorities then put on display the wreckage of the U-2 and paraded its pilot before the world's press. Khrushchev gave Eisenhower the opportunity to blame the Pentagon for the incident, but the President refused to pass the buck, publicly defending the flights as essential to U.S. security, though adding that there would be no more of them.

Khrushchev arrived in Paris in a truculent mood. He had antagonized hawks in the Kremlin by his willingness to meet Eisenhower and was embarrassed by the U-2 incident, which seemed to confirm their suspicions about America's intentions. He demanded American apologies and the punishment of those responsible, warning that the summit would have to be postponed until the atmosphere had cleared. With Eisenhower dismissing any idea "that I'm going to crawl on my knees to Khrushchev,"[19] the summit broke up on May 16, 1960, without any formal sessions being convened.

Macmillan remained publicly loyal, driving around Paris in an open car with the President, ostensibly sight-seeing, in reality displaying Anglo-American solidarity. Yet Sir Philip de Zulueta, the Prime Minister's private secretary, had "never seen Harold Macmillan so depressed,"[20] and in the Foreign Office there was "amazement that the United States had not found a face-saving way out." Khrushchev, it was believed, "would have accepted almost any excuse. He even came to the British delegation in Paris to plead with the British to intervene with the U.S. and find some way out."[21]

Though publicly unabashed, Eisenhower, too, was shaken by the collapse of the summit. The last months of his presidency were pervaded by a sense of regret and lost opportunity. On November 10, 1960, Macmillan wrote to Eisenhower recalling almost two decades of partnership. "I can only assure you that I will try my best to keep our governments and our two countries on the same course. But," he predicted dolefully, "I cannot of course ever hope to have anything to replace the sort of relations that we have had."[22] It was a sad end to a long and distinguished partnership.

"Let the word go forth from this time and place, to friend and foe alike, that the torch has been passed to a new generation of Americans, born in this century, tempered by war, disciplined by a hard and bitter peace. . . ."[23] John F. Kennedy's words at his inauguration, with their implication that the older generation's days were over, gnawed at Macmillan. He had been born in the nineteenth century, Kennedy in the twentieth. There was a gap of twenty-three years between them, and Kennedy was only forty-three. How could Macmillan reproduce, for the benefit of Britain and the Western Alliance, the easy partnership he had enjoyed with Eisenhower, his old comrade-in-arms? He had known Kennedy's father, American ambassador to Britain from 1938 to 1940, as an appeaser and a defeatist. Macmillan, a prominent critic of Munich, could not easily forgive him. And the Kennedys were Catholics, of Irish descent, who had made their way in Boston Democratic politics, where to be anti-British was a badge of political respectability. The attractive new leader, with his polished Harvard manner, his photogenic wife and children, and an entourage said to contain the best and the brightest from business and the universities, was eager to break through a New Frontier into the modern age. According to his private secretary, Sir Philip de Zulueta, Macmillan "was afraid that he might be overtaken by this brilliant young man of a different generation and that he would not be relevant to Kennedy."[24]

The relationship turned out better than Macmillan expected. Kennedy had lived in Britain during his father's ambassadorship and was intrigued by the patrician world of British high politics. He liked Macmillan's style, the deceptive "Victorian languor" that concealed a shrewd, subtle politician.[25] He admired Macmillan's obvious commitment to arms control and to greater social justice. For his part Macmillan was flattered by Kennedy's charm and impressed by his sense of history. Both men shared a sharp, ironic sense of humor. After early disagreements over Kennedy's confrontational reaction to Soviet intransigence on Berlin and to Communist insurgency in Laos, there developed, according to the President's aide the historian Arthur Schlesinger, "Kennedy's closest personal relationship with a foreign leader."[26]

The turning point came after Kennedy's first meeting with Khrushchev in Vienna in June 1961. Now that Eisenhower had broken the ice, America no longer needed Britain to point the way to Moscow. Macmillan was unhappy about this development, particularly since the young President might prove no match for his wily and experienced opponent. When Kennedy and Khrushchev met, they disagreed on almost every world issue, particularly Berlin. "I want peace," said Khrushchev, "but, if you want war, that is your problem." Kennedy gave as good as he got: "It is you, and not I, who wants to force a change."[27] But the President was shaken by Khrushchev's intransigence. There seemed to be no meeting of minds, no hint of progress. Secretary of State Dean Rusk recalls that Kennedy was "disturbed that Mr. Khrushchev thought he could intimidate this new young President of the United States."[28]

Next stop after Vienna was Paris. Kennedy could not speak French, unlike his glamorous wife, Jacqueline, who stole the show, captivating even the stony heart of Charles de Gaulle, the French president. With a touch of bitter wit, Kennedy announced himself at a press luncheon as "the man who accompanied Jacqueline Kennedy to Paris."[29] When they arrived in London, their last European stop before returning home, the President was in low spirits and suffering acute pain from his weak back. He was under attack from the world's press as a young and callow leader who had bungled the Bay of Pigs invasion of Cuba in April and had now been worsted by Khrushchev in Vienna. The "Jackie cult" had invaded England as well. People seemed more impressed with the First Lady than with the President. The Lord Chamberlain, in those days Britain's official censor, prohibited a satirical revue from including a sketch in which an actress portraying Mrs. Kennedy sang:

> *"While Jack fumbles with Russia, I use all my guile,*
> *So the press and public won't guess for a while,*
> *He is just like Ike dressed up Madison Avenue style."*[30]

On June 5, 1961, tired and tense, Kennedy arrived at 10 Downing Street. Macmillan immediately saw that a formal conference, flanked by advisers, was inappropriate. With his habitual weary fling of the hand he said, "Let's not have a meeting—the Foreign Office and all that. Why not have a peaceful drink and chat by ourselves?"[31] Gratefully Kennedy sat back and poured out his impressions of Khrushchev. He was not seeking advice on policy: America had long since followed its own road. He needed help on psychology, baffled at how to deal with a man who seemed unwilling to negotiate about anything. Macmillan spoke the same language, offering wisdom and sympathy, sharing confidences, helping Kennedy feel less alone in the burdens of world leadership. In the words of Macmillan's private secretary, the relationship became as "uncle to nephew, or something like that."[32]

The new friendship was reinforced by Macmillan's choice of British ambassador to succeed Sir Harold Caccia. One of Kennedy's

oldest British friends, David Ormsby Gore was a minister of state
at the Foreign Office. Kennedy let Macmillan know that he was
"emphatic for David Gore,"[33] and an unconventional but inspired
appointment followed. Ormsby Gore was not a career diplomat but
was of the same generation as Kennedy and operated on the President's wavelength. Soon he became almost a White House insider,
mixing easily with the Kennedy clan and their staff, as ready to play
touch football on Cape Cod as to discuss high policy in Washington.

In 1961 Britain therefore had a prime minister and an ambassador
who got on exceptionally well with President Kennedy. Macmillan
hoped that these personal relationships could help advance the goals
of British foreign policy. He had a clear idea of what this should be.
There were three key elements. Britain should, first, maintain a
special relationship with the United States, working for agreement
on policy by using her influence and experience. She should also
have an independent power base, an entitlement to the top table of
world affairs, based on the possession of nuclear weapons. And lastly
she should start to play a full part in the affairs of Europe by joining
the European Economic Community. These three ambitions, while
in theory compatible, came into conflict in practice, and each, in its
different way, was blighted in the few months between the autumn
of 1962 and the spring of 1963.

First to be tested was the special relationship, on which Macmillan
set so much store. In 1962 Khrushchev attempted to place nuclear
missiles in Cuba, ninety miles from the United States. This led to
a crisis that brought the United States and Russia nearer to nuclear
war than ever before or since.

From the moment he gained power in Cuba in 1959 Fidel Castro
had distanced himself from the United States, diminishing American economic domination and seizing American assets. Washington's growing enmity forced Castro into complete dependence on
the Soviet bloc. The United States saw his actions as a threat to the
Pax Americana in Central America. Following the example of Eisenhower's coup against a leftist regime in Guatemala in 1954, the
CIA proposed to the newly elected President Kennedy that a similar
strike against Cuba should be attempted. Eisenhower had already
agreed and a skeptical Kennedy gave his approval, but the subsequent Bay of Pigs invasion by Cuban exiles, supported by the CIA,
ended in disaster. Cubans stayed loyal to Castro, his forces hit back
hard with their Russian equipment, and the invaders were pinned
down on the beaches and forced to surrender. Wryly Kennedy

observed that under parliamentary government in Britain he would have been obliged to resign, whereas in America failure had enhanced his charm. Shown a poll indicating 82 percent backing for his administration, he quipped: "It's just like Eisenhower. The worse I do, the more popular I get."[34]

But Kennedy paid a price for the Bay of Pigs fiasco when, in the following year, Khrushchev decided to exploit Russia's newly dominant position in Cuba. The Soviet Union, in spite of Khrushchev's boasts in 1957 about a missile gap, had fallen behind in the nuclear arms race. The United States was deploying the new intercontinental Minuteman missiles, and already had ground-to-air missiles in Britain and, close to the Russian border, in Turkey. Khrushchev decided to counter these threats by installing Russian missiles in Cuba. It was a gambler's throw that, if successful, would humiliate President Kennedy, provide the missile advantage Khrushchev was seeking, and give him a dramatic propaganda victory over the West.

American U-2 spy planes detected the construction work taking place on Cuba. On October 16 the photographic intelligence was put before the President. All the missiles had not yet arrived, but it was obvious that if the United States was to react, it must do so fast. Amid deepest secrecy Kennedy convened a special crisis-management committee known as ExCom. It agreed that the United States could not accept Soviet missiles ninety miles off the coast of Florida. The options available were narrowed down to two. Most of the Joint Chiefs of Staff favored an air strike to destroy the missile sites, which risked escalating the crisis and might not be successful. Kennedy, dubious of military advice after the failure of the Bay of Pigs, chose the alternative proposal. On Saturday afternoon, October 20, he decided to blockade rather than bomb Cuba, a choice that would defer an immediate confrontation and give the Soviets time to retreat.

The crisis was kept secret. No allies were consulted or informed, so anxious was Kennedy not to give Russia prior warning of his plans. At lunchtime on Sunday, his decision already made, he summoned his friend Ormsby Gore, the British ambassador, to the White House. He explained the situation and outlined the two options that had been presented to him at ExCom, asking Gore which he favored. The ambassador, to Kennedy's satisfaction, plumped for the blockade. That evening Kennedy spoke to Macmillan in London and explained the decision and the background. On the following Monday, October 22, the crisis was publicly revealed

OVER THE GARDEN WALL

The British magazine Punch *voices British doubts early in the Cuban missile crisis of October 1962.
Why should Kennedy be so exercised about Cuba when Khrushchev's Russia has
long been overshadowed by U.S. bases?*

to the American people by television. The United States, the President announced, was imposing "a strict quarantine on all offensive military equipment under shipment to Cuba." Any nuclear missile launched from Cuba against any country in the Western Hemisphere would be regarded as a direct attack "by the Soviet Union on the United States, requiring a full, retaliatory response upon the Soviet Union."[35]

The reaction in London to Kennedy's announcement was not initially enthusiastic. Since 1959 Britain had disputed America's interpretation of the threat posed by Castro's Cuba, and had refused to bow to American pressure to cut off trade. In October 1962 Macmillan initially doubted whether the blockade was wise, unlike de Gaulle, who refused to look at the photographic evidence for the missile buildup, saying that America's word was good enough for him. In the British Parliament and in the press there were suspicions that the crisis was not genuine but was another machination against Castro. It was asked why Kennedy had not resorted to the United Nations, as the Americans had been so keen to do over Suez, and it was even suggested by some on the left of the Labour party that Kennedy, with congressional elections imminent, was "risking blowing the world to hell in order to sweep a few Democrats into office."[36] Ormsby Gore was concerned at the skepticism being shown in Britain, and he persuaded Kennedy to release the photographic evidence. Together the two men selected photographs that looked most convincing to the nonexpert eye, and when these were published the British press changed its tune.

Throughout the crisis Kennedy kept in close touch with Macmillan, speaking to him by telephone every evening. On some days there were several conversations. Kennedy brought Macmillan up to date on events and listened to his views. He wanted, according to George Ball, under secretary of state, to maintain the unity of the West by keeping in close touch with Britain, but "also wanted the sense of reassurance that he got from talking to an old experienced political leader for whom he had great respect."[37] It was the same need that Macmillan had satisfied after Vienna in June 1961. But Britain was not consulted so much as informed about American policy. "We did not ask London for guidance or advice," explained Secretary of State Dean Rusk, "because this was an issue primarily between ourselves and the Russians."[38] The nearest Britain came to wielding any direct influence was the continual presence of Ormsby Gore at crisis meetings. He was responsible for persuading the President to reduce the area of the blockade from eight hundred to five hundred miles to allow Khrushchev more time to decide how to respond.

In a state of apprehension bordering on terror, the world waited to see what effect Kennedy's ultimatum to Khrushchev would have. The news that the ships steaming toward the quarantine zone had turned back, with missiles clearly visible on their decks, was greeted with universal relief. On October 28 Khrushchev announced that the Soviet Union would withdraw all missile bases from Cuba. In return, Moscow received an assurance that the United States would not again try to invade Cuba and that Jupiter missiles in Turkey, coming to the end of their natural life, would be withdrawn. The crisis had ended in triumph for the President.

Macmillan, in the House of Commons, insisted, "It is not true that we in this country played an inactive role in this great trial of strength."[39] But the reality was obvious. The world had been on the brink of disaster, and Britain, like everyone else, had been entirely dependent on the conduct of the Big Two. The pretension that her membership of the nuclear club gave her any special influence had been shown to be a sham. Russia and America had been eyeball to eyeball, with Britain an almost impotent observer.

The euphoria in Washington over the successful outcome of the Cuba crisis was partly responsible for a dramatic confrontation between Britain and America in the last weeks of 1962. This was over Britain's possession of her own nuclear deterrent, the second element in Macmillan's strategy. Eisenhower's decision in March 1960 to offer Britain the air-to-ground missile Skybolt as her independent nuclear deterrent had not been universally approved in Washington. There was a powerful lobby inside the State Department which believed dogmatically that Britain should not be a nuclear power and that America was doing itself a disservice by providing the missile. The "theologians," as they became known, were convinced that America should pay more attention to France and West Germany, both now revived and united within the European Community. America's unique nuclear partnership with Britain was, they believed, a major obstacle to good transatlantic relations at a time when France had just entered the nuclear club and West Germany was chafing at its exclusion. "We must try to eliminate the privileged British status," urged two of the "theologians," Henry Owen and Henry Rowen, in April 1961. "In matters nuclear, the road to Paris may well be through London."[40] In the Pentagon there were others who wanted to "denuclearize" Britain for different reasons. They believed that the world would be safer if only Russia and America had the bomb. Nuclear proliferation should be prevented. In June 1962 Kennedy's defense secretary, Robert McNamara, publicly criticized "limited nuclear capacities operating independently" as "dangerous, expensive, prone to obsolescence, and lacking in credibility as a deterrent."[41]

The Europeanists in the State Department proposed an alternative to the British unilateral nuclear deterrent in the form of a Multilateral Force (MLF). This would be a naval force, crewed by members of all the NATO countries and carrying nuclear weapons. The United States would retain control over the actual decision to fire a nuclear missile, but everyone, particularly the Germans, would feel more involved. It seems in retrospect a slightly absurd idea, a transparently political device, which offered no substantial role to its non-American participants.

Macmillan would have none of it. Britain's nuclear capability was, he believed, an insurance policy against America failing to honor its nuclear guarantee of Europe. Now that the Soviets could strike directly at the United States, making any American nuclear defense of Europe suicidal, this seemed a real possibility. He also argued, despite the evidence of the Cuban crisis, that membership in the nuclear club would give Britain a voice in world affairs that she would otherwise be denied. Suggestions by McNamara and others that America's allies should not have their own nuclear weapons were therefore deeply embarrassing to Macmillan. Pressed by Labour critics in the Commons in June 1962 as to whether Britain's nuclear forces were truly independent, he insisted that "these forces, although we with our allies make joint plans, are constitutionally under the sovereignty of the Government of the day. That is the point, and in that sense they are independent."[42] Labour was not impressed, particularly since Britain's nuclear force would soon be American missiles, not British bombers, but for many Tories Britain's "independent nuclear deterrent" had become an article of patriotic faith—a symbol that she still remained a great power.

All might have been well had Skybolt proved a success. When it was offered to Britain by Eisenhower in 1960 it was in the development stage. The U.S. Air Force was supporting it to keep the nuclear deterrent in its hands rather than see it transferred to the U.S. Navy with its new submarine-launched Polaris missiles. But by 1962 Skybolt was behind schedule. The tests were proving unsatisfactory, and it failed the new criteria of "cost-effectiveness" introduced by McNamara at the Pentagon. He saw it as a candidate for cancellation, but was reluctant to come clean to the British government for fear that premature publicity would allow Skybolt's sup-

porters in Congress to frustrate his plans. Hints were dropped to the
British that all was not well, but Whitehall assumed that the U.S.
Air Force and its industrial allies would be a sufficiently powerful
lobby to safeguard Skybolt. There was little understanding of Pentagon politics or the impact of McNamara's determination to cut
unnecessary costs. Anyway, it was argued, Kennedy had assured
Macmillan that there would be "no publicity before decision and no
decisions before consultation" with Britain.[43]

But by the time McNamara visited London for talks on December
11, 1962, the likelihood of cancellation was being openly discussed
in the British and American press. MacNamara, at an airport press
conference on his arrival, blithely announced that Skybolt's five
tests had all ended in failure and went on to inform the British
government of the proposed cancellation. The British minister of
defence, Peter Thorneycroft, was "furious with this decision," according to Paul Nitze who accompanied McNamara. The reaction,
Nitze said, was "stronger than expected," though he had not exactly
anticipated "hugs and kisses from the British."[44]

Secretary of State Dean Rusk was taken aback by the furor in
Britain. "If I may say, with a smile, I think it is possible that the
surprise in London was somewhat exaggerated as part of the bargaining position in order to get further nuclear cooperation from the
United States."[45] But if Whitehall was at fault for having failed to
realize that Skybolt was in jeopardy, Kennedy's men seemed equally
incapable of grasping how much Macmillan had invested politically
in Skybolt. The Cuban crisis was behind them, and in their bullish
confidence about having saved the world, they cared little for what
seemed to be the minor details of an ally's defense spending. In the
last weeks of 1962, with their eyes on other issues, they allowed a
crisis in the Alliance to develop unchecked.

An Anglo-American summit had been arranged at Nassau, in the
Bahamas, for the week before Christmas. This now became the
venue for a showdown on the future of the nuclear "special relationship." Macmillan arrived tired and depressed. Anti-American sentiment was running high in London and, just before his departure,
more than one hundred Conservative MPs had signed a motion
calling on him to safeguard their deterrent. Particularly striking was
the reaction to a speech by Dean Acheson, the former secretary of
state, on December 5, in which he commented that "Great Britain
has lost an Empire and has not yet found a role. The attempt to play
a separate power role—that is, a role apart from Europe, a role based

on a 'special relationship' with the United States, a role based on being the head of a 'Commonwealth' which has no political structure, or unity, or strength . . . this role is about to be played out."[46] Anger in Britain was intense. Acheson had touched a raw nerve. Macmillan let it be known publicly that in appearing "to denigrate the resolution and will of Britain and the British people, Mr. Acheson has fallen into an error which has been made by quite a lot of people in the course of the last four hundred years, including Philip of Spain, Louis XIV, Napoleon, the Kaiser and Hitler."[47]

Many in London suspected that the speech had been inspired by the White House, but in fact Kennedy moved quickly to distance himself from Acheson. With the full authority of the President, White House aide McGeorge Bundy instructed the State Department to brief the press that "US-UK relations are not based only on a power calculus, but also on deep community of purpose and long practice of close cooperation. Examples are legion. . . . 'Special relationship' may not be a perfect phrase, but sneers at Anglo-American reality would be equally foolish."[48]

But the State Department "theologians" were now ready to sever

"ER, COULD I BE THE HIND LEGS, PLEASE?"

British cartoonist Vicky, in the Evening Standard, *December 6, 1962.*

the relationship for good. George Ball, who, as Rusk's deputy, headed the State Department delegation at Nassau, believed that the cancellation of Skybolt offered an opportunity to terminate the nuclear alliance with Britain. He was against providing Polaris as an alternative. The advantage of Skybolt was that it would not last very long, but Polaris was another matter. "It seemed to me we should avoid doing anything that would extend Britain's nuclear deterrent for another generation. . . . I was very determined to have the British begin to get out of the feeling that they were a great power because they had an Empire, which they no longer had, and they had a nuclear weapon which the others didn't have, and they had a relationship with the United States which nobody else had. This seemed to me not very healthy even from the British point of view."[49] But Macmillan still had no time for a mixed NATO multilateral force. He asked Ball disdainfully, "You don't expect our chaps to share their grog with Turks, do you?"[50] The mood in the British camp at Nassau, according to veteran journalist Henry Brandon, writing soon afterward, was "resentment and suspicion of American intentions such as I have never experienced in all the Anglo-American conferences I have covered over the past twenty years."[51]

Belatedly Kennedy grasped what was at stake for Macmillan. On the flight to Nassau he talked at length to the British ambassador, Ormsby Gore, and studied the State Department's briefing book compiled by its British desk. This warned that "the special Anglo-American relationship is threatened as it has not been since Suez by the cancellation of Skybolt. . . . The Prime Minister needs a successful meeting for . . . political survival."[52] At Nassau Kennedy offered Britain various choices. She could develop Skybolt herself on generous terms. Macmillan demurred. The missile was no longer credible, he told Kennedy. After all the public comment "the virginity of the lady must now be regarded as doubtful."[53] The offer of an alternative American air-to-ground missile was also rejected: How, Macmillan asked, could be go back to the House of Commons and explain that Britain's much vaunted independent deterrent would now be called Hound Dog? Nor was the Prime Minister interested in an Anglo-American joint study to examine future options. There was only one thing he would accept, and that was Polaris.

The Macmillan who argued Britain's case at Nassau was a man President Kennedy had not seen before. His government was unpopular. It had just lost two by-elections, and was being mocked for its lack of influence over Cuba and the absurdity of its claim to own a nuclear deterrent that was at the mercy of the United States. He spoke with the skill and determination of a politician in mortal danger, convinced that his survival depended on the success of the conference. Movingly he outlined the vicissitudes of the nuclear relationship since the war, emphasizing that Britain had kept her side of the agreements. He reminded Kennedy of the promises made by Roosevelt to Churchill, of the McMahon Act and of the bargain struck in 1960 with Eisenhower: Skybolt in return for Holy Loch. He hinted that if nothing was done to replace Skybolt there would be a grave anti-American backlash in Britain with the possibility of a neutralist government coming to power. In his own words he "had to pull out all the stops."[54] It was a formidable performance, and by the end of the oration, according to de Zulueta, "there wasn't a dry eye in the house, including mine . . . I think it swung the day."[55]

Reluctantly Kennedy accepted that only Polaris would satisfy the British, but responding to those like Ball who wanted to use the Skybolt crisis to bolster the MLF, he tried to mesh the Polaris deal into that policy. The final agreement reached at Nassau on December 21, 1962, was flexible but confusing. It offered Britain Polaris, but committed the weapon in principle to "a NATO multilateral force" while reserving the right of the British government to operate independently whenever it "may decide that supreme national interests are at stake."[56] Macmillan was delighted. He had obtained a nuclear deterrent superior to Skybolt, which, being launched by submarine instead of bomber, would be far less vulnerable. He had also acquired it on favorable terms, with Britain obliged to make only a small contribution to research and development in addition to the price of each missile. A damaging clash with America had been avoided, and Britain could remain in the nuclear club. There was, however, as the European "theologians" in the State Department anticipated, a price to pay. For the Polaris deal helped to undermine the third pillar of Macmillan's foreign policy—Britain's bid to enter the EEC.

In January 1958 France, West Germany, Italy, Belgium, the Netherlands and Luxembourg had formed themselves into the European Community. The British government remained aloof, in line with the policy it had adopted toward the Schuman Plan of 1950 and the Messina conference of 1955. It believed that Britain's economic future lay with the Commonwealth and the countries of the Sterling Area, and regarded the integration of Western Europe mainly as a way of reconciling France and Germany and thus

preventing a third European war. But by 1960 Germany was producing nearly a fifth of the world's manufacturing output, and her
economic miracle was transforming not just German society but
also those of her European neighbors as wealth began to flow freely
across reduced tariff barriers. The British had been wrong-footed.
They assumed that postwar prosperity would depend on rising
prices for the world's raw materials, many of which they still controlled. They did not expect the rejuvenation of continental Europe,
based on industries that started afresh after 1945. Germany, many
Britons observed sourly, had lost the war but was winning the peace.
And Britain, the German leader Konrad Adenauer joked in 1958,
was like "a rich man who has lost all his property but does not realise
it."[57]

Macmillan did realize what was happening. A convinced Euro-
peanist, by 1960 he could see compelling economic reasons for
Britain joining the EEC, even though the Labour party was opposed
and many Conservatives were distinctly unenthusiastic about the
Community's long-term political objective of a united Europe. Yet
Macmillan, like his predecessors Churchill and Eden, believed that
Britain was not irreducibly European, that she must maintain her
special links with the Commonwealth, the Sterling Area and the
United States. In April 1961 Macmillan received an assurance from
the Kennedy administration, in line with long-standing American
policy, that "relations between the United States and the United
Kingdom would be strengthened, not weakened, if the UK moved
toward membership."[58] The following August Macmillan formally
applied for Britain to join.

By December 1962 the negotiations for British membership of the
EEC were making progress, particularly on the special position to
be given to Britain's trading partners in the Commonwealth. There
were still substantial issues to be resolved and informed diplomats
differed in their predictions of the likely outcome. But then the
French President Charles de Gaulle made his position brutally clear.
At a meeting at Rambouillet in mid-December, just before the Nassau conference, he told Macmillan that he did not consider Britain
to be European and strongly implied that he would veto her application to join the Community. Fearful that this information would
strengthen the hand of those in Washington who wanted to end
Britain's special nuclear relationship with the United States, Macmillan did not reveal the news to Kennedy at Nassau.

De Gaulle's motives were no mystery. He did not want a rival power usurping France's leadership of the EEC. As one French minister put it to his British counterpart: "It's very simple, my dear chap. At present in the Six there are five hens and one cock. If you join, with the other countries, there will be perhaps seven or eight hens. But there will be *two* cocks. Well—that's not so pleasant."[59]

There was also a deeper reason for de Gaulle's opposition—his antipathy to the Anglo-American axis dating back to World War II. As leader of the Free French forces, he had been consistently snubbed by Roosevelt, who had no time for France and her imperial pretensions. For as long as possible FDR had blocked the Free French claim to be the provisional government of France and to share in the occupation of Germany. Although the British, particularly Eden, interceded where they could for France, Churchill generally sided with the Americans. In his memoirs de Gaulle recalled one bitter row on the eve of the D-Day landings, when Churchill finally exploded: "This is something you ought to know: each time we have to choose between Europe and the open sea, we shall always choose the open sea. Each time I have to choose between you and Roosevelt, I shall always choose Roosevelt."[60]

These were words de Gaulle did not forget when he regained office in 1958. Since the war France had seen a succession of weak ministries, unable to cope with economic stagnation and with the bitter wars in Indochina and Algeria. De Gaulle produced a new constitution, which gave the President much greater power. He ended the Algerian conflict by granting the country independence and set about rebuilding France's position in Europe. This meant reducing America's influence. Americans, he believed, had not provided adequate help during France's colonial crises, and their strategic guarantee was dubious in the post-Sputnik era of *mutual* assured destruction. Britain's close relationship with the United States meant, in France's view, that she would be a Trojan horse in the EEC, guaranteeing continued American domination of Western Europe.

De Gaulle had made up his mind long before Nassau. He had virtually given Macmillan his verdict at Rambouillet. But the Polaris deal provided him with a convenient additional justification, and he was not diverted by the belated American offer of a similar nuclear arrangement for France. In a magnificently staged press conference on January 14, 1963, the General vetoed the British application for membership. He dismissed Britain as not yet a true European: her economy and trading links were very different from those of the Six, and the result of her membership would, he said, probably be "a colossal Atlantic Community under American dependence and leadership."[61] Macmillan was near despair, noting in his diary that "all our policies at home and abroad are in ruins."[62]

For Macmillan in 1963, like his old friend Eisenhower in 1960, the last months in office were a sad anticlimax. His government was buffeted by security crises, particularly the sex scandal involving his war minister, John Profumo, and the defection of Soviet agent Kim Philby. The Premier's patrician manner, once Super Mac's great asset, was now savagely lampooned by the satirists. He was often compared unfavorably with the vibrant Kennedy, who had become a hero among the liberal youth of Europe. That summer Macmillan's rating in the opinion polls was the lowest for any premier since Chamberlain, and his last meeting with Kennedy in June 1963 was not a success. After a triumphal visit to Berlin, the President found Macmillan jaded and devoid of new ideas. Gossip about his imminent resignation was rampant. It was a far cry from their meeting of minds after the Vienna summit only two years before.

There was one consolation for Macmillan during 1963: the signing of the first nuclear test-ban treaty by America, Russia and Britain. Since 1957 Macmillan had been arguing indefatigably for a ban, continually raising the issue with both Moscow and Washington, however unpropitious their moods. In the wake of the Cuban missile crisis Khrushchev finally decided that it was in Russia's interests to have an agreement with America. Macmillan also whittled away at the American demand for extensive inspections. One British diplomat recalled that "we looked at Britain as being in the position of being able to bring the two sides together."[63] Kennedy himself was deeply engaged, but on the admission of one leading American official, Macmillan deserved "much of the credit for the . . . ultimately decisive step" in the negotiations—a joint proposal with Kennedy for high-level but not summit talks, which was made in April 1963.[64] This broke the diplomatic impasse and paved the way for the eventual agreement signed the following August.

Although the treaty did not prohibit underground tests, it was the first major arms control agreement of the nuclear age. Macmillan viewed it as one of his greatest achievements, and in August Ormsby Gore told Kennedy that the Prime Minister was "in such a state of euphoria that Alec [Douglas-Home, the foreign secretary] doubts whether he now has any intention of resigning."[65] But the triumph was short-lived. In October 1963 sudden surgery forced Macmillan to give up, and the Conservative leadership chose Douglas-Home as his successor.

In America, too, power changed hands in the autumn of 1963. On Friday, November 22, President Kennedy was shot dead as his motorcade drove through Dallas. Americans were stunned, near panic, as rumors spread of a possible Communist conspiracy. In Britain, too, the shock was palpable and unprecedented. Thousands waited to sign a book of condolence at the American embassy, the Catholic Westminster Cathedral was packed to overflowing for a Requiem Mass, and Kennedy became only the third American president after Abraham Lincoln and Franklin Roosevelt to have a monument erected in his memory in London. Despite less than three years in office, his vivid personality and his martyr's death left an indelible impression on the British public.

With Kennedy's assassination and Macmillan's retirement an era in Anglo-American relations came to an end. Macmillan's close friendships, first with Eisenhower and then with Kennedy, had restored a relationship that had nearly been destroyed over Suez. He played an important role in helping thaw the cold war as intermediary between the superpowers. His premiership also left durable legacies, particularly the unique nuclear partnership between the United States and its transatlantic ally. Nevertheless, Macmillan's last year in office had demonstrated Britain's growing impotence in the superpower world, the test-ban treaty notwithstanding, and the "special relationship" had proved a major stumbling block to Britain's attempted entry into the New Europe. For the next decade, as America became enmeshed in the most disastrous war of its history, Britain remained in suspense, contracting as a world power yet excluded from the EEC, in limbo "between Europe and the Open Sea."

CHAPTER 13

DRIFTING
APART
1963–1973

"For millions of Americans," Lyndon Baines Johnson later recalled, "I was . . . a pretender to the throne, an illegal usurper."[1] Yet
the Vice President stepped into the dead Kennedy's shoes and,
reassuring the country, led it through its mourning and into a new
era of social reform. It was an impressive feat for which Johnson was
rewarded by a landslide victory in the November 1964 elections,
which secured the Democrats not only the presidency but a two-to-
one majority in both houses of Congress. A month earlier Harold
Wilson took office, Britain's first Labour prime minister since 1951.
He had run what many commentators thought to be a presidential-
style campaign. "What we are going to need," Wilson declared in
the summer of 1964, "is something like what President Kennedy
had after years of stagnation—a programme of a hundred days of
dynamic action."[2]

As in 1945 many in Washington found the prospect of dealing
with a socialist government unappealing. Wilson had said during his
campaign that he intended to renegotiate the Polaris agreement. His
Tory opponents claimed that he would abandon control over Britain's nuclear weapons and "surrender all our authority in world
affairs."[3] In America advocates of the NATO multilateral nuclear
force, the MLF—"zealots," according to Secretary of State Dean
Rusk—were determined that Britain would agree to participate be-

fore the year was out. An early confrontation between the two newly elected leaders seemed likely.

In December 1964 Wilson and his senior colleagues arrived in Washington. Britain's new minister of defence, Denis Healey, had already decided that Polaris was too far advanced to be worth canceling. The promised renegotiation of the Nassau agreement therefore amounted to no more than a cut in the number of submarines from five to four. Next on the agenda was the MLF. Healey was skeptical of the concept, which he mocked as "artificial dissemination," a way of "pretending to give Europe a voice in America's nuclear strategy without actually doing so." According to Healey, American support for the MLF was a last attempt to produce a mechanism that could lead to a federated Europe, "the grain of sand round which the pearl of European unity would develop."[4]

For eighteen months an experimental MLF had been in operation on a U.S. destroyer, the *Claude V. Ricketts*. The captain and executive officer were American, together with half the crew, but the rest were British, German, Dutch, Italian, Greek and Turkish. There were marked cultural differences to overcome. The British grumbled at going without their daily tot of rum, to conform with the U.S. Navy, which had been dry since the First World War. The Greeks did not welcome being served sweet corn, an American favorite, which they considered "something for chickens to eat."[5] Discipline, according to the American skipper of the *Ricketts*, was the trickiest problem: it was not easy to persuade a foreigner to accept the austere American naval punishment of three days' solitary, on bread and water, with only a Bible to read. The common language was English, but a vocabulary of only eight hundred words, "including some good old-fashioned Anglo-Saxon swear words," was apparently sufficient for most practical purposes.[6]

The experiment itself was a success, but the concept behind it a failure. "It died a natural death," Dean Rusk said, "because our NATO allies, particularly Britain and Germany, could not agree on it."[7] There was also opposition from Congress and a distinct lack of enthusiasm from President Johnson. Wilson offered Washington a substitute proposal, the ANF, or Atlantic Nuclear Force, an amalgam of existing national nuclear forces, with minimal mixed manning. "We put it for the sake of courtesy," said Denis Healey, "after making a very strong case against the [MLF] proposal." Johnson, relieved to be free of the MLF, agreed to explore the ANF idea and then allowed it to slip into oblivion during 1965. Healey did not think there was "much weeping in Washington over it."[8] America had now abandoned the attempt to restrict the nuclear power of its allies and resigned itself to the continued existence of both British and French nuclear forces.

Washington's first encounter with the new British government had passed off well. Wilson gave the impression of being committed to Anglo-American cooperation while deriding Tory yearnings for the days of empire and transatlantic equality. At the White House dinner on December 7, 1964, he told Johnson: "Some of those who talk about the special relationship, I think, are looking backwards and not looking forward. They talk about the nostalgia of our imperial age. We regard our relationship with you not as a *special* relationship, but as a *close* relationship, governed by the only things that matter, unity of purpose, and unity in our objectives."[9]

But no personal rapport developed between the rough-spoken Texan President and the wily British Prime Minister, nothing like the relationship that had been built up by Macmillan with Eisenhower and Kennedy. George Ball, then under secretary of state, recalls that "LBJ had been impressed with Macmillan," but Wilson "lacked Macmillan's consummate ability to deal on a friendly but slightly condescending basis. He wore no patrician armor, was too ordinary, too much like other politicians with whom LBJ had to deal, and Johnson took an almost instant dislike to him."[10] In the Macmillan era cordial transatlantic friendships had cushioned the shock of conflicting policies and offset the decline of Britain's power. In the mid-1960s, a time of strained personal relations, the decline accelerated and the differences over policy became severe.

The foreign policy issue that eclipsed all others for America by the mid-1960s was the conflict in Vietnam. It spilled over into American domestic politics and fundamentally changed the perception of the United States in Britain. It demonstrated to America the limits of its power, and also the limits of its friendship with Britain, for in this long conflict Britain consistently failed to come up to Washington's expectations.

The partition of Vietnam, masterminded by Anthony Eden in 1954, had produced two rival states: the South, under Ngo Dinh Diem, and the North, under the Communist Ho Chi Minh. The 1954 agreement had provided for elections throughout the country in 1956, but Diem refused to go along with this plan and the North-South divide continued. Ho had expected to win the elections and had no intention of allowing partition to become permanent, as it had in Korea. He insisted that the country must be reunited under Communist rule, and in the late 1950s he exploited Vietnamese opposition to Diem's corrupt government to create the Vietcong, a guerrilla force raised in the South but trained and controlled by the North.

Diem had been supported by America since 1954 as a bastion of democracy against the totalitarian regime in the North. Dulles had backed Diem's obstructionism, arguing that free elections were impossible in the areas controlled by the Communists. He had never accepted the Geneva Accords of 1954 and told Eisenhower in February 1956 that "our policy in Vietnam is directed toward . . . the continued strengthening of the position of Free Vietnam under President Diem . . . and . . . the eventual weakening of North Vietnam by political and psychological warfare."[11] Faced with the threat from the Vietcong, Diem naturally asked America for further help and Kennedy agreed to provide it. Overt military intervention was rejected in favor of American "advisers," whose job was to train Diem's men in counterinsurgency tactics and psychological warfare to defeat the Vietcong. At the time of Kennedy's death there were already fifteen thousand American "advisers" in Vietnam and the United States was bearing most of the cost of the war. Yet both militarily and politically the situation was deteriorating.

Kennedy believed that the fate of South Vietnam would decide U.S. influence in Southeast Asia, and that its allies around the world would be watching to see how America discharged its responsibilities, but the lack of popular support for Diem was the weakness at the heart of the strategy. After attempts to encourage and enforce reform had proved ineffective, his administration covertly supported Diem's overthrow in November 1963. Kennedy accepted that the military commitments America had now embarked upon were dangerous. If one stage failed, the next would be an escalation. "It's like taking a drink," he told one aide. "The effect wears off, and you have to take another."[12]

Johnson inherited the makings of a disaster. In the early days of his presidency he gave little attention to Vietnam. He was ambitious for domestic reform, the field in which he had made his reputation in Congress. He wanted to take his place in history by introducing the welfare and civil rights program known as the Great Society. He was reluctant, he said later, to leave "the woman I really loved— the Great Society—in order to get involved with that bitch of a war on the other side of the world." But the war could not be ignored.

Johnson was sensitive to Republican criticism that he, as a liberal Democrat, was soft on Communism. If South Vietnam fell, he feared there would be a national inquest far worse than the one after China went Communist in 1949, which would "shatter my Presidency . . . and damage our democracy."[13] He accepted, as Kennedy had done, that Vietnam was a test case of America's credibility; pull out, he commented in 1965, and we "might as well give up everywhere else—pull out of Berlin, Japan, South America."[14] Under these pressures Johnson started to ignore the advice of State Department doves like George Ball, who argued for a more cautious policy, and listened instead to the Joint Chiefs of Staff, who believed that direct American military intervention would bring the enemy to the negotiating table.

In January 1965 the deteriorating situation in South Vietnam led most of Johnson's inner circle of advisers to advocate selective bombing in the North. A new Communist offensive, in early February, provided the pretext for a series of air attacks on specific targets, code-named Rolling Thunder. By avoiding an outright declaration of war, Johnson was able to circumvent Congress. In July he took a further step, again on his own authority as commander in chief. He accepted the open-ended commitment of U.S. combat troops. By the end of 1965 nearly two hundred thousand Americans were in South Vietnam.

Johnson did less than his military advisers wanted: "Enough, but not too much" was his motto.[15] He dared not risk all-out war with China, as had happened over Korea. So he escalated the war cautiously, behind the backs of the Congress. But Ho Chi Minh, skillfully exploiting the rivalry between Russia and China, and America's antagonism to both, was able to match each step Johnson took. During the next two years U.S. restrictions on bombing targets were gradually lifted. From the spring of 1967 regular raids were mounted on targets in the cities of Hanoi and Haiphong, despite the danger of incurring Russian or Chinese casualties, and the troop commitment rose to nearly half a million men. Johnson had become so deeply entangled that he could no longer extricate himself. As George Ball had warned in 1964, "Once on the tiger's back we cannot be sure of picking the place to dismount."[16] As long as Ho retained the support of Moscow and Peking he held the initiative. Simply by refusing to negotiate he could suck America deeper and deeper into the mire.

Throughout the war Johnson hoped for Britain's help. Increasingly beleaguered at home, he needed support from America's allies and, if possible, their military backing. He did not expect a major contingent from Britain, since she was already engaged in a counterinsurgency war against the forces of Sukarno's Indonesian government, which were trying to infiltrate and destroy the Malaysian federation. But Wilson refused to send even a token force, and earned Johnson's contempt for proffering advice from the sidelines and trying to act, in the Macmillan tradition, as mediator between the two sides in Vietnam.

When Wilson came to Washington for talks in December 1964, he was aware, according to William Bundy, one of Johnson's principal advisers on Vietnam, that American raids on North Vietnam were being planned. In his memoirs Wilson merely says that Johnson raised the question of British participation "without excessive enthusiasm."[17] On the night of February 10–11, 1965, Wilson called Johnson from London to express concern over the first bombing raids. He proposed coming to Washington to discuss the issue. Johnson retorted that unless he cared to send some British troops Wilson should mind his own business. "I won't tell you how to run Malaysia, and you don't tell us how to run Vietnam."[18] Bundy thinks Wilson "overreacted and made out more surprised than he should have done. The time to have spoken was when he was in Washington in December, if he really felt the way he expressed himself in February." In Bundy's view the incident affected Johnson's judgment of Wilson. He decided that the British Prime Minister did not really have his mind on the problem of ensuring stability and peace in Southeast Asia, and showed that he was not "what the French would call *un homme serieux.*"[19]

The disagreements between Britain and America over Southeast Asia had surfaced before, over the handling of the war in Korea in the 1950s. Asian Communism was consistently perceived in Britain as less of a threat to world peace than it was in America. The British government did not believe Communism was monolithic, and thought that the Americans, by treating it as such, missed the opportunity of dividing Russia from China and thereby undermining Ho Chi Minh. But on Korea, Britain had remonstrated with the Americans from the position of an ally, with her own troops fighting alongside the Americans. Over Vietnam she was standing on the sidelines.

To have sent troops to Vietnam would have been impossible for Wilson's government. There was not only resistance in the Labour

"O wad some pow'r the giftie gie us / To see oursels as others see us!"

World statesman or American stooge? Garland, in the Daily Telegraph, *July 19, 1966, quotes*
Burns—a favorite of Kosygin—to mock Wilson.

party but also growing public hostility to the war. London witnessed some of the most violent demonstrations ever seen there. On
October 27, 1968, thousands of young people battled with mounted
police in Grosvenor Square. They broke the windows of the American embassy and threatened to ransack it.

Wilson's solution to the dilemma was a typical compromise. He
refused to condemn his ally outright, continuing to support American policy in general terms, but tried to assuage critics at home by
criticizing specific actions, such as the bombing of Hanoi and Haiphong. Meanwhile he made repeated efforts to bring both sides to
the peace table. In December 1965, for instance, he pressed Johnson
to call a halt to the bombing of Vietnam as a test of Ho's goodwill.
In July of the following year he flew to Moscow to urge the Kremlin
to dissuade Hanoi from putting captured U.S. bomber pilots on
trial. But his most sustained effort at mediation came in February
1967, when the Soviet premier, Alexei Kosygin, was visiting Britain.

Washington was in contact with Hanoi and had put forward a
tentative proposal for a permanent halt to U.S. bombing in return
for Hanoi's ending its troop infiltration of the South. Wilson told
Kosygin of the plan and seemed to be winning his support, when
Washington, without letting London know, abruptly changed the
negotiating terms. Wilson cabled Johnson that he had been placed
in a "hell of a situation" with Kosygin,[20] and begged the President

to give him a proper chance to enlist Soviet help. As a gesture, the bombing had been halted for the duration of the Vietnamese holiday of Tet, and Wilson believed there was a chance of exploiting this pause to begin real negotiations.

Johnson and the National Security Council deliberated in Washington as Kosygin spent Sunday evening, February 12, 1967, at a final meeting at Chequers, the Prime Minister's official residence in Buckinghamshire. Wilson talked on and on, about everything from high tech to geology, in an effort to prevent the Russians from leaving. The American diplomat Chester Cooper sat in a garret with an open telephone line to the White House, waiting for Washington's response. Trying to force a decision, he held the telephone out of the window to prove that the Russian motorcade was revving up, ready to leave. But no reply came from Washington, and a peeved Kosygin left Chequers to drive back to his London hotel. After his departure Washington abruptly agreed to suspend the bombing if Hanoi would open negotiations before the Tet truce ended on the following day. Wilson rushed to Kosygin's hotel with the news at 1:00 A.M., but there was no time for a response from Hanoi within the deadline set by the Americans, and the fighting began again. An angry Wilson put a good face on it, assuring his Cabinet that he enjoyed the "absolute confidence" of both Johnson and Kosygin and that they had been "on the edge of peace."[21]

Wilson had been let down by Johnson's failure to keep him informed and by the impossible final deadline, but although the Russians showed more interest than before in the peace process, Hanoi remained unresponsive. The American administration, for its part, never saw Wilson as a serious intermediary. It tolerated his involvement, as it did that of many others, somewhat skeptically. Bundy believed that Wilson was "overwhelmingly minded to get into a negotiation at almost any cost, regardless of where that negotiation might lead and without having thought through how immensely difficult it was going to be."[22] Many in Washington thought his main aim was to win the Nobel Peace Prize. In his memoirs LBJ remarked tartly: "I have no doubt . . . that the British government's general approach to the war and to finding a peaceful solution would have been considerably different if a brigade of Her Majesty's forces had been stationed . . . in Vietnam."[23]

Johnson's conception of politics was intensely personal: loyalty was the highest virtue, betrayal the deadliest sin. Wilson's failure to send troops was seen as dereliction of duty. It was also politically damaging to Johnson. Daily TV news reports from Vietnam showed America's headquarters in Saigon, in front of which flew the flags of its fellow combatants, with the Union Jack conspicuously absent. Administration officials like Bundy argue that a British commitment "would have made a considerable psychological difference . . . particularly in liberal circles, which was where the main criticism of the war came from."[24] The Americans stressed that they only needed a token force. In Washington, in July 1966, LBJ told Wilson that "a platoon of bagpipers would be sufficient, it was the British flag that was wanted."[25] Dean Rusk also applied pressure. Rusk was an Anglophile and a former Rhodes scholar, who was deeply distressed by the British attitude. According to Louis Heren, a British correspondent in Washington, Rusk asked him at a cocktail party why the British couldn't manage "just one battalion of the Black Watch?" Patiently Heren explained British policy. Rusk glowered: "When the Russians invade Sussex, don't expect us to come and help you."[26]

Tangible evidence of British loyalty might have made Johnson more tolerant of Wilson's efforts to mediate in Vietnam, but even if British opinion had been supportive, it is unlikely that she could have played a significant role. Prime Minister Attlee's influence in Korea in 1950–51 was as much a reflection of Britain's strength as of her loyalty. In the early 1950s Britain was the world's third largest military power, with nearly a million men under arms. From 1954 four divisions and a tactical air force were committed to NATO in the defense of Western Europe. But a decade later the balance had shifted. West Germany overtook Britain's armed forces in 1964, with 430,000 men to her 425,000.[27] During the intervening years, as Britain brought conscription to an end, Germany had replaced her as the main military pillar of NATO in Europe. Although France, discontented with America's leadership, had withdrawn her forces from NATO in 1966, Germany and France had developed close ties and were becoming the effective leaders of the European side of the Atlantic Alliance.

The shift in military and political strength coincided with a similar shift in economic power. In 1953 Britain had the third strongest economy in the world, although it was only half as big as Russia's and one-eighth the size of the United States'. By 1963 Britain had fallen to fifth place, with Germany third and France fourth.[28] Her economic performance had suffered from her continued exclusion from the EEC. De Gaulle remained implacably opposed to her entry when, overcoming Labour opposition, Wilson investigated anew the possibility of membership in 1967.

Despite this relative decline, Wilson was determined to uphold a world role for Britain. Although she had given up most of her colonies, she still maintained bases and troops in Singapore, Aden and the Persian Gulf, which protected important pro-Western states and ensured access to vital European oil supplies. "We are a world power, and a world influence, or we are nothing," Wilson proclaimed in 1964, within a month of taking office.[29] Quick to deride the Tories as jingoists, he nevertheless believed Britain's ideals and interests were inextricably bound up with her presence in Southeast Asia and the Middle East, and that the Commonwealth was still an effective instrument for British influence. The United States, heavily committed in Vietnam, welcomed British involvement east of Suez. In December 1964 Denis Healey, back from Washington, told the Cabinet that America wanted Britain "to keep a foothold in Hong Kong, Malaya, the Persian Gulf, to enable us to do things for the alliance which they can't do. They think our forces are much more useful to the alliance outside Europe than in Germany."[30] The following summer the Chancellor of the Exchequer, James Callaghan, was lectured on the dangers of excessive defense cuts during a visit to Washington. U.S. Defense Secretary Robert McNamara told him that America was already overcommitted in Asia and would certainly not assume additional commitments both there and in the Middle East if Britain pulled out. He insisted that "the American Congress would not tolerate a situation in which the United States was the sole world policeman."[31]

But the high cost of her commitments soon forced Britain to ignore America's wishes and reexamine her role overseas. Labour had come to power anxious to maintain the value of sterling, which, still standing at the $2.80 level adopted in 1949, was now grossly overvalued. In the era of fixed exchange rates the level of the currency was seen as a status symbol, much as it had been when an earlier Labour government under MacDonald had struggled with the consequences of too high a rate in the 1920s. In 1964 the result of its overvalued level, combined with a lack of competitiveness in Britain's economy, was persistent trade deficits and runs on the pound, as overseas investors lost confidence in sterling. Reductions in government spending became inevitable, with overseas commitments a prime target.

Britain's role east of Suez, with its echoes of imperialism, was particularly unpopular among Labour's left-wingers. In February 1966, as part of general reductions in defense spending, the Cabinet agreed to pull out of Aden in 1967–68. It reaffirmed, at the same time, its commitment to stay in the Gulf and in the Far East until the mid-seventies. More defense cuts followed in July 1967, but Wilson still refused to devalue sterling. One left-wing member of the Cabinet, Richard Crossman, was convinced that "the decision not to devalue the pound and the East of Suez policy were very closely united." Crossman felt that both were part of an essentially Tory foreign policy of maintaining Britain's world role and her credibility in Washington. "It's my view," he wrote, "that this determination to cling to parity and keep Britain great has been the basic reason for all our economic troubles."[32]

In the mid-1960s Britain defended the pound with the help of repeated credits from American banks and from the International Monetary Fund. James Callaghan denies that this help was given only in return for British support of American policy in Vietnam. "Emphatically I must record that I encountered nothing said or implied to this effect."[33] De Gaulle was trying to undermine America's financial hegemony, and he regarded sterling as the dollar's first line of defense. It was therefore in America's financial interest, Callaghan claims, to protect the pound.

But the assistance was in vain. In the autumn of 1967 another devastating run on sterling finally forced Wilson to accept devaluation. New government spending cuts followed. Social policies close to Labour's heart, such as the provision of free drugs and medicines on the National Health Service, were affected, and further defense cuts became politically unavoidable. The cost of Britain's presence in the Gulf was not a major part of total defense spending, and the oil-rich Gulf states, where British troops were stationed, indicated their willingness to bear the entire cost themselves. But, as *The Times* commented, "the defence cuts are the *sine qua non* of a package which will involve the wholesale slaughter of sacred cows."[34] Only Polaris and the British Army of the Rhine were sacrosanct as the Cabinet announced that Britain would withdraw from all its east-of-Suez bases, except Hong Kong, by March 1971.

The State Department was aghast. In February 1967 some middle-level officials in Washington had suggested offering Britain a multibillion-dollar loan, or even gift, to fund her sterling debts and end for good the speculation against the pound. What they wanted in return was a firm British commitment to remain east of Suez—a

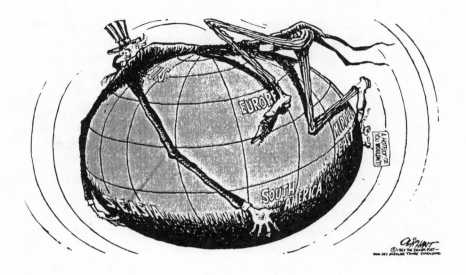

Uncle Sam overextended. Oliphant's view in 1967.

demand Callaghan dismissed as "unacceptable."[35] When the British foreign secretary, George Brown, visited Washington in January 1968 to explain the withdrawal decision, one official pleaded: "Be British, George, be British—how can you betray us?"[36] Johnson made a personal appeal to Wilson to reconsider his decision, and there were even hints of American economic retaliation, but to no avail. The Cabinet agreed to defer Britain's departure until December 1971, but no further.

The withdrawal could not have come at a worse time for Anglo-American relations. Johnson was facing the most devastating Vietcong assault so far in Vietnam and had no forces to spare to fill the vacuum in the Gulf. He was obliged to turn to Iran and Saudi Arabia to maintain the West's influence. Denis Healey, as the minister of defence responsible for implementing the British decision, had no doubt that it was right, arguing that it was too expensive to stay east of Suez and that had she stayed Britain would have become the target of nationalist opposition in the area. "The Americans change their mind about Britain all the time. They spent the whole of the war trying to get us to give up the empire everywhere and being very nasty to us when we didn't. Eisenhower and Dulles tried to torpedo the Anglo-French intervention in Suez, quite rightly in my opinion. Then they changed their position."[37] Dean Rusk, secretary

of state, disagrees: "I personally believe . . . that Britain overreacted
to the loss of empire and has underestimated its own position and
influence in the world, its own ability to influence the course of
events. . . . In Washington we were disappointed, disturbed, regret-
ful."[38]

When Wilson visited the United States in February 1968, there
was a sense that an era in British and world history had passed.
Britain had withdrawn east of Suez and had devalued the pound.
Such was the mood that the American press read a deliberate snub
into the choice of songs for the White House dinner in Wilson's
honor—"On the Road to Mandalay" and "I've Got Plenty of Nothing." Johnson's wife, Lady Bird, called it "the most ridiculous international furor so far," and Wilson brushed it off, claiming that the
songs were his favorites. At the dinner Wilson once again played
the role of world statesman, chatting easily with "Lyndon" and
"Lady Bird" and discoursing at length on his plans for peace in
Vietnam. Afterward Johnson saw the Wilsons to their car, but his
mind was on other things. As the limousine drew away he ran up
the stairs to his "war room" saying, "I've got to get back to Khe
Sanh."[39]

Khe Sanh was in danger of becoming America's Dien Bien Phu.
The U.S. marines in this remote base near the Laotian border were
besieged by two North Vietnamese divisions. LBJ insisted that Khe
Sanh must be held at all costs, sending in reinforcements and laying
waste the surrounding countryside with bombs. As he did so the
Vietcong launched devastating new offensives throughout South
Vietnam at the end of the Tet holiday in January 1968. Film of
fighting inside the grounds of the American embassy in Saigon and
of the besieged U.S. marines in Khe Sanh was shown nightly on
American television, providing proof that, despite administration
claims, the war was not being won. It was being lost, and in a
particularly disturbing way, as though to oppose evil America had
been forced to resort to evil methods itself.

Hearings by Senator William Fulbright's Foreign Relations
Committee early in 1968 suggested that Johnson had consistently
deceived Congress about the nature of the war, the scale of American involvement and the results of its efforts. Pictures shown around
the world of the Saigon police chief summarily executing a Vietcong suspect on the street led many to wonder what kind of democracy the United States was really fighting for. In March these
feelings surfaced during the first stage of the presidential election

campaign, when Senator Eugene McCarthy, running on an antiwar ticket, came a strong second to the President in the New Hampshire Democratic primary, prompting John Kennedy's brother Robert to join the race against Johnson. America's premier newscaster, Walter Cronkite, back from his own tour of Vietnam, told viewers:

> It seems now more certain than ever that the bloody experience of Vietnam is to end in a stalemate. This summer's almost certain stand-off will either end in real give-or-take negotiations or terrible escalation; and for every means we have to escalate the enemy can match us. . . . And with each escalation, the world comes close to the brink of cosmic disaster.[40]

Such a judgment from the most trusted man in America was a staggering indictment of the administration's policy.

The political challenges he faced at home prompted an extraordinary decision by President Johnson. McNamara, exhausted and disillusioned, had resigned as defense secretary and had been replaced by Clark Clifford, an adviser of Democratic presidents since the Truman era. Clifford cast a fresh eye over U.S. policy and persuaded Johnson that the war could not now be won on terms that would be acceptable to the American people. If he insisted on pursuing it and agreed to the request of the Joint Chiefs of Staff for another two hundred thousand troops to be drafted to Vietnam, he would split the Democratic party and inflict terrible damage on the country. What was needed, Clifford was advised, was "not a war speech, but a peace speech."[41] Johnson, the consummate politician, knew he was beaten. On March 31 he announced that nearly all air and ground operations against North Vietnam would be halted, that he would not seek reelection as president, and that his last months in office would be devoted to the search for peace. Some Americans half wondered whether it was an early April Fool, but the shattered President was in earnest.

Yet the summer of 1968 brought peace neither in Vietnam nor at home. Under the merciless eye of television it sometimes looked as if American society itself was on the verge of collapse. Johnson had previously insisted that the war against poverty at home and the war against Communism in Vietnam could be fought without increases in taxation. "We are a rich Nation," he told Congress in 1966, "and can afford to make progress at home while meeting obligations abroad."[42] But his fiscal policy proved irresponsible.

Heavy government borrowing undermined confidence in the dollar
abroad and fueled roaring inflation at home. Soon the war in Vietnam was spilling its violence onto America's streets. A few days
after Johnson's withdrawal from the presidential race the black civil
rights leader Martin Luther King was assassinated, causing riots
across the country, some of them only a few blocks from the White
House and the Capitol. In June Robert Kennedy, by now leading
the Democratic race, was shot and killed in a San Francisco hotel.
In August, at the Democratic convention in Chicago, Mayor
Daley's police force beat up peace protesters and innocent bystand-
ers in full view of television cameras, and tear gas brought conference delegates running from their hotels. As horror succeeded
horror America's reputation as the bastion of liberty, as a free and
fair society, came under question. Only the brutal Russian invasion
of Czechoslovakia in August reminded the world that the other
superpower did not accept even the principle of civil liberty.

The election of Republican Richard Nixon in November 1968
led to a reassessment of the Vietnam War. With his national security
adviser, Henry Kissinger, a German-born Harvard professor,
Nixon evolved a scheme for ending the war swiftly, with minimum
protest at home, but without incurring an obvious military defeat.
To mollify domestic opinion he began to withdraw American
troops, substituting a policy of "Vietnamization" with the retrain-
ing of South Vietnam's own army. The air war, which caused few
American casualties, was, however, intensified. In an attempt to
force Hanoi to the conference table, North Vietnamese sanctuaries
in Cambodia were bombed, bringing that country into the war
directly for the first time, and raids on the North continued, including periodic saturation bombings of the cities of Hanoi and Haiphong. "I can't believe," Kissinger told his aides in 1969, "that a
fourth-rate power like North Vietnam doesn't have a breaking
point."[43] Nixon's efforts to secure "peace with honor" included
military strikes on the ground against Cambodia and Laos and the
dropping on Indochina of a greater tonnage of bombs than had
fallen under Johnson, who had himself dropped more than America
used in the whole of World War II.[44]

Nixon and Kissinger did not intend to rely on brute force alone.
America's crisis of the late 1960s prompted them to review the
country's relations with the Communist world, thus clearing the
way for a peace settlement in Vietnam. By the early 1960s Russia
and China were openly at odds, contrary to America's image of

Communism as a global monolith. While Kennedy and Johnson failed to exploit the rift, Ho adroitly played off Moscow and Peking against each other and enlisted the aid of both against the United States. As long as he could continue to do so he would have the support he needed to fight the war. But Nixon, despite his history as a pro-McCarthy cold warrior, believed it was time for America to "come . . . to grips with the reality of China" and stop pretending that Mao's regime did not exist.[45] China was now emerging from its Cultural Revolution and seeking new contacts with the West.

After secret diplomacy by Kissinger, Nixon struck a deal with Peking. In return for Chinese pressure on Hanoi, the United States would gradually extricate itself from support for Chiang Kai-shek on his outpost island of Taiwan. America was at last beginning to acknowledge that Mao, not Chiang, was the real ruler of China. To seal the bargain and demonstrate the thaw in relations, Nixon flew to Peking in February 1972 and was greeted at the airport by Premier Chou En-lai. Mindful of how Dulles had snubbed Chou by refusing to shake hands at the Geneva conference on Indochina in 1954, Nixon walked down the steps of his aircraft with arm thrust forward. Later Chou said, "Your handshake came over the vastest ocean in the world—twenty-five years of no communication."[46]

Nixon also opened up a new relationship with Russia. Shocked by its rebuff in Cuba in 1962, the Soviet Union had built up its stock of nuclear missiles to near parity with America. An arms control agreement now seemed attractive to the United States, and Russia, for its part, was keen to acquire American goods and technology for its backward economy. In May 1972, less than three months after his historic trip to Peking, Nixon became the first U.S. president to visit Moscow. There he and the Soviet leader, Leonid Brezhnev, signed the Strategic Arms Limitation Treaty, SALT I, which froze existing missile systems at their current levels. A related agreement restricted the deployment of anti-ballistic missile defenses. Moscow, too, would be encouraged to distance itself from North Vietnam.

By this combination of brute force and subtle diplomacy Nixon and Kissinger wore down Hanoi's resistance at the peace talks in Paris. Finally in January 1973 an agreement was reached that could be called "peace with honor," even though few thought it would last, as long as Hanoi yearned for a united country. Under the settlement American troops were withdrawn, but air and naval forces were kept in the region to prevent any North Vietnamese movement into the South. South Vietnam was to be protected by

America from a distance while funds were provided for internal reconstruction. The policy was not given long to work. Congress, in the wake of the Watergate scandal, halved U.S. aid to Saigon, and passed the War Powers Act to curtail the president's power to wage limited war without congressional approval. In 1975 a new Vietcong offensive began, and on May Day victorious Vietcong troops swept into Saigon. The last that was seen of the Americans was a desperate scramble for helicopters lifting them and a few of their luckier Vietnamese supporters from the roof of the U.S. embassy. Fifty-five thousand Americans had died, apparently to no avail. Shaken and embittered, the United States was ready to turn in on itself, to lick its wounds, and to ask hard questions about its many other responsibilities around the world.

Nixon, like Johnson, had been destroyed by the war. To implement his Vietnam policy he had adopted obsessive secrecy as a protection against domestic opposition. The State Department was bypassed, Democrats were subjected to dirty-tricks campaigns and leaks of information were plugged by illegal means. When the activities of the White House "plumbers," burgling opponents on behalf of the President, were revealed, Nixon sacked his own attorney general in an effort to conceal the evidence on tape recordings of White House conversations. When these were finally made public, the President, abandoned by his party and facing impeachment, was forced to resign in August 1974.

The manner of Nixon's departure, reduced to a tearful, rambling eulogy of his mother on worldwide television, belied the significance of his presidency. In three historic months in 1972 he had broken the frozen grip of the cold war by being the first U.S. president to visit Peking and Moscow, capitals of the Communist world. The United States was finally beginning to acknowledge the legitimacy of these two alien regimes. It was also conceding to the Soviet Union equal status as a military power.

In the agreements with China and Russia, unlike the moves toward détente in the 1950s or the test-ban treaty of 1963, Great Britain played no part. Finished as a world power, she had slipped out of the major league and was now in search of a new relationship with the continent of Europe.

The Labour government of Harold Wilson had decided that for commercial reasons Britain should join the European Community, even though the party remained suspicious of being tied too tightly to Europe. As long as General de Gaulle remained in power, however, France vetoed the application. His retirement in 1969 allowed negotiations to begin in earnest, conducted by a new Conservative government, led by Edward Heath, which came to office in 1970. Heath was unique among Britain's postwar prime ministers in being deeply skeptical of Britain's obsession with America. He had been an ardent pro-Marketeer for many years, cutting his diplomatic teeth as Macmillan's chief negotiator in 1961–63. In 1970 he returned with relish to the task of preparing for Britain's entry, convinced that her destiny lay in Europe, and that Europe's destiny was to develop as a continent friendly to America but separate from it. In October 1971 he was rewarded with a House of Commons majority in favor of entry on the terms he had negotiated. The treaty was signed with much ceremony, and took effect on New Year's Day, 1973. Denmark and Ireland joined as well. The Six became the Nine.

America's attitude to the enlarged EEC had changed in the years since it first hoped to see a federal Europe emerge from the ruins of the Second World War. In 1945 it produced half the world's manufactured goods; in 1970, less than a third. During the 1960s the EEC had emerged as a serious economic rival. As America's share of world production and of exports fell, Europe's rose, until, by 1970, although still producing only half the output of the United States, the Six accounted for 29 percent of world exports against America's 14 percent. EEC tariff barriers were keeping out American farm produce; her internal subsidies helped European steel and other products undercut America in world markets. Together with Japan the EEC was posing a serious challenge to American economic supremacy.

The loss of trade affected America's financial standing too. It had grown used to the position of dominance assumed after World War II. U.S. trade surpluses, based on the production of essential goods and raw materials, had been reinvested outside America in economic aid and military expenditure. The rest of the world was driven by the great dynamo of the American economy. America benefited in return by bolstering friendly countries as bastions against Communism. But as the world recovered from World War II America's share of total international reserves fell from 50 percent in 1950 to only 16 percent twenty years later. By the late 1960s the United States could no longer afford the role of world leader.

As America's reserves fell and the competitiveness of its products declined the dollar became overvalued. The costs of the Vietnam

War and the inflation it spawned increased the pressure on the dollar, but since fixed exchange rates were still the international trading norm, there was no easy way of making the necessary adjustment. In August 1971 Nixon unilaterally decided that the dollar would no longer be automatically convertible into gold. At the same time he imposed a temporary 10 percent surcharge on all foreign imports. Over the next eighteen months successive currency crises resulted in the dollar and most other major world currencies floating—left to find their own levels in response to market forces—as central banks tried to adjust to the new era. Bretton Woods had served the postwar world well, but after twenty-five years it no longer fitted the new distribution of economic power. Just as the gold standard had depended on British supremacy, so Bretton Woods had rested on the hegemony of the dollar.

The United States remained the most powerful nation on earth, but it was no longer impregnable. Economically it was being challenged by the newly enlarged EEC and by Japan. Militarily, with SALT I, it had conceded parity with the Soviet Union. Diplomatically an atmosphere of détente with Russia and the new links with China seemed to signal, if not the end of the cold war, at least a marked thaw. Nixon propounded the argument that the language of two superpowers, of East versus West, no longer served to describe international relations. "It would be a safer world and better world," he said in 1972, "if we have a strong, healthy United States, Europe, Soviet Union, China, Japan; each balancing the other, not playing one against the other, an even balance."[47]

Logically, this new philosophy demanded a reassessment of America's relationship with Europe, which had barely been examined since the establishment of NATO after the war. If Europe was back on her feet again, and even challenging the United States, it made sense to ask whether she should not take more responsibility for her own defense. Senator Mike Mansfield had focused attention on the point ever since 1966, when he first put down a resolution calling for reductions in American troops in Europe. He asked in 1970 why "the 250 million people of Western Europe, with tremendous industrial resources and long military experience, are unable to organize an effective military coalition to defend themselves against 200 million Russians who are contending at the same time with 800 million Chinese, but must continue after 20 years to depend upon 200 million Americans for their defense."[48]

With the war in Vietnam coming to an end, Nixon, encouraged

by his secretary of state, Henry Kissinger, decided to turn his attention to Europe. The initiative was ill fated from the start. Kissinger
announced that 1973 would be the Year of Europe. The very title
stuck in the craw of many Europeans, suggesting as it did that
having sorted out Vietnam and the two Communist giants, Washington wanted to sort out Europe, and thought it could all be done
in twelve months. To the leaders of Europe that seemed a presump-
tuous and arrogant approach. The British foreign secretary, Sir Alec
Douglas-Home, did not even hear about the proposal from Kissinger or the State Department, but read it on the news agency tapes,
and rang the French foreign minister to see if he could throw any
light on it, but Paris knew no more than London.

The news tape Douglas-Home read was a report of a keynote
speech given by Kissinger in New York on April 23. It called for
negotiations leading by the end of the year to "a new Atlantic
charter" between the United States and its European allies. The aim
was to reduce economic rivalry, negotiate a more equitable sharing
of defense burdens, and at the same time reassure the Europeans that
their interests would not be overlooked in America's moves toward
détente with the Soviet Union. Remembering the European condemnation of the Christmas bombing of Hanoi a few months earlier,
Kissinger drew a contrast between the postcolonial countries of
Western Europe and their superpower ally: "the United States has
global interests and responsibilities. Our European allies have regional interests." The time had come for a comprehensive stock-
taking. America "must strike a new balance between self-interest
and the common interest."[49]

The inauspicious start should have warned Kissinger that all was
not well. He admits now that although the idea was "based on a
correct analysis" it "misfired." He concedes that it was put forward
in "too dramatic a form" and was unfortunately proposed two
weeks after the Watergate scandal broke. "I think that the desire of
European leaders to be seen at a summit with President Nixon was
not as great as it would have been two months earlier." But he
blames the European allies, and in particular Heath, for not simply
saying to Washington, " 'For God's sake, let's drop this for six
months' . . . but nobody said no and nobody said yes."[50]

In past transatlantic misunderstandings, Britain had often
adopted the role of go-between, interpreting America to Europe and
moderating U.S. policy. But this did not happen in 1973. Kissinger
believes that, with Britain just entering the EEC, Heath did not

want to be stigmatized as an American agent or a Trojan horse. Contrary to Kissinger's expectations, Heath refused to discuss the American proposals privately with Washington before they were put to the other European partners. Heath's view is that the U.S. initiative was misguided. Kissinger was publicly trying to make out that there should now be one Europe to whom he could talk, while privately he "sometimes still tried to play one [country] off against the other. None of us were prepared to play that game."[51] On July 25, 1973, Heath cabled Nixon that all discussions must be conducted with the nine members of the EEC as a single group. Kissinger was furious. He believed that close consultation between Britain and America was invaluable. He told Sir Burke Trend, the influential secretary to the Cabinet, that "Atlantic—and especially Anglo-American—relations had thrived on intangibles of trust and communication" and warned that if Britain's current Europeanist tendencies continued, "we were at a turning point in Atlantic relations."[52]

The other countries of the EEC were no warmer toward Kissinger's proposals than Britain. Led by the French, they resented being dismissed as purely regional powers and rejected the link, implicit in Kissinger's speech, between continued American military commitments to Europe and European economic concessions to America. Reluctantly the Europeans started negotiating, but progress was slow, and, against Kissinger's wishes, economic and military questions were kept separate.

The talks were finally killed by a new outbreak of war in the Middle East, which served further to deepen the Atlantic divide. On October 6, 1973, the sacred Jewish holiday of Yom Kippur, Egypt and Syria mounted simultaneous attacks on Israel to avenge their defeat in 1967. Faced with what looked like the imminent destruction of an ill-prepared Israel, one of America's key client states, a round-the-clock airlift of supplies was mounted by Washington. America's European allies were asked if their NATO bases could be used to help the operation. All but the Netherlands and Portugal refused. German objections were overridden. Depending heavily on Arab oil supplies, the Europeans argued that the war was a non-NATO affair—"out of area" in the jargon—and that they could not provide help.

Britain, unlike Greece and Turkey, did not announce her decision publicly, but quietly intimated to Washington that a request to use British bases would be unwelcome. Reports that Britain had refused the use of the RAF base at Akrotiri in Cyprus for reconnaissance flights could thus be "staunchly denied" by Whitehall.[53] As Kissinger observes, "there was never a formal refusal on the airlift because it had been made plain that we should not ask."[54] He adds: "We took it publicly more or less stoically" but we "cursed to each other."[55] Heath believes that it was not necessary for the Americans to involve Britain in the first place. They could perfectly well have used their own facilities all the time. Their motive was simply "that they wanted to have someone else with them in doing what they wanted to do." British policy was to be "even handed" between Israel and the Arab states, and it was not in her interest, according to Heath, "to lean more to one side than the other."[56]

Worse was to come for transatlantic relations. Israel recovered from its initial surprise and gradually drove the Egyptian armies back across Sinai. By late October, faced with Egypt's virtual destruction, Moscow seemed to be threatening direct military intervention. On October 24, 1973, Nixon and Kissinger decided that the Russians must be warned off. At 11:41 P.M. all U.S. military commands around the world were placed on DefCon III alert—in Kissinger's words, "the highest state of readiness for essentially peacetime conditions."[57] The next Defense Condition, DefCon II, covers a situation in which attack is imminent. DefCon I means war.

The object was to send an unambiguous warning to Moscow. The administration did not want to dilute the effect by telling its allies in advance, since the information would almost inevitably leak out. But, as in 1962 over Cuba, Washington did accord the British special treatment. Just after 1:00 A.M. on October 25 Kissinger informed the British ambassador, Lord Cromer, of the alert and of Nixon's latest letter to Moscow. He hoped that Britain would use her influence on the NATO allies when the latter were told of the American action a few hours later. Heath's reluctance to do so again infuriated Kissinger.

From London's point of view the fact that it had been "informed" but not "consulted" about the alert revived anxiety about the status of American bases in Britain. In a stormy House of Commons, Douglas-Home was left arguing that "if the bases were to be *used* for any purpose, there would be consultation. But the Americans must be allowed to *alert* their forces the world over, just as we might in certain circumstances."[58] This distinction between the actual use of the bases in war and simply putting them on alert—the first requiring British consent under the 1952 agreement, the second not—seemed a little tenuous in the worst superpower crisis since Cuba. Heath believes America should have consulted Britain in advance. It was "mythology" that with modern intelligence devices and satellites there was no warning of the buildup, and in any case "we didn't feel that the situation required a nuclear alert."[59] Kissinger is adamant that there was no time to "wait for British approval," but hints at another explanation: "After all, the Europeans had disassociated themselves from us . . . all through the crisis."[60]

Faced with America's warning, the Soviet Union backed down and a cease-fire was arranged. But the crisis left its mark on Anglo-American relations, reinforcing fears in Britain that the United States thought it could treat Britain and Europe as pawns in its game of superpower politics. For Secretary of State Kissinger the lesson was different. "I objected then, and I object today, wherever allies try to turn the alliance into a unilateral American guarantee of what they consider to be their vital interests without reciprocity."[61] NATO, he believed, could not survive as a one-way street.

In the rapidly changing world of the early 1970s Britain and America seemed further apart than at any time since Suez or even the end of the Second World War. It was perhaps a consequence of both countries trying to redefine their roles in the world and discovering that the old relationship no longer seemed suitable to their changed circumstances. Britain was finally coming to terms with the end of her era of world power. In seeking a new future inside Europe, the Heath government was prepared for a hard-headed reexamination of the old "special relationship." The United States, for its part, was also adjusting to a relative decline in its economic and military superiority. After a quarter of a century of struggle against Russia and China there was a new, if tentative, acceptance of their right to exist as major Communist states. And America's defeated enemies of 1945, Germany and Japan, were now economic rivals. As power became diffused it seemed fair to redistribute the burdens of global security more equitably with America's allies—an ambition that Britain, along, with her European allies, appeared to have thwarted.

By 1973, in short, there were many signs that America and Britain were drifting apart diplomatically. The "special relationship" seemed to be a thing of the past. But the Anglo-American connection has always been more than diplomacy, greater than a few transatlantic links between politicians, soldiers and bureaucrats. Despite political storms the tides of economic and cultural change were ebbing to and fro across the Atlantic with unprecedented intensity, bringing the two peoples, if not the two governments, into closer contact than ever before.

CHAPTER 14

LIVING IN THE AMERICAN AGE

BUSINESS AND SOCIETY FROM THE 1940s TO THE 1970s

No account of American life in the nineteenth century can avoid frequent references to Britain—the role of British products, investment and ideas in the expansion and development of the United States. By the end of the century America was in turn making its mark on the industrial and cultural life of Britain, but even in the 1920s and 1930s influences remained two-way. After 1945, however, the current ran strongly from west to east—a flow of commerce, capital and culture that led to a new British furor in the 1960s about an American "invasion." While American firms penetrated deep into British industrial life, a new generation of Britons, dismayed by the cautious, sedate and stuffy mood of the Establishment, took their cue from their counterparts across the ocean. Their spirits were lifted by the new wave of popular music, and their rebelliousness was nurtured by the American example. But what they believed to be the norms of modern American life had only recently been established. The United States had itself been transformed in two decades after 1945.

The postwar world saw the greatest sustained improvement in living standards ever experienced. In the United States, the richest country on earth, the wartime boom began a remarkable expansion in the economy and in personal wealth. There were periodic setbacks: growth was sluggish in the late 1940s and late 1950s, and in the 1970s recession bit hard. But in 1956—when Eisenhower's election slogan was "Everything's booming but the guns"—the income of the average American was 50 percent higher in real terms than in 1929. By 1960 it was 35 percent more than in the war boom year of 1945.

The growth was largely fueled by consumer demand: America's population grew from 131 million in 1940 to 226 million forty years later. Its purchasing power was revolutionized by the expansion of personal credit, such as easy installment plans and the ubiquitous credit card. Much of the 1950s growth was based on the needs of the modern home, particularly for electrical goods. By 1953 two-thirds of American families had a TV set; by 1960 98 percent of homes with electrical wiring had a refrigerator. In the 1960s teenagers sustained the boom by their demand for clothes, soft drinks, transistors and records. Much of the economy became geared to satisfying the tastes of this new consumer culture, and to shaping those tastes through multimillion-dollar advertising that spread the gospel of happiness through possessions, satisfaction from novelty.

To produce these new, sophisticated goods required massive and expensive investment in research and development. As a result America moved further away from the small-scale, individualist values espoused by nineteenth-century liberals. In key industries, such as automobiles, chemicals, aerospace and electronics, size was everything. "The proportion of total corporate assets owned by the two hundred leading manufacturing concerns increased from 47.2 percent in 1947 to 60.9 percent in 1968."[1] The consumer culture was also the corporate culture. Charles E. Wilson, the president of General Motors who became Eisenhower's defense secretary, provided the classic statement about the identity of interests: "What's good for our country is good for General Motors, and vice versa."[2]

Industrial consolidation was not the only sign that the age of economic individualism was over. Even the biggest companies could not sustain unaided the vast costs of research and development. But the U.S. government, pursuing its cold war strategy, was ready to spend an unprecedented amount on defense and related areas, such as electronics and computers. At its peak the Korean War had pushed defense spending to nearly 40 percent of GNP and 66 percent of the total expenditure of the federal government. After the shock of Russia winning the race into space with Sputnik in 1957, the impetus was maintained by the missile program and by Kennedy's pledge in 1961 to put a man on the moon before the end

of the decade. Technical resources and skilled manpower were
mobilized for the project. Lyndon Johnson explained America's
motivation: "Failure to master space means being second best in the
crucial arena of our Cold War world. In the eyes of the world, first
in space means first, period; second in space is second in everything."[3] On July 20, 1969, an estimated one billion TV viewers all
over the world watched Neil Armstrong become the first man on
the moon. It was a triumph of American skill and determination, but
testimony also to the expanding role of government in the economy.
By the mid-1960s the federal government was funding 80 percent
of all R & D in the United States, and all but 10 percent of the
R & D by the Defense Department, the National Aeronautical and
Space Agency and the Atomic Energy Commission.

   Not everyone benefited from the boom in the economy created
by government and the consumer. As for much of the twentieth
century, the lowest fifth of America's population received only
about one-twentieth of the national income. The poorest of the poor
were mainly black, and the 1960s saw their belated effort to gain for
themselves what whites had long denied them. Led by Martin Luther King, Jr., the civil rights movement, through its marches and
protests in the early 1960s, helped eliminate much of the formal
segregation that had existed in the South since the late-nineteenth
century, including separate toilets, eating places and seating on
public transport. In 1965 it also won federal protection for blacks'
right to vote. But by 1960 only half of the black population was still
in the South and three-quarters lived in urban areas. In Northern
cities they organized for action, and glimpsed in the neighboring
white suburbs what American society offered its favored beneficiaries. But they could do little through marches and protests to deal
with the underlying urban problems of discrimination in employment, housing and education. The big-city riots each summer from
1964 to 1968 were the result of their pent-up anger and frustration.

   The civil rights movement provided the model and the inspiration for other agitation in the 1960s. Women began to organize,
pressing for an end to sex discrimination and demanding an amendment to the Constitution guaranteeing equal rights. Even more
potent were the youth protests, centered on the Vietnam War but
expressing a more general reaction against the values of the consumer society. The emphasis was on personal fulfilment through
sexual freedom, the use of drugs and experiments with various forms

of Eastern mysticism, new values that were spread by the popular music of the day.

Already in the 1950s the revolt of the young against the life-style of their parents had been symbolized by rock 'n' roll. This was a shrewdly marketed adaptation of black rhythm and blues, with white singers shouting out their lyrics against a continuous band accompaniment and an insistent beat. Parents of the fifties, accustomed to the decorous swing music of the big-band era, were often alarmed or outraged, while their children responded with wild enthusiasm. The pioneers of this new era in popular music and culture were Bill Haley and His Comets, but they were quickly outshone by Elvis Presley, the farm boy from Mississippi, who had a vocal talent and sexual charisma that Haley lacked. Elvis, with his gyrating pelvis and greased-down hair, became the cult figure of the late fifties and early sixties. The leadership in American popular music was then taken over by the more politicized folk rock of Joan Baez and Bob Dylan, both of whom were closely associated with the protest movement against the Vietnam War. By the mid-sixties a significant British influence was making itself felt. With the Beatles and the Rolling Stones, popular music became the symbol of an international youth culture.

The protest movements, whether political or musical, did not seriously challenge the dominant consumer culture. Women and blacks sought not its elimination but the extension of its benefits. By global standards even America's poor were "staggeringly well off"; the per capita income of Harlem, New York's black ghetto, "ranked with that of the top five nations in the world."[4] The most disadvantaged families often had telephones, cars and televisions. Even the young of the mammoth Woodstock music festival in 1969 or the Haight-Ashbury ("Hashbury") hippie colony of San Francisco depended on the affluent society for their wealth, leisure and life-style. Furthermore, the main focus of youth protest was the university campus—itself testimony to the success of the American way. By 1970 40 percent of eighteen- to twenty-one-year-olds were attending college or university (compared with 16 percent in 1940). The counterculture was "contemptuous of this world's goods as only people who take them for granted can be."[5]

The federal government's response to poverty and protest also exhibited distinctively American characteristics. Socialism, let alone Communism, remained a minority movement. In postwar America there was nothing comparable to the nationalization programs seen

in Britain and much of Western Europe, and the idea of a national
health service remained anathema to most Americans. In the United
States health care continued to be the concern of the individual
through private insurance schemes. Nevertheless, just as the U.S.
government had become more involved in the economy in the 1940s
and 1950s, so the 1960s saw a vast increase in government welfare
provisions. LBJ's Great Society introduced such programs as food
stamps, Medicare (funded health insurance for the aged) and Medi-
caid (medical help for those in particular need). The consequences
of this "welfare revolution" were profound. By 1974 welfare payments were consuming 16 percent of GNP, and their share of the
federal government's budget, over 40 percent, had outstripped defense.

The welfare state of the 1960s reinforced the impact of the warfare state created in the 1940s and 1950s. Both depended on a vast
increase in government expenditure and on the revolutionary assumption that such expenditure was both normal and essential for
a healthy economy and society. In short, Keynesianism was taking
root in America.

John Maynard Keynes, the British economist and government
adviser, was one of the most influential thinkers of the twentieth
century. His ideas about the role of government investment in
promoting economic growth and full employment and his criticism
of the dogma of balanced budgets had found their American advocates since the New Deal. They had been put into practice intermit-
tently since the 1930s—Roosevelt's reluctant deficit spending
during the depression, the arms booms of World War II and Korea,
and Eisenhower's fueling of the "military-industrial complex." But
Roosevelt, Truman and Eisenhower were all instinctively fiscal
conservatives who regarded unbalanced budgets as temporary aber-
rations, occasional necessary evils, and Keynes was distrusted by
many American businessmen and economists as a dangerous left-
winger.

It was not until the 1960s that policy caught up with practice. By
this time Keynes's thought had been widely disseminated in economic circles and popularized through textbooks like the best-seller
by Professor Paul Samuelson, which had sold over two million
copies by 1965. Kennedy's Council of Economic Advisers was
staffed by Keynesians led by Walter Heller. They persuaded the
President to embark on a program of tax cuts, which, he assured
business leaders in a major speech in December 1962, was not in-

tended "to incur a budget deficit, but to achieve the more prosperous, expanding economy which can bring a budget surplus." Afterward Kennedy called the speech "straight Keynes and Heller," adding that "they loved it."[6] In 1965, with Kennedy's tax cuts and Johnson's wage and price restraint, the U.S. economy grew by 5 percent in real terms. Personal incomes rose 7 percent, corporate profits were up 21 percent, and unemployment was only 4 percent. With Keynesianism it now seemed possible to manage the economy to ensure long-term prosperity. Johnson's budget director, Charles Schultze, said, "We can't prevent every little wiggle in the economy, but we now can prevent a major slide." Even Milton Friedman, America's leading conservative economist, admitted, "We are all Keynesians now."[7]

Kennedy and Johnson were Democrats, more inclined than the Republicans to permit heavy government spending. At the end of the decade Richard Nixon tried to dampen inflation by a return to Republican fiscal orthodoxy, but his attempts to balance the budget helped create a recession that led him to adopt deficit spending in 1971. Acknowledging this U-turn, Nixon, too, confessed his conversion: "I am now a Keynesian."[8]

Although Keynesianism was more than, and often very different from, what Keynes intended, it was perhaps Britain's most important intellectual export to America in the postwar era. This economic philosophy served to legitimize the vastly increased role of government in the economic life of the country—a process that has helped transform America more profoundly in the last forty years than in the previous two hundred.

For Britain the postwar story was in some respects similar to the American. The British population also experienced a dramatic improvement in living standards, so that in 1959 Macmillan could justly campaign on the slogan "You've never had it so good." And yet Britain's "age of affluence" was different in that it occurred during a period of decline in the competitiveness of the national economy compared with those of her rivals. In both affluence and decline the hand of America was very evident.

It took Britain years to shake off the austerity of war. Thanks to her foreign exchange problems and the Korean conflict, rationing continued well into the 1950s, with meat not being fully de-rationed until 1956. But from the mid-1950s Britain began to cultivate a taste for American living. With the easing of exchange controls from 1958, American goods flowed into Britain and British manufacturers geared up to satisfy the growing demand. By 1971 two-thirds of British homes had refrigerators and washing machines and 91 percent had televisions, whereas, two decades before, all these "consumer goods" had been rarities. Household appliances helped revolutionize the lives of women, while television transmitted into every home previously unimagined attitudes and life-styles. The growth in consumer demand was sustained by a credit explosion emulating America—"hire purchase" and later "plastic money." In this, as in much else, Britain was following America, a decade or so behind.

The most striking feature of the American invasion was popular music—the decisive influence in shaping the new British teenage culture. In the year of Suez Jimmy Porter, in John Osborne's play *Look Back in Anger*, grumbled: "I must say it's pretty dreary living in the American Age—unless you're an American of course. Perhaps all our children will be Americans. That's a thought isn't it?"[9]

It was a prophecy that already seemed to be coming true. In September of the same year, 1956, Bill Haley's film *Rock Around the Clock* took Britain by storm. The *New York Times* reported that "Britons are puzzled by the riotous behavior of the teen-agers who have been moved by rock 'n' roll music to sing and dance wildly in the streets, to slug inoffensive Bobbies and in general to behave in a most un-British fashion."[10] The relentless music provoked the young audiences to dance in the aisles of cinemas and to jive and sing their way in groups through the center of British towns, often clashing with the police in the process. Many cities, including Birmingham, Liverpool, Bristol and Belfast, banned the film from being shown. Sometimes it sparked off blatant hooliganism. When it was shown in the Gaiety Cinema in Manchester, fifty youths threw light bulbs and lighted cigarettes down from the gallery and turned fire extinguishers on members of the audience. A magistrate told those arrested: "It would be very much better if the police were allowed to deal with you in the way which would give you something to rock and roll about for a bit."[11]

While the courts passed down stiff sentences, guardians of high culture scoffed at the new youth heroes. *The Times* mocked Elvis Presley for his "combination of a hill-billy style of wailing with bodily contortions that are supposed to suggest the 'fundamental human drive.' . . . Mr. Presley, now the proud owner of three Cadillacs and hundreds of the violent sports shirts he affects, says: 'I don't want no regular spot on no TV programme. I love to act.

I don't care nothing whatsoever about singing in no movie.'" *The Times* commented: "Mr. Presley adds, by way of illustration, that English was what he liked best at school."[12]

But Establishment contempt had no effect. The following year Bill Haley and His Comets, already burning out in the States, had a spectacularly successful tour of Britain, traveling around in a special train. Rock 'n' roll caught on as the reaction of the young to their parents—in most extreme form through the adoption by "Teddy boys" of the Comets' dress code. British teenagers now tuned in to the ever-changing, high-decibel sounds of the American music scene. It led to an explosion in the British record industry, as it had in the United States from the early fifties. By 1973 the United Kingdom came fifth in the world-league table of record and tape sales—spending the equivalent of $38 million or $6.86 for every person in the country. (The United States headed the list with retail sales of over $2 billion, or $9.70 per head.)[13] Capitalizing on the pop music craze was a whole array of leisure industries, particularly clothing, often modeled on American fashions, such as blue jeans.

In other ways the loosening up of British life owed much to the American example: the development of commercial television in the mid-1950s, the spread of drugs in the 1960s, and the proliferation in the 1970s of pressure groups using American techniques of protest and lobbying. The American civil rights movement provided a particularly influential model, most of all for the Catholic minority in Northern Ireland. From 1968 they began to protest openly against decades of discrimination by Protestant Unionists, who dominated Ulster and who were determined to keep it part of the United Kingdom. The new sectarian violence, encouraging and encouraged by the Irish Republican Army (IRA), reopened an unsolved problem that successive British governments had chosen to ignore since the 1920s. It also reintroduced the Irish dimension into Anglo-American relations as U.S. politicians with Irish American constituencies, such as Edward Kennedy and Thomas "Tip" O'Neill, repeatedly raised the issue of Northern Ireland on Capitol Hill. Combating Irish American agitation became a major concern of British diplomats in the United States in the 1970s.

Britain was also being shaped by the presence of American servicemen. Since the arrival of the B-29 bombers during the Berlin crisis in 1948, U.S. military bases had become a small but significant reminder that Britain now sheltered under the eagle's wing. The greatest concentration of American servicemen was in East Anglia.

Many of the professional airmen had been there already in World
War II. Some had married East Anglian women, whom they
brought back with them in the fifties, while many of the locals had
friends or relatives in the United States. It was almost "an American
community," recalls Donald Griffiths of USAF Counterintelli-
gence: "You could go into a pub and have ice in your drink which
you couldn't get anywhere else in England at the time. . . . We used
to call it the forty-ninth state."[14]

Despite periodic incidents, East Anglia became relatively used to
the Americans—many of whom were married and therefore lived
more stable lives than the "oversexed, overpaid" bachelor GIs of
World War II. Much more intrusive and controversial was the U.S.
Polaris submarine base established at Holy Loch on the Clyde from
March 1961. The news was sprung on the inhabitants without
consultation or warning—feeding Scottish nationalist anger, arousing widespread fears about radiation dangers. For the first year or
so the local resort town of Dunoon attracted hundreds of CND
antinuclear demonstrators, who conducted American-style sit-ins
around the base. Some locals, more alienated by the "beatnik" protesters than by the Americans, sported posters reading "Go Home
Weirdies,"[15] and the local business community gleefully anticipated
an economic boom. But others were disturbed at the nuclear presence and upset by the conduct of some of the bachelor sailors from
the depot ship who vented their frustrations at the boring work and
long, dark winters by roisterous behavior in town, causing a sharp
increase in the local statistics for VD and illegitimacy.

The American command, facing problems that were familiar
around the military bases of every nation, quickly imposed a curfew
for their men and mounted an intensive campaign to promote good
community relations. Senior officers wined and dined local community leaders, while their wives entertained local women's groups
with slide shows about the United States. In dealing with protesters
the policy was to "out-Gandhi Gandhi," in the words of the first
base commander, Captain Richard Laning. On one occasion a CND
protester paddled his canoe up to one of the submarines and climbed
aboard. Instead of provoking an incident in front of eager ranks of
press photographers, Laning simply let him sit on the tail-fin of the
submarine until he got "blue and shivering." He was then taken to
the quarterdeck of the depot ship, where he was given "not the
third-degree treatment he expected but hot cocoa and a blanket,
before being allowed to go."[16]

But the U.S. military presence in Britain was small compared with that of World War II. It usually averaged between sixty thousand and seventy thousand base personnel and dependents from the early 1960s onward.[17] Furthermore, Pentagon policy was generally to minimize contact with the local population by creating an all-American environment on base.

More pervasive in its effects on Britain was the new "invasion" of American capital. The initial impetus was Britain's postwar dollar shortage, which limited her ability to import direct from the United States and therefore encouraged American firms to set up in Britain. But the real growth in U.S. investment came after exchange controls were eased in 1958. American companies were quick to exploit the consumer boom and envisaged Britain, with its shared language, as an easily accessible entry point into the EEC. By 1966 there were more than sixteen hundred American subsidiaries or Anglo-American-financed firms in the United Kingdom, with a total investment stake of nearly $6 billion—about one-tenth of all U.S. corporate investment overseas. Only Canada had more. In 1965 these companies employed 6 percent of the labor force in British manufacturing industry and produced 10 percent of the total goods made in British factories. Two-fifths of all the American investment was in five big companies: Esso (the tenth largest firm in Britain), Ford, Woolworth's, Vauxhall Motors and the tobacco giant Gallahers.[18]

There was little U.S. investment in Britain's declining industries, such as textiles, steel and shipbuilding. Nor were many dollars seen in the north, with the significant exception of Scotland. Most American money was concentrated in the new consumer-goods industries and in those linked with advanced technology, such as computers. These sixteen hundred companies produced more than half the cars, cosmetics, office machinery and vacuum cleaners purchased in Britain and nearly the half the drugs sold to the National Health Service, while IBM supplied two-fifths of the British computer market. American companies such as Hoover, Heinz and Kodak had become household names in Britain. Ideas borrowed from America, ranging from TV dinners to opinion polls, from barbecues to frozen vegetables, were revolutionizing daily life.

The statistics about U.S. investment and particularly the well-publicized American takeovers of British household names such as Smiths Crisps, Gallahers and Rootes, one of the "big three" car manufacturers, gave rise in the 1960s to a rash of polemics about "the

American invasion," reminiscent of those in the early 1900s and late 1920s. One such book asked: "Need alliance involve occupation? Must we become Americans to save Western civilization?"[19] Another, *The American Take-Over of Britain*, set out the British predicament with dramatic starkness: "From the moment an English baby is weaned on American-owned baby food, until he is carted away in an American-owned funeral car, he is, to that extent, American-orientated from the cradle to the grave. Must it now be universal? Is it to be 'all the way with LBJ'?"[20]

Some commentators emphasized the beneficial effects of American investment. Britain was gaining an infusion of new capital, technology and marketing skills, and many of the companies concerned, such as Ford, were high exporters who helped ease the country's balance of payments problem. American-owned companies accounted for over 17 percent of Britain's manufacturing exports in 1966. Against this, critics stressed the loss of national control over key sectors of the economy. The American parent company would inevitably decide future strategy in the light of its worldwide interests, not those of local workers or of the British economy. The car industry was a prime example. Chrysler's take-over of Rootes in 1967 meant that each of America's "big three" automobile manufacturers owned a subsidiary or plant in Britain as well as one on the Continent. Chrysler had Rootes, plus Simca in France; GM controlled Vauxhall together with Opel in Germany; and Ford had major plants in Dagenham and Cologne. They soon began to "rationalize" operations at Britain's expense, taking account of the country's peripheral geographical position and the labor problems in her car industry.

While American capital moved east, it seemed that British talent was going west. The so-called brain drain of engineers and scientists to the United States became a lively topic of public debate in mid-1960s Britain. A special government inquiry reported that in 1966 Britain lost 4,200 engineers and technologists, half of them to North America. This represented over 40 percent of the "new supply" of engineers and technologists leaving higher education three years before. Two thousand scientists also emigrated, equivalent to nearly a quarter of the new supply three years earlier. Even allowing for immigration from the Commonwealth and the return of some of those who had worked in North America, Britain experienced a net loss of 2,700 engineers, technologists and scientists in 1966.[21]

Politicians and pundits debated the causes of the brain drain. Tory politician Quintin Hogg fulminated that "the richest country in the world has been plundering the educational systems of Western Europe," because, he explained "in such a way as to cause the maximum offence . . . , the American high school system is not sufficiently good to produce high-class graduates on the scale required by American industry, American universities and the American Government."[22] U.S. Defense Secretary Robert McNamara put it differently, suggesting that "brains on the whole are like hearts— they go where they are appreciated."[23] He was referring not merely to American salary levels, up to three times those of young engineers in Britain, but to the availability of challenging work and the higher status accorded to industrial researchers in the United States. In the words of one British aeronautical engineer, exiled with dozens of colleagues in the Pacific Northwest of America: "This is a cultural wilderness. Deep down we all prefer England, its way of life, its people." But, he went on, "to be an engineer in England is to live on the edge of existence," treated as "just a factory worker. The poor image of the engineer in England results in poor pay. . . . In America we [the engineers] are on more equal terms with the other professions. . . . An engineer is respected in America."[24]

At root, the brain drain reflected the far greater expenditure on research and development in the United States compared with Western Europe—$24 billion as against $6 billion in 1966, according to one estimate[25]—despite the rough equivalence in total population. The most voracious appetites were in defense-related industries, particularly those connected with the space program. Commentators warned that, if unmatched, America's concentration of resources and skills in these high-tech areas would open an unbridgeable gap between the United States and its competitors. Prime Minister Harold Wilson feared that Britain and Europe could be "left in industrial terms as the hewers of wood and the drawers of water" while the Americans came to monopolize advanced technology.[26]

At the heart of the debate about America's economic challenge in the 1960s was British aircraft manufacture. This was a key national industry, central to Britain's defense interests and to her export drive. It also produced a high-tech fallout for the civilian economy in technologies such as electronics, computers and metallurgy. It was extremely expensive, requiring vast government support to remain competitive, but it was America's major rival in the Western world. The aircraft industry epitomized Britain's increasingly complex relationship with the United States.

By the early 1960s the industry seemed in reasonable shape to meet the American challenge. The Tories had forced it to consolidate from the extravagance of the twenty airframe companies that existed in 1958. By 1963 only two major groups were left, the British Aircraft Corporation (BAC) and Hawker Siddeley, while Westland became the main helicopter manufacturer. Hawker had RAF orders to develop the P1154 supersonic fighter and the HS 681 transport, and BAC were working on the TSR2 high-speed, low-level strike aircraft with its sophisticated computer guidance system. The P1154 and HS 681 were still on the drawing board, but the TSR2, despite technical problems and severe cost overruns, was ready ahead of its American rival, the F-111, and its first test flight took place in September 1964.

Within six months, however, all three aircraft had been abandoned, the prototypes of the TSR2 ending up as scrap or gunnery targets for the army. In their place the new Labour government had committed itself to buying more than a billion dollars' worth of American planes. After the Tories had "gone American" over strategic missiles in 1960 and 1962, it seemed that Labour was now selling out the British aircraft industry to the United States.

The abrupt change of policy was caused partly by the usual interservice rivalry. The Royal Navy, ruthlessly backed by Lord Mountbatten, chief of the Defence Staff, was determined to safeguard its own aircraft-carrier program at the expense of the RAF's planes. But the British Treasury had long believed that the aircraft industry drained too much public money for too little return. Complex modern aircraft were enormously costly and took a decade or more to produce. Until proven they depended largely on government subsidies and domestic orders to cover the vast R & D investment, and the Treasury judged that Britain simply could not compete with the United States in either respect. It therefore advised the government to purchase U.S. aircraft where possible, preferably manufactured under license in Britain to reduce dollar costs, and to concentrate British energies on aircraft engine production by Rolls-Royce. When Labour came to power in October 1964, faced with a grave financial crisis and pledged to get "value for money" in defense, it accepted this Treasury advice. It immediately axed the P1154 and HS 681, substituting orders for American Phantoms and Hercules C130 transports.

But simple cost may not have been the only factor. In addition there was Wilson's determination not to devalue the pound—because of the effect he feared on Britain's financial reputation and, it was said, on her relationship with the United States. Supporters of the TSR2 allege that the plane's cancellation was the price America extracted in return for an IMF loan to shore up sterling in December 1964. According to Julian Amery, the former Tory aviation minister, the Americans said, in effect, " 'Look here—yes, we'll let you have the money but we don't see why we should subsidize prestige projects like the Concorde.' " The government agreed to review the supersonic Concorde program being carried out jointly by Britain and France but discovered that Amery had made it part of a treaty that would have been almost impossible to break. "And it was at that point, as far as I understand it," claims Amery, that "the Americans said, 'Well, what else could you cancel? You've got this very expensive TSR2, which is much the same as our F-111—why don't you cancel the TSR2 and we'll let you have the F-111 fairly cheap." '27

Such pressure would, of course, have been in line with standard IMF policy of dissuading debtors from what it regarded as unessential spending, but it would also have suited the interests of the U.S. aircraft industry in eliminating major rivals. On the other hand, Labour's defense minister at the time, Denis Healey, dismisses allegations of American pressure as "quite untrue." While admitting that McNamara once "not very seriously" suggested "a disarmament agreement" whereby neither country would produce a Concorde-style supersonic transport, he insists that "there was never any pressure from the Americans on us so far as the TSR2 was concerned" and says that the RAF was "delighted" to have a cheap, secure source of planes from the United States.28 Nevertheless the Americans appear to have heavily subsidized the price of the Hercules as an inducement to Britain: Australia paid nearly twice as much for the same aircraft. The F-111s, also attractively priced in the initial agreement, soon escalated dramatically in cost and were canceled by the Labour government, which had only just ordered them, in the postdevaluation cuts of 1967–68.

The benefits to Britain from the episode are far from clear, and any final judgment on the controversy must await the opening of the official British archives. But the determination to preserve the value of the pound, in part to help maintain Britain's world role and her influence in Washington, does seem to have made the country more dependent on the American-directed IMF and therefore more vulnerable to any American commercial pressure. The TSR2 affair highlighted a growing tension between Britain's economic interests and the idea of a continuing special relationship with the United States. Was economic domination the price that had to be paid for the American alliance?

Initially Wilson had tried to match the Americans at their own game. He cultivated a technocratic, Kennedyesque style, mocking Macmillan's Edwardian, grouse-moor image and the relevance of "the fourteenth Earl of Home" in the Swinging Sixties. His first administration, 1964–66, saw the most determined effort of the post-war years to modernize the British economy—with a National Plan, a new Ministry of Technology to promote a high-tech revolution, and heavy government investment in industrial mergers, on the grounds that size made for competitiveness. But these attempted remedies fell afoul of Britain's deepening economic crisis and Wilson's method of handling it.

Compared with its own past performance the British economy did not decline in the 1950s and 1960s. "Between 1948 and 1968 real gross domestic product increased at an average annual rate of 2.7 percent"[29]—a better performance than in the interwar years or indeed the period before 1913. Even more striking was the unemployment rate, which for a quarter-century from 1945 remained almost always below 3 percent, compared with 10 percent or more in the interwar years. In British terms, therefore, the postwar period saw impressive growth.

But relative to Britain's competitors, the picture looked very different. British GDP grew at roughly half the rate of most of the EEC, and by the late 1970s the country that had once been the richest in Western Europe was nearly on a par with Italy in per capita output and income. At the heart of the problem was the collapse in Britain's share of world exports in manufactured goods, at a time when the consumer boom was sucking an ever-increasing flow of imports into the country. The result was a chronic payments deficit throughout the 1960s, which, in an era of fixed exchange rates, meant repeated runs on the pound.

Wilson could have devalued in 1964, as soon as he entered office, but he and his advisers refused to do so, convinced that they could support the pound and believing that the level of sterling was one of Britain's last status symbols as a world power. Wilson soon found, however, that the only alternative to devaluation was deflationary measures that directly conflicted with the need for investment and growth. Finally, after deflation at home and defense cuts abroad had both failed to save sterling, he was forced to devalue in November 1967—when it was too late to save Britain's commercial competitiveness.

The failure of national economic policy made a joint European response to America's economic threat seem more attractive. Although Britain was particularly open to American economic penetration—not only because of its industrial weakness, but because the common language made it easier for American companies to set up in the United Kingdom or to poach British talent—"the American challenge" was a problem for most of Western Europe. Jacques Servan-Schreiber, in his 1967 best-selling book with that title, was only the most prominent of commentators calling for a concerted response. He proposed Europe-wide companies, concentrating on high-tech industries, within a truly integrated Europe. "This integration will be carried out by American big business if Europe does not do it herself," he warned. "Either we build a common European industrial policy, or American industry will continue taking over the Common Market."[30]

By the mid-1960s even Labour, previously deeply suspicious of the EEC, was coming around to this point of view. After the aircraft cancellations of 1964–65, Healey turned to Anglo-French collaboration on a trainer/tactical strike aircraft and on swing-wing supersonic technology. The former resulted in the successful Jaguar, while the latter eventually became the Anglo-German-Italian Tornado developed in the 1970s.

More fundamentally, the American challenge and the failure of the British response were considerations that helped push Labour into applying for membership of the EEC in 1967. "Let no one here doubt Britain's loyalty to NATO and the Atlantic Alliance," Wilson told the Council of Europe in Strasbourg in January 1967. "But . . . loyalty must never mean subservience. Still less must it mean an industrial helotry under which we in Europe produce only the conventional apparatus of a modern economy while becoming increasingly dependent on American business for the sophisticated apparatus which will call the industrial tune in the 70s and 80s."[31] America's economic threat had proved more effective as an instrument of European integration than two decades of persuasive noises from Washington.

Like earlier scares, the sixties furor about the American invasion gradually abated. With the European media full of America's assassi-

nations, protests and racial violence, many decided that "poverty
and peace in Britain were preferable to riches and riots in America,"[32] and the brain drain became only a trickle. Britain's balance
of payments improved after devaluation, and the belated success of
Britain's EEC application between 1969 and 1972 gave a new and
hopeful focus for British aspirations. It was also possible to gain
some perspective on the extent of American economic penetration:
even in 1966 the total investment by foreign companies in the
United Kingdom was less than half that of British companies overseas, and British direct investment in the United States amounted
to nearly half the American stake in Britain.[33] And it became clear
that European countries experienced much less interference in their
economic and political life from U.S. companies than did developing states in South America, Southeast Asia and the Middle East. In
the 1950s Iran had been a particular target for British and American
oil multinationals, but the most notorious example in the 1970s was
the role of the American communications giant IT&T in Chile in
1973–74, when it helped to undermine the Socialist government of
Salvador Allende and encouraged General Augusto Pinochet's military coup. Nothing like that happened in Europe.

By the 1970s the anti-American reaction that had swept much of
Europe during the previous decade, particularly on the political left,
gave way to a more considered policy. No one followed Japan's
long-standing practice of excluding virtually all foreign capital, but
most developed countries tried to impose more stringent conditions
on potential investors so as to minimize the costs and maximize the
benefits. The 1970s also saw the beginnings of a significant reverse
flow of investment, as multinationals from Western Europe and
Japan, particularly banks, started to set up on a large scale in the
United States.

The world economy of the sixties and seventies, freed from many
of the exchange and trade controls of the immediate postwar era and
stimulated by the resurgence of Japan and Western Europe, was
demonstrating that the impetus for "modernization" no longer
came predominantly from the United States. America led, but others followed. The modern age was no longer exclusively the American age.

The erosion of American leadership was most apparent in pop
music, where the American invasion of Britain in the fifties by Bill
Haley and Elvis Presley gave way to a British cultural invasion of
America in the sixties. The most potent musical force of the decade

was the Beatles, who developed from a Liverpool skiffle group to dominate the British music scene by 1962. When they arrived for the first time at Kennedy Airport, New York, in February 1964, they were greeted by more than three thousand screaming girls, bearing posters reading "Beatles, we love you." Two hundred reporters and photographers turned the press conference into chaos as they scrambled for close-ups and quotes. One airport official shook his head in amazement: "We've never seen anything like this before. Never. Not even for kings and queens."[34] Americans liked the group's distinctive accents, "mop" haircuts and perky humor: asked at Kennedy Airport what he thought of Beethoven, Ringo Starr replied, "I love him, especially his poems." Even politicians jumped on the bandwagon. Sir Alec Douglas-Home, then the British prime minister, commended what the group was doing for Britain's balance of payments. "They are my secret weapon," he quipped.[35] Until their breakup in 1969 the group was probably the most important single influence in pop music not just in Britain and the United States but worldwide. In the 1970s the Rolling Stones took over the Beatles' mantle as the best-known British group in America.

As the United States became bogged down in the Vietnam War, with the draft or draft-dodging a major preoccupation of many young Americans, Britain seemed to offer the prospect of a freer, more civilized society. In reality what Americans saw was little more than a mirror image of what America had pioneered. By the mid-sixties England's capital was portrayed by the American media as a mecca for America's youth. *Time*, America's premier current-affairs weekly, featured "London—The Swinging City" as its cover story in April 1966.[36] In the 1900s Vienna had been in the vanguard of culture, in the twenties Paris, in the forties New York. "Today," *Time* told its readers, "it is London, a city steeped in tradition, seized by change, liberated by affluence. . . . In a decade dominated by youth, London has burst into bloom. It swings, it is the scene." This was the city of Beatles music, Mary Quant fashions and Vidal Sassoon hairstyles, of miniskirts, admen and biting satire.

Backing its analysis with eight pages of color photos, largely taken around Carnaby Street, the center of the youth fashion industry, *Time* insisted that "today Britain is in the midst of a bloodless revolution. This time, those who are giving way are the old Tory-Liberal Establishment that ruled the Empire from the clubs along Pall Mall and St. James's, the still-powerful City of London, the church and Oxbridge. In their stead is rising a new and surprising leadership community: economists, professors, actors, photographers, singers, admen, TV executives and writers—a swinging meritocracy . . . mostly under 40." Symbolizing the change, *Time* suggested, was Harold Wilson, at fifty Britain's youngest prime minister of the century, his Yorkshire tones a sign that "it is no longer necessary to affect an Oxford accent to get ahead."

Britain *was* changing in the sixties, but *Time*'s eulogy of Swinging London, like British fears of American economic domination, was exaggerated. Much of British life proved resistant to the influences of the modern American Age. Britain remained a country with its own distinctive attitude to work and a skeptical view of the American philosophy of hustle and bustle. It was accepted that Americans worked harder, but Britain's relative indolence was justified on the grounds that her quality of life was superior. The geographical mobility of labor, whether managers or blue-collar workers, which was essential to America's rapid economic growth, was not evident in Britain, where housing shortages and wide regional disparities in house prices made it harder for families to move, even if they had wanted to. Most Britons, however, put down deep roots in their local communities, preferring to accept lower rewards as the price of remaining with family and friends among whom they had grown up. White American society was much more homogeneous than Britain's, despite the vastly greater size of the United States. A Briton moving to another part of the country found himself among strangers, and disliked it. There was far greater difference between the ways of life in Conservative Cheltenham and the Labour-dominated Welsh mining town of Ebbw Vale, sixty miles away, than, say, between Wolfeboro, New Hampshire, and Wenatchee, Washington, three thousand miles across America in the Pacific Northwest.

In Britain "class" remained a national obsession. To some extent the sixties did see the rise of the meritocracy, as a new and more prosperous generation exercised its economic power and political influence. Businesses and professions began to open up, accepting the products of expanding universities regardless of their social background. But at the top the country remained dominated by a small elite, linked if not by shared background at least by a common route to the top, through the public schools and the two ancient universities of Oxford and Cambridge. Their source of wealth was now more often industry or finance instead of land; their origins

Prime Minister Harold Wilson and President Lyndon B. Johnson at the White House (December 1964). *Popperfoto*

Demonstration against the Vietnam War, near the U.S. embassy in Grosvenor Square, London (November 1968). *BBC Hulton Picture Library*

Queen Elizabeth, accompanied by Edward Heath, chats with President Richard Nixon and his wife, Pat, at Chequers (October 1970). *Popperfoto*

Bill Haley (right, kneeling) and his Comets (1957). *BBC Hulton Picture Library*

The Beatles during their American trip of August 1966. *Rex Features*

Right: America's youth culture of the sixties invades Britain: hippie love-in in London's Hyde Park. *Rex Features*

British rock music goes West: A Rolling Stones concert in America. *Rex Features*

A British cultural export to America: BBC TV's *The First Churchills*. *BBC*

Alistair Cooke, transatlantic interpreter. *BBC*

An American cultural export to Britain: *Dallas*. *Rex Features*

President Jimmy Carter with Prime Minister James Callaghan in Newcastle (May 1977). *Rex Features*

London's Leicester Square during the Winter of Discontent (1978–79). *BBC*

Secretary of State Alexander Haig at London's Heathrow Airport during the Falklands crisis (April 1982). *Rex Features*

Prime Minister Margaret Thatcher and President Ronald Reagan at Camp David. *Rex Features*

Brits out of Ireland: pro-IRA demonstration in America (July 1983). *Rex Features*

Yanks out of Britain: British demonstration against the raid on Libya (April 1986). *Rex Features*

Hands across the Ocean: simultaneous rock concerts in Britain and America, linked by television, raise money for Ethiopian famine relief. *London Features International*

Mixed up together? British bobbies watch American football in London's Hyde Park. *Allsport Photographic*

were more diverse than in earlier decades. But the British experience was still in marked contrast to that of America, where elites were regional rather than national, and class was largely a matter of money instead of involving accent, education and manners as well. Lower down the British social scale the sense of class manifested itself in fraught industrial relations, riddled with demarcations of status and role, and in confrontation between management and unions, often centered on the use of new technology. American companies that tried to introduce their own methods of management often provoked conflict, as at Vauxhall in 1966, or, like Esso, found that it took years to reach a streamlined agreement on wages and conditions.

Perhaps the most striking survival of British tradition was the monarchy, which, despite periodic debate, went from strength to strength during the postwar years, making Britain the most celebrated exception in a predominantly republican world. Since 1910 the country has had only four monarchs, one of whom, Edward VIII, lasted less than a year. The other three—George V, George VI and Elizabeth II—could all be held up as paragons of morality and family values while also displaying in full splendor the pomp and circumstance of Britain's past. Edward VIII was the great exception to this "synthesis of private probity and public grandeur,"[37] consorting with married women and scoffing at court protocol. Significantly, the Jazz Age prince was the most "Americanized" member of the House of Windsor.

Ironically, it was radio and particularly television, usually the harbingers of change, that assisted in this consecration of the Royal Family as the nation's symbol. Christmas messages from the monarch, the broadcasting of state occasions and the opening up of royalty's private life to the TV cameras—all this helped confirm the popularity of the Crown at a time when the rest of the landed aristocracy was declining rapidly in influence and prestige. Thirteen opinion polls (another American invention) taken between 1953 and 1976 suggested that on average only "11% of the population was opposed to a monarchy throughout this period."[38] For most British people their virtuous, politically neutral, long-lived monarchs came to symbolize the continuity of national values in an era of change and decay, despite the fact that the adulation of royalty was a relatively recent phenomenon.

Britain, then, remained at root resistant to the winds of change blowing across the Atlantic. The most controversial cultural influ-

ence on Britain in the 1960s was not America but the growing
numbers of nonwhite migrants from the "New Commonwealth."
By the end of the decade their presence had aroused a powerful
political backlash, of which the principal spokesman was Tory MP
Enoch Powell. The proportion of nonwhites in the population was
only about 3.3 percent by the mid-1970s, but in numerical terms the
1.8 million New Commonwealth residents constituted a far larger
colored population than the eight thousand or so in Britain before
World War II, and many white Britons refused to accept the new
immigrants and their offspring as members of the community. Yet
by the 1970s 40 percent of nonwhites had been born in Britain.[39]
Talk of "sending them home" ignored this simple fact.

The American race problem was repeating itself in Britain, albeit
on a smaller scale, with nonwhite communities overwhelmingly
concentrated in the decaying inner cities and increasingly alienated
from the norms of a society of which they were members but not
full beneficiaries. Yet, unlike American blacks, the British colored
population did not develop its own protest movement or political
organization. Resentment exploded in sporadic communal violence,
often directed at the police. And because the nonwhite population
was located in a few urban areas, much of the country felt able to
turn a deaf ear to its demands for equal treatment.

During the 1960s, at a time when the United States and Great
Britain seemed to be drifting apart diplomatically, the American
imprint on British life became more apparent than ever before—in
industry, life-style and music. Britain's response was ambivalent,
much as America's had been toward British influence on its own
development in the nineteenth century: welcoming the material
benefits but resenting the sense of dependence. Yet in the sixties,
although living in the American Age, Britain was not "Americanized"—any more than the United States a century or two before had
been "Anglicized." For the modern world was becoming a "global
village" in which the winds of change blew from many directions,
not just one. And Britain retained its own distinctive social character, sometimes shaped by new forces, such as racial diversity, usually
drawing self-consciously on the legacy of the past. In the last analysis the fear of Americanization was more pronounced than the reality—evidence of a country losing its power, pride and sense of
direction in a new and unfamiliar world.

CHAPTER 15

ALL
AT SEA
1973-1980

From the 1970s onward the story of Anglo-American relations no longer lies at the heart of world affairs. Britain and America, as allies or as rivals, had shaped the first half of the twentieth century, but as America matured as a superpower much of its diplomacy was conducted independently of the British influence that had helped direct its rise to world leadership. As Britain declined in global power her foreign policy and her relations with the United States became peripheral to the vital issues of international affairs. Where Britain did matter, it was often as one of the Western European states, as a member of NATO or the EEC, rather than by herself.

But Britain did not become completely European. If Edward Heath's vision of a Britain playing its full role in Europe had become a reality, the 1970s and 1980s would have been very different. Britain would have been integrated with her European neighbors, pursuing a coherent European foreign policy. There would have been little to say about America and Britain that could not equally have been said about America's relations with France or West Germany. But the vision of 1973 was deceptive, or perhaps premature. A united Western Europe and a stable superpower détente were hard to achieve. The late seventies saw the world reverting to the patterns of the fifties and sixties, with Anglo-American relations restored—albeit diminished in importance—Britain still distant from continental Europe, and global politics dominated by hostile superpowers.

The last year of Edward Heath's Conservative government had put the Anglo-American relationship under acute strain, first over Henry Kissinger's call for the "Year of Europe" and then over Britain's refusal to support American policy during the Yom Kippur war. When Heath was defeated in the election of February 1974, Harold Wilson's new Labour government worked to restore ties with Washington. His foreign secretary, James Callaghan, recalls that "Mr Heath's deep and lasting commitment to Europe had weakened our relations with the United States, and as a strong believer in the Atlantic Alliance, I was determined that these must be strengthened."[1] In his first major statement of policy Callaghan criticized "anti-American tinges" in European opinion and urged that Europe should engage in the "fullest and most intimate" cooperation with the United States, adding that "we repudiate the view that Europe will emerge only after a process of struggle against America."[2]

Behind the scenes the two governments continued to foster the close defense ties that had characterized the Anglo-American relationship since the 1950s. Although Labour was officially pledged not to develop a new generation of nuclear weapons, Wilson and Callaghan renewed the agreements originally made with Eisenhower in 1958–59 for the exchange of nuclear information and materials. They also secretly continued the Tories' expensive modernization program for Polaris. Wilson told his Cabinet that nuclear weapons amounted to only 2 percent of Britain's defense budget, that they gave her "a unique entrée to US thinking" and that it was important for Britain's diplomatic influence to remain a nuclear power.[3]

The habits of close consultation between London and Washington were also resumed. Wilson visited Washington in February 1975, meeting Nixon's successor, Gerald Ford. One of Wilson's Cabinet ministers, Barbara Castle, noted in her diary afterward that "he could not resist a little touch of the old self-satisfaction at the way he had been received by President Ford. Relations with the United States, he said, were 'as good as they have ever been,' adding typically, 'The ceremonies of welcome went far beyond anything I have had before.' "[4] Callaghan succeeded Wilson as premier in March 1976 and soon established a particularly good rapport with Jimmy Carter, who became president in January 1977. When Carter visited Britain that spring, Callaghan deliberately took him away from London and the South to see Newcastle and the industrial northeast of England. Carter visited Washington Old Hall, the ancestral home of the first president of the United States, and delighted the Newcastle crowds by shouting the local rallying cry "Haaway the Lads" in a passable Geordie accent. Carter and his UN ambassador, Andrew Young, worked closely with Callaghan's government in its efforts to find a settlement in Rhodesia.

Although Britain no longer played a major global role, many American leaders considered these close contacts to be invaluable. The common language made communication easy, and the breadth of Britain's international connections and experience still enabled her to offer authoritative advice. Henry Kissinger, who believed that this "consultative relationship" was particularly useful to the United States, went so far as to say of his years as national security adviser in the White House: "I kept the British Foreign Office better informed and more closely engaged than I did the American State Department."[5]

Heath had been cold toward America, passionate about Europe. The Labour government's greater warmth toward the United States reflected its coolness to the EEC. Michel Jobert, the French foreign minister, remarked that while Heath was "a man of the Rhine," Wilson was "a man of the Scilly Isles."[6] On the EEC, as on most issues, Labour was divided, and, to secure party unity, Wilson campaigned in 1974 on a commitment to renegotiate the terms of Britain's entry and to submit the result to a national referendum. As with Labour's earlier pledge in the 1964 campaign to "renegotiate" the Polaris agreement, the performance did not live up to the promise. Britain's partners offered only limited concessions and Wilson's Cabinet was still divided, but he went ahead with the referendum. His own ministers were free to campaign as they liked, and Britain was treated to the extraordinary spectacle of senior Cabinet colleagues arguing in public for and against membership. Barbara Castle commented in March 1975: "Cabinet government barely exists any more and is certainly broadly in abeyance until the referendum is over."[7] On June 5, 1975, two-thirds of the electorate voted and, by a majority of two to one, indicated its desire to stay within the European Community. Wilson announced that "fourteen years of national argument are over."[8]

Membership of the Common Market did not mean, however, that the British public thought of itself as European. In June 1979 inter-

est in the new direct elections to the European Parliament was
lukewarm. Nor was there much enthusiasm for the idea of a federal
Europe, which the United States had envisaged at the time of the
Marshall Plan and which had been the dream of the EEC's founding
fathers. As the decade progressed public attitudes toward the Community became, if anything, more antagonistic. Britain had joined
at a bad moment. The long postwar European boom had ended, and,
in the recession that followed, the economic benefits promised by
pro-Marketeers were slow to materialize. The British were also
paying the price for joining after the Community's institutions had
been created. The common agricultural policy, designed to protect
the Continent's many small farmers, was an expensive burden for
Britain, whose agricultural sector was less significant and relatively
efficient.

Hopes that Europe would prove a new force in world affairs were
also dashed. Since late 1972 the heads of government of the Community countries had developed the practice of regular summit meetings to coordinate policy, and in 1973 Kissinger's call for a new
Atlantic Charter had united Western Europe against him. But when
the Arabs quadrupled the price of oil after the Yom Kippur war, the
EEC's common front disintegrated. At their summit in Copenhagen
in February 1974 the Community leaders bickered openly, unable
to agree on whether to negotiate with the Arabs and whether to
cooperate with the United States in an effort to stabilize oil prices.
The result was "a kind of *sauve-qui-peut*, a scurrying for advantage
through bilateral negotiations with this or that oil-producing country."[9] Ironically, only under Kissinger's leadership was Europe
eventually able to establish some kind of joint oil policy. Unity on
monetary policy proved equally elusive. In 1977 France and Germany developed a European Monetary System, designed to keep
national currency and interest rates in harmony in Europe at a time
when the Americans were allowing the dollar to slide. But Britain
refused to join.

The vision of a united and influential European Community,
which had inspired many in the early 1970s, had soon faded. The
other new powers envisaged in the early 1970s, China and Japan,
also failed to develop political and military strength to match their
population and industrial resources. The two superpowers, America
and Russia, still dominated world affairs. They remained the only
nuclear giants and arms limitation talks were a matter for them
alone. And, by the end of the 1970s, the détente that seemed so

hopeful a few years before had degenerated into renewed confrontation between them.

Jimmy Carter was one of the best-educated men to occupy the White House since World War II. He was hardworking, experienced in business and trained as a nuclear engineer. But he was a Washington outsider, who remained naive in the ways of political management and often failed to translate his almost visionary idealism into viable policies. Starting from the assumption that détente would continue, the President was anxious to shift the focus of American foreign policy away from superpower rivalry to issues that he thought had been neglected: human rights, Third World development and nuclear nonproliferation. After the brutality of Vietnam, after the corruption of Watergate, he wanted the United States to behave in a more principled way.

Carter's inauguration dramatically symbolized his approach to the presidency. He saw himself in the mold of Woodrow Wilson, as the moral leader of his country. In his address, on the steps of the Capitol, he expressed the hope that he could build "a lasting peace, based not on weapons of war but on international policies which reflect our own most precious values." Then he and his family were driven back toward the White House in a motorcade of long black limousines. But suddenly the cars stopped in the middle of Pennsylvania Avenue, the Carters jumped out and, amid gasps and then cheers from the crowd, walked the rest of the way to the White House, the President and his wife hand in hand. He wrote later: "I felt a simple walk would be a tangible indication of some reduction in the imperial status of the President and his family."[10]

Carter soon began to act on his belief that the United States should stop behaving like a militaristic superpower. Despite protests from conservatives, he imposed a brake on the modernization of America's strategic forces. The B-1 bomber was canceled, naval spending reduced and the MX missile program slowed down. He tried to increase the momentum of arms control talks. The 1972 SALT I treaty was only a temporary freeze on missile launchers. A comprehensive agreement had been drafted under Ford, but its approval was delayed because Carter wanted deeper cuts.

The President also tried to improve America's image among developing countries. In 1903 the United States had pressured the new Panamanian republic to be allowed to build a canal through the isthmus and to exercise perpetual sovereignty over it. America's position in Panama had long been deeply resented in Central America, much as the Suez Canal had been in Egypt earlier in the century. Carter believed it essential to right an injustice and dispose of the criticism that America was an imperialist power. In 1977 he concluded a treaty with Panama, pledging U.S. withdrawal at the end of the century with rights of return in an emergency. Despite the opposition of the Republican right, led by Ronald Reagan, who had repeatedly insisted that "we built it, we paid for it, it's ours and ... we are going to keep it,"[11] Carter forced the canal treaty through the Senate in a long and bitter battle.

The Panama Canal treaty was Carter's major diplomatic success, although he also helped bring Egypt and Israel to the negotiating table and completed the normalization of relations with Communist China. But the foundation of his foreign policy was soon undermined because of the breakdown of détente.

By the time the SALT II arms limitation treaty was signed by Carter and Leonid Brezhnev in Vienna in June 1979, détente had become a dirty word in the United States. Many Americans had assumed that Moscow would now behave as the United States wanted. But the Soviets saw détente not as an end to rivalry but as competition by other means. They continued their efforts to gain parity with the global power and influence of the United States, shifting the focus away from Europe and nuclear weapons to the Third World. The seventies saw a rapid growth of the Soviets' influence in Africa, where they used Cuban troops in countries like Angola, and the expansion of the Soviet Navy into the Pacific and Indian oceans. Russia had now become not merely a major land power but, for the first time, a global sea power as well. Carter's national security adviser, Zbigniew Brzezinski, warned the President that he was underestimating the Soviet threat and argued from U.S. history that a foreign policy of moral principle could work only if there was prior respect for American power. "You first have to be a Truman before you are a Wilson," he told the President.[12]

Carter's conversion occurred at Christmas, 1979. On December 27 the President cut short his holiday and returned to the White House because of reports that the Soviet Union was airlifting troops and supplies into Afghanistan—over two hundred flights in the previous twenty-four hours. The Russians had invaded to shore up their Marxist client regime on the USSR's southern borders. After a tense meeting with his advisers on December 28 Carter sent Brezhnev on the hot line what he considers "the sharpest message of my Presidency," warning the Russian leader that the invasion was "a clear threat to the peace" and that it "could mark a fundamental and long-lasting turning point in our relations."[13]

In public Carter was equally blunt. Under attack at home over his management of the economy, he struck out at Russia, calling this "the greatest threat to peace since World War II" and claiming that it had "made a more dramatic change in my own opinion of what the Soviets' ultimate goals are than anything they've done in the previous time I've been in office."[14] With Afghanistan's neighbor Iran in turmoil following the fall of the Shah, there seemed a real Russian threat to the Persian Gulf, which was vital for the West's oil supplies. Carter quickly imposed sanctions on Russia, including an embargo on grain sales and a ban on American participation in the Moscow Olympics. More seriously, he also withdrew the SALT II treaty from Congress. Even before Afghanistan it faced strong opposition; after the invasion there was no hope of ratification. By 1980 the talk was not of détente but of a new cold war.

America's European allies watched the twists and turns of U.S. policy with disquiet. In the mid-1970s the economic friction between the United States and the EEC had intensified. The Americans protested that European subsidies and tariffs were undercutting key sectors of their economy. In 1977–78 the Europeans resented the decline of the dollar, which was encouraged by the administration to make U.S. exports more competitive but which damaged their own trade. Western European governments were even more disturbed about arms control. As the SALT talks progressed during the 1970s there were fears in European capitals that a deal might be reached over their heads. This could leave them outnumbered by the Warsaw Pact's conventional forces and outclassed by the newly modernized Soviet intermediate nuclear missiles. These fears were acute in West Germany, which would be the battleground if the bluff of deterrence was called and conventional war broke out again.

After long negotiations the NATO Allies therefore announced on December 12, 1979, that new American intermediate-range nuclear weapons would be deployed in Western Europe: 108 Pershing II missiles in West Germany and 464 ground-launched Cruise missiles, 160 of which would be based in Britain. This was not a U.S. initiative, forced on Europe, but Washington's response to the fears of European governments, particularly Bonn. Brzezinski commented later: "I was personally never persuaded that we needed [the new weapons] for military reasons. I was persuaded reluctantly that we needed [them] to obtain European support for SALT."[15]

Yet the European governments, again with the Germans in the lead, did not seek renewed confrontation with the Russians. They lived in closer proximity than the Americans to the Soviet Union and, as countries with few remaining global interests, they were less concerned than the United States about superpower rivalries in Africa or Asia. They wished to maintain the momentum of détente as long as their security was assured. So on December 12, 1979, NATO also affirmed its determination to negotiate substantial reductions in nuclear forces on both sides in Europe. NATO policy, therefore, was "dual-track": deploying new missiles while seeking long-term arms reductions. The idea was negotiation from a position of security.

A few weeks later came Afghanistan and Carter's withdrawal of SALT II from the Senate. America's sudden shift into renewed confrontation with Russia was profoundly unsettling for Western Europe. There was little enthusiasm for sanctions and a widespread suspicion that Carter was exaggerating the threat to peace in order to strengthen his chances of reelection. Helmut Schmidt, the West German chancellor, was particularly critical of what he called Carter's "deadly game," even suggesting that Germany and France might serve as "interpreters" between the two superpowers in an effort to maintain détente.[16]

But Carter and America were in no mood to listen. By 1980 they were preoccupied with a single diplomatic crisis that demonstrated, more vividly than any words of Carter, the limits of American power. Early in 1979 the Shah of Iran, America's bulwark in the Persian Gulf since the British withdrawal, was overthrown and a fundamentalist Islamic regime installed. That autumn Carter admitted the Shah into the United States for medical treatment. Incensed, Iranian "students" took over the U.S. embassy in Tehran on November 4, 1979. Some of its inmates were later released, but fifty-two were held hostage for 444 days, victims of visceral anti-American feeling welling up after years of forced Westernization imposed, with Washington's backing, by the Shah's regime. Negotiations for the hostages' release failed, as did an attempted rescue mission in April 1980.

Carter, the media and the public were mesmerized by these fifty-two Americans. Their prospects were analyzed on every news bulletin, their memory perpetuated by ubiquitous yellow ribbons. It was testimony to the high value placed by Americans on the security and freedom of their citizens. But few other countries would have become so obsessed. By defining foreign policy almost exclusively in terms of this one issue, Carter had allowed America itself to be taken hostage. The rest of his presidency was overwhelmed by the crisis, and the growing mood of frustration at American impotence was a major reason for Carter's defeat in the November 1980 election.

Both American and British diplomacy displayed a similar lack of direction in the later 1970s, appearing all at sea in unfamiliar waters—sometimes following old bearings, sometimes setting course anew. Britain looked to Europe, then to America; the United States explored détente, then swung back to cold war confrontation. But the source of their confusion was not simply the unsettled state of the world. It was also due to the collapse of the Western economic boom that had lasted for most of the period since 1945. Both countries were shaken by the recession, and its larger ramifications helped to push them further apart in the late 1970s.

The experience of virtually continuous economic growth had been a feature of life in much of the developed world in the quarter-century after 1945. A generation had grown up that took for granted prosperity, full employment and government largess. Few were therefore prepared for the economic recession of the 1970s, which began to bite in 1973–74, when the Arab oil producers quadrupled oil prices and struck at one of the foundations of the postwar boom: cheap, secure energy supplies. The developed world soon faced an unprecedented problem, "stagflation"—a combination of stagnant growth and roaring inflation, which Keynesian orthodoxy seemed incapable of explaining, let alone of curing.

The U.S. economy still grew in the 1970s and the living standards of Americans improved by nearly a quarter. But unemployment climbed to over 6 percent, with blacks disproportionately hit, and prices more than doubled during the decade—four times as large an increase as in the fifties and sixties.[17] America was now less able than in the past to insulate itself from the ups and downs of the world economy. For much of the century, foreign trade had been of little importance to the U.S. economy as a whole, but during the 1970s it grew to over one-fifth of the Gross National Product. Exports alone constituted nearly 13 percent of total GNP by 1981.[18] Key industries, such as cars, steel, textiles and electronics, were therefore vulnerable to competition from Europe, Japan and developing

Pacific nations like South Korea. The "national mood" was intro-
spective and uncertain. Economic sluggishness, the energy crisis
and the growth of foreign competition all suggested that the era of
American abundance and supremacy might be coming to an end.

The recession of the mid-1970s also exposed a fundamental shift
of power within the United States, which had been developing since
World War II. By 1980 one-tenth of Americans lived in California,
which had overtaken New York during the 1960s as the most populous state, while Texas now came third, having nearly doubled in
numbers during the previous thirty years. The "Sunbelt" of states
from Florida to California was the location of much of the new
high-tech and defense-related industries, in contrast with the "Rust-
belt" of the Northeast and Midwest where many of the older, less
competitive industries, such as steel and automobiles, were concentrated. The collapse of these industries, in the seventies recession,
accelerated the migration south and west—away from the Atlantic
seaboard, the area most shaped by European and particularly British
influences and connections, toward the Pacific, where America's
new trading partners and rivals, notably Japan, were to be found.

The changing ethnic balance of America reinforced this shift in
its economic geography. New leaders were challenging the old
white Anglo-Saxon Protestant leadership with its natural affinity for
Britain. The great waves of immigrants from Eastern and Southern
Europe that had crossed the Atlantic in the early twentieth century
had gradually been assimilated into American society. They became
a force first in the politics of big Northern cities, such as Boston and
Chicago, and then in the Democratic party, from the New Deal
onward. After the war they left their mark on Washington itself,
including its diplomacy. By the seventies American foreign policy
was being made by men with names such as Kissinger and Brzezinski. Much had changed since the era of Marshall and Acheson,
whose view of Britain had been influenced by British ancestry and
their experiences of the wartime alliance.

Yet the assimilation of the European Americans did not mean that
the United States was no longer a nation of immigrants. It was just
that the influx from across the Atlantic, which had shaped America
in earlier centuries, had now dried up. In the 1970s over 6 percent
of Americans had been born abroad, a marked increase on each of
the previous two decades. Forty percent of them came from Asia,
from countries such as Vietnam and South Korea, and another 40
percent from the Spanish-speaking countries of Central and South

America. The Hispanic Americans were the fastest growing minority group in the United States. Officially they were calculated at 6.5 percent of the population, but that was probably a considerable underestimate because the United States had a 1,500-mile border with Mexico, largely uncontrolled, which enabled thousands to slip in illegally.[19] By 1970 one in six Americans claimed to have a mother tongue that was not English. Nearly a quarter of these spoke Spanish, and they had now overtaken German speakers as the most numerous group with a non-English mother tongue.[20]

Many Hispanics and blacks did not want to assimilate completely into American life: they sought its economic and social benefits while retaining their cultural distinctiveness. This new pride in ethnic diversity was a spinoff from the civil rights movement of the 1960s, from slogans such as "Black is beautiful." The America these minorities wanted was a pluralist one in which different ethnic groups lived together, not fusing their identity in the WASP culture. Their ideal was "the salad bowl," not "the melting pot."

For Hispanics, in particular, language was a vital part of their effort to retain their cultural identity. In the 1960s the federal government had enacted legislation intended to improve minority groups' proficiency in English by teaching it to them in their mother tongue. In the 1970s this was often exploited by local Hispanic communities to promote Spanish as the primary teaching language in schools. In the past the United States had survived as a unified country because of its insistence that all newcomers must accept a common national language—English. Back in the early twentieth century German Americans had battled against the dominant English-speaking culture; the draft protest in New Ulm in 1917 had been one example. In the 1970s, assisted by much broader legal recognition for minority rights, the growing Hispanic population posed a new challenge to the "Anglo" ethos of America. These new Americans felt no special affinities with Britain.

Even those Americans who naturally looked across the Atlantic felt little but dismay at the state of Britain during the seventies. The country seemed incapable of grappling with the problems that it had been facing for several decades. They were easy to describe but hard to cure: declining old industries, lack of new investment, bad management, poor productivity, embattled labor relations and the absence of incentives. Growth in the rest of the world was sluggish; in Britain it was nonexistent. In the mid-seventies, British living

standards fell for the first time since 1945 and inflation was running
at 25 percent in 1975.

Although the economy failed to grow, the demands of its
beneficiaries increased. Welfare payments and government subsidies to industry took an increasing proportion of national income,
while labor unions competed in self-defeating wage claims, which
only fueled inflation. Twice governments were brought down after
conflict with the unions. In 1974 the Conservatives lost the election
after Heath confronted the miners on the issue of pay restraint.
Labour returned to power, but its "social contract" with the unions
eventually collapsed in the "winter of discontent" of 1978–79.
Americans had believed Britain, for all its failings, to be one of the
world's most civilized societies. Now the media showed a country
in which, it seemed, the dead lay unburied, the sick were turned
away from hospitals and the refuse was piled high in the streets.

Not only was the United Kingdom hard to govern, it seemed to
be breaking apart. The escalating sectarian violence in Northern
Ireland forced Westminster to replace provincial government with
direct rule from 1972, but no solution could be found. Tit-for-tat
shootings increased, and the British Army, hated by the Catholics
and distrusted by Loyalist Protestants, was drawn into an apparently unending commitment. In Wales and Scotland nationalist
political parties were on the march, albeit more peacefully. They
demanded a devolution of powers from London and won increasing
support among voters. Labour, with a slim parliamentary majority,
was reliant on their backing to keep itself in power in the mid-1970s,
and it eventually conceded referenda on Welsh and Scottish devolution in 1979.

To many Americans the United Kingdom seemed disorderly and
disunited. Commentator Eric Sevareid, who had lauded Britain's
defiance of Hitler in 1940, told television viewers in May 1975 that
"Britain is drifting towards a condition of ungovernability." Economist Milton Friedman insisted in November 1976 that a military
coup, like that of General Pinochet in Chile, was "the only outcome
that is conceivable."[21] Others claimed that Britain had "become the
latest version of the Sick Man of Europe,"[22] a humiliating comparison with the old Turkish empire before the First World War. Many
American conservatives pointed to Britain as an indictment of socialism, Keynesianism and the welfare state—vices to which, they
judged, America itself had become dangerously attached.

Britain had become used to America no longer taking her seriously as a world power. But it was deeply distressing to realize that she was also losing her reputation for political sagacity. In the late-nineteenth century Woodrow Wilson had praised the British system of Cabinet government as superior to America's separation of powers, which often made it hard for president and Congress to reach agreement on policy. In the 1950s American liberals had argued that in Britain the tighter party discipline and deference to political leaders would prevent grass-roots paranoia like McCarthyism. The author of an American textbook on British politics published in 1965 wrote: "Just as Alexis de Tocqueville travelled to America in 1831 to seek the secrets of democracy, so today we might travel to England in search of the secrets of stable representative government."[23]

But the turmoil of the seventies cast Britain in a different light. "As it once showed the way to democratic success," wrote one Harvard professor, "today it blazes the trail towards democratic failure."[24] Britain's institutions seemed incapable of coping with the demands of the seventies—vested interests apparently blocking industrial regeneration, pressure groups demanding greater shares of a diminishing national cake. Across the Atlantic, Americans, with Watergate and Vietnam behind them, regained faith in the wisdom of their own political institutions. An unfettered press and an independent legislature seemed essential to check the "imperial presidency," exposing the iniquities of the Nixon administration and reining in the President's power to wage war behind Congress's back. The comment of Woodrow Wyatt, a British political columnist and former MP—"Don't think a Watergate couldn't happen here. You just wouldn't hear about it"—was noted with approval in America.[25]

By the mid-1970s Britain no longer mattered, even to Anglophile Americans, as a world power or as a political example. It was her past, not her present, that now seemed attractive, and in the seventies more and more Americans were ready to cross the ocean to sample, for a few weeks, the world they were glad to have lost.

Crossing the Atlantic by sea had always been the preserve of a few, mostly the rich or the migrants. The start of commercial air travel did little initially to change that. But during the 1960s, with greater affluence and more competitive fares, transatlantic travel began to be feasible for ordinary people. In 1965 Britain and France had each drawn about 670,000 American visitors. But thereafter Britain became the principal attraction. In 1970, 1.4 million Ameri-

MEET WINSTON

Winston is the Poundstretcher 'mascot' and he's as
British as the Union Jack he wears. Winston is your
friend and he's around to make sure all your travel
arrangements meet his most exacting demands in
value-for-money flights and holidays. Winston is
strong, faithful, tenacious, appealing. He's everything
that Poundstretcher is and stands for.

*Britain's Churchillian past becomes copy for the admen: British Airways
"poundstretcher" promotion for transatlantic flights.*

cans visited the country, a figure that had doubled by 1984. Even
more striking were the economic benefits. In 1960 Britain earned
about $120 million from American tourists, in 1971 $344 million,
and by the early 1980s over a billion dollars.[26]

Americans showed little interest in modern Britain, struggling to
emerge from the ruins of the old. They came not to see new towns
and new factories but to visit the relics of Britain's past: ancient
cities, country houses, literary haunts. Above all, tourists were fas-
cinated by the monarchy, Britain's most distinctive national symbol,
which had been given additional appeal through Queen Elizabeth II's Silver Jubilee in 1977 and the media's obsession with the
lives and loves of her children. The marketing of Britain as a tourist
attraction, an increasingly slick business operation, deliberately concentrated on these past glories. One of Britain's most successful
promoters in the United States during the 1970s was actor Robert

"Say—it's really great to be invited into a typical English home."

The illusions of American tourists, according to Punch, *March 1, 1972.*

Morley, on advertisements for British Airways. His blimpish but genial Briton seemed like a parody of Churchill. Later the airline adopted bulldog "Winston" as one of its marketing emblems. For "postindustrial" Britain, tourism had developed into a major service industry. The country's past was becoming its future.

Television reinforced these impressions. In the 1930s British news bulked large on the pages of serious American newspapers. By the 1970s Britain was rarely mentioned at all by the American media, with the exception of the royal family. But upmarket American television was keenly interested in things British. Many historical series produced by British television were bought up by American public stations—*The Forsyte Saga, The First Churchills, Upstairs, Downstairs.* They were shown under the umbrella of *Masterpiece Theater,* hosted by the transplanted English journalist Alistair Cooke, who explained the essential historical background to puzzled American viewers, much as he had edified a generation of British radio listeners with his *Letter from America.* In the 1970s *Masterpiece Theater* was conveying the same archaic impressions of Britain as had movies of the 1930s, such as *The Private Life of Henry*

VIII or *A Yank at Oxford*. Television, like the tourism industry, perpetuated the image of Britain as a country that relished being behind the times, not one desperately trying to keep up with them.

The portrait of the United States presented on British television was no more flattering. British TV acquired action series from the United States: Westerns such as *The Lone Ranger* or *Laramie*, crime stories like *Perry Mason* and *Cagney and Lacey*, and those grotesque flauntings of American materialism—*Dallas* and *Dynasty*. These programs played on familiar British stereotypes of America: a country of vice, violence and conspicuous wealth. This was the America that Britons loved—or loved to hate. As with the cinema of the 1930s, whose pernicious effects Ambassador Joseph Kennedy had castigated in 1939, so with television: a generation in Britain derived their main impressions of the United States from "the box," unbalanced by any awareness of the real Americans whose life-style was almost as far removed from the screen image as was their own.

In the 1970s tourism and television helped to bridge the Atlantic divide. They offered ordinary Britons and ordinary Americans an unprecedented opportunity to get acquainted with the other country. But they could do little to counter America's sense that Britain was now irrelevant to the modern world; on the contrary, they often reinforced it. Stripped of her empire and her wealth, torn by strife and dissension, Britain seemed at best a living museum. One Labour member of Parliament, Andrew Faulds, envisaged her in the future as "a sort of Switzerland with monuments in place of mountains . . . to provide the haven, heavy with history, for those millions . . . who will come seeking peace in a place away from the pulsating pressures and the grit and grievances of their own industrial societies."[27]

But despite the shocks of the seventies, not everyone in Britain was ready to write her off. In May 1979 conservative Britain elected her first woman prime minister, at a time when no American woman had even been a candidate for president or vice-president. Margaret Thatcher did not accept that decline was irreversible. She set out to regenerate Britain at home and rebuild British influence abroad. In doing so, she looked across the Atlantic for support, to a new American president whose ideals were similar to her own and who was equally determined to restore his country's power and pride. Together they established one of the closest personal bonds in the history of Anglo-American cooperation and breathed new life into the "special relationship."

CHAPTER 16

A RELATIONSHIP
RENEWED
1981–1987

At noon on Tuesday, January 20, 1981, Ronald Reagan was inaugurated as the fortieth president of the United States. Forty minutes later news came through that the fifty-two American hostages had left Tehran airport after 444 days of captivity. Carter's efforts to secure their release had finally borne fruit, aided by Algerian diplomacy and by a large financial settlement. But he was no longer in office to welcome them home. Reagan reaped the benefits of the mood of national rejoicing and capitalized on a widespread feeling that America must not be humiliated again. The new President was determined that his country should "walk tall" once more, after the drift and self-doubt of the 1970s.

Reagan's inauguration marked a turning point not only for the United States but also for Anglo-American relations. He found a natural ally in Margaret Thatcher, Britain's prime minister since May 1979, despite their marked differences of temperament. Mrs. Thatcher, although often hesitant and cautious about her political judgments, adopted in public a defiant tone. In the face of opposition her instinct was to respond not with discussion but with a forceful restatement of her views, as though repetition would be enough to reveal their self-evident truth. She prided herself on being a "conviction" politician, a stance that was novel and appealing to

many in an electorate that had become so accustomed to compromise that it had almost ceased to believe that a radical attempt to
solve Britain's problems could succeed.

Mrs. Thatcher had a quick mind and a brisk manner. Her energy
was indefatigable, her appetite for work voracious. Ronald Reagan
was very different. With his friendly, informal style of conversation,
his short attention span, his occasional slips of the tongue and lapses
of memory, he gave the impression of an easygoing leader, content
to lay down the guidelines of policy and leave others to sort out the
details. While Mrs. Thatcher bullied and cajoled her advisers into
agreement, insisting that she "could not waste time having any
internal arguments,"[1] President Reagan was protected by his aides
from the press and the public, except in carefully controlled circumstances. If he muddled two countries or forgot his facts, he would
shrug his shoulders, grin amiably and leave it to a staff member to
explain what he had really meant. It was not an attitude Mrs.
Thatcher would have tolerated in her own Cabinet. Responding to
a speech she gave in Washington in February 1981, the President
joked: "You are a hard act to follow."[2]

For all his insouciance, however, the President was a man of
tenacity and courage, displayed within months of his inauguration
when he was the target of attempted assassination. He knew what
he wanted and how to get his way, winning the affection and respect
of the American people to a degree unknown since Franklin Roosevelt. Both he and Margaret Thatcher had won high office in the face
of snobbish contempt. Reagan, a former movie actor, was mocked
for his presumption in even seeking the presidency. Mrs. Thatcher,
as a woman, had to endure the condescension of politicians within
her own party as well as outside. Both had triumphed over these
attempts to humiliate them and believed that they had made it to the

British cartoonist Steve Bell satirizes President Reagan's (and America's) view of the world.

top through their own efforts. Once in power they were determined to put their principles into practice.

For both leaders the central tenet of their faith was "freedom," which they believed was endangered at home and abroad. The enemy within was seen as big-spending, Keynesian government, which throttled enterprise and stifled self-reliance. They wanted the freedom of the individual increased at the expense of the encroaching state. Abroad, they believed that Communist Russia posed a threat to freedom, and that the West, deluded by détente, had become complacent about the danger. They doubted that an accommodation could be reached with the Soviet Union on the basis of mutual self-interest and argued that negotiation could take place only from a position of much greater military strength.

Their aims, though seemingly conservative, were radical—to resurrect the principles of the past in order to reshape the present. Both were trying to turn back the tides of recent history, to reverse the policies of Keynesianism and détente, to rekindle national pride, to check the sense of impotence and decline afflicting both their countries. Facing intense opposition at home, they leaned on each other for support. "It is widely known that I share many of your ideals and beliefs, Prime Minister Thatcher," the President observed two months after he had assumed office.[3] No previous president and prime minister had coincided so closely in their political philosophies—certainly not the anticolonial Franklin Roosevelt and the diehard imperialist Winston Churchill, nor even the liberal John Kennedy and the progressive Harold Macmillan.

Their economic policies were commonly described as "monetarist," but neither leader was a serious disciple of theory. They were practical politicians, using the language of economics to justify gut instincts, derived from personal experience, about how to make their countries prosperous again. As Mrs. Thatcher observed, "Economics are the method; the object is to change the heart and soul . . . of the nation."[4] Both denounced Keynesian solutions—in particular, increased government spending—as a counter to the recession of the early 1980s. But their priorities were different. For Reagan, the prime aim was to reduce taxes. So-called supply-side economists predicted that this would stimulate growth, thereby generating greater tax revenues, which the United States could spend on modernizing its armed forces against the Soviet Union. For Thatcher, rampant inflation was the principal danger, and her immediate goal was therefore to control government borrowing. The Prime Minister also wanted to curb the power of the big unions, whose wage claims, she believed, had fueled inflation and brought the country to its knees in 1979. More fundamentally, she wanted to reverse the march of socialism. "Each time you go further along the Socialist road," she warned in 1977, "nearer and nearer to the Communist State, then the consequences of the Communist State will follow."[5]

The Thatcher Revolution proved more radical than the Reagan Revolution. No president can serve more than eight years, and Reagan's own authority diminished rapidly from January 1987, when he lost effective control of Congress to the Democrats and was undermined by the Iran-contra scandal. Mrs. Thatcher, by contrast, secured reelection in 1983 and 1987, each time with healthy working majorities in Parliament, which enabled her to push through her policies in a way President Reagan must often have envied.

In Britain, inflation was running at 21 percent in 1979; by 1987 it had stabilized at between 4 and 5 percent. The government had reduced Britain's nationalized sector by half, raising £25 billion in the process and greatly widening the spread of share ownership, though without breaking up the existing monopolies to more competition. It had also weakened the union movement by legislation and, in 1984–85, by defeating the strike by the National Union of Mineworkers, which had brought down the previous Conservative government of Edward Heath a decade before. This victory and the recession helped force a more flexible union attitude to pay claims and new technology, not just in coal mining but in other industries, such as cars and newspapers. By 1987 the government could point to 4 percent growth and rapidly increasing productivity. The British economy, boasted Chancellor of the Exchequer Nigel Lawson, was "on top of the world."[6]

The price some Britons paid for this revolution was high. Unemployment soared from 6 percent of the work force in 1979, when Mrs. Thatcher took office, to 13 percent by 1983—the worst level for half a century. And industrial production fell even more sharply in 1979–81 than it did in the slump of 1929–32.[7] The world recession was partly to blame, but so was the government's policy of keeping interest rates high to control inflation, thereby raising the value of the pound and pricing British manufactures out of many foreign markets. Under Mrs. Thatcher, the apostle of business enterprise, the progressive "de-industrialization" of Britain spread to affect not just long-declining areas like the northeast but also previously prosperous regions, such as the West Midlands. Critics pointed to a widening gap between the "two nations"—a thriving southeast and a decaying north.

Britain's underlying economic problems remained. After the 1987 election, Mrs. Thatcher made the rejuvenation of the inner cities and the older industrial areas primary objectives, together with increased spending on education and health. Yet the government could expect less income in the future, now that most marketable nationalized industries had been sold off and North Sea Oil, which had fueled government spending and covered Britain's worsening trade balance in the 1970s and 1980s, was beginning to dry up. Mrs. Thatcher had changed Britain more than any prime minister since the 1940s; whether she had achieved a long-term reversal of the country's economic decline was not yet clear.

In America, the Reagan Revolution saw different successes and failures. The centerpiece of the President's program was a dramatic cut in income tax, a tax he believed to be a fundamental evil. Back in the 1960s he had claimed that "we have received this progressive tax direct from Karl Marx," who intended it "to tax the middle class out of existence, because you can't have socialism where you have a strong middle class."[8] By 1987 the top rate of federal income tax was reduced to 28 percent, only 1 percent above the *lowest* rate then obtaining in Britain. The highest British rate, even after the Thatcher government's cuts, was 60 percent.

But, as in Britain, government spending was not so easy to curb. Retirement pensions and Medicare (health care for those over sixty-five) were left largely intact, despite the fact that their ever-increasing costs took up nearly two-thirds of the welfare budget. It would have been hard to reduce them against the wishes of so many of Reagan's Republican supporters. In America, as in Britain, spending cuts tended to fall on those in society without organization and influence—the low-income families and ethnic minorities, particularly in the inner cities, who bore the brunt of the recession. And the Reagan Revolution did little to confront America's underlying economic problem: its lack of competitiveness internationally. The nation that had given the world Ford, Hoover and Coca-Cola was now buying its consumer goods—cars, televisions and computers— from Japan and other Pacific industrial nations. Imports exceeded exports for the first time in the twentieth century, and in 1986 the U.S. trade deficit was about $160 billion.

But the gravest consequence of "Reaganomics" was the soaring budget deficit. On the face of it a policy of tax cuts and increased

defense spending seemed to guarantee an unbalanced budget, but
the President believed the assurances of supply-side economists that
big tax cuts would boost the economy so dramatically that it would
soon generate the extra tax revenue needed to balance the books.
Nothing of the sort happened. Supply-side theory proved utopian;
the beneficiaries of government spending and their congressional
spokesmen blocked significant spending cuts; and Budget Director
David Stockman made serious blunders in his haste to get the economic reforms through Congress while Reagan's postelection influence was at its peak in early 1981. Looking back, Stockman
admits that "designing a comprehensive plan to bring about a
sweeping change in national economic governance in forty days is
a preposterous, wantonly reckless notion," but he "reckoned that
the 'window' for successfully launching sweeping change in national economic policy would be exceedingly brief."[9]

The worst muddle was the defense budget. At 7:30 P.M. on Friday, January 30, 1981, Stockman met Defense Secretary Caspar
Weinberger and his aides in the Pentagon. There they agreed upon
the outlines of the defense budget, Stockman doing the arithmetic
on his pocket calculator. The meeting lasted less than half an hour.
When they had finished, Weinberger looked at his watch, yawned
and said, "I call this a good night's work." Stockman, whose day had
begun at 4:30 A.M. and would not end until after midnight, rushed
off to his next engagement. Only when the figures were processed
by the Budget Office computer a few weeks later did he realize
that he had let the Pentagon get away with a defense budget of
$1.5 trillion over five years. This meant a 10 percent increase in
defense spending in real terms, double even Reagan's campaign
promise.[10]

By the time this and other errors were appreciated, little could be
done. The budget had to be ready for Congress by mid-February,
and Reagan was not interested in the details. Faced with problems
or disagreements among his advisers, he would smile and say,
"Okay, you fellas work it out." It was a far cry from Mrs. Thatcher's
interventionist style of leadership. As predictions of the future government deficit poured out of the Budget Office computer, they
were fudged by what became known as the "magic asterisk"—
"Future savings to be identified."[11]

When savings were not made, and, as predicted, the budget deficit soared, the President refused to curb defense spending, despite
reports of extravagance and waste among the Pentagon's contrac-

tors. Nor would he abandon his cherished tax cuts, let alone increase income tax rates to generate the necessary revenue. With the White House abdicating responsibility, Congress stepped in with a program of mandatory spending cuts if the deficit exceeded specified limits. Even so, the budget deficit was running at an unprecedented $220 billion per annum by July 1986. Reagan, America's most conservative president for decades, had piled up a national debt three times as large as that accumulated by all his thirty-nine precedessors.

The consequences for the rest of the world were profound. Since World War II American capital in the form of foreign investment, economic aid and military commitments had helped sustain the world economy. Now the process had gone into reverse. Because the U.S. government could not pay for its spending through tax revenue, it had to borrow. By 1985 the inflow of funds, particularly from Japan, to cover the budget and trade deficits had turned the United States into a net debtor nation, borrowing more than it lent, for the first time since the First World War. One of the world's most powerful economies was importing capital rather than exporting it.

The relationship between American and British business was also being reversed. British firms started taking over American companies on a large scale, a transatlantic invasion in a direction opposite from that of the 1960s. In the early 1980s many British businesses made large profits and were looking for new areas in which to invest. In 1979 the Thatcher government had ended all exchange controls, allowing British capital to move freely abroad. With a favorable pound-dollar exchange rate and growing expertise in the City of London about American opportunities, British capital began to flow across the Atlantic. In 1985 British companies spent over $5 billion in takeovers in the United States; the following year the figure nearly trebled. Among the U.S. corporations acquired were Moosehead Beer, J. Walter Thompson, the advertising giant, and Smith & Wesson, makers of the guns that won the West. In Britain, some asked whether the money should not have been spent at home, revitalizing the depressed north, but by the mid-1980s, with capital free to choose its destination, Britain was the top direct foreign investor in the United States, owning about as much in America as the United States owned in Britain.

Critics in America and Europe warned that the eventual consequences of America's trade and budget deficits would be disastrous, but little was done in Washington. The economy seemed strong, the stock market was booming. Most Americans paid little attention to the effects of U.S. policy on the rest of the world. Some of Mrs. Thatcher's ministers added their voices to the criticism, but the Prime Minister was not among them. For her the "special relationship" was an article of faith. To rebuke America in public went against all her natural instincts. Sir Anthony Parsons, Mrs. Thatcher's special adviser on foreign affairs in 1982–83, thinks she "believes very strongly that the United States is absolutely vital to us, and that obviously one of the cardinal planks of our policy must be the best possible relations with the United States. By the same token, I think she believes that we can only hope to influence the United States in private and affect their judgments over various issues where we may disagree, if the basic relationship is extremely good."[12]

Margaret Thatcher stood in marked contrast to her Conservative predecessor Edward Heath. Although no anti-Marketeer, she showed little enthusiasm for the European Community. Her early years in office were spent demanding a rebate on Britain's excessive budget contribution—"I cannot play Sister Bountiful to the Community"; "We want our money."[13] Whereas Heath had espoused the ideal of a united Europe, it seemed to Helmut Schmidt that Mrs. Thatcher "saw her main European mission as reducing as close to zero as possible Britain's net contribution to the financing of the European Community."[14] The lack of affection was mutual. Mrs. Thatcher had little time for the Continental leaders, many of them socialists, with whom she had to deal. Born in 1925, reaching maturity in the era of the wartime Anglo-American alliance and the cold war, she had no doubt that Britain's closest ties still lay with America—English-speaking, free enterprise, fervently anti-Communist. By comparison Europe seemed disunited, left-wing and irredeemably foreign.

At the heart of the Thatcher foreign policy was the renewal of Britain's nuclear special relationship, established by Macmillan two decades before. By the late 1970s the Polaris submarine-launched deterrent was nearing the end of its useful life. Labour had been ready to modernize Polaris but not to acquire a new generation of strategic missiles, although Callaghan secretly opened negotiations with Carter in February 1979. Mrs. Thatcher had no such inhibitions. She was determined that Britain should remain a nuclear power into the twenty-first century. In July 1980 it was announced that Britain would purchase Trident C-4 missiles from the United States for its new fleet of submarines, an agreement made with

Carter. When Reagan decided to upgrade the Trident program and develop the more powerful D-5 missiles, the Thatcher government, fearful of another Skybolt fiasco, quickly arranged an agreement for these instead. This was concluded in an exchange of letters between the two leaders in March 1982.

On the face of it Britain had secured an exceptional bargain. Unlike Polaris, Trident missiles would be installed and serviced in the United States. Britain was given the use of them at little more than cost price. Under the Polaris and Trident I agreements the British government had agreed to pay 5 percent of the total research and development costs of the programs. For Trident II it was simply asked to pay a fixed R & D charge of $116 million (at 1982 prices) and to man the Rapier air defense system around the U.S. Air Force bases in Britain. And, as with Polaris, Mrs. Thatcher promised that the Trident force would be assigned to NATO "except where the United Kingdom Government may decide that supreme national interests are at stake."[15] Again Britain would get the fruits of American technology for its own use and at minimum cost. No other country was allowed these benefits.

The uniqueness of these arrangements and the generosity of the terms indicated the Reagan administration's urgent desire to strengthen NATO's defenses. In the 1960s and for most of the 1970s, Washington had been lukewarm at best about Britain having its own nuclear force. But in his letter to Mrs. Thatcher the President observed that "the United States readiness to provide these systems is a demonstration of the great importance which the United States Government attach to the maintenance by the United Kingdom of an independent nuclear deterrent capability."[16]

Yet the special relationship was being used to provide a weapon that would probably be employed, if at all, only when that relationship had broken down. The ultimate justification for Britain having its own strategic deterrent lay in doubts about American reliability: Was the United States likely to honor its guarantee of European security by launching its own missiles when it would be faced in return with the threat of devastating Soviet retaliation on American cities? The British Ministry of Defence preferred to pose the dilemma less bluntly, professing "great confidence in the depth of resolve underlying the United States commitment." But, it suggested, a Soviet government, "perhaps much changed in character from today's, perhaps also operating amid the pressures of turbulent internal or external circumstances, might believe that it could im-

pose its will on Europe by military force without becoming involved in strategic nuclear war with the United States."[17] The
government insisted that Britain's modernized nuclear force, using
missiles sold and serviced by the United States, provided an independent insurance.

The Trident decision was sharply attacked by the Opposition in
Parliament. They argued that no British nuclear deterrent could
ever be credible, since its use would invite instant obliteration of a
small and densely populated island. To remain a nuclear power
simply showed, they claimed, that Mrs. Thatcher harbored delu-
sions of past grandeur. Labour MP Robin Cook commented: "It is
time that we adjusted ourselves to the fact that we are a declining
medium-range power and looked first and foremost at how we use
our desperately scarce industrial resources to commercial advantage
rather than on grandiose projects which we have inherited from the
past."[18]

Others attacked the cost of Trident, which had soared by 1985 to
about £10 billion. The government argued that, spread over the total
duration of the program, Trident would represent only about
6 percent of Britain's defense equipment budget, but the Commons
Defence Committee claimed the proportion would be more than
12 percent in the peak years of expenditure in the late 1980s.[19]
Given Britain's underlying economic problems, the government's
determination to cut borrowing and expenditure, and its commitment, reaffirmed as part of the Trident II deal, to increase spending
on conventional forces in Europe, many defense analysts predicted
a looming crisis in the defense budget if Trident went ahead. There
was not enough money for all these defense commitments. Britain,
they argued, could not afford to stay in the nuclear club, even with
America paying so much of the bill.

Even those who believed in nuclear deterrence had their doubts
about Trident. Trident I had double the range and four times the
warheads of Polaris. Yet Trident II had nearly five times the "yield,"
or explosive power, of Trident I and was even more accurate, perhaps to within four hundred feet.[20] This might suit America's need
for a weapon that could travel all the way from the United States
to Russia and could there penetrate hardened Soviet missile silos.
But Britain, whose targets were Soviet cities and who was much
closer to Russia, did not need such power, range and pinpoint
accuracy. Because she was reliant on American technology, however, Britain had to take whatever the United States had in stock—

Skybolt, Polaris, Trident I, Trident II—regardless of her specific
needs. France, by contrast, had developed her own nuclear deterrent, tailored to French needs. Critics, such as the then Social Democrat leader David Owen, urged that Britain's nuclear future lay in
collaboration with France on a deterrent appropriate to European
needs, rather than being tied to the vagaries of Pentagon policy.

Within weeks of the Trident II deal, however, the benefits of a
close military relationship with America seemed amply demonstrated. In April 1982 the repressive Argentine military junta, faced
with growing domestic unrest, decided to divert attention to Argentina's long-standing grievance, the British occupation of the Falklands. The ownership of these remote South Atlantic islands, with
their 1,800 British settlers, had been in dispute for a century and a
half. In late 1980 the Thatcher government, then in the process of
negotiating an agreement to give Hong Kong back to China, had
been talking to the Argentines about a similar scheme whereby they
would be given freehold to the islands, which would then be leased
back to the inhabitants for a period of time. But the minister responsible, Nicholas Ridley, was howled down by MPs of all parties in
the House of Commons. Later, angry and shaken, he told one critic:
"If we don't do something, they will invade."[21] No further negotiations followed, but meanwhile, to save money for Trident, the
defence minister, John Nott, had been cutting hard at the Royal
Navy's surface fleet. One of the casualties was HMS *Endurance,* a
small patrol ship deployed in the South Atlantic as a symbol of
Britain's commitment to the Falklands. The Foreign Office protested, but in vain: Nott had the backing of the Prime Minister.

General Leopoldo Galtieri's government read these moves as
signals that although Britain refused to talk, she would not resist an
Argentine takeover. It was a grave miscalculation. The Argentine
invasion of the islands, protected only by a small garrison of marines, on April 2, 1982, provoked a wave of patriotic fury in Britain.
MPs of all parties attacked Mrs. Thatcher's government for incom-
petence, and the foreign secretary, Lord Carrington, felt obliged to
resign. Incensed at the humiliation to Britain's pride and with her
own political survival in jeopardy, the Prime Minister immediately
dispatched a Royal Navy task force to the South Atlantic. At its
head were Britain's two aircraft carriers, *Hermes* and *Invincible,*
which, until recently, had been high on Mr. Nott's list for disposal.
When the task force, packed with soldiers, supplies and aircraft,
started on its long journey southward, there were still hopes that a

demonstration of military force might be enough to persuade the Argentines to back down. But during April 1982 repeated attempts to secure a peace formula failed, and it became clear that Britain faced a war to recover the islands.

Publicly the United States was slow to support Britain. Between the Argentine invasion and the start of full-scale hostilities, Washington sat on the fence. "We're friends with both of the countries engaged in the dispute," the President observed in his first comments on the crisis. Asked if America would act as "honest broker," he said: "If we can be of help in doing that, yes, anything that would bring about a peaceful solution to what seems to be an unnecessary disagreement."[22] London was dismayed and angry, but the Reagan administration faced a genuine conflict of loyalties. The Argentine junta was the linchpin of its anti-Communist strategy in Latin America. President Carter's arms embargo had been lifted and General Galtieri assured of American backing. Faced with a conflict between its main supporter in South America and its closest NATO ally, the United States was in an impossible position. As former Secretary of State Henry Kissinger observed: "Sometimes you come up against a situation where you can't win."[23]

The Thatcher government had no sympathy for America's dilemma. In its view, fundamental issues of principle were at stake— British sovereignty, the rights of the islanders, the illegal use of force. Particular wrath was reserved for Jeane Kirkpatrick, U.S. ambassador to the United Nations, who wanted to avoid alienating Argentina. "The Argentinians have been claiming for 200 years that they own those islands," she declared. "If they own those islands, then moving troops into them is not armed aggression."[24] Meanwhile Secretary of State Alexander Haig, sympathetic to Britain, engaged in intensive shuttle diplomacy between Washington, New York, London and Buenos Aires, traveling 33,000 miles in twelve days in search of a peaceful settlement. For their efforts his team was denounced by Mrs. Kirkpatrick as "Brits in American clothes." She asked, "Why not disband the State Department and have the British Foreign Office make our policy?"[25] It was not until fighting started at the end of April that the United States sided publicly with Britain. On April 30 the President noted that "the aggression was on the part of Argentina in this dispute . . . and I think the principle that all of us must abide by is, armed aggression of that kind must not be allowed to succeed."[26]

But although it took Washington all April to come out publicly against the Argentine, behind the scenes the Pentagon had been backing Britain from the start, and its aid increased dramatically once America came off the fence. Directed by Caspar Weinberger, the Anglophile defense secretary, the United States provided Britain's ill-equipped and overextended forces with crucial help at a speed rarely achieved by the Pentagon's cumbersome bureaucracy. Weinberger set up a central clearinghouse, with direct access to his office. Fifteen stages were eliminated from the supply-authorization process and matériel was transferred from inventories in twenty-four hours instead of the normal two weeks. The assistance provided included ammunition, equipment, twelve million gallons of aviation fuel and two hundred of the latest Sidewinder air-to-air missiles. Most useful of all, Britain was given vital military intelligence from intercepted signals and from one of America's surveillance satellites, which, it was alleged, had been specially moved away from its orbit over Russia for the purpose.[27]

This help was given without any special permission being sought. Dr. John Lehman, U.S. secretary of the navy at the time, explains: "One has to understand the relationship of the United States Navy and the Royal Navy—there's no other relationship, I think, like it in the world between two military services." Channels had existed since the Second World War for regular naval exercises, exchanges of personnel, sharing of equipment, weapons and intelligence. "There was no need to establish a new relationship. . . . it was really just turning up the volume . . . almost a case of not being told to stop rather than crossing a threshold to start."[28] Britain was reaping the benefits of agreements dating back over decades, including the U.K.-U.S. intelligence treaty of 1947. The President himself hinted at this. "There are no new agreements that have come out of this at all," he remarked in late May 1982. "There are certain bilateral agreements and our relationship in the North Atlantic Alliance that we fulfill regardless of what's going on."[29]

But there was more to the relationship than formal agreements. The Americans would probably not have done as much for any other NATO ally. John Lehman, who confesses, "I had traveled to England twenty times before I got west of the Mississippi," observes that "the special relationship is very special indeed. There are not those channels with other countries that are operating day to day where you pick up the phone to call somebody at the other end and he's been at your home and you've been at his home, and you know him by his first name and you know his children's names and that kind of thing. I mean it's a different kind of a relationship." And Lehman believes that the relationship was decisive for Britain. Without American help, he says, "I think that Britain would have had to have withdrawn from the Falklands."[30]

Although American help was crucial for Britain's success, victory was won by the skill and courage of her own forces, who, at the cost of 255 lives, retrieved the mistakes made by politicians and civil servants. On June 14, 1982, six weeks after the first British landings on the Falklands, the Argentines surrendered. Most of the American public cheered the British victory. Three to one they supported Britain against the dictatorial Argentine junta and made no secret of their admiration for the way the operation had been conducted. Americans were also surprised at the outpouring of patriotic fervor from the supposedly phlegmatic British, and many revised their seventies judgments about Britain going the same way as Chile. "Great Britain is great again," Mrs. Thatcher proclaimed.[31] The war also resuscitated her own reputation, previously in the doldrums. Those closely involved all agreed: "It was Mrs. Thatcher's war. She held us to it. She never seemed to flinch from her conviction about its course. She took the risks on her shoulders and she won."[32] In Britain and America, among her critics as well as her friends, Mrs. Thatcher was confirmed as "the iron lady," one of the West's most decisive leaders.

America was not blindly supporting Britain's cause, however. Once the fighting was over and Galtieri had been shown that force did not pay, the administration assumed that Britain would return to the negotiating table. But British blood had been spilled and Mrs Thatcher was not about to give away what had been so expensively recovered, particularly when the "Falklands factor" had played a part in her political recovery. She now insisted that the wishes of the islanders were paramount and that Britain would not relinquish sovereignty. She embarked on a costly Fortress Falklands policy, developing the airport and providing a permanent garrison for the islands. Washington was concerned at this diversion of Britain's limited resources from her main commitments to NATO. It was sure that Britain's colonial claims could not be sustained indefinitely.

For all the rhetoric about "alliance" and "friendship," America had not been consulted over Britain's policy in the spring of 1982. Under extreme duress Mrs. Thatcher simply acted, and President Reagan was left to respond in a way that minimized the damage to the United States. In October 1983 a similar tension between British and American interests arose, but this time it was the Americans who acted on their own—in Grenada.

Washington anticipated a Marxist takeover in this nearby Caribbean island. Fearing another Iran-style hostage crisis, it was also concerned about the welfare of the six hundred Americans there. Critics of the operation suspected that the administration was even more anxious to divert public attention from the recent horrific terrorist attack on the U.S. Marine barracks in Beirut in which 241 died. And so, with token military support from other Caribbean states, U.S. troops were sent in to take control. Grenada was a former British colony and member of the Commonwealth. Its head of the state was Queen Elizabeth II. Yet British government objections were ignored, despite last-minute representations by Mrs. Thatcher. According to Langhorn Motley, the State Department official handling the operation, "There were two telephone calls to Mrs. Thatcher from President Reagan," one before the final decision was taken, the other soon after. In both, he says, "I am told that the majority of the talking was done by Mrs. Thatcher. . . . It was vintage Mrs. Thatcher. Forceful!" But in neither case was the Prime Minister able to change the President's mind, and, Motley judged, Reagan was "surprised and a little disappointed" at her reaction. Motley adds that some members of the administration resented her lack of support after the help she had received over the Falklands. "When she needed us we were there. . . . we just didn't understand, and I still don't understand to this day, this strong feeling that we shouldn't have done this."[33]

It was a bitter humiliation for the Prime Minister, because it suggested that she had little influence in Washington, and her critics made the most of it. Denis Healey, Labour's shadow foreign secretary, claimed that she "had made something of a cult of her special relationship with the American President, at the expense of British interests, of her relations with our European partners and our relations with the Commonwealth." Lambasting her "servility to the American President," he dubbed her Reagan's "obedient poodle."[34]

Trident, the Falklands and Grenada together summed up the complex state of Anglo-American relations in the early 1980s. The special defense ties remained extremely close and the British could still exert considerable leverage on American policy in a major crisis, such as the Falklands. But both the Falklands and Grenada also illustrated the growing importance to the United States of relations outside the Atlantic alliance, particularly in Latin America, and the fact that ever since the Second World War the Anglo-American relationship had been asymmetrical: America mattered far more to the British than Britain did to the United States. "An enduring alliance with the United States is fundamental to our beliefs and our objectives," Mrs. Thatcher declared in 1981.[35] For President Reagan, however, ties with Britain were only one facet of his diplomacy. Despite his warm regard for Mrs. Thatcher, her country was no longer a decisive force in world affairs and only one of several allies with whom he kept in close touch. The underlying question was whether Mrs. Thatcher was leaving Britain too dependent on the United States and too remote from her European partners, who, collectively, might help keep the transatlantic relationship in balance. This issue came to a head in the new cold war between America and Russia.

Like Margaret Thatcher, Ronald Reagan came into office determined to restore his country's power and prestige after what he considered the drift of the 1970s. He quickly reinstated the MX missile and the B-1 bomber, both suspended by Carter, and promised substantial funds for the U.S. Navy to help it face the expanded Soviet fleet. The President took a much harder line than Carter on arms control. "So far detente's been a one-way street that the Soviet Union has used to pursue its own aims," the President observed in January 1981.[36] He condemned the SALT treaties concluded in the 1970s and showed no hurry to get back to the negotiating table until American defenses were stronger. Meanwhile he denounced the Soviet Union in language not heard from the White House since the depths of the cold war. "The Soviet Union underlies all the unrest that is going on," he claimed in 1980. "If they weren't engaged in this game of dominoes, there wouldn't be any hot spots in the world."[37]

In 1981 the President's anti-Soviet rhetoric helped get his defense budget through Congress, but it aroused alarm at home and abroad. In the United States antinuclear groups proliferated, demanding a freeze on the weapons systems of both sides, and an estimated half-million people attended a rally in Central Park, New York, in June 1982. In Western Europe there was a similar grass-roots revolt against government policies. In the détente of the 1970s the European allies had been fearful that the United States would leave them defenseless. The December 1979 decision to deploy Cruise and Pershing missiles had been NATO's answer. From 1982 European public opinion woke up to what had happened, just at the time when

"Farewell, Sir Ronald, and jolly good luck on the crusade!"

Off on the Holy War against the Communists. (JAK in the London Standard, June 10, 1982.)

Reagan's cold war rhetoric suggested that the United States had no interest in arms control negotiations—the other part of the dual-track decision in December 1979. Antinuclear protests spread across Western Europe.

In Britain, the decisions to deploy Cruise and buy Trident revived the Campaign for Nuclear Disarmament (CND), which had lain dormant since the 1960s. At the American base of Greenham Common, one of the sites for Cruise missiles, a permanent camp of women protesters was established. Nuclear weapons were not the only issue. There was also intense anti-American feeling, fostered by Britain's growing inferiority complex toward the United States and by the doubts about American reliability. Even supporters of Cruise were critical of the government's decision, on grounds of cost, not to install a "dual-key" mechanism, like that on the Thor missiles of twenty years before. This, critics argued, would have been an insurance against a trigger-happy U.S. president. Instead the government reaffirmed the old Churchill-Truman "joint decision" agreement of 1952, insisting that this was a sufficient safeguard for British interests. The government's unspoken anxiety, reflected in its desire for Trident, was that America might renege on its commitments. Many of the British public feared that "Rambo" Reagan was all too ready to honor those commitments—and blow Europe to pieces in the process.

In the British election of 1983 the Labour party campaigned for a non-nuclear Britain—stripped of U.S. bases and of her own nuclear force. It also repudiated NATO's dual-track decision of 1979 because, in the words of its leader, Michael Foot, it was "absolutely opposed to . . . the deployment of cruise missiles."[38] Labour insisted that these would be matters for negotiation and that de-nuclearization would help pay for a stronger British conventional role in NATO. But in Washington, recalls Richard Perle, then assistant secretary of defense, "no one believed that it was the intention of the Labour party to increase defense spending on conventional forces." And "no one could see a way that Europe could be defended only with conventional forces, even at greatly increased levels, which were unlikely, and therefore you had a major party, in . . . perhaps the key country of the alliance, off on an excursion that led to no coherent Western strategy."[39] General Bernard Rogers, the American supreme commander of NATO's forces in Europe at this time, anticipated a U-turn if Labour took office, as had happened over Polaris in 1964. But he claims that if the non-nuclear policy had been implemented "the United States would have withdrawn its forces completely from Western Europe. . . . it would have unraveled the Alliance."[40]

Both Perle and Rogers, like Mrs. Thatcher, believed that a non-nuclear defense of Europe was impossible. Despite its economic resurgence, Western Europe remained incapable of defending itself. That was not true, of course, in the crude sense sometimes expressed in the United States, where there was mounting public irritation at European "free-riding." The Western Europeans *did* contribute substantially to their own security—providing between 80 and 90 percent of NATO's manpower and conventional equipment. But, insists General Rogers, "the real world was and is that NATO's conventional forces have always been out of balance with those of the Warsaw Pact, even for an alliance whose mission . . . is deterrence. . . . Within days after a conventional attack by the Soviet Union," Rogers argues, he would have had "no option but to request the release of nuclear weapons, and that would come in less than two weeks."[41] The only nuclear deterrent of sufficient size was

American: the small nuclear forces of Britain and France were inadequate by themselves.

If the Western Europeans desired a greater say in their own security, they had two options. Either they had to develop their own nuclear force, as the Foreign Office had urged dramatically in 1957 after Suez, or they had to make non-nuclear defense a real possibility by vastly increasing the size and sophistication of their conventional forces. Each course would require higher defense spending and far greater political unity than the Western Europeans had shown to date. Without such a change of policy, they were left impotently waiting for the latest swings of U.S. policy—alternately fearing desertion or domination, American isolationism or renewed cold war.

By the summer of 1983 the Cruise and Pershing furor was abating. Mrs. Thatcher's reelection in Britain and the victory of Helmut Kohl's Christian Democrats in West Germany ensured that the weapons were deployed. But then a new American initiative left its allies wrong-footed once again, and posed a fundamental challenge to the theory of extended deterrence upon which NATO strategy rested.

In March 1983 the President outlined the idea of a space-based defensive shield against nuclear missiles—the so-called Strategic Defense Initiative (SDI), popularly known as Star Wars. This would marshal the latest laser technology to destroy nuclear missiles in space before they reached their targets. Instead of protecting America by threatening to obliterate Russia—the strategy of deterrence—the President was proposing a defense against Soviet missiles, which, he said, would eventually "render these nuclear weapons impotent and obsolete."[42] He even suggested that the technology might be shared with the Soviet Union. The administration quickly mounted an advertising campaign about an astrodome defense under which American children could sleep soundly at night.

SDI proved a shrewd tactic for undercutting the American "Freeze" campaigners: the President was presenting himself as more peace-loving than them because he wanted total disarmament and not just a halt to the arms race. Reagan himself believed passionately in the idea of complete defense, but a majority of American scientists did not take it seriously. Two-thirds considered it "improbable" or "very unlikely" that SDI could be comprehensive enough to defend American cities from Soviet attack.[43] Many defense experts believed that deterrence was more sensible, because neither side dared attack and risk the other unleashing nuclear retaliation. If, they argued, America felt secure and Russia did not, a dangerous instability would have been introduced.

Few Pentagon officials believed in the President's vision of total defense. They saw SDI mainly as a way of protecting America's own offensive missiles: "the defense of America's capacity to retaliate," in the words of Richard Perle.[44] For them the astrodome imagery was largely public relations—an effective way to get money from a tightfisted Congress for protracted and costly research into new generations of weapons. This work on lasers, optics, satellites and computers might well have valuable commercial spin-offs. For America's high-tech industries, dependent on federal government funds for research and development, SDI therefore seemed an ideal successor to the lucrative Apollo moon program of the 1960s. Senator William Proxmire remarked that big corporations like Boeing, Rockwell and Lockheed "look at SDI as an insurance policy that will maintain their prosperity for the next two decades."[45]

Though shrewd politics for the Reagan administration, SDI had little attraction for Western Europe. If the President was right, the United States could become totally secure. This risked "decoupling" America from Europe, no longer treating the defense of America and the defense of Western Europe as indivisible. Europe might then be threatened by Soviet conventional forces and short-range nuclear missiles without America stepping in. Alternatively, if SDI only resulted, as the Pentagon expected, in America's anti-missile defenses being strengthened, the arms race might spiral, with Russia increasing its nuclear arsenal and trying to match America in space-based defenses. This could breach the 1972 Anti-Ballistic Missile Treaty, one of the main guarantees of mutual assured destruction, the philosophy on which deterrence rested. Equally alarming for Europe were the commercial implications of SDI. Persuaded by the President's vision, Congress began to allocate billions of dollars for research. If the United States alone developed the program, it might open up a new Atlantic technological divide and start a brain drain far worse than that of the 1960s.

Mrs. Thatcher's response demonstrated again her faith in the Anglo-American relationship. Publicly she welcomed SDI as a prudent hedge against similar Soviet research, but in private she tried to influence the direction of the project to protect British interests. On December 22, 1984, during a visit to the President at Camp David, she secured a joint statement on SDI. Against the wishes of the Pentagon, both leaders pledged that any attempt to move from SDI research to the deployment of new systems "would, in view of treaty obligations, have to be a matter for negotiation."[46] It was the first major American statement setting the SDI program in the context of arms control. In December 1985 Britain became the first European state formally to join the SDI project. British support gave the Reagan administration useful leverage in getting money out of Congress, while the Thatcher government hoped to be rewarded with a substantial slice of the high-tech work.

Mrs. Thatcher's approach to SDI was a classic example of the British conception of the "special relationship"—trying to influence America discreetly in private rather than carping noisily in public. It was the opposite approach to that of the French government, which in 1983 had publicly questioned the American project and proposed a rival European scheme, "Eureka." Britain eventually did participate in Eureka, but its commitment to SDI, and similar support from West Germany, undermined whatever chance the French project had of becoming the focus for a major European high-tech initiative. Whether Mrs. Thatcher's approach was more prudent is unclear. The Pentagon had never liked the Camp David guidelines, and its efforts to accelerate the SDI program were frustrated not by British diplomacy but by Congress's unwillingness to vote the funds. Nor did Britain gain the substantial commercial benefits for which she had hoped. By February 1987 British SDI contracts amounted to only £24 million—a far cry from the £1 billion predicted by the Ministry of Defence when Britain joined the project.[47]

In Britain the "Europe versus America" debate was given a vivid focus by the Westland Affair. At the end of 1985 Westland, Britain's only helicopter firm, was on the verge of collapse. Its Continental rivals were unwilling to come to the rescue, until an American competitor, the multinational United Technologies, which owned Sikorsky helicopters, put forward a bid. Britain's Minister of Defence, Michael Heseltine, was particularly concerned. He had helped cement Britain's new American connections, implementing the Cruise deployment and negotiating the SDI collaboration. But he had long believed in the need for European cooperation in defense projects to counterbalance American technological dominance, and in 1985 he played a major part in securing a five-nation agreement to build the European Fighter Aircraft. His anxieties about the American offer were shared by other senior Cabinet ministers, including Norman Tebbit, the Prime Minister's closest ad-

viser. With Heseltine's encouragement, a European bid for Westland was hastily put together by a Franco-Italian-British consortium.

But the Westland board supported Sikorsky, and the Prime Minister agreed. Asked to choose, as she saw it, between a dynamic
American enterprise and an eleventh-hour salvage operation involving a collection of Continentals, she had no doubts. Her Cabinet fell
into line, except for Michael Heseltine. A bitter political row followed, with the policy differences reinforced by a clash of strong
personalities. Heseltine refused to accept her judgment and backed
the European offer with flamboyant defiance, using all his skills with
the media. She, equally determinedly, tried to undermine his arguments and silence his public opposition, employing every technique
at the disposal of a prime minister. "We'll take care of Heseltine,"
she is reported to have told Westland.[48] The defense secretary was
forced to resign and the Sikorsky offer was eventually accepted.

The most dramatic example of Mrs. Thatcher's identification
with America rather than Europe came later in 1986. Both President
and Prime Minister had vigorously denounced international terrorism, particularly when connected with the Palestinian question, and
Reagan had repeatedly identified the Libyan leader, Muammar el-
Qaddafi, as its ultimate source. Just after Christmas 1985 sixteen
passengers were killed in Palestinian terrorist attacks on Rome and
Vienna airports. On April 2, 1986, four died when a bomb exploded
on a TWA flight from Rome to Athens, and on the fifth another
explosion wrecked a discotheque in West Berlin frequented by
American servicemen and their families. One American died and
sixty were injured.

Qaddafi denied involvement in all these atrocities, but Reagan
claimed that evidence of Libyan complicity was irrefutable. Over
the previous few months he had imposed economic sanctions on
Libya, moved the U.S. Sixth Fleet close to the Libyan coast, and fed
the media with diatribes against Qaddafi. After the April bombings
the administration was under mounting domestic pressure to take
military action. The country was incensed at these atrocities and its
"can do" spirit had also been buffeted by the loss of the space shuttle
Challenger a few months before. The administration prepared plans
for air strikes against targets in Libya, and European leaders were
secretly asked for support.

Only three months earlier, on January 10, 1986, Mrs. Thatcher
had spoken out emphatically against American talk of military ac-

tion against Libya. "I must warn you that I do not believe in retaliatory strikes that are against international law," she told American journalists in London. A British policewoman had been killed by shots from the Libyan embassy in London, and the country had suffered over two thousand deaths as a result of IRA terrorism, but, she said, there had never been any question of Britain making "retaliatory strikes" or going in "hot pursuit." "Once you start to go across borders," she said, "then I do not see an end to it. And I uphold international law very firmly."[49]

Three months later Mrs. Thatcher took a different line. On the night of April 14–15 she gave the U.S. Air Force permission to use F-111s from its British bases to attack Tripoli. Simultaneously the U.S. Navy's A-6 attack aircraft from the nearby Sixth Fleet bombed Benghazi. American opinion overwhelmingly supported the President, and Mrs. Thatcher was applauded by the American media as America's only loyal European ally. France, who had refused America the use of its airspace, was roundly condemned, as was the European Community, which had spent days arguing about sanctions when America wanted immediate action.

John Hughes, press and information officer at the British embassy in Washington, was overwhelmed by the American reaction. On the morning after the raid "we received so many telephone calls that our switchboard was sort of jammed. . . . In my time at the embassy, and I think in most people's time at the embassy, we've never seen quite anything like it. . . . Overall, not just Washington but our consulates right across the country, we had in the week after the Libyan bombing raid four thousand telephone calls, about ninety-eight percent of which were favorable to the action taken by the British government." Some of those phoning added, "I'll be calling your French colleague immediately after this telephone call and delivering a rather different message."[50]

The official reason given in America and Britain for the use of the F-111s was that their superior accuracy was essential for the success of the raid. Some Pentagon sources were soon admitting, however, that President Reagan mainly wanted political support in Europe.[51] Mrs. Thatcher justified her decision in the House of Commons in language rather different from that she had used in January: "The United States has hundreds of thousands of forces in Europe to defend the liberty of Europe. In that capacity they have been subject to terrorist attack. It was inconceivable to me that we should refuse United States aircraft and pilots the opportunity to defend their people."⁵² As compelling, perhaps, was the obligation to repay President Reagan for his support over the Falklands, so important to her government four years before, particularly since he had felt let down by her over Grenada.

But Mrs. Thatcher knew she would pay a price at home for her loyalty to the President. General Vernon Walters was sent to brief her about the operation at 10 Downing Street. At the end of their meeting he said, "You know, Prime Minister, my normal job is United States representative to the United Nations, and when I go back there I'm going into the eye of the storm." Mrs. Thatcher replied, "General, when I go back to the British electorate I'm going into the eye of the storm."⁵³

Mrs. Thatcher was right. Opinion polls suggested that over two-thirds of the public condemned her involvement in the raid. Labour leader Neil Kinnock called the Prime Minister "supine in her support for the American President," asserting "she has not acted in the interests of Britain."⁵⁴ Her supporters noted that, after the raids, little more was heard from Qaddafi, but opponents were able to add to her embarrassment when it was revealed at the end of 1986 that, despite his calls for a tough line on terrorism, the President had agreed to covert arms sales to Iran in an attempt to effect the release of American hostages held by pro-Iranian Arab terrorists in Lebanon. Ronald Reagan seemed to be operating a double standard on terrorism: negotiating with some, bombing others. So, critics asked, why should Britain be dragged in?

Mrs. Thatcher's reaction in 1986 was in striking contrast to that of Edward Heath in 1973. Faced with a similar request from President Nixon to use British bases during the Yom Kippur war, the Heath government had demurred. It was judged to be an operation outside the NATO area and at odds with British policy. In 1986 Mrs. Thatcher could also have refused the American request. But to have done so, she said, would have been "inconceivable." Her commitment to the American alliance, her regard for the President and her debts to him over the Falklands were too strong. The two crises dramatized the differences between a prime minister whose instincts were European and one who was an Atlanticist.

Behind the scenes in Whitehall, "Europeanist" ideas were gaining favor by 1987. Even the Treasury had deserted Mrs. Thatcher in her rearguard action against Britain becoming a full member of the European Monetary System. Civil servants in the Foreign Office and Ministry of Defence were strengthening political and military

Special relationship or Her Master's Voice? (British satirical weekly Private Eye *after the Libyan raid.)*

links with France and West Germany and even looking ahead to the possibility of a joint Anglo-French nuclear deterrent in the twenty-first century, when Trident was finished. In public Foreign Secretary Sir Geoffrey Howe noted the pressures on the U.S. defense budget and the shift in American interests toward the Pacific among "trends in American thinking which might diminish our security—perhaps not today or tomorrow, but possibly in the longer term," and suggested "a greater responsibility on the part of Europeans for the defence of Western Europe."[55]

But the problem for those such as Germany's Helmut Schmidt, who criticized Mrs. Thatcher for failing to support European initiatives, was that "Europe" was still being created. Prone to bickering and indecision, unable to reform even its own wasteful agricultural policy, the European Community showed little capacity to organize its own defense. As Schmidt himself admitted, to expect Mrs. Thatcher to use her rapport with President Reagan to advance European political and security interests "would presuppose that the Europeans had a common analysis of their interests in these fields which obviously they lack right now."[56]

Yet the problems of transatlantic relations would not go away. In the early 1980s, when Margaret Thatcher and Ronald Reagan were new to office, the world seemed to be returning to the patterns of the 1940s and 1950s—with two hostile superpowers dominating the stage and Britain throwing in her lot with America rather than Europe. By 1987 it was clear that although both leaders had restored their countries' pride and established a remarkable personal alliance, they had not answered the fundamental questions about the future that had been raised in the early 1970s during the era of détente and Britain's entry into Europe.

By the mid-1980s a second phase of détente was developing. Having walked out of arms control negotiations at the end of 1983, the Russians started talking again two years later. Part of the reason was a new, energetic leader, Mikhail Gorbachev, who was anxious to reduce the defense burden on the inefficient Russian economy. President Reagan was also keen for an agreement before he left office. And he and Mrs. Thatcher could also plausibly point to the Cruise and Pershing deployment and to the threat of SDI in forcing the Soviets back to the negotiating table. In November 1985 Reagan and Gorbachev were chatting like old friends around the fireside in Geneva.

The momentum of arms control faltered a year later at Reykjavik when Soviet opposition to Reagan's SDI program proved a major obstacle to agreement. Government officials in America and Europe were alarmed at the President's apparently invincible belief that the elimination of nuclear weapons was an achievable goal, which would ensure a safer world. Mrs. Thatcher invited herself to the United States after Reykjavik to try to modify the President's stance, much as she had done over SDI two years before. Their statement "confirmed that NATO's strategy . . . would continue to require effective nuclear deterrents" and that "reductions in nuclear weapons would increase the importance of eliminating conventional disparities." And whatever was agreed between the superpowers on strategic arms limitation, the President "confirmed his full support for the arrangements made to modernise Britain's independent nuclear deterrent with Trident."[57]

Richard Perle, one of Reagan's principal arms negotiators at Reykjavik, was relieved that, as before, Mrs. Thatcher was prepared to challenge the President's non-nuclear creed. "Some of us, learning that Mrs. Thatcher was coming, were rather pleased at the prospect that some of the more intemperate and visionary views of the President might be modified, as indeed they were. So many of us regarded her as a voice of calm reason, and a much needed one, in particular on this issue of a world without nuclear weapons, which is dangerous nonsense. The President gives expression to it too frequently, but never in close proximity with a visit from Mrs. Thatcher. So we get a brief respite from that rubbish when she comes."[58]

Although SDI destroyed the Reykjavik summit, it did not prove an insuperable barrier to arms control. Quiet negotiation behind the scenes laid the ground for further progress. By the end of 1987 Gorbachev had visited the United States and an agreement had been reached on eliminating from Europe all intermediate-range missiles, including Cruise, Pershings and the Russian SS-20s. Prospects for a strategic arms treaty between the superpowers seemed good, though, as always, the attitude of the U.S. Senate could not be taken for granted.

But the détente of the late 1980s raised the same problems as the first era of détente fifteen years before. NATO had introduced the intermediate-range missiles at Europe's request, responding to fears, particularly in West Germany, that, as America came to terms with Russia, Europe would be left vulnerable to Soviet conventional strength. Once the missiles were removed, the same problem would reemerge. General Bernard Rogers, recently retired as NATO's supreme commander and a vigorous critic of the Intermediate Nuclear Forces (INF) agreement, believes that "what we're doing is making Western Europe safe for conventional war again. And that's exactly what the Soviets want."[59] So although European leaders publicly welcomed the INF accord between America and Russia, behind the scenes there was much anxiety about NATO's European strategy for the future. Should Europe strengthen its own nuclear forces or develop a more effective conventional defense? How long could it safely shelter under the American umbrella?

The second phase of détente, like the first, also coincided with new doubts about America's ability to bear all the global burdens it had accumulated since World War II. No longer supreme economically, the United States was still trying in the 1980s to persuade Japan and Germany to assume more responsibility for the health of the world economy, much as Britain had tried, in vain, to influence American policy in the 1920s and 1930s. And by 1987 the budget deficit, reduced since 1986 but still running at over $150 billion, had finally sparked off an economic crisis at home as Americans lost confidence in the President's powers of leadership. On Black Monday, October 19, share values on the Dow Jones Industrial Average dropped by 23 percent, nearly twice the size of the record one-day fall during the Great Crash of 1929. As further falls followed and shock waves spread around the financial markets of the world, Congress and President finally started to address the budget crisis, talking seriously about cutting spending and, against all Ronald Reagan's instincts, of increasing taxes. But whatever curbs were imposed, the deficit would not vanish overnight, and America's belt-tightening, as in the early 1970s, raised the question of why the United States was still undertaking so many overseas commitments while its economic rivals—Japan, Germany and Western Europe as a whole—got away with so little defense spending in proportion to their now substantial wealth. There was renewed talk of reducing America's three hundred thousand troops in Europe.

Ronald Reagan and Margaret Thatcher had effected remarkable changes in the character of their countries and in their national self-esteem. But the underlying problems they had inherited still remained. Was the United States contracting as a superpower? How long would it feel able to honor its nuclear and conventional commitments in Europe? Was Britain wise to still rely so heavily on the United States? Should she be seeking to build a stronger Europe, capable of doing more for its own defense, or was Western Europe incapable of managing its own affairs without American direction? Despite the upheavals of the seventies and eighties the questions for the future remained essentially the same and the answers equally elusive.

CONCLUSION

The rise of the United States to become the world's leading super-power was predictable. Once the country had won its independence, had spread west to the Pacific and had sealed its unity in the blood of Civil War, its preeminence was assured. Size, population and abundant resources guaranteed America's supremacy. Britain's rapid decline was less easy to predict. A small European island, her world power depended on control of her empire, trade and investments. No one at the beginning of this century expected her to retain that position indefinitely, but few anticipated how quickly her grip on the world would slacken.

Two great wars accelerated this process of rise and decline. Britain faced a variety of foes, eager to take a share of her power and prosperity, and against Germany, twice in a quarter-century, she had to fight for her empire and for her very survival. From both of these wars she emerged on the winning side. But she lost a sixth of her wealth in World War I and a quarter of what remained in World War II. The United States, on the other hand, emerged from the First as a creditor nation rather than a debtor and from the Second as the producer of half the world's manufactured goods.

Yet America had not intended to embroil itself in either of these conflicts, hoping at the outset of each to remain insulated from European quarrels. The connections with Britain—economic, ideo-

logical and cultural—helped make this impossible, drawing the
United States into commitments it would not otherwise have under-
taken. And the power that accrued to America in the course of
World War II ruled out a return to isolationism, however desirable
this might have seemed to some. In the 1940s America's new
strength could have been mainly asserted in the Pacific, against
Japan, but once again the British connection helped draw it into
Europe, culminating in the North Atlantic Treaty of 1949.

These involvements were not simply attributable to ties of sentiment, language and common heritage, important though they were
for some Americans. There was no automatic Anglo-Saxon alliance.
The United States had established its independence at Britain's
expense, defining many of its values in antithesis to those of the
monarchical, aristocratic, imperialist mother country. It remained
suspicious of Britain's motives even in the period of their greatest
intimacy during World War II, and tried to break apart Britain's
commercial and financial empire. Britain never willingly relin-
quished power or influence, but her position was so exposed, her
resources so inadequate, that she had no choice but to treat the least
menacing of her foes as a potential friend.

In these great crises of the twentieth century Britain had to accept
whatever help the Americans were willing to offer, on the terms
they proposed. If that meant trading the right to build bases on
Caribbean islands for some old destroyers, or sacrificing Imperial
Preference for financial aid, so be it. From the 1940s onward Britain
was living beyond her means, while still desperately trying to remain a great power. She stayed at the top table only by virtue of
American assistance, ranging from dollar loans to the provision of
nuclear missiles.

Although this was a hardheaded relationship, it was also remarkably close, particularly between 1941 and 1945. No modern allies
have fused their war efforts so successfully. The ties of language and
culture, though they could not eliminate friction, at least acted as
emollients, allowing deep personal friendships to develop whose
importance lasted well after 1945. And in both world wars the
liberal values that the two countries shared seemed more important
than the different interpretations sometimes put on them. Personal
freedom, private property, government under the law—these were
liberties established long before in Britain, inherited by America,
and then championed by both countries in the twentieth century
against autocrats, fascists and communists alike.

This relationship with the United States has inevitably complicated Britain's recent adjustment to her destiny as a middle-ranking European power. The contrast with France is striking. After 1945 the French faced many of the same problems as the British—imperial decline, industrial stagnation, the search for a European identity. Both relied on America for economic and military help. Yet, despite sheltering under the eagle's wing, modern France developed much more self-consciously than Britain in opposition to the United States and things American. Under de Gaulle the French created a truly independent nuclear deterrent, not one using missiles bought from and serviced by the United States. They pulled out of an alliance that they deemed too heavily dominated by America, while working energetically to promote a Franco-German axis that is now the linchpin of the European Community. They also struggled to preserve the integrity of their culture, purging their language of Americanisms and trying to promote a francophone community around the world.

The divergent experiences of France and Britain in World War II are part of the explanation for the different courses they have taken after 1945. In the war France was humiliated and occupied, while Britain emerged victorious in alliance with the Americans and her "kin across the seas." These seemed her natural allies for a generation. But at a deeper level the British find it hard to identify with the continent of Europe. Everything that makes the transatlantic relationship seem natural makes links with the Continent seem unnatural. In particular, Britain and America share the same tongue, and because of their combined influence around the world English has become the premier international language of the twentieth century—the lingua franca of science, technology and culture, used by perhaps a fifth of the world's population as their first or second tongue. Language pulls Britain away from Europe, but although she is particularly affected, language and related cultural differences are barriers between all the nations of Western Europe, reinforced by lingering animosities from so many centuries of war. Scorn for a disunited European Community has led many, including Prime Minister Thatcher, to believe that Britain's interests are best served by maintaining her ties with the United States at almost any cost.

But, to survive, a relationship has to be two-way. In the past Britain mattered to America as its front line of defense, its entry point to the continent of Europe and its ally in the containment of communism around the world. But Britain's power has waned,

America's interests are shifting, and the relationship has become less important to the United States. America, reflecting its changing economic interests and ethnic balance, is again concentrating attention on Japan and the Pacific basin rather than on Europe. Its transatlantic commitment after World War II sprang directly from its hostility to the Soviet Union. The decision to defend Western Europe against Russia was taken to ensure American, not European, security, for fear that the resources of one of the most important economic regions of the world would fall under Soviet control or influence. Out of it have come NATO, forever in crisis but still the most durable peacetime alliance in modern history, and a tight bond with Britain, which serves as a vital base for air, submarine and missile defense, as well as for sophisticated intelligence gathering.

This role of "unsinkable" aircraft carrier, which Britain has played for so long, could change if the process of détente with the Soviet Union continues and America's budget and trade crises are not solved. In future strategic arms negotiations Britain's American-made nuclear deterrent, at present guaranteed by both the British and U.S. governments, may be in jeopardy. Demands from the American Congress and public opinion for withdrawal of the three hundred thousand U.S. troops in Europe could lead to major reductions and new doubts about the reliability of the American guarantee of European security. This would force Western Europe into taking more responsibility for its own defense—by strengthening conventional forces, developing its own nuclear capability, or negotiating its own arms reduction agreements with the Soviet Union and Eastern Europe.

None of this may happen—pundits have written NATO's obituary many times before—but it would be shortsighted to assume that the transatlantic alliance is the same now as it was in the 1940s. It would also be unwise to assume that the relationship between Britain and America will continue indefinitely in its present form. Close personal friendships alone will not insulate traditional policies against changing international realities. In the 1980s the rapport between Ronald Reagan and Margaret Thatcher has been as close as any in Anglo-American history, but it cannot conceal the signs, apparent since the early 1970s, that the interests of the two countries are growing further apart and the imbalance in their power has become more pronounced.

Today America is painfully adapting to the loss of its economic supremacy and, at the same time, establishing a more structured if still adversarial relationship with the Soviet Union as the cold war appears to thaw. Britain is slowly facing up to the loss of her world power and her reversion after three centuries to a largely European role. If America reduces its foreign burdens and tilts toward the Pacific, becoming less willing to help defend Europe and more aggressive in protecting its struggling economy, then Britain's future, some politicians argue, may lie in closer relations with her European partners. It will not be easy to turn a fractious, wasteful Economic Community into a united political force, let alone an alliance largely responsible for its own security. But in the twenty-first century the links with continental Europe may come to seem as appropriate to new generations of Britons as those with the United States seemed to British leaders after the Second World War.

Britain will always have a special relationship with the United States. The bonds of history, culture and language are too strong for it to be otherwise, and they have been strengthened in recent years by the impact of tourism and television. In the past, cultural values have pulled in the same direction as national interest, tying Britain and America in a double bond. But in the future, Britain's feeling of cultural affinity with America may have to be balanced against a growing sense of common political and economic interest with the rest of Europe. These need not be incompatible. The United States has itself often expressed the hope that Britain would play a significant part in building a more united Europe. Greater Western European cooperation, particularly in defense, could relieve America of some of its burdens. America's latest economic problems and the second phase of détente confirm trends apparent since the early 1970s and will give new impetus to the difficult search for greater European unity. But that lies in the future—apparently easier for the United States to confront than for Britain, a country accustomed to celebrating the triumphs of its past. For the generation of Britons who have lived through World War II and the cold war, it is not surprising that the Atlantic Ocean often seems narrower and less forbidding than the English Channel.

NOTES AND
FURTHER READING

This book draws on the many scholarly studies of Anglo-American relations published in recent years, on original research in archives on both sides of the Atlantic and on interviews conducted for the BBC television series of the same title. These notes give sources for quotations and important statistics, together with guidance for further reading. It is hoped that this will help to make the book a survey that will prove of long-term use to students of the relationship.

INTRODUCTION

Note

1. Winston S. Churchill, *The Second World War*, 6 vols (London: Cassell, 1948–54), vol. 3, p. 609.

Background Reading

General

H.C. Allen, *Great Britain and the United States, 1783–1952* (London: Odhams, 1954). Still the best overview, but it does not cover recent events and has proved too sanguine about Britain's continuing power and the harmony of her relationship with the United States.

H.G. Nicholas, *The United States and Britain* (Chicago: University of Chicago Press, 1975). Readable and more up-to-date but brief.

David Frost and Michael Shea, *The Rich Tide: Men, Women, Ideas and their Transatlantic Impact* (London: Collins, 1986). The stories of people who shaped the economic, cultural and social life of the two countries, particularly in the eighteenth and nineteenth centuries.

Surveys of the Twentieth Century

Basil Collier, *The Lion and the Eagle: British and Anglo-American Strategy, 1900–1950* (London: Macdonald, 1972). The scope is indicated by the subtitle.

Bruce M. Russett, *Community and Contention: Britain and America in the Twentieth Century* (Cambridge, Mass.: MIT Press, 1963). A distinctive analysis of cultural and economic relations by a political scientist, seeking to determine the "mutual responsiveness" of the two societies.

D. Cameron Watt, *Succeeding John Bull: America in Britain's Place, 1900–1975—A Study of the Anglo-American Relationship and World Politics in the Context of British and American Foreign-Policy-Making in the Twentieth Century* (New York: Cambridge University Press, 1984). A work of enormous scholarship, synthesizing virtually all the recent monographs, but primarily a study of foreign-policy elites and not a history of Anglo-American relations as a whole.

General Interpretations of the "Special Relationship"

Max Beloff, "The Special Relationship: An Anglo-American Myth," in Martin Gilbert, ed., *A Century of Conflict, 1850–1950: Essays for A.J.P. Taylor* (London: Hamish Hamilton, 1966), pp. 151–71. Sees it as a myth developed by the British elite to help cope with the decline of British power.

A.E. Campbell, "The United States and Great Britain: Uneasy Allies," in John Braeman, Robert H. Bremner, and David Brody, eds., *Twentieth-Century American Foreign Policy* (Columbus, Ohio: Ohio State University Press, 1971), pp. 471–501. A relationship founded on a common interest in the maintenance of peace, which lasted as long as Britain remained a great power.

Coral Bell, "The 'Special Relationship,' " in Michael Leifer, ed., *Constraints and Adjustments in British Foreign Policy* (London: George Allen & Unwin, 1972), pp. 103–19. Stressing the capacity to discern common interests.

Alastair Buchan, "Mothers and Daughters (or Greeks and Romans)," *Foreign Affairs*, vol. 54 (1976), pp. 645–69. A superb survey of the previous two hundred years and the shifting balance of the relationship.

CHAPTER I: THE STRUGGLE FOR INDEPENDENCE, C. 1620–1865

Notes

1. William Bradford, *Of Plymouth Plantation, 1620–1647*, ed. Samuel E. Morison (New York: Modern Library, 1952), quotations respectively from pp. 76, 77 and 62. This account also draws on the annotated passenger list in the older two-volume edition of Bradford's *History* (New York: Russell & Russell, 1912), pp. 399–412, and George D. Langdon, *Pilgrim Colony: A History of New Plymouth, 1620–1691* (New Haven: Yale University Press, 1966), esp. chs. 1–2.

2. Michael Heale, *The Making of American Politics, 1750–1850* (London: Longman, 1977), p. 23.

3. John Kenyon, *The History Men: The Historical Profession in England since the Renaissance* (London: Weidenfeld & Nicolson, 1983), pp. 51–52.

4. James A. Henretta, *The Evolution of American Society, 1700–1815* (Lexington, Mass.: D.C. Heath, 1973), p. 9.

5. Hamilton (1774) in Bernard Bailyn, ed., *Pamphlets of the American Revolution*, vol. 1 (Cambridge, Mass.: Harvard University Press, 1965), p. 74.

6. J.R. Pole, ed., *The Revolution in America, 1754–1788: Documents and Commentaries* (London: Macmillan, 1970), pp. 36–39.

7. Madison's message to Congress, June 1, 1812, in James D. Richardson, ed., *A Compilation of the Messages and Papers of the Presidents, 1789–1897*, 10 vols. (Washington, D.C.: U.S. Government Printing Office, 1896–1899), vol. 1, p. 504.

8. Washington's farewell address, Sept. 17, 1796, in Richardson, ed., *Messages and Papers of the Presidents*, vol. 1, pp. 222–23.

9. Jefferson's inaugural address, March 4, 1801, in Richardson, ed., *Messages and Papers of the Presidents*, vol. 1, p. 323.

10. Jefferson to Monroe, Oct. 24, 1823, in Dexter Perkins, *The Monroe Doctrine, 1823–1826* (Cambridge, Mass.: Harvard University Press, 1927), p. 91.

11. Adams in Cabinet, Nov. 7, 1823—Ernest R. May, *The Making of the Monroe Doctrine* (Cambridge, Mass.: Harvard University Press, 1975), p. 199.

12. Monroe's annual message, Dec. 2, 1823, in Richardson, ed., *Messages and Papers of the Presidents*, vol. 2, pp. 218–19.

13. Canning's speech of Dec. 12, 1826, in Harold Temperley, *The Foreign Policy of Canning, 1822–1827: England, the Neo-Holy Alliance and the New World* (London: Frank Cass, 1966 ed.), p. 154.

14. Jefferson to Abigail Adams, June 21, 1785, in Lester J. Cappon, ed., *The Adams-Jefferson Letters*, 2 vols (Chapel Hill: University of North Carolina Press, 1959), vol. 1, pp. 33–34.

15. Noah Webster, *Dissertations on the English Language* (Boston: Isaiah Thomas, 1789), pp. 20, 22–23.

16. Sydney Smith in *Edinburgh Review*, vol. 65 (Jan. 1820), pp. 79–80.

17. Frances Trollope, *Domestic Manners of the Americans* (1832), ed. Richard Mullen (Oxford: Oxford University Press, 1984), p. 314.

18. Alexis de Tocqueville, *Democracy in America*, ed. J.P. Mayer (New York: Anchor Books, 1969), p. 9.

19. Thomas Colley Grattan (1859), in Walter Allen, ed., *Transatlantic Crossing: American Visitors to Britain and British Visitors to America in the Nineteenth Century* (London: Heinemann, 1971), p. 270.

20. J.S. Mill in *Edinburgh Review*, vol. 72 (Oct. 1840), p. 40.

21. The Chartist newspaper, *Weekly Chronicle*, March 12, 1837, in G.D. Lillibridge, *Beacon of Liberty: The Impact of American Democracy upon Great Britain, 1830–1870* (Philadelphia: University of Pennsylvania Press, 1954), p. 31.

22. Thomas Hamilton to Dugald Bannatyne, Feb. 15, 1831, in Hamilton's *Men and Manners in America* (1843 ed.), quoted in David P. Crook, *American Democracy in English Politics, 1815–1850* (Oxford: Clarendon Press, 1965), p. 127.

23. *Hansard's Parliamentary Debates*, 3rd series, vol. 183, columns 103–4, April 27, 1866.

24. John L. O'Sullivan, New York *Morning News*, Dec. 27, 1845, in Albert K. Weinberg, *Manifest Destiny: A Study of Nationalist Expansionism in American History* (Baltimore: Johns Hopkins Press, 1935), p. 145.

25. 1839 "Maine Battle Song," quoted in Thomas G. Paterson, J. Garry Clifford, and Kenneth J. Hagan, *American Foreign Policy: A History to 1914* (Lexington, Mass.: D.C. Heath, 1983), p. 101.

26. De Tocqueville, *Democracy in America*, p. 413.

27. Augusta *Chronicle and Sentinel*, quoted in Michael F. Holt, *The Political Crisis of the 1850s* (New York: John Wiley, 1978), p. 241.

28. Senator James H. Hammond (South Carolina) to M.C.M. Hammond, April 22, 1860, in William R. Brock, *Conflict and Transformation: The United States, 1844–1877* (Harmondsworth: Penguin Books, 1973), p. 173.

29. Lincoln's inaugural address, March 4, 1861, in Richardson, ed., *Messages and Papers of the Presidents*, vol. 6, p. 5.

30. Rev. William Croke Squier, in Mary Ellison, *Support for Secession: Lancashire and the American Civil War* (Chicago: University of Chicago Press, 1972), p. 38.

31. *Harper's Weekly*, Nov. 16, 1861, in Carl Sandburg, *Abraham Lincoln: The War Years*, 4 vols. (New York: Harcourt, Brace & Co., 1939), vol. 1, p. 363.

32. According to his private secretary. See Kenneth Bourne, *Britain and the Balance of Power in North America, 1815–1908* (London: Longmans, 1967), p. 219.

33. Palmerston in House of Commons, July 18, 1862, in D.P. Crook, *The North, the South, and the Powers, 1861–1865* (New York: John Wiley, 1974), p. 216.

34. Lyons to Russell, April 19, 1864, in Charles S. Campbell, *From Revolution to Rapprochement: The United States and Great Britain, 1783–1900* (New York: John Wiley, 1974), p. 110.

Background Reading

General

W. A. Speck, *British America, 1607–1763* (London: British Association for American Studies, 1985). A useful little pamphlet, comparing British and colonial societies.

R. C. Simmons, *The American Colonies: From Settlement to Independence* (New York; W.W. Norton, 1976). A thorough, informed and readable survey.

David G. Allen, *In English Ways: The Movement of Societies and the Transferal of English Local Law and Custom to Massachusetts Bay in the Seventeenth Century* (Chapel Hill: University of North Carolina Press, 1981). A meticulous case study of five New England communities and their Old England antecedents.

Surveys of Anglo-American Relations after Independence

Charles S. Campbell, *From Revolution to Rapprochement: The United States and Great Britain, 1783–1900* (New York: John Wiley, 1974). The best overview of the relationship in this period.

R.B. Mowat, *The Diplomatic Relations of Great Britain and the United States up to 1913* (London: Edward Arnold, 1925). A much older book, concentrating on diplomacy, but still useful.

Frank Thistlethwaite, *The Anglo-American Connection in the Early Nineteenth Century* (Philadelphia: University of Pennsylvania Press, 1959). Still the best study of economic, social and cultural relations in the first half of the century.

CHAPTER 2: LEARNING TO LIVE TOGETHER, C. 1865–1914

Notes

1. James Russell Lowell, "On a Certain Condescension in Foreigners," *Atlantic Monthly*, Jan. 1869, p. 94.

2. Lord Illingworth in "A Woman of No Importance," *The Complete Works of Oscar Wilde* (London: Collins, 1968), p. 436.

3. Quotations from Wesley and Douglass in Frank Thistlethwaite, *The Anglo-American Connection in the Early Nineteenth Century* (Philadelphia: University of Pennsylvania Press, 1959), pp. 108–9.

4. Quoted in Merle Curti, *The American Peace Crusade, 1815–1860* (Durham, N.C.: Duke University Press, 1929), p. 116.

5. John Hay to Henry Adams, July 7, 1897, Hay Papers, vol. 3 (Library of Congress, Washington, D.C.).

6. Quoted in Paul M. Kennedy, *The Rise of the Anglo-German Antagonism, 1860–1914* (London: George Allen & Unwin, 1980), p. 467.

7. Quoted in Michael Howard, *The Continental Commitment: The Dilemma of British Defence Policy in the Era of the Two World Wars* (Harmondsworth: Pelican Books, 1974), p. 11.

8. Henry Carey, *The Way to Outdo England without Fighting Her: Letters to the Hon. Schuyler Colfax* (Philadelphia: H.C. Baird, 1865).

9. Quoted in Edward P. Crapol, *America for Americans: Economic Nationalism and Anglophobia in the Late Nineteenth Century* (London: Greenwood Press, 1973), p. 4.

10. Note of July 20, 1895, in U.S. Dept. of State, *Foreign Relations of the United States, 1895* (Washington, D.C.: U.S. Government Printing Office, 1896), part I, p. 558.

11. Quoted in J.A.S. Grenville, *Lord Salisbury and Foreign Policy at the Close of the Nineteenth Century* (London: Athlone Press, 1970), p. 66.

12. Sir Julian Pauncefote to Lord Salisbury, Dec. 24, 1895, Foreign Office correspondence, FO 80/364, f. 269 (Public Record Office, London).

13. Quoted in Charles S. Campbell, *From Revolution to Rapprochement: The United States and Great Britain, 1783–1900* (New York: John Wiley, 1974), p. 183.

14. *The Spectator*, May 7, 1898, quoted in A.E. Campbell, *Great Britain and the United States, 1898–1905* (London: Longmans, 1960), p. 152.

15. Annual message, Dec. 6, 1904, in Fred L. Israel, ed., *The State of the Union Messages of the Presidents, 1790–1966*, 3 vols. (New York: Chelsea House/Robert Hector, 1966), vol. 2, p. 2134.

16. J.L. Garvin, *The Life of Joseph Chamberlain*, 3 vols (London: Macmillan, 1932–34), vol. 2, p. 334, and vol. 3, p. 302.

17. Quoted from Josiah Strong, *Our Country* (1885), in Stuart Anderson, *Race and Rapprochement: Anglo-Saxonism and Anglo-American Relations, 1895–1904* (London: Associated Universities Press, 1981), p. 34.

18. A.J. Balfour to Joseph H. Choate, June 1, 1905, Choate papers, box 11 (Library of Congress, Washington, D.C.).

19. Balfour (1903), in Charles S. Campbell, *Anglo-American Understanding, 1898–1903* (Baltimore: Johns Hopkins Press, 1957), p. 299.

20. Lord Selborne, memo of Feb. 24, 1905, in Kenneth Bourne, *Britain and the Balance of Power in North America, 1815–1908* (London: Longmans, 1967), p. 381.

21. See John H. Dunning, *American Investment in British Manufacturing Industry* (London: George Allen & Unwin, 1958), esp. ch. 1.

22. T.C. Barker and Michael Robbins, *A History of London Transport*, vol. 2 (London: George Allen & Unwin, 1976), p. 61.

23. Joseph Chamberlain to the Duke of Devonshire, Sept. 22, 1902, in Vivian Vale, *The American Peril: Challenge to Britain on the North Atlantic, 1901–1904* (Manchester: Manchester University Press, 1984), p. 191.

24. B.W.E. Alford, *W.D. & H.O. Wills and the Development of the U.K. Tobacco Industry, 1786–1965* (London: Methuen, 1973), p. 258.

25. F.A. McKenzie, *The American Invaders* (London: Grant Richards, 1902), pp. 142–43.

26. W.T. Stead, *The Americanisation of the World* (London: Review of Reviews, 1902), p. 13.

27. W.D. Rubinstein, ed., *Wealth and the Wealthy in the Modern World* (London: Croom Helm, 1980), pp. 18–19.

28. Henry Pelling, *America and the British Left: From Bright to Bevan* (London: A. and C. Black, 1956), p. 65.

29. The standard study remains Maldwyn A. Jones, *American Immigration* (Chicago: University of Chicago Press, 1960). See also Stephan Thernstrom, ed., *Harvard Encyclopedia of American Ethnic Groups* (Cambridge, Mass.: Harvard University Press, 1980).

30. Lodge to Theodore Roosevelt, Feb. 2, 1900, Roosevelt papers, series I (Library of Congress, Washington, D.C.).

31. Quotations from Hay to Henry White, Sept. 24, 1899, and Hay to J.W. Foster, June 23, 1900, in William Roscoe Thayer, *The Life and Letters of John Hay*, 2 vols. (London: Constable, 1915), vol. 2, pp. 221, 234–35.

32. Howard K. Beale, *Theodore Roosevelt and the Rise of America to World Power* (Baltimore: Johns Hopkins Press, 1956), p. 447.

33. *The Education of Henry Adams: An Autobiography* (Boston: Houghton, Mifflin, 1961), p. 363. (The book was written in 1905.)

34. Sir Eyre Crowe, memo of July 31, 1914, in Zara S. Steiner, *Britain and the Origins of the First World War* (London: Macmillan, 1977), p. 228.

Background Reading

See also the reading for chapter 1, especially C.S. Campbell and Mowat.

Bradford Perkins, *The Great Rapprochement: England and the United States, 1895–1914* (New York: Atheneum, 1968). This remains the basic survey of this period, concentrating on diplomacy.

A.E. Campbell, *Great Britain and the United States, 1898–1905* (London: Longmans, 1960). Case studies of British policy, with perceptive analysis of the underlying interests and ideology.

Richard H. Heindel, *The American Impact on Great Britain, 1898–1914* (Philadelphia: University of Pennsylvania Press, 1940). An old book, but full of fascinating detail on the economic and social contacts.

CHAPTER 3: TO FIGHT OR NOT TO FIGHT? 1914–1917

Notes

1. "An Appeal to the American People," Aug. 18, 1914, *The Papers of Woodrow Wilson*, ed. Arthur S. Link et al., multivolume edition, still in progress (Princeton: Princeton University Press, 1966–), vol. 1, pp. 393–94.

2. Ibid.

3. Arthur S. Link, *Wilson: The Struggle for Neutrality, 1914–1915* (Princeton: Princeton University Press, 1960), p. 56.

4. Ibid., p. 53.

5. "An Appeal," Aug. 18, 1914.

6. Dimbleby, BBC 1 interview with Sonny Powers.

7. *New York American*, Aug. 8, 1914, in Jeffrey J. Safford, *Wilsonian Maritime Diplomacy, 1913–1921* (New Brunswick, N.J.: Rutgers University Press, 1978), p. 38.

8. Jefferson to Edward Rutledge, July 4, 1790, *The Papers of Thomas Jefferson*, ed. Julian P. Boyd (Princeton: Princeton University Press, 1961), vol. 16, p. 601.

9. Patrick Devlin, *Too Proud to Fight: Woodrow Wilson's Neutrality* (London: Oxford University Press, 1974), p. 200.

10. New York *Nation*, May 13, 1915, in Link, *Wilson, 1914–15*, p. 373.

11. Address in Philadelphia, May 10, 1915, Wilson, *Papers*, vol. 33, p. 149.

12. First *Lusitania* note, May 12, 1915, Wilson, *Papers*, vol. 33, pp. 174–78.

13. Devlin, *Too Proud to Fight*, p. 325.

14. Statement of Aug. 15, 1914, in Link, *Wilson, 1914–15*, p. 64.

15. Lansing to Wilson, Sept. 6, 1915, in U.S. Dept. of State, *Foreign Relations of the United States: The Lansing Papers, 1914–20* (Washington D.C.: U.S. Government Printing Office, 1939), vol. 1, p. 146.

16. House-Grey memorandum, Feb. 22, 1916, in Devlin, *Too Proud to Fight*, p. 437.

17. Quoted by C.M. Mason, "Anglo-American Relations: Mediation and 'Permanent Peace,'" in F.H. Hinsley, ed., *British Foreign Policy under Sir Edward Grey* (Cambridge: Cambridge University Press, 1977), p. 479.

18. Walter Hines Page to Col. E.M. House, May 23, 1916, in Charles Seymour, *The Intimate Papers of Colonel House*, 4 vols. (London: Ernest Benn, 1926–28), vol. 2, p. 256.

19. Page to Edwin A. Alderman, June 22, 1916, in Burton J. Hendrick, *The Life and Letters of Walter H. Page, 1855–1918*, vol. 2 (Garden City, N.Y.: Garden City Publishing Co., 1927), p. 143.

20. Arthur Bullard to Col. E.M. House, May 23, 1916, in Arthur S. Link, *Wilson: Campaigns for Progressivism and Peace, 1916–1917* (Princeton: Princeton University Press, 1965), p. 13.

21. Wilson to House, July 23, 1916, Wilson, *Papers*, vol. 37, p. 467.

22. House diary, Nov. 15, 1916, Wilson, *Papers*, vol. 38, p. 658.

23. Keynes, "The Financial Dependence of the United Kingdom on the United States of America," Oct. 10, 1916, FO 371/2796, 205593 (Public Record Office, London).

24. McKenna, "Our Financial Position in America," Oct. 24, 1916, CAB 24/2, G-87 (PRO).

25. FRB statement of Nov. 27, 1916, Link, *Wilson, 1916–1917*, p. 202.

26. Sir Cecil Spring Rice to FO, Dec. 3, 1916, in Wilson, *Papers*, vol. 40, p. 137.

27. Note of Dec. 18, 1916, Wilson, *Papers*, vol. 40, pp. 273–76.

28. Address to the Senate, Jan. 22, 1917, Wilson, *Papers*, vol. 40, pp. 533–39.

29. Interview with Roy Howard, published Sept. 28, 1916, in John Grigg, *Lloyd George: From Peace to War, 1912–1916* (London: Methuen, 1985), pp. 424–28.

30. Sir Cecil Spring Rice to Sir Eric Drummond, Oct. 13, 1916, FO 800/242, f. 253 (PRO).

31. Lord Hankey, *The Supreme Command*, 2 vols. (London: George Allen & Unwin, 1961), vol. 2, p. 557, diary entry for Nov. 9, 1916.

32. Address in Milwaukee, Jan. 31, 1916, Wilson, *Papers*, vol. 36, p. 57.

33. *Lord Riddell's War Diary, 1914–1918* (London: Ivor Nicholson & Watson, 1933), Feb. 4, 1917, p. 238.

34. Patrick Beesly, *Room 40: British Naval Intelligence, 1914–1918* (Oxford: Oxford University Press, 1984), p. 216, text of complete copy of telegram obtained by Room 40 on Feb. 19, 1917.

35. Address to Joint Session of Congress, April 2, 1917, Wilson, *Papers*, vol. 41, pp. 519–27.

36. *Memoirs of Mrs. Woodrow Wilson* (London: Putnam, 1939), p. 159.

Background Reading

General

Keith Robbins, *The First World War* (Oxford: OPUS, 1985). A succinct but comprehensive study of war, diplomacy, attitudes and social change.

James L. Stokesbury, *A Short History of World War I* (New York: William Morrow, 1981). Concentrates on battles and diplomacy.

Trevor Wilson, *The Myriad Faces of War: Britain and the Great War, 1914–1918* (New York: Blackwell, 1986). A massive study of the battlefronts and the home front, of origins, impact and consequences.

Daniel M. Smith, *The Great Departure: The United States and World War I, 1914–1920* (New York: John Wiley, 1965). Still a good overview of the whole period of U.S. neutrality, war and peacemaking.

Ross Gregory, *The Origins of American Intervention in the First World War* (New York: W.W. Norton, 1971). A useful introduction on 1914–17.

Biographical

Kenneth O. Morgan, *Lloyd George* (London: Weidenfeld & Nicolson, 1974). A short, readable biography. (The detailed studies of Lloyd George's life and foreign policy, respectively by John Grigg and Michael Fry, have not yet reached his premiership.)

Arthur S. Link, *Woodrow Wilson: War, Revolution and Peace* (Arlington Heights, Ill.: AHM, 1979). The best short account, by Wilson's principal biographer.

J.A. Thompson, "Woodrow Wilson and World War I: A Reappraisal," *Journal of American Studies*, vol. 19 (1985), pp. 325–48. A stimulating survey, arguing that Wilson was not a rigid idealist but did his best to match foreign policy to domestic politics.

Studies of the Anglo-American Relationship

Ernest R. May, *The World War and American Isolation* (Cambridge, Mass.: Harvard University Press, 1959). This remains an outstanding account, integrating American, British and German policy.

Patrick Devlin, *Too Proud to Fight: Woodrow Wilson's Neutrality* (New York: Oxford University Press, 1974). A vast book, stressing Wilson's idealism, but also including much detail on British policy and Anglo-American relations. Particularly good on neutral rights and the law of blockade.

John M. Cooper, Jr., "The Command of Gold Reversed: American Loans to Britain, 1915–1917," *Pacific Historical Review*, vol. 45 (1976), pp. 209–30. Detailed yet dramatic on Britain's financial dependence.

Kathleen Burk, *Britain, America and the Sinews of War, 1914–1918* (London: George Allen & Unwin, 1985). A study of munitions and finance, using British and American sources, and emphasizing the shift of economic power across the Atlantic.

CHAPTER 4: VICTORY WITHOUT PEACE, 1917–1920

Notes

1. Spring Rice to Balfour, Dec. 7, 1917, in Robert H. Ferrell, *Woodrow Wilson and World War I, 1917–1921* (New York: Harper & Row, 1985), p. 46.

2. Dimbleby, BBC 1 interviews in New Ulm. See also Frederick C. Luebke, *Bonds of Loyalty: German-Americans and World War I* (De Kalb, Ill.: Northern Illinois University Press, 1974), esp. ch. 8.

3. Wilson to House, July 21, 1917, *The Papers of Woodrow Wilson*, ed. Arthur S. Link et al., Multivolume edition, still in progress (Princeton: Princeton University Press, 1966–), vol. 43, p. 238.

4. Senator Thomas S. Martin, in David M. Kennedy, *Over Here: The First World War and American Society* (New York: Oxford University Press, 1980), p. 144.

5. Dimbleby, BBC 1 interview with Winston Roche.

6. Dimbleby, BBC 1 interview with William Bruder.

7. Dimbleby—Roche interview.

8. David F. Trask, *Captains and Cabinets: Anglo-American Naval Relations, 1917–1918* (Columbia: University of Missouri Press, 1972), p. 55.

9. Dimbleby, BBC 1 interview with "Tanky" Taylor.

10. David R. Woodward, "Did Lloyd George Starve the British Army of Men Prior to the German Offensive of 21 March 1918?" *Historical Journal* vol. 27 (1984), p. 250.

11. Robert Blake, ed., *The Private Papers of Douglas Haig, 1914–1918* (London: Eyre & Spottiswood, 1952), p. 307, diary for May 1, 1918.

12. Fourteen Points, Jan. 8, 1918, Wilson, *Papers*, vol. 45, pp. 534–39.

13. Smuts in Imperial War Cabinet, Aug. 14, 1918, David R. Woodward, *Lloyd George and the Generals* (Newark: University of Delaware Press, 1983), p. 328.

14. Admiralty memo for War Cabinet, Dec. 1918, in V.H. Rothwell, *British War Aims and Peace Diplomacy, 1914–1918* (Oxford: Clarendon Press, 1971), p. 258.

15. Col. Edward House, diary, Nov. 4, 1918, Colonel Edward M. House papers (Sterling Library, Yale University).

16. Remarks on Oct. 29, 1918, in Sterling Kernek, *Distractions of Peace during War: The Lloyd George Government's Reactions to Woodrow Wilson, December 1916 to November 1918* (Philadelphia: American Philosophical Society Transactions, 1975), p. 104.

17. Dimbleby, BBC 1 interview with Edith Sowerbutts.

18. John Maynard Keynes, *The Economic Consequences of the Peace* (1919), in *The Collected Writings of John Maynard Keynes* vol. 2 (London: Macmillan, 1971), p. 24.

19. Dr. Cary Grayson, diary, Dec. 27, 1918, in Wilson, *Papers*, vol. 53, p. 521.

20. David Lloyd George, *The Truth about the Peace Treaties* (London: Victor Gollancz, 1938), vol. 1, p. 181.

21. Quoted in Lloyd C. Gardner, *Safe for Democracy: The Anglo-American Response to Revolution, 1913–1923* (New York: Oxford University Press, 1984), pp. 2–3.

22. A. Lentin, *Lloyd George, Woodrow Wilson and the Guilt of Germany: An Essay in the Pre-History of Appeasement* (Leicester: Leicester University Press, 1984), pp. 16–29.

23. Harold Nicolson, *Peacemaking, 1919* (London: Constable, 1933), p. 152.

24. Michael L. Dockrill and J. Douglas Goold, *Peace without Promise: Britain and the Paris Peace Conferences, 1919–23* (London: Batsford, 1981), p. 59.

25. Wilson to House, March 3, 1919, in Wilson, *Papers*, vol. 55, p. 392.

26. Sen. Frank Brandegee, in Ralph Stone, *The Irreconcilables: The Fight against the League of Nations* (New York: W.W. Norton, 1973), p. 63.

27. Charles Seymour, *The Intimate Papers of Colonel House*, 4 vols. (London: Ernest Benn, 1926–28), vol. 4, p. 405.

28. J.M. Keynes to Florence Keynes, May 14, 1919, *The Collected Writings of John Maynard Keynes*, ed. Elizabeth Johnson, vol. 16 (London: Macmillan, 1971), p. 458.

29. Peter Rowland, *Lloyd George* (London: Barrie & Jenkins, 1975), p. 495.

30. Alan J. Ward, *Ireland and Anglo-American Relations, 1899–1921* (London: Weidenfeld & Nicolson, 1969), p. 176.

31. *Philadelphia Irish Press*, May 24, 1919, in Joseph P. O'Grady, ed., *The Immigrants' Influence on Wilson's Peace Policies* (Lexington: University of Kentucky Press, 1967), p. 77.

32. Woodrow Wilson, *War and Peace: Presidential Messages, Addresses, and Public Papers, 1917–1924*, eds. Ray Stannard Baker and William E. Dodd, 2 vols. (New York: Harper & Brothers, 1927), vol. 1, p. 640 (St. Louis, Sept. 5, 1919), vol. 2, pp. 52 (Sioux Falls, Sept. 8) and 212 (Portland, Sept. 15).

33. Thomas A. Bailey, *Woodrow Wilson and the Great Betrayal* (Chicago: Quadrangle Books, 1945), p. 185.

34. George W. Egerton, "Britain and the 'Great Betrayal': Anglo-American Relations and the Struggle for United States Ratification of the Treaty of Versailles, 1919–1920," *Historical Journal*, vol. 21 (1978), p. 911.

Background Reading

See also the reading for chapter 3. Some books overlap both chapters.

General

Robert H. Ferrell, *Woodrow Wilson and World War I, 1917–1921* (New York: Harper & Row, 1985). A good, recent survey of war, diplomacy and the home front.

Charles L. Mee, Jr., *The End of Order: Versailles, 1919* (New York: Dutton, 1980). A vivid, readable account of the Paris peace conference.

Studies of the Anglo-American Relationship

Sterling Kernek, *Distractions of Peace during War: The Lloyd George Government's Reactions to Woodrow Wilson, December 1916 to November 1918* (Philadelphia: American Philosophical Society Transactions, 1975). The debates about rival peace plans.

Wilton B. Fowler, *British-American Relations, 1917–1918: The Role of Sir William Wiseman* (Princeton: Princeton University Press, 1969). Based on the Wiseman papers, but providing good insights into British and U.S. policy on finance, war aims and the use of U.S. troops.

Edward B. Parsons, *Wilsonian Diplomacy: Allied-American Rivalries in War and Peace* (St. Louis, Mo.: Forum Press, 1978). Covers 1916–18. Trade, shipping and what to do with Pershing's army.

George W. Egerton, *Great Britain and the Creation of the League of Nations: Strategy, Politics, and International Organization, 1914–1919* (Chapel Hill: University of North Carolina Press, 1979). The Anglo-American negotiations about the League.

Lloyd C. Gardner, *Safe for Democracy: The Anglo-American Response to Revolution, 1913–1923* (New York: Oxford University Press, 1984). The attempts of Wilson and Lloyd George to find an ordered liberal alternative to revolution. Concentrates on policy toward Russia and China from 1917.

CHAPTER 5: THE BIG TWO, 1921–1935

Notes

1. Speech in Des Moines, Iowa, Sept. 6, 1919, in Woodrow Wilson, *War and Peace: Presidential Messages, Addresses, and Public Papers, 1917–1924*, eds. Ray Stannard Baker and William E. Dodd, 2 vols. (New York: Harper & Brothers, 1927), vol. 2, p. 18.

2. Klaus Hildebrand, " 'British Interests' und 'Pax Britannica': Grundfragen englischer Aussenpolitik im 19. und 20. Jahrhundert," *Historische Zeitschrift*, 221 (1975), p. 625.

3. Lord Northcliffe to Geoffrey Robinson, July 1, 1917, quoted in Kathleen Burk, "Great Britain in the United States, 1917–1918: The Turning Point," *International History Review*, vol. 1 (1979), p. 228.

4. Cecil, memo for War Cabinet, Sept. 18, 1917, CAB 24/26, doc. 2074 (Public Record Office, London).

5. Wiseman, memo on U.S. attitudes to the peace conference, c. Oct. 20, 1918, Sir William Wiseman papers, I/9/213 (Sterling Library, Yale University).

6. House to Wilson, July 30, 1919, in Charles Seymour, *The Intimate Papers of Colonel House*, 4 vols. (London: Ernest Benn, 1926–28), vol. 4, p. 510.

7. Memorandum for the Cabinet, July 20, 1927, in Martin Gilbert, *Winston S. Churchill*, vol. 5, Companion Part I (London: Heinemann, 1979), p. 1033.

8. Mark Sullivan, quoted in Thomas H. Buckley, *The United States and the Washington Naval Conference, 1921–22* (Knoxville: University of Tennessee Press, 1970), p. 72.

9. U.S. Navy General Board report, April 21, 1927, in Stephen Roskill, *Naval Policy between the Wars*, vol. 1 (London: Collins, 1968), p. 502.

10. Hugh Gibson to William Castle, Sept. 30, 1928, in Frank Costigliola, *Awkward Dominion: American Political, Economic, and Cultural Relations with Europe, 1919–1933* (Ithaca, N.Y.: Cornell University Press, 1984), p. 189.

11. Christopher Hall, *Britain, America and Arms Control, 1921–1937* (London: Macmillan, 1987), p. 58. The congressman was Fred Britten, chairman of the House Naval Affairs Committee.

12. Vansittart, minute, Oct. 19, 1927, FO 371/12040, A6057/133/45 (Public Record Office, London).

13. Hankey to Thomas Jones (Prime Minister Baldwin's private secretary), Oct. 11, 1928, in Thomas Jones, *Whitehall Diary, 1926–30*, vol. 2 (London: Oxford University Press, 1969), pp. 147–48.

14. *New York Times*, Oct. 13, 1929, quoted in David Marquand, *Ramsay MacDonald* (London: Jonathan Cape, 1977), p. 508.

15. Christopher Thorne, *The Limits of Foreign Policy: The West, the League and the Far Eastern Crisis of 1931–1933* (London: Heinemann, 1972), quoting respectively from pp. 262, 260.

16. William Allen White to Lord Lothian, March 16, 1939, Lothian papers, GD 40/17/387 (Scottish Record Office, Edinburgh).

17. Emile Moreau, governor of the Bank of France, in Andrew Boyle, *Montagu Norman* (London: Cassell, 1967), p. 198.

18. Sir Cecil Hirst, Oct. 12, 1925, in D. Cameron Watt, *Succeeding John Bull: America in Britain's Place, 1900–1975* (Cambridge: Cambridge University Press, 1984), p. 57.

19. Frank C. Costigliola, "Anglo-American Financial Rivalry in the 1920s," *Journal of Economic History*, vol. 37 (1977), p. 913.

20. Speech of Aug. 5, 1925, in *Winston S. Churchill: His Complete Speeches, 1897–1963*, ed. Robert Rhodes James, vol. 4 (New York: Chelsea House, 1974), p. 3742.

21. Diane B. Kunz, *The Battle for Britain's Gold Standard in 1931* (London: Croom Helm, 1987), p. 82.

22. Message of Aug. 23, 1931, in CAB 23/67, f. 365. (PRO). Apparently this was described to the Cabinet as a message from Benjamin Harrison and the Federal Reserve, perhaps because MacDonald feared that to mention the name of Morgan's would only further incense his critics. See Kunz, *Battle for Britain's Gold Standard*, p. 105.

23. Cabinet meeting, Cab. 46 (31), Aug. 23, 1931, CAB 23/67, f. 360. (PRO).

24. R. Bassett, *Nineteen Thirty-One: Political Crisis* (London: Macmillan, 1958), pp. 175, 173.

25. Dimbleby, BBC 1 interview with C. Douglas Dillon.

26. Neville Chamberlain to Ida Chamberlain, July 15, 1933, Neville Chamberlain papers, NC 18/1/836 (Birmingham University Library).

27. Charles P. Kindleberger, *The World in Depression, 1929–1939* (Berkeley: University of California Press, 1973), p. 292.

28. Quoted in W. Roger Louis, *British Strategy in the Far East, 1919–1939* (Oxford: Clarendon Press, 1971), p. 77.

29. Memo of Nov. 1927, in B.J.C. McKercher, *The Second Baldwin Government and the United States, 1924–1929* (Cambridge: Cambridge University Press, 1984), p. 1.

30. Both Baldwin quotations in Keith Middlemas and John Barnes, *Baldwin: A Biography* (London: Weidenfeld & Nicolson, 1969), p. 729.

31. Minute of Feb. 5, 1934, in Norman Rose, *Vansittart: Study of a Diplomat* (London: Heinemann, 1978), p. 126–27.

32. John E. Wiltz, *In Search of Peace: The Senate Munitions Inquiry, 1934–1936* (Baton Rouge: Louisiana State University Press, 1963), p. 15.

33. Quoted in Cushing Strout, *The American Image of the Old World* (New York: Harper & Row, 1963), p. 205.

Background Reading

General

Graham Ross, *The Great Powers and the Decline of the European States System, 1914–1945* (New York: Longman, 1983). A succinct if dry introduction to the diplomacy of the period.

Arnold A. Offner, *The Origins of the Second World War: American Foreign Policy and World Politics, 1917–1941* (New York: Krieger reprint, 1986). First published in 1975, but still a good overview of U.S. policy.

F.S. Northedge, *The Troubled Giant: Britain among the Great Powers, 1916–1939* (London: G. Bell, 1966). Still a useful survey.

Derek H. Aldcroft, *From Versailles to Wall Street, 1919–1929* (Berkeley: University of California Press, 1977). A good introduction to the economic history of the 1920s.

Studies of the Anglo-American Relationship: Navies

Roger Dingman, *Power in the Pacific: The Origins of Naval Arms Limitation, 1914–1922* (Chicago: University of Chicago Press, 1976). Thorough study of British, American and Japanese naval policy.

B.J.C. McKercher, *The Second Baldwin Government and the United States, 1924–1929* (New York: Cambridge University Press, 1984). Mainly on the naval race and freedom of the seas before and after the Geneva conference of 1927.

Christopher Hall, *Britain, America and Arms Control, 1921–1937* (London: Macmillan, 1987). A lucid account, concentrating on the naval conferences between 1927 and 1935.

Studies of the Anglo-American Relationship: Finance

Jon Jacobson, "Is There a New International History of the 1920s?" *American Historical Review*, vol. 88 (1983), pp. 617–45. A good introduction to the new literature on Europe in the 1920s and the American role.

Stephen V.O. Clarke, *Central Bank Cooperation, 1924–1931* (New York: Federal Reserve Bank of New York, 1967). Still the basic study of British and U.S. policy, although it predates the opening of the British archives.

D.E. Moggridge, *British Monetary Policy, 1924–1931: The Norman Conquest of $4.86* (Cambridge: Cambridge University Press, 1972). Basic study of British financial policy during the period of the return to gold.

Frank C. Costigliola, "Anglo-American Financial Rivalry in the 1920s," *Journal of Economic History*, vol. 37 (1977), pp. 911–34. A succinct survey, based on British and American archives.

Diane B. Kunz, *The Battle for Britain's Gold Standard in 1931* (New York: Croom Helm, 1987). This is the best study of the financial diplomacy of the crisis, using British and American archives.

CHAPTER 6: AMERICANIZATION

BUSINESS AND SOCIETY BETWEEN THE WORLD WARS

Notes

1. G. Lowes Dickinson, *Appearances: Being Notes of Travel* (London: J.M. Dent, 1914), p. 160.

2. Alanson Houghton to Owen Young, Feb. 13, 1926, in Frank Costigliola, *Awkward Dominion: American Political, Economic, and Cultural Relations with Europe, 1919–1933* (Ithaca, N.Y.: Cornell University Press, 1984), p. 144.

3. Thomas Jones, *Whitehall Diary*, ed. Keith Middlemas, vol. 2 (London: Oxford University Press, 1969), p. 177, entry for March 8, 1929.

4. BBC 1 interview with Raymond Firestone.

5. Sir Arthur Willert, *Aspects of British Foreign Policy* (New Haven: Yale University Press, 1928), p. 15—lecture given by Willert, the head of the Foreign Office News Dept., in Williamstown, Mass., in July 1927.

6. Joan Hoff Wilson, *Herbert Hoover: Forgotten Progressive* (Boston: Little, Brown, 1975), p. 177.

7. Sir Esme Howard to Sir Austen Chamberlain, April 26, 1928, in Michael J. Hogan, *Informal Entente: The Private Structure of Cooperation in Anglo-American Economic Diplomacy, 1918–1928* (Columbia: University of Missouri Press, 1977), p. 208.

8. Elie Garcia report, Aug. 1920, in E. David Cronon, *Black Moses: The Story of Marcus Garvey and the Universal Negro Improvement Association* (Madison: University of Wisconsin Press, 1969), p. 124.

9. Telegram of May 22, 1925, in U.S. Dept. of State, *Foreign Relations of the United States, 1925* (Washington, D.C.: U.S. Government Printing Office, 1940), vol. 2, p. 432.

10. Raymond L. Buell, *The Native Problem in Africa*, 2 vols. (New York: Macmillan, 1928), vol. 2, p. 837.

11. BBC 1 interview with Charles L. James, former assistant to Garvey.

12. Ludwell Denny, *America Conquers Britain: A Record of Economic War* (New York: Alfred A. Knopf, 1930), p. 407.

13. Swope to Docker, Feb. 16, 1928, in Robert Jones and Oliver Marriott, *Anatomy of a Merger: A History of G.E.C., A.E.I. and English Electric* (London: Jonathan Cape, 1970), p. 98.

14. R.P.T. Davenport-Hines, *Dudley Docker: The Life and Times of a Trade Warrior* (Cambridge: Cambridge University Press, 1984), p. 179.

15. Jones and Marriott, *Anatomy of a Merger*, p. 99.

16. *New York Times*, March 31, 1929, in Denny, *America Conquers Britain*, p. 142.

17. *Manchester Guardian*, Feb. 15, 1929, p. 11.

18. Leslie Hannah, *Electricity before Nationalisation: A Study of the Development of the Electrical Supply Industry in Britain to 1948* (London: Macmillan, 1979), p. 229.

19. J. Ellis Barker, *America's Secret: The Causes of Her Economic Success* (London: John Murray, 1927), p. 412.

20. BBC 1 interview with Winifred Davis.

21. Chris Goddard, *Jazz Away from Home* (New York: Paddington Press, 1979), p. 219.

22. BBC 1 interview with Doreen Evans.

23. Board of Education memo, July 1941, in David Reynolds, "Whitehall, Washington and the Promotion of American Studies in Britain during World War Two," *Journal of American Studies*, vol. 16 (1982), p. 174.

24. *Daily Express*, March 18, 1927, p. 6.

25. Herbert Williams, in House of Commons, *Debates*, March 16, 1927, vol. 203, col. 2086.

26. Oliver Stanley, in House of Commons, *Debates*, Nov. 4, 1937, vol. 328, col. 1173.

27. *Morning Post* (1923), quoted in Edward G. Lowry, "Trade Follows the Film," *Saturday Evening Post*, Nov. 7, 1925, p. 12.

28. Quoted by Thomas H. Guback, "Hollywood's International Market," in Tino Balio, ed., *The American Film Industry* (Madison: University of Wisconsin Press, 1976), p. 394.

29. Quoted in Peter Stead, "Hollywood's Message for the World: The British Response in the Nineteen Thirties," *Historical Journal of Film, Radio and Television* vol. 1 (1981), p. 22.

30. C.E.M. Joad, *The Babbitt Warren* (London: Kegan, Trench, Trubner, 1926), esp. pp. xii, 4, 188, 190–91.

31. Nicolson to Vita Sackville-West, Nov. 17, 1934, in Harold Nicolson, *Diaries and Letters, 1930–1939*, ed. Nigel Nicolson (London: Collins, 1966), p. 189.

32. BBC 1 interview with John Carberry.

33. Fitzgerald to Edmund Wilson, May 1921, in Andrew Turnbull, ed., *The Letters of F. Scott Fitzgerald* (London: Bodley Head, 1964), p. 326.

34. Quotations from *Europa und Amerika* (1926) in Isaac Deutscher, *The Prophet Unarmed: Trotsky, 1921–1929* (London: Oxford University Press, 1959), p. 215.

35. Robert H. Ferrell, *Woodrow Wilson and World War I, 1917–1921* (New York: Harper & Row, 1985), p. 210.

36. John L. Gaddis, *Russia, the Soviet Union and the United States: An Interpretive History* (New York: Alfred A. Knopf, 1978), p. 113.

37. Werner Sombart, in Daniel Bell, *Marxian Socialism in the United States* (Princeton: Princeton University Press, 1967), p. 4.

38. Article of Feb. 1933, in Frank Freidel, *Franklin D. Roosevelt: Launching the New Deal* (Boston: Little, Brown, 1973), p. 12.

39. Arthur M. Schlesinger, Jr., *The Age of Roosevelt: The Crisis of the Old Order, 1919–1933* (Boston: Houghton Mifflin, 1957), p. 155.

40. William E. Leuchtenburg, *Franklin D. Roosevelt and the New Deal, 1932–1940* (New York: Harper & Row, 1963), p. 28, recounting a story from the spring of 1931.

41. James MacGregor Burns, *Roosevelt: The Lion and the Fox* (New York: Harcourt, Brace & World, 1956), p. 163.

42. In 1930 total British long-term foreign investment (direct and portfolio) was estimated at $18.2 billion; American at between $14.7 billion and $15.4 billion. See Mira Wilkins, *The Maturing of Multinational Enterprise: American Business Abroad from 1914 to 1970* (Cambridge, Mass.: Harvard University Press, 1974), p. 156, note.

43. Comment of 1926 in Roy Church and Michael Miller, " 'The Big Three': Competition, Management and Marketing in the British Motor Industry, 1922–1939," in Barry Supple, ed., *Essays in British Business History* (Oxford: Clarendon Press, 1977), p. 169.

44. *Fortune*, July 1937, in D.C. Coleman, *Courtaulds: An Economic and Social History*, vol. 2 (Oxford: Clarendon Press, 1969), pp. 384–85.

45. Freidel, *Launching the New Deal*, p. 346 (Securities Act); Barry Supple, "The Political Economy of Demoralization: The State and the Coalmining Industry in America and Britain between the Wars," n. 116, *Economic History Review*, forthcoming, 1988.

46. Sir Arthur Willert, memo of conversations with FDR in Jan. and March 1936, April 14, 1936, Willert papers, box 14, folder 59 (Yale University).

47. Henry Pelling, *America and the British Left: From Bright to Bevan* (London: Adam & Charles Black, 1956), p. 136.

48. Comments of Dec. 1934 in Peter Rowland, *Lloyd George* (London: Barrie & Jenkins, 1975), p. 713.

49. E.g., Sir Ronald Lindsay to Lord Halifax, despatch 360, April 1937, FO 371/21546, A 3440/1202/45 (Public Record Office, London),

50. Frank Ashton-Gwatkin, report on U.S. economic situation in May 1938, CAB 24/277, CP 161 (38) (PRO).

51. Richard H. Heindel, *The American Impact on Great Britain, 1898–1914* (Philadelphia: University of Pennsylvania, 1940), pp. 15–18. He surveyed the press in 1936–37 and concluded that there had not been much change in quantity or quality since the First World War.

52. *The Times*, May 19, 1939, p. 18.

53. H. Morse Stephens (1916) in Bruce M. Russett, *Community and Contention: Britain and America in the Twentieth Century* (Cambridge, Mass.: MIT Press, 1963), p. 133.

54. Frances Donaldson, *Edward VIII* (London: Weidenfeld & Nicolson, 1974), p. 232.

55. *New York Journal*, Oct. 26, 1936, in Brian Inglis, *Abdication* (London: Hodder & Stoughton, 1966), pp. 193–94.

56. House of Commons, *Debates*, vol. 318, col. 2179, Dec. 10, 1936.

Background Reading

General Histories of Anglo-American Economic Relations

Philip S. Bagwell and G.E. Mingay, *Britain and America: A Study of Economic Change, 1850–1939* (London: Routledge & Kegan Paul, 1970).

Graeme M. Holmes, *Britain and America: A Comparative Economic History, 1850–1939* (New York: Barnes & Noble, 1976).

Studies of Anglo-American Economic Relations in the Interwar Period

See also background reading for chapter 5.

Michael J. Hogan, *Informal Entente: The Private Structure of Cooperation in Anglo-American Economic Diplomacy, 1918–1928* (Columbia: University of Missouri Press, 1977). Analyzes policy on finance, oil, cables and radio, possibly exaggerating the ententes achieved.

Michael D. Goldberg, "Anglo-American Economic Competition, 1920–1930," *Economy and History*, vol. 16 (1973), pp. 15–36. Surveys the global competition, with full statistical detail, but not official policy.

The American Impact on British Society

John Dizikes, *Britain, Roosevelt and the New Deal: British Public Opinion, 1932–1938* (New York: Garland, 1979). Reprint of 1964 Harvard Ph.D., based on books and newspaper sources.

Jeffrey Richards, *The Age of the Dream Palace: Cinema and Society in Britain, 1930–1939* (London: Routledge & Kegan Paul, 1984). The best study, with much discussion of American films and Americanization.

George H. Knoles, *The Jazz Age Revisited: British Criticism of American Civilization during the 1920s* (Stanford, Calif.: Stanford University Press, 1955). A detailed survey of British comment.

John H. Dunning, *American Investment in British Manufacturing Industry* (London: George Allen & Unwin, 1958). Concentrates on the 1950s, but with good background on earlier decades.

CHAPTER 7: BRITAIN ALONE, 1935–1941

Notes

1. Winston S. Churchill, *The Second World War*, 6 vols. (London: Cassell, 1948–54), vol. 1, viii–ix.

2. Speech of Aug. 14, 1936, in Edgar B. Nixon, ed., *Franklin D. Roosevelt and Foreign Affairs*, (Cambridge, Mass.: Harvard University Press, 1969), vol. 3, p. 380.

3. James M. Burns, *Roosevelt: The Soldier of Freedom, 1940–1945* (New York: Harcourt Brace Jovanovich, 1970), p. 606.

4. Admiral Sir Ernle Chatfield to Sir Warren Fisher, June 4, 1934, Chatfield papers, CHT/3/1 (National Maritime Museum, Greenwich).

5. Neville Chamberlain to Hilda Chamberlain, Dec. 17, 1937, Chamberlain papers, NC 18/1/1032 (Birmingham University Library).

6. Richard N. Kottman, *Reciprocity and the North Atlantic Triangle, 1932–1938* (Ithaca, N.Y.: Cornell University Press, 1968), p. 117.

7. Jay Pierrepont Moffat to Norman Davis, Oct. 7, 1936, Davis papers, box 41 (Library of Congress, Washington, D.C.).

8. Chamberlain, diary, Feb. 19, 1938, NC 2/24A.

9. Dimbleby, BBC 1 interview with Lord Home.

10. Eden to Chamberlain, draft, Jan. 18, 1938, Foreign Office correspondence, FO 371/21526, A 2127/64/45 (Public Record Office, London).

11. Churchill, *Second World War*, vol. 1, p. 199.

12. J.R.M. Butler, *Lord Lothian* (London: Macmillan, 1960), p. 213.

13. Roosevelt to Chamberlain, Oct. 5, 1938, in William L. Langer and S. Everett Gleason, *The Challenge to Isolation, 1937–40* (New York: Council on Foreign Relations, 1952), p. 138.

14. Roosevelt to Roger B. Merriman, Feb. 15, 1939, President's Secretary's File, PSF 46: "Great Britain" (Roosevelt Library, Hyde Park, N.Y.).

15. Robert Dallek, *Franklin D. Roosevelt and American Foreign Policy, 1932–1945* (New York: Oxford University Press, 1979), p. 199.

16. Neville Chamberlain to Ida Chamberlain, Jan. 27, 1940, Chamberlain papers, NC 18/1/1140.

17. Broadcast of May 10, 1940 in Edward Bliss, Jr, ed., *In Search of Light: The Broadcasts of Edward R. Murrow, 1938–61* (London: Macmillan, 1968), p. 22.

18. Dimbleby, BBC 1 interview with Sir John Colville.

19. Harold L. Ickes, diary, May 12, 1940 (Library of Congress, Washington, D.C.).

20. Speech of June 4, 1940 in Robert Rhodes James, ed., *Winston S. Churchill: His Complete Speeches, 1897–1963* (New York: Chelsea House, 1974), vol. 6, p. 6231.

21. Warren F. Kimball, ed., *Churchill and Roosevelt: The Complete Correspondence*, 3 vols. (Princeton: Princeton University Press, 1984), vol. 1, pp. 43, 51, 57, messages of June 11, 15, and July 31, 1940.

22. Kennedy to Roosevelt, May 15, 1940, State Dept. records, RG 59, 740.0011 EW 1939/2952 (National Archives, Washington, D.C.).

23. Christopher Thorne, *The Far Eastern War: States and Societies, 1941–1945* (London: Unwin Paperbacks, 1986), pp. 211–212.

24. War Cabinet minutes, Aug. 21, 1940, CAB 65/8, WM 231 (40) 1 (PRO).

25. Churchill to Roosevelt, Aug. 25, 1940, Kimball, *Correspondence*, vol. 1, p. 65.

26. Dimbleby, BBC 1 interview with Graham Hutton.

27. Dimbleby, BBC 1 interview with Douglas Fairbanks, Jr.

28. Dimbleby, BBC 1 interview with Kingman Brewster.

29. Sir Ronald Lindsay to Rex Leeper, March 17, 1939, FO 395/648b, pp. 569–70 (PRO).

30. Edward R. Murrow, *This is London*, ed. Elmer Davis (New York: Simon & Schuster, 1941), p. 167.

31. Frank Gillard, "Goodnight, and good luck," *Listener*, May 1, 1975, p. 565.

32. Dimbleby—Fairbanks interview.

33. Quotations in this paragraph from Robert Divine, *Foreign Policy and U.S. Presidential Elections* (New York: New Viewpoints, 1974) vol. 1, pp. 80, 82–83.

34. Churchill, *Second World War*, vol. 2, p. 501.

35. Kimball, ed., *Correspondence*, vol. 1, pp. 101–9.

36. Quotations in this and the previous paragraph from press conference of Dec. 17, 1940, in Samuel Rosenman, ed., *The Public Papers and Addresses of Franklin D. Roosevelt, 1940* (New York: Macmillan, 1941), esp. pp. 604 and 607.

37. Dimbleby, BBC 1 interview with Claude Pepper.

38. Churchill, *Second World War*, vol. 2, p. 506.

39. Draft of Dec. 28, 1940, Prime Minister's Papers, PREM 4/17/1 (PRO).

40. W. Averell Harriman and Elie Abel, *Special Envoy to Churchill and Stalin, 1941–1946* (New York: Random House, 1975), p. 19.

41. Churchill, *Second World War*, vol. 2, p. 503.

42. Dimbleby—Pepper interview.

43. Churchill to Roosevelt, May 4, 1941, Kimball, *Correspondence*, vol. 1, p. 182.

44. Churchill to Queen Elizabeth, Aug. 3, 1941, PREM 3/485/6, p. 16 (PRO).

45. Dimbleby, BBC 1 interview with Elliott Roosevelt.

46. U.S. Dept. of State, *Foreign Relations of the United States, 1941* (Washington, D.C.: U.S. Government Printing Office, 1958), vol. 1, p. 368.

47. War Cabinet Minutes, Aug. 19, 1941, CAB 65/19, WM 84 (41)1, Confidential Annex (PRO).

48. Hadley Cantril, ed., *Public Opinion, 1935–1946* (Princeton: Princeton University Press, 1951), p. 977.

49. Dimbleby—Hutton interview.

50. Letters from Leonard N. Conrad, in Susan Winslow, ed., *Brother, Can You Spare a Dime?* (New York: Paddington Press, 1976), p. 159.

51. Roosevelt to Churchill, Dec. 8, 1941, in Kimball, ed., *Correspondence*, vol. 1, p. 283.

52. Churchill, *Second World War*, vol. 3, p. 540.

Background Reading

General

William Carr, *Poland to Pearl Harbor: The Making of the Second World War* (Baltimore: Edward Arnold, 1985). A genuinely global study, taking Asia as seriously as Europe. Strongest on 1939–41.

Robert A. Divine, *The Reluctant Belligerent: American Entry into World War II* (New York: Alfred A. Knopf, 1979). The best survey of American policy.

Roy Douglas, *In the Year of Munich* (London: Macmillan, 1977), *The Advent of War, 1939–1940* (1978), and *New Alliances, 1940–1941* (1982), offer good summaries of British policy based on the official documents.

Biographical

Robert Dallek, *Franklin D. Roosevelt and American Foreign Policy, 1932–1945* (New York: Oxford University Press, 1979). The basic text on FDR's foreign policy.

Martin Gilbert, *Finest Hour: Winston S. Churchill, 1939–1941* (New York: Houghton Mifflin, 1983). The pertinent volume of the vast official biography.

Joseph Lash, *Roosevelt and Churchill, 1939–1941: The Partnership that Saved the West* (New York: W.W. Norton, 1976). A vivid account of their relationship, based on British and American archives.

Studies of the Anglo-American Relationship

C.A. MacDonald, *The United States, Britain and Appeasement, 1936–1939* (London: Macmillan, 1980). A good, short analysis, based on British and U.S. archives, emphasizing the economic rivalries.

Ritchie Ovendale, *Appeasement and the English-Speaking World: Britain, the United States, the Dominions and the Policy of 'Appeasement', 1937–1939* (Cardiff: University of Wales Press, 1975). British policy toward the United States and the Commonwealth. More sympathetic to Chamberlain, to British policy and to the idea of an "English-speaking world" than most recent studies.

James R. Leutze, *Bargaining for Supremacy: Anglo-American Naval Relations, 1937–1941* (Chapel Hill: University of North Carolina Press, 1977). Naval rivalry, especially in 1940–41.

Malcolm H. Murfett, *Fool-Proof Relations: The Search for Anglo-American Naval Cooperation during the Chamberlain Years, 1937–40* (Singapore: Singapore University Press, 1984). Fuller on British side than Leutze, and, like Ovendale, sympathetic to Chamberlain.

David Reynolds, *The Creation of the Anglo-American Alliance, 1937–1941: A Study in Competitive Co-operation* (Chapel Hill: University of North Carolina Press, 1982). Survey of the whole relationship: diplomatic, military and economic. Used as the foundation for this chapter.

CHAPTER 8: MIXED UP TOGETHER, 1941–1945

Notes

1. Arthur Bryant, *The Turn of the Tide: A Study Based on the Diaries and Autobiographical Notes of Field Marshal the Viscount Alanbrooke, KG, OM* (London: Collins, 1957), p. 282.

2. Robert E. Sherwood, *Roosevelt and Hopkins: An Intimate History* (New York: Harper & Brothers, 1948), p. 442.

3. War Cabinet minutes, WM 8 (42) 1, Jan. 17, 1942, CAB 65/25 (Public Record Office, London).

4. Roosevelt to Churchill, Jan. 30, 1942, in Warren F. Kimball, ed., *Churchill and Roosevelt: Their Complete Correspondence*, 3 vols. (Princeton: Princeton University Press, 1984), vol. 1, p. 337.

5. Winston S. Churchill, *The Second World War*, 6 vols. (London: Cassell, 1948–54), vol. 2, p. 22.

6. Churchill to Eden, Nov. 5, 1942, Prime Minister's Correspondence, PREM 4/27/1 (PRO).

7. Alex Danchev, *Very Special Relationship: Field Marshal Sir John Dill and the Anglo-American Alliance, 1941–1944* (London: Brassey's Defence Publishers, 1986), p. 3.

8. House of Commons, *Debates*, vol. 364, col. 1171, Aug. 20, 1940.

9. H. Duncan Hall, *North American Supply* (London: HMSO, 1955), p. 353.

10. Joint memo, "American and British Strategy," WW1 (Final), Jan. 20, 1942, Annex I, CAB 80/33 (PRO).

11. Martin Gilbert, *Road to Victory: Winston S. Churchill, 1941–1945* (London: Heinemann, 1986), p. 44.

12. Marshall's memo in J.R.M. Butler, *Grand Strategy*, vol. 3, part II of *History of the Second World War: UK Military Series* (London: HMSO, 1964), p. 675.

13. Meeting with Marshall, April 14, 1942, CAB 79/56 (PRO).

14. Bryant, *Turn of the Tide*, p. 357.

15. Roosevelt to Churchill, April 3, 1942, and Churchill to Roosevelt, April 12, 1942, in Kimball, ed., *Correspondence*, vol. 2, pp. 441, 448.

16. Dimbleby, BBC 1 interview with General Albert C. Wedemeyer.

17. Chiefs of Staff 65th (42) (0) meeting, July 6, 1942, CAB 79/56 (PRO).

18. Richard W. Steele, "American Popular Opinion and the War against Germany: The Issue of a Negotiated Peace," *Journal of American History* vol. 65 (1978), p. 708.

19. Mark A. Stoler, *The Politics of the Second Front: American Military Planning and Diplomacy in Coalition Warfare, 1941–1943* (Westport, Conn.: Greenwood Press, 1977), p. 58.

20. Harry C. Butcher, *My Three Years with Eisenhower* (New York: Simon & Schuster, 1946), p. 29, diary entry for July 23, 1942.

21. Henry L. Stimson, diary, vol. 43, June 1, 1943 (Sterling Library, Yale University).

22. Stoler, *Politics of the Second Front*, p. 55.

23. Earl of Halifax, "Secret Diary," July 15, 1942, Hickleton Papers, A 7.8.19 (Borthwick Institute, York).

24. Dimbleby—Wedemeyer interview.

25. Dimbleby, BBC 1 interview with Sir Ian Jacob.

26. Wm. Roger Louis, *Imperialism at Bay, 1941–1945: The United States and the Decolonization of the British Empire* (Oxford: Clarendon Press, 1977), p. 226.

27. *Life*, Oct. 12, 1942, in Louis, *Imperialism at Bay*, p. 198.

28. Churchill, *Complete Speeches*, vol. 6, p. 6695, Nov. 10, 1942.

29. Adolf A. Berle, diary, VIII.2.109, memo, Feb. 28, 1942 (Franklin D. Roosevelt Library, Hyde Park, N.Y.).

30. Kimball, ed., *Churchill and Roosevelt: Correspondence*, vol. 1, p. 447.

31. Christopher Thorne, *Allies of a Kind: The United States, Britain, and the War against Japan, 1941–1945* (London: Hamish Hamilton, 1977), pp. 337, 453.

32. Churchill to Eden, Aug. 25, 1944, PREM 4/30/11 (PRO).

33. Eisenhower to General Thomas T. Handy, Jan. 28, 1943, in Alfred D. Chandler, Jr., ed., *The Papers of Dwight David Eisenhower: The War Years, 1941–1945*, 5 vols. (Baltimore: Johns Hopkins University Press, 1970), vol. 2, p. 928.

34. Dimbleby, BBC 1 interview with Joseph Curtis.

35. David Reynolds, "The Churchill Government and the Black American Troops in Britain during World War II," *Transactions of the Royal Historical Society*, 5th series, vol. 35 (1985), p. 121.

36. Memo, "United States Negro Troops in the United Kingdom," Oct. 17, 1942, WP (42) 473, CAB 66/30 (PRO).

37. Dimbleby, BBC 1 interview with John Wilson.

38. Foreign Office memo, July 10, 1943, in David Reynolds, "GI and Tommy in Wartime Britain: The Army 'Inter-Attachment' Scheme of 1943–4," *Journal of Strategic Studies*, vol. 7 (1984), p. 412.

39. Dimbleby, BBC 1 interview with Margaret Whiting.

40. Dimbleby, BBC 1 interviews with William Stock and John Wilson.

41. See Keith Sainsbury, *The Turning Point: Roosevelt, Stalin, Churchill, and Chiang-Kai-Shek, 1943. The Moscow, Cairo, and Teheran Conferences* (Oxford: Oxford University Press, 1985).

42. Roosevelt to Churchill, March 18, 1942, in Kimball, ed., *Correspondence*, vol. 1, p. 421.

43. John Grigg, *1943: The Victory That Never Was* (London: Methuen, paperback ed., 1985), p. 79.

44. Dimbleby, BBC 1 interview with Elliott Roosevelt.

45. Churchill to Richard Law, Feb. 17, 1944, PREM 4/27/10 (PRO).

46. Dimbleby—Jacob interview.

47. Anderson to Churchill, July 30, 1942, PREM 3/139/8A (PRO).

48. Stimson to Roosevelt, Oct. 29, 1942, in Martin J. Sherwin, *A World Destroyed: The Atomic Bomb and the Grand Alliance* (New York: Vintage Books, 1977), p. 72.

49. Churchill to Hopkins, Feb. 27, 1943, PREM 3/139/8A (PRO).

50. Margaret Gowing, *Britain and Atomic Energy, 1939–1945* (London: Macmillan, 1964), p. 439.

51. Sir Ronald Campbell to Sir John Anderson, Jan. 29, 1945, quoted by Margaret Gowing, "Nuclear Weapons and the 'Special Relationship,' " in Wm. Roger Louis and Hedley Bull, eds., *The 'Special Relationship': Anglo-American Relations since 1945* (Oxford: Clarendon Press, 1986), p. 120.

52. Leslie R. Groves, *Now It Can Be Told: The Story of the Manhattan Project* (New York: Da Capo ed., 1983), p. 408.

53. Arthur Bryant, *Triumph in the West, 1943–1946: Based on the Autobiographical Notes of Field Marshal the Viscount Alanbrooke, KG, OM* (London: Collins, 1957), pp. 205–6.

54. Roosevelt to Churchill, June 29, 1944, in Kimball, ed., *Correspondence*, vol. 3, p. 222.

55. Churchill to Smuts, Dec. 3, 1944, in Gilbert, *Road to Victory*, p. 1081.

56. Memo by H.B. Butler, May 15, 1942, WP (42) 208, CAB 66/24 (PRO).

57. Joint Staff Mission to AMSSO, tel. 96, June 1944, FO 371/38696, AN 2423/2113/45 (PRO).

58. *Chicago Tribune*, Aug. 2, 1944, in Thorne, *Allies of a Kind*, p. 392.

59. Churchill to Eden, Jan. 16, 1944, PREM 3/399/6 (PRO).

60. Churchill to Eden, May 8, 1944, FO 954/20 (PRO).

61. Memorandum of Kremlin meeting, Oct. 9, 1944, in Graham Ross, ed., *The Foreign Office and the Kremlin: British Documents on Anglo-Soviet Relations, 1941–45* (Cambridge: Cambridge University Press, 1984), p. 174.

62. FDR's meeting with senators, Jan. 1945, in Robert Dallek, *Franklin D. Roosevelt and American Foreign Policy, 1932–1945* (New York: Oxford University Press, 1979), pp. 507–8.

63. Sir John Colville, *The Fringes of Power: Downing Street Diaries, 1939–1955* (London: Hodder & Stoughton, 1985), p. 555, entry for Jan. 23, 1945.

64. Diane Shaver Clemens, *Yalta* (New York: Oxford University Press, 1970), p. 306.

65. Sherwood, *Roosevelt and Hopkins*, p. 870.

66. Hugh Dalton, diary, vol. 32, p. 28, Feb. 23, 1945 (British Library of Political and Economic Science, London).

67. Churchill, *Second World War*, vol. 6, pp. 413 and 417.

68. Eden to Churchill, May 8, 1945, in Gilbert, *Road to Victory*, p. 1351.

69. Appeal of Dec. 27, 1941, in R.J. Bell, *Unequal Allies: Australian-American Relations and the Pacific War* (Melbourne: Melbourne University Press, 1977), p. 47.

70. Ronald H. Spector, *Eagle Against the Sun: The American War with Japan* (New York: Vintage Books, 1985), p. 544.

71. Recalled by Alger Hiss in Michael Charlton, *The Eagle and the Small Birds. Crisis in the Soviet Empire: From Yalta to Solidarity* (London: BBC Publications, 1984), p. 46.

72. *New York Herald Tribune*, Aug. 15, 1945, in Thorne, *Allies of a Kind*, p. 503. Understandably, the debate on the use of the bomb rumbles on—Were the Japanese about to surrender? How far did the United States have Russia in mind? For the "revisionist" case, see Gar Alperovitz, *Atomic Diplomacy: The Use of the Atomic Bomb and the American Confrontation with Soviet Power* (New York: 2nd ed., Penguin, 1985).

73. Brooke diary, April 1, 1945, in Bryant, *Triumph in the West*, p. 455.

Background Reading

General

James L. Stokesbury, *A Short History of World War II* (New York: William Morrow, 1980). A lively narrative.

Peter Calvocoressi and Guy Wint, *Total War: Causes and Courses of the Second World War* (New York: Penguin, 1974). A big yet vivid book, as strong on Asia as on Europe.

Henry Pelling, *Britain and the Second World War* (London: Fontana, 1970). An excellent short study of the war at home and abroad.

Gaddis Smith, *American Diplomacy during the Second World War, 1941–1945* (New York: John Wiley, 1965). A useful survey.

Biographical

James MacGregor Burns, *Roosevelt: The Soldier of Freedom, 1940–1945* (New York: Harcourt Brace Jovanovich, 1970). Still the best biography of FDR in this period. (See also Dallek, cited in reading to chapter 7.)

Martin Gilbert, *Road to Victory: Winston S. Churchill, 1941–1945* (New York: Houghton Mifflin, 1986). Day-by-day account of Churchill's war, with extensive quotation from his papers.

Studies of the Anglo-American Relationship

David Reynolds, "Roosevelt, Churchill, and the Wartime Anglo-American Alliance, 1939–1945: Towards a New Synthesis," in Wm. Roger Louis and Hedley Bull, eds., *The 'Special Relationship': Anglo-American Relations since 1945* (New York: Oxford University Press, 1986), pp. 17–41. An interpretation of the relationship in its various facets, synthesizing recent scholarship.

Christopher Thorne, *Allies of a Kind: The United States, Britain, and the War against Japan, 1941–1945* (New York: Oxford University Press, 1977). Vast yet incisive analysis of how the two allies conducted the Pacific war, with particular attention to China, India, Southeast Asia and Australasia.

Wm. Roger Louis, *Imperialism at Bay, 1941–1945: The United States and the Decolonization of the British Empire* (Oxford: Clarendon Press, 1977). Detailed study of the debates about colonies, trusteeship, etc.

Alan P. Dobson, *US Wartime Aid to Britain, 1940–1946* (New York: Croom Helm, 1986). Monograph on the tangled diplomacy of Lend-Lease.

Norman Longmate, *The G.I.'s: The Americans in Britain, 1942–1945* (London: Hutchinson, 1975). Readable account, based on oral history and some British archives.

CHAPTER 9: UNITING AGAINST RUSSIA, 1945–1949

Notes

1. Dimbleby, BBC 1 interview with Donald Worby.

2. Dimbleby, BBC 1 interview with Barbara Markus.

3. Winston S. Churchill, *The Second World War*, 6 vols. (London: Cassell, 1948–54), vol. 6, p. 583.

4. Sir Orme Sargent, soon to become permanent under secretary at the Foreign Office, quoted in Kenneth O. Morgan, *Labour in Power, 1945–1951* (Oxford: Oxford University Press, 1985), p. 42.

5. Quotations from Bevin, in Commons, *Debates*, vol. 437, col. 1965, May 16, 1947, and from David Dilks, ed., *The Diaries of Sir Alexander Cadogan, OM, 1938–1945* (London: Cassell, 1971), Aug. 2, 1945, p. 778.

6. Treasury memo, Aug. 14, 1945, CP (45) 112, CAB 129/1 (Public Record Office, London).

7. Dimbleby, BBC 1 interview with Claude Pepper.

8. Dimbleby, BBC 1 interview with Marion T. Bennett (Republican congressman from Missouri, 1943–49).

9. Gen. Robert E. Wood to Will Clayton, Nov. 26, 1945, in Richard N. Gardner, *Sterling-Dollar Diplomacy in Current Perspective* (New York: Columbia University Press, 1980), p. 197.

10. Speech to businessmen in Detroit, May 21, 1945, in Robert A. Pollard, *Economic Security and the Origins of the Cold War, 1945–1950* (New York: Columbia University Press, 1985), p. 2.

11. Armand van Dormael, *Bretton Woods: Birth of a Monetary System* (London: Macmillan, 1978), p. 133.

12. *New York Herald Tribune*, March 31, 1946, in David Rees, *Harry Dexter White: A Study in Paradox* (New York: Macmillan, 1973), p. 138.

13. Quotations from Robert Boothby and Jennie Lee, Dec. 12 and 13, 1945, in House of Commons, *Debates*, vol. 417, cols. 468 and 669.

14. *Economist*, Dec. 15, 1945, p. 850.

15. Rep. Emmanuel Celler, in Gardner, *Sterling-Dollar Diplomacy*, p. 237.

16. Memo of Sept. 19, 1944, in Margaret Gowing, *Britain and Atomic Energy, 1939–1945* (London: Macmillan, 1964), p. 447.

17. Agreement of Nov. 15, 1945, in Margaret Gowing, assisted by Lorna Arnold, *Independence and Deterrence: Britain and Atomic Energy, 1945–1952*, 2 vols. (London: Macmillan, 1974), vol. 1, p. 76.

18. A.V. Alexander, memo of Oct. 12, 1949, on meeting with Senator McMahon, Oct. 8, PREM 8/1097 (PRO).

19. Acheson memo of March 1946, in Gregg Herken, *The Winning Weapon: The Atomic Bomb in the Cold War, 1945–1950* (New York: Vintage Books, 1982), p. 145.

20. Bevin, Oct. 26, 1946, as recalled by Sir Michael Perrin, in Alan Bullock, *Ernest Bevin: Foreign Secretary, 1945–1951* (London: Heinemann, 1983), p. 352.

21. Speech in June 1946, in Wm. Roger Louis, *The British Empire in the Middle East, 1945–51* (Oxford: Clarendon Press, 1984), p. 428.

22. Bevin, in conversation with Molotov, Sept. 23, 1945. Faced with Molotov's indignation, he later retracted, but the remark shows his state of mind. Bullock, *Bevin*, p. 132.

23. Sir Orme Sargent, minute, Oct. 1, 1945, FO 371/44557, AN 2560/22/45 (PRO).

24. Pierson Dixon, minute, Sept. 24, 1945, in Graham Ross, ed., *The Foreign Office and the Kremlin: British Documents on Anglo-Soviet Relations, 1941–45* (Cambridge: Cambridge University Press, 1984), p. 252.

25. Memo-letter of Jan. 5, 1946, in Robert L. Messer, *The End of an Alliance: James F. Byrnes, Roosevelt, Truman, and the Origins of the Cold War* (Chapel Hill: University of North Carolina, 1982), p. 158. Truman said in his memoirs that he read out this passage as a stinging rebuke to Byrnes, a claim Messer convincingly refutes. But Messer acknowledges that the memo did broadly represent Truman's thinking by early 1946.

26. Churchill to Attlee, March 7, 1946, in Fraser J. Harbutt, *The Iron Curtain: Churchill, America, and the Origins of the Cold War* (New York: Oxford University Press, 1986), p. 180.

27. Robert Rhodes James, ed., *Winston S. Churchill: His Complete Speeches* (New York: Chelsea House, 1974), vol. 7, pp. 7285–93.

28. Thomas H. Etzold and John L. Gaddis, eds., *Containment: Documents on American Policy and Strategy, 1945–1950* (New York: Columbia University Press, 1978), pp. 50–63.

29. JCS 1641/3, March 13, 1946, in Richard A. Best, Jr., *"Co-operation with Like-Minded Peoples": British Influences on American Security Policy, 1945–1949* (New York: Greenwood Press, 1986), p. 121.

30. John L. Gaddis, *The United States and the Origins of the Cold War, 1941–1947* (New York: Columbia University Press, 1972), p. 309.

31. *Wall Street Journal*, March 19, 1946, in Robin Edmonds, *Setting the Mould: The United States and Britain, 1945–1950* (Oxford: Clarendon Press, 1986), p. 6.

32. Kennedy (March 1946), in Gardner, *Sterling-Dollar Diplomacy*, p. 250.

33. Memo by Chancellor of the Exchequer, March 21, 1947, in Sir Richard Clarke, *Anglo-American Economic Collaboration in War and Peace, 1942–1949* (Oxford: Clarendon Press, 1982), p. 156.

34. British embassy to State Dept., Feb. 21, 1947, in Terry H. Anderson, *The United States, Great Britain, and the Cold War, 1944–1947* (Columbia: University of Missouri Press, 1981), p. 169.

35. Memo of Feb. 21, 1947, in Lawrence S. Wittner, *American Intervention in Greece, 1943–1949* (New York: Columbia University Press, 1982), p. 67.

36. Recollection of meeting of Feb. 27, 1947, in Dean Acheson, *Present at the Creation: My Years in the State Department* (London: Hamish Hamilton, 1970), p. 219.

37. Quoted in Best, "*Co-operation between Like-Minded Peoples,*" p. 134.

38. *Public Papers of the Presidents of the United States: Harry S Truman, 1947* (Washington, D.C.: U.S. Government Printing Office, 1963), pp. 176–80.

39. Clayton, memo, May 27, 1947, in U.S. Dept. of State, *Foreign Relations of the United States, 1947* (Washington, D.C.: U.S. Government Printing Office, 1972), vol. 3, pp. 230–32.

40. Speech of June 5, 1947, in *Foreign Relations, 1947,* vol. 3, p. 239.

41. Speech in Washington, April 1, 1949, in Bullock, *Bevin,* p. 405. For U.S. priming, see Walter Lipgens, *A History of European Integration, vol. 1, 1945–47* (Oxford: Clarendon Press, 1982), p. 507.

42. Ben T. Moore to Clair Wilcox, July 28, 1947, in *Foreign Relations, 1947,* vol. 3, p. 239.

43. Quotations from Truman and Clay in Robert J. Donovan, *Conflict and Crisis: The Presidency of Harry S Truman, 1945–1948* (New York: W.W. Norton, 1977), pp. 359–60.

44. Bevin, memo, "The Threat to Western Civilisation," March 3, 1948, CP (48) 72, CAB 129/25 (PRO).

45. Marshall to Lord Inverchapel, March 12, 1948, in U.S. Dept. of State, *Foreign Relations of the United States, 1948* (Washington, D.C.: U.S. Government Printing Office, 1974), vol. 3, p. 48.

46. Internal State Dept. policy statement, Aug. 26, 1948, in Etzold and Gaddis, eds., *Containment,* p. 130.

47. Quoted in Avi Shlaim, *The United States and the Berlin Blockade, 1948–1949* (Berkeley: University of California Press, 1983), pp. 195–96.

48. Dimbleby, BBC 1 interview with Gen. Leon Johnson.

49. Quoted in *The World Today,* vol. 16 (Aug. 1960), p. 320.

50. Walter Millis, ed., *The Forrestal Diaries* (London: Cassell, 1952), July 15, 1948, pp. 429–30.

51. Simon Duke, *US Defence Bases in the United Kingdom: A Matter for Joint Decision?* (London: Macmillan, 1987), p. 40.

52. Except the vice-chief of the Air Staff, Sir William Dickson. Gowing, *Independence and Deterrence,* vol. 1, pp. 250–51.

53. Bevin to State Dept., April 9, 1948, in Alan K. Henrikson, "The Creation of the North Atlantic Alliance, 1948–1952," *U.S. Naval War College Review,* vol. 32 (May–June 1980), p. 15.

54. Acheson, quoted in Timothy P. Ireland, *Creating the Entangling Alliance: The Origins of the North Atlantic Treaty Organization* (New York: Greenwood Press, 1981), p. 110.

55. North Atlantic Treaty, April 4, 1949, article 5, in U.S. Dept. of State, *Foreign Relations of the United States, 1949* (Washington, D.C.: U.S. Government Printing Office, 1975), vol. 4, p. 282.

56. Remarks on April 4, 1949, in *Public Papers of the Presidents of the United States: Harry S Truman, 1949* (Washington, D.C.: U.S. Government Printing Office, 1964), pp. 196–98.

57. Gardner, *Sterling-Dollar Diplomacy,* p. xiii.

58. Douglas to SecState, Aug. 11, 1948, in U.S. Dept. of State, *Foreign Relations of the United States, 1948* (Washington, D.C.: U.S. Government Printing Office, 1974), vol. 3, p. 1113.

Background Reading

General Books on the Origins of the Cold War

Martin McCauley, *The Origins of the Cold War* (London: Longman, 1983). A brief introduction, with documents, concentrating on the years 1941–48.

Thomas G. Paterson, *On Every Front: The Making of the Cold War* (New York: W.W. Norton, 1979). A short, readable analysis of US policy, 1945–50.

Elisabeth Barker, *The British between the Superpowers, 1945–50* (London: Macmillan, 1983). Useful narrative based on official British archives.

General Studies of Anglo-American Relations since 1945 (Useful background for this and subsequent chapters)

John Baylis, *Anglo-American Defence Relations, 1939–1984* (London: Macmillan, 1984). The best survey of military matters.

Wm. Roger Louis and Hedley Bull, eds., *The 'Special Relationship': Anglo-American Relations since 1945* (New York: Oxford University Press, 1986). A wide range of essays on all aspects of the relationship—by historical period and theme (military, economic and in the Third World).

Jeffrey T. Richelson and Desmond Ball, *The Ties that Bind: Intelligence Cooperation between the UKUSA Countries* (London: Allen & Unwin, 1985). Recent study of the vital intelligence relationship; full of detail, but not always very revealing.

David Reynolds, "A 'special relationship'?: America, Britain and the International Order since World War Two," *International Affairs*, vol. 62 (Winter 1985/86), pp. 1–20. An interpretative survey.

Studies of the Anglo-American Relationship

Robin Edmonds, *Setting the Mould: The United States and Britain, 1945–1950* (New York: W.W. Norton, 1986). The best survey, synthesizing recent scholarship.

Robert M. Hathaway, *Ambiguous Partnership: Britain and America, 1944–1947* (New York: Columbia University Press, 1981). Covers the general relationship from the autumn of 1944 to the spring of 1947.

Terry H. Anderson, *The United States, Great Britain, and the Cold War, 1944–1947* (Columbia: University of Missouri Press, 1981). Covers a similar period but concentrates on British influence on U.S. policy toward Russia.

Henry B. Ryan, *The Vision of Anglo-America: The US–UK Alliance and the Emerging Cold War, 1943–1946* (New York: Cambridge University Press, 1987). British policy toward the United States in the Greek and Polish crises.

Fraser J. Harbutt, *The Iron Curtain: Churchill, America, and the Origins of the Cold War* (New York: Oxford University Press, 1986). An incisive account, focusing on the winter of 1945–46, but probably exaggerating Churchill's impact on U.S. diplomacy.

Richard A. Best, Jr., *"Co-operation with Like-Minded Peoples": British Influences on American Security Policy, 1945–1949* (New York: Greenwood Press, 1986). Examines U.S. strategic planning; also probably overstates British influence.

Michael J. Hogan, *The Marshall Plan: America, Britain and the Reconstruction of Western Europe, 1947–1952* (New York: Cambridge University Press, 1987). A major new assessment of the origins and impact of the plan.

CHAPTER 10: GLOBAL COLD WAR, 1949–1954

Notes

1. Robert J. Donovan, *Tumultuous Years: The Presidency of Harry S Truman, 1949–1953* (New York: W.W. Norton, 1982), p. 191.

2. Acheson remarks of Feb. 24, 1949, in Ritchie Ovendale, *The English-Speaking Alliance: Britain, the United States, the Dominions and the Cold War, 1945–51* (London: George Allen & Unwin, 1985), p. 187.

3. Mundt, speech of April 18, 1949, in Justus D. Doenecke, *Not to the Swift: The Old Isolationists in the Cold War Era* (London: Associated Universities Press, 1979), p. 179.

4. Wheeling speech, Feb. 9, 1950, in Thomas C. Reeves, *The Life and Times of Joe McCarthy: A Biography* (New York: Stein & Day, 1982), pp. 224–47.

5. Acheson to Douglas for British govt., June 27, 1950, in Peter Lowe, *The Origins of the Korean War* (London: Longman, 1986), p. 162.

6. Press conference, Nov. 30, 1950, in *The Public Papers of the Presidents: Harry S Truman, 1950* (Washington, D.C.: U.S. Government Printing Office, 1965), p. 727.

7. Dimbleby, BBC 1 interview with Paul Nitze.

8. Pierson Dixon, minute, July 12, 1950, in M.L. Dockrill, "The Foreign Office, Anglo-American Relations and the Korean War, June 1950–June 1951," in *International Affairs*, vol. 62 (1986), p. 462.

9. George Orwell, *Nineteen Eighty-Four* (London: Secker & Warburg, 1949), p. 7.

10. MOD, brief for Defence Committee meeting of Jan. 31, 1950, in DEFE 7/516 (PRO).

11. Bevin, draft dispatch to Washington, Nov. 26, 1949, in DEFE 7/516.

12. C.A.E. Shuckburgh, draft FO memo, "United States Air Force Groups in the United Kingdom," Jan. 4, 1950, in DEFE 7/516.

13. Dimbleby, BBC 1 interview with David Rolain.

14. Comments in Chiefs of Staff meeting, July 27, 1950, in N.J. Wheeler, "British Nuclear Weapons and Anglo-American Relations," *International Affairs*, vol. 62 (Winter 1985–86), p. 74.

15. Dimbleby, BBC 1 interview with Clark Clifford.

16. Philip Jessup, memorandum for the record, Dec. 7, 1950, in U.S. Dept. of State, *Foreign Relations of the United States, 1950* (Washington, D.C.: U.S. Government Printing Office, 1976), vol. 7, p. 1462.

17. Dimbleby, BBC 1 interview with Gordon Arneson.

18. Copy of communiqué, Dec. 8, 1950, in PREM 8/1200 (PRO).

19. Exchange of March 7, 1951, in John Baylis, "American Bases in Britain: The 'Truman-Attlee' Understandings," *The World Today*, vol. 42 (Aug./Sept. 1986), p. 156.

20. Dimbleby, BBC 1 interview with Lucius Battle.

21. Bevin to Attlee, Jan. 12, 1951, PREM 8/1439 (PRO).

22. Ben Pimlott, ed., *The Political Diary of Hugh Dalton, 1918–40, 1945–60* (London: Jonathan Cape, 1986), p. 505.

23. Quoted in Dean Acheson, *Present at the Creation: My Years in the State Department* (London: Hamish Hamilton, 1969), p. 399.

24. Geoffrey Bing et al., *Keep Left* (London: New Statesman, May 1947), pp. 33, 42. The authors included Richard Crossman and Michael Foot.

25. House of Commons, *Debates*, Jan. 23, 1948, vol. 446, col. 566.

26. House of Commons, *Debates*, April 23, 1951, vol. 487, col. 38.

27. *Daily Sketch*, quoted in Michael Foot, *Aneurin Bevan: A Biography* (London: Davis-Poynter, 1973), vol. 2, p. 339.

28. Memo of June or July 1952, in Philip M. Williams, ed., *The Diary of Hugh Gaitskell, 1945–1956* (London: Jonathan Cape, 1983), pp. 316–17.

29. Dimbleby, BBC 1 interview with Sir Evelyn Shuckburgh.

30. Robert Ferrell, ed., *The Eisenhower Diaries* (New York: W.W. Norton, 1981), Jan. 6, 1953, p. 223.

31. House of Commons, *Debates*, Feb. 15, 1951, vol. 484, col. 630.

32. Arneson to Secretary of State, Oct. 18, 1951, in Baylis, "American Bases in Britain," p. 158.

33. Statement of Jan. 9, 1952, in FO 371/97592, AU 1051/12 (PRO).

34. Arneson, memo on proposed UK statement, Oct. 17, 1951, in Baylis, "American Bases in Britain," p. 157. The Foreign Office, for instance, was telling peace groups in 1955 that, as a result of the statement, "it would be impossible for the Americans in this country to take any military action without the consent of Her Majesty's Government." R.P. Pinsent to Mrs. E.F. Ineson, Mar. 2, 1955, FO 371/114415, AU 11917/2 (PRO).

35. Sir Eyre Crowe, quoted in Michael J. Hogan, *Informal Entente: The Private Structure of Cooperation in Anglo-American Economic Diplomacy, 1918–1928* (Columbia: University of Missouri Press, 1977), p. 172.

36. Michael B. Stoff, *Oil, War, and American Security: The Search for a National Policy on Foreign Oil, 1941–1947* (New Haven: Yale University Press, 1980), p. 209.

37. Roosevelt to Churchill, March 3, 1944, and Churchill to Roosevelt, March 4, 1944, in Warren F. Kimball, ed., *Churchill and Roosevelt: The Complete Correspondence*, 3 vols. (Princeton: Princeton University Press, 1984), vol. 3, pp. 14, 17.

38. CM 60 (51) 6, CAB 128/20 (PRO).

39. Sir Francis Shepherd, in Wm. Roger Louis, *The British Empire in the Middle East, 1945–51: Arab Nationalism, the United States and Postwar Imperialism* (Oxford: Clarendon Press, 1984), p. 651.

40. Acheson, *Present at the Creation*, p. 503.

41. Stephen Ambrose, with Richard Immerman, *Ike's Spies: Eisenhower and the Espionage Establishment* (New York: Doubleday, 1981), p. 200.

42. Ritchie Ovendale, *The Origins of the Arab-Israeli Wars* (London: Longman, 1984), p. 136.

43. Dimbleby, BBC 1 interview with George McGhee.

44. Sir Roger Makins, memo, Jan. 25, 1954, quoted in Wm. Roger Louis, "American Anti-Colonialism and the Dissolution of the British Empire," in Wm. Roger Louis and Hedley Bull, eds., *The 'Special Relationship': Anglo-American Relations since 1945* (Oxford: Clarendon Press, 1986), p. 260.

45. Record of JCS-State Dept. meeting, Nov. 21, 1951, in U.S. Dept. of State, *Foreign Relations of the United States, 1951* (Washington, D.C.: U.S. Government Printing Office, 1983), vol. 4, p. 985.

46. Acheson, *Present at the Creation*, pp. 387–88.

47. NSC 48/1, Dec. 23, 1949, in Thomas H. Etzold and John L. Gaddis, eds., *Containment: Documents on American Policy and Strategy, 1945–1950* (New York: Columbia University Press, 1978), p. 259.

48. Eisenhower, Feb. 7, 1954, in George C. Herring and Richard H. Immerman, "Eisenhower, Dulles and Dienbienphu: 'The Day We Didn't Go to War' Revisited," *Journal of American History*, vol. 71 (1984), p. 346.

49. Eisenhower to Churchill, April 5, 1954, PREM 11/1074 (PRO).

50. Dulles-Eden memcon, April 25, 1954, in U.S. Dept. of State, *Foreign Relations of the United States, 1952–4* (Washington, D.C.: U.S. Government Printing Office, 1981), vol. 16, p. 555.

51. George C. Herring, *America's Longest War: The United States and Vietnam, 1950–1975* (New York: John Wiley, 1979), p. 34.

52. Evelyn Shuckburgh, *Descent into Suez: Diaries, 1951–56* (London: Weidenfeld & Nicolson, 1986), p. 187, diary for May 2, 1954.

53. The comment of biographer Townsend Hoopes, *The Devil and John Foster Dulles* (London: Andre Deutsch, 1974), p. 222.

54. Shuckburgh, *Descent into Suez*, p. 164, diary entry for April 12, 1954.

55. *New Statesman*, July 24, 1954, in James Cable, *The Geneva Conference of 1954 on Indochina* (London: Macmillan, 1986), p. 128.

56. Dulles, statement to North Atlantic Council, Dec. 14, 1953, in U.S. Dept. of State, *Foreign Relations of the United States, 1952–4* (Washington, D.C.: U.S. Government Printing Office, 1983), vol. 5, p. 868.

57. Butterworth to State Dept., Sept. 8, 1954, in *Foreign Relations of the United States, 1952–4*, vol. 5, p. 1154.

58. Edward Fursdon, *The European Defence Community: A History* (London: Macmillan, 1980), pp. 321–22.

Background Reading

Studies of the Anglo-American Relationship

We are now entering the no-man's-land between memoir and history, when either the archives are not yet opened or their materials are still undigested in book form. But two studies are already available:

Ritchie Ovendale, *The English-Speaking Alliance: Britain, the United States, the Dominions and the Cold War, 1945–51* (London: George Allen & Unwin, 1985). From a British perspective the book examines the Anglo-American relationship over such issues as China, Korea and the Middle East.

Simon Duke, *US Defence Bases in the United Kingdom: A Matter for Joint Decision?* (London: Macmillan, 1987). Covers the whole postwar period, though fullest on the years 1948–54.

See also background reading for chapter 9, especially Wm. Roger Louis and Hedley Bull, eds, *The 'Special Relationship': Anglo-American Relations since 1945* (New York: Oxford University Press, 1986)—essays by Bradford Perkins on the Truman era and D. Cameron Watt on the Eisenhower era.

Biographical

Stephen Ambrose, *Eisenhower: The President* (New York: Simon & Schuster, 1984). The best recent one-volume survey of his presidency.

Townsend Hoopes, *The Devil and John Foster Dulles* (Boston: Little, Brown, 1973). A detailed and critical evaluation of his diplomacy.

David Carlton, *Anthony Eden: A Biography* (London: Allen Lane, 1981), is a recent account, often very critical of Eden.

Robert Rhodes James, *Anthony Eden* (New York: McGraw-Hill, 1987). The more sympathetic official biography, based largely on Eden's papers.

CHAPTER II: THE EMPIRE'S LAST GASP, 1955–1956

Notes

1. Lord Moran, *Winston Churchill: The Struggle for Survival, 1940–1965* (London: Sphere Books, 1968), April 28, 1953, p. 428.

2. Dimbleby, BBC 1 interview with Sir John Colville.

3. Moran, *Churchill*, June 25, 1953, p. 433.

4. Speech in the Commons, May 11, 1953, in Anthony Seldon, *Churchill's Indian Summer: The Conservative Government, 1951–1955* (London: Hodder & Stoughton, 1981), p. 400.

5. Evelyn Shuckburgh, *Descent to Suez: Diaries, 1951–56* (London: Weidenfeld & Nicolson, 1986), p. 147, entry for March 15, 1954.

6. Speech in Bloomfield, N.J., Oct. 10, 1952, in Townsend Hoopes, *The Devil and John Foster Dulles* (London: Andre Deutsch, 1974), p. 131.

7. Eden to Churchill, Nov. 21, 1952, PREM 11/323 (Public Record Office, London).

8. Churchill to Eisenhower, April 5, 1953, PREM 11/1074 (PRO).

9. Shuckburgh, *Descent to Suez*, p. 277, entry for Aug. 31, 1955, recording Harold Macmillan on a conversation with Churchill in June.

10. CM 28 (55) 10, Aug. 15, 1955, CAB 128/29 (PRO).

11. Harold Macmillan, *Tides of Fortune, 1945–1955* (London: Macmillan, 1969), pp. 616, 621.

12. Moran, *Churchill*, pp. 462, 536, entries for July 19 and Dec. 7, 1953.

13. Dimbleby, BBC 1 interview with Sir Philip de Zulueta.

14. Stephen E. Ambrose, *Eisenhower the President* (New York: Simon & Schuster, 1984), p. 265.

15. Article on "The United States of Europe," Feb. 15, 1930, in Michael Wolff, ed., *The Collected Essays of Sir Winston Churchill*, 4 vols. (London: Library of Imperial History, 1976), vol. 2, pp. 184–85.

16. Recalled by Sir Anthony Nutting in Edward Fursdon, *The European Defence Community: A History* (London: Macmillan, 1980), p. 77.

17. Shuckburgh, *Descent to Suez*, p. 18.

18. Speech at Columbia University, New York, Jan. 11, 1952, in David Carlton, *Anthony Eden: A Biography* (London: Allen Lane, 1981), p. 311.

19. Peter Foot, "Defence Burden-Sharing in the Atlantic Community, 1945–1954," *Aberdeen Studies in Defence Economics*, vol. 20 (Summer 1981), p. 13.

20. E.G. Compton (HM Treasury), brief for Churchill, Dec. 15, 1951, in PREM 11/313 (PRO).

21. "Report by Officials" for Cabinet, CP (55) 55, June 29, 1955, CAB 129/76 (PRO).

22. Moran, *Churchill*, p. 504, entry for Oct. 10, 1953.

23. Eden to Lord Hankey (a director of the Suez Canal Company), Feb. 1953, copy in PREM 11/636 (PRO).

24. Shuckburgh, *Descent to Suez*, p. 327, entry for Jan. 29, 1956.

25. Ibid., p. 346, entry for March 12, 1956.

26. William J. Burns, *Economic Aid and American Policy toward Egypt, 1955–1981* (Albany, N.Y.: SUNY Press, 1985), Appendix 2, p. 214.

27. Selwyn Lloyd, *Suez, 1956: A Personal Account* (London: Jonathan Cape, 1978), p. 69.

28. Dimbleby, BBC 1 interview with William Macomber.

29. *Keesing's Contemporary Archives*, p. 15001.

30. Egypt Committee, EC (56) 3rd mtg., July 30, 1956, CAB 134/1216 (PRO).

31. Eden to Eisenhower, July 27, 1956, PREM 11/1177 (PRO).

32. Ibid., Aug. 5, 1956, PREM 11/1177 (PRO).

33. Eisenhower, meeting of July 31, 1956, in Ambrose, *Eisenhower: The President*, p. 331.

34. John Colville, *Footprints in Time: Downing Street Diaries, 1939–1955* (London: Hodder & Stoughton, 1985), p. 686, entry for Dec. 6, 1953.

35. Washington embassy to Foreign Office, telegram 2046, Oct. 2, 1956, PREM 11/1174 (PRO). Dulles later apologized, calling the press conference "a really bad blunder" (tel. 2052, Oct. 3, 1956), but Eden never forgave him.

36. Dimbleby, BBC 1 interview with Sir Anthony Nutting.

37. CM 34 (55) 8, Oct. 4, 1955, CAB 128/29 (PRO).

38. Sir Leslie Rowan, note on "Economic and financial measures in the event of war with Egypt," Sept. 11, 1956, Treasury records, T 236/4188 (PRO).

39. Emmett John Hughes, *The Ordeal of Power: A Political Memoir of the Eisenhower Years* (London: Macmillan, 1963), p. 217, diary entry for Oct. 30, 1956.

40. Dimbleby, interview with William Clark. Clark told this story often—it may well have become exaggerated over time. See Robert Rhodes James, *Anthony Eden* (London: Weidenfeld & Nicolson, 1986), p. 568.

41. Staff notes, Oct. 6, 1956, in Stephen Ambrose, with Richard Immerman, *Ike's Spies: Eisenhower and the Espionage Establishment* (New York: Doubleday, 1981), p. 240.

42. Eisenhower to Eden, Sept. 3, 1956, PREM 11/1177 (PRO).

43. Dulles at NSC, Nov. 1, 1956, in Wm. Roger Louis, "American Anti-Colonialism and the Dissolution of the British Empire," in Wm. Roger Louis and Hedley Bull, *The 'Special Relationship': Anglo-American Relations since 1945* (Oxford: Clarendon Press, 1986), p. 277.

44. Meeting with J.E. Coulson, Oct. 29, 1956, in Ambrose, *Eisenhower: The President*, p. 359.

45. Ambrose, *Eisenhower: The President*, p. 364.

46. CM 80 (56), Nov. 6, 1956, CAB 128/30 (PRO).

47. Lloyd, *Suez*, p. 219, also pp. 257–58.

48. Dwight D. Eisenhower, *The White House Years: Waging Peace, 1956–1961* (London: Heinemann, 1966), p. 93.

49. Eisenhower to Eden, Nov. 7, 1956, PREM 11/1137 (PRO).

50. Harold Macmillan, *Riding the Storm, 1956–1959* (London: Macmillan, 1971), p. 149. After talking to Eisenhower, Macmillan recorded in his diary: "On Suez, he was sure that we must get Nasser down" (p. 134).

51. Sir Harold Caccia to Foreign Office, tel. 2272, Nov. 9, 1956, T 236/4189 (PRO).

52. Caccia to FO, Nov. 27, 1956, tel. 2352, T 236/4190 (PRO).

53. CM 90 (56), Nov. 28, 1956, CAB 128/30 (PRO).

54. Moran, *Churchill*, pp. 743–44, entries for Nov. 26 and Dec. 6, 1956.

55. House of Commons, *Debates*, vol. 562, col. 1094, Dec. 18, 1956.

56. " 'The Grand Design' (Co-operation with Western Europe)," CP (57) 6, Jan. 5, 1957, CAB 129/84 (PRO).

57. Cabinet minutes, CM (57) 3, Jan. 8, 1957, CAB 128/30 (PRO).

Background Reading

See also general reading cited in chapter 9 and the biographies listed in chapter 10. Rhodes James's biography of Eden is the first non-memoir to use the British Cabinet documents extensively.

Studies of Suez (all before the archives were opened)

Hugh Thomas, *The Suez Affair* (London: Weidenfeld & Nicolson, 1986). Originally published in 1966 and based on extensive interviews, this remains a very good account.

Richard E. Neustadt, *Alliance Politics* (New York: Columbia University Press, 1970). Suez as a case study in Anglo-American misperceptions.

Selwyn Lloyd, *Suez, 1956: A Personal Account* (London: Jonathan Cape, 1978). Posthumous apology, glossing over the full extent of collusion.

Donald Neff, *Warriors at Suez: Eisenhower Takes America into the Middle East* (New York: Linden Press/Simon & Schuster, 1981). A full account from an American perspective.

CHAPTER 12: DEPENDENCE AND DETERRENCE, 1957–1963

Notes

1. Richard E. Neustadt, *Alliance Politics* (New York: Columbia University Press, 1970), p. 21.

2. Dimbleby, BBC 1 interview with General Andrew Goodpaster (Eisenhower's staff secretary and closest foreign policy aide).

3. Harold Macmillan, *Riding the Storm, 1956–1959* (London: Macmillan, 1971), pp. 253–54, record for March 21, 1957.

4. Makins, quoted in Douglas MacArthur II, memo, Dec. 2, 1953, in *Foreign Relations of the United States, 1952–4* (Washington, D.C.: U.S. Government Printing Office, 1983), vol. 5, p. 1726.

5. Dimbleby—Goodpaster interview.

6. Churchill to Eden, tel. T2/53, Jan. 6, 1953, PREM 11/373 (Public Record Office, London).

7. Understanding of Jan. 9, 1952, FO 371/97592, AU 1051/12 (PRO). See also above, ch. 10.

8. House of Commons, *Debates*, April 1, 1957, vol. 568, col. 56.

9. Dwight D. Eisenhower, *The White House Years: Waging Peace, 1956–1961* (London: Heinemann, 1966), p. 124.

10. Robert A. Divine, *Blowing on the Wind: The Nuclear Test Ban Debate, 1954–1960* (New York: Oxford University Press, 1978), p. 170.

11. Comments of Jan. 1, 1957, in Robert A. Divine, *Eisenhower and the Cold War* (Oxford: Oxford University Press, 1981), p. 90.

12. Stephen E. Ambrose, *Eisenhower: The President* (New York: Simon & Schuster, 1984), p. 471.

13. Quoted in Macmillan, *Riding the Storm*, p. 534.

14. Harold Macmillan, *Pointing the Way, 1959–1961* (London: Macmillan, 1972), p. 252, diary entry for March 29, 1960.

15. Denis Healey, article in *Commentary*, May 1961, quoted in Philip M. Williams, *Hugh Gaitskell* (Oxford: Oxford University Press, 1982), p. 341.

16. House of Commons, *Debates*, Nov. 1, 1960, vol. 629, col. 122.

17. Commons, *Debates*, Nov. 8, 1960, vol. 629, col. 831.

18. Dimbleby—Goodpaster interview.

19. Michael R. Beschloss, *MAYDAY: Eisenhower, Khrushchev and the U-2 Affair* (New York: Harper & Row, 1986), p. 278.

20. Dimbleby, BBC 1 interview with Sir Philip de Zulueta.

21. Robert H. Estabrook, interview with John Russell of FO, Oct. 18, 1961, Estabrook papers (John F. Kennedy Library, Boston).

22. Macmillan to Ike, Nov. 10, 1960, in Macmillan, *Pointing the Way*, p. 284.

23. Quotations from Kennedy inaugural, Jan. 21, 1961, in Theodore C. Sorensen, *Kennedy* (London: Hodder & Stoughton, 1965), pp. 245–48.

24. Dimbleby—de Zulueta interview.

25. The phrase comes from David Bruce, Kennedy's ambassador to Britain. See Bruce to State Dept., telegram 2295, Dec. 12, 1961, National Security File, NSF 170/12 (Kennedy Library).

26. Arthur M. Schlesinger, Jr., *A Thousand Days: John F. Kennedy in the White House* (New York: Fawcett Books, 1971), p. 350.

27. Ibid., p. 348.

28. Dimbleby, BBC 1 interview with Dean Rusk.

29. Herbert S. Parmet, *JFK: The Presidency of John F. Kennedy* (Harmondsworth: Penguin, 1984), p. 187.

30. *New York Times*, June 6, 1961, p. 14.

31. Schlesinger, *Thousand Days*, p. 350.

32. Dimbleby—de Zulueta interview.

33. Macmillan, *Pointing the Way*, p. 339.

34. Schlesinger, *Thousand Days*, p. 273.

35. Robert F. Kennedy, *Thirteen Days: The Cuban Missile Crisis* (London: Pan, 1969), pp. 134–35.

36. *Tribune*, quoted in David Nunnerley, *President Kennedy and Britain* (London: Bodley Head, 1972), p. 73.

37. Dimbleby, BBC 1 interview with George Ball.

38. Dimbleby—Rusk interview.

39. House of Commons, *Debates*, Oct. 30, 1962, vol. 666, col. 34.

40. Henry Owen (State Dept.) and Henry Rowen (Defense Dept.), draft memo, "A New Approach to France," April 21, 1961, NSF 70 (Kennedy Library).

41. Speech at Ann Arbor, Michigan, June 16, 1962, in John D. Steinbruner, *The Cybernetic Theory of Decision: New Dimensions of Political Analysis* (Princeton: Princeton University Press, 1974), p. 206. The title conceals a very useful study of the MLF idea in American policymaking.

42. House of Commons, *Debates*, June 26, 1962, vol. 661, col. 957.

43. Richard E. Neustadt, report to the President, Nov. 15, 1963, "Skybolt and Nassau," p. 52, NSF 322 (Kennedy Library). This is a "sanitized" version of Neustadt's postmortem on the crisis, but it reveals considerably more than the published account in Richard E. Neustadt, *Alliance Politics* (New York: Columbia University Press, 1970), although that remains the best published source. The interpretation offered here has also benefited greatly from Professor Neustadt's conversations with David Reynolds in Washington and at Harvard in May 1985.

44. Dimbleby, BBC 1 interview with Paul Nitze.

45. Dimbleby—Rusk interview.

46. Acheson's speech, West Point, Dec. 5, 1962, in Ian S. McDonald, ed., *Anglo-American Relations since the Second World War* (New York: St. Martin's Press, 1974), pp. 181–82.

47. Published letter to Lord Chandos, Dec. 7, 1962, in Harold Macmillan, *At the End of the Day, 1961–1963* (London: Macmillan, 1973), p. 339.

48. McGeorge Bundy to Robert J. Manning, Dec. 7, 1962, NSF 170A/34 (Kennedy Library).

49. Dimbleby—Ball interview.

50. George W. Ball, *The Past Has Another Pattern: Memoirs* (New York: W.W. Norton, 1982), p. 267.

51. Henry Brandon, "SKYBOLT: The Full Inside Story of How a Missile Nearly Split the West," *Sunday Times*, Dec. 8, 1963, pp. 29–31.

52. State Dept., British desk, "Current Political Scene in the UK," Dec. 13, 1962, NSF 238: Nassau (Kennedy Library).

53. Macmillan, *At the End of the Day*, p. 358.

54. Ibid., p. 360.

55. Dimbleby—de Zulueta interview.

56. Joint statement, Dec. 21, 1962, in *Public Papers of the Presidents of the United States: John F. Kennedy, 1962* (Washington, D.C.: U.S. Government Printing Office, 1963), p. 909.

57. Richard J. Barnet, *Allies: America, Europe and Japan since the War* (London: Jonathan Cape, 1983), p. 181.

58. Assurance to Macmillan recorded in McGeorge Bundy, memo for the President, April 7, 1961, NSF 170/2 (Kennedy Library).

59. French agriculture minister, in Macmillan, *At the End of the Day*, p. 365, diary entry for Jan. 12, 1963.

60. Charles de Gaulle, *War Memoirs: Unity, 1942–1944*, trans. Richard Howard (London: Weidenfeld, 1956), p. 227.

61. De Gaulle's press statement, Jan. 14, 1963, official French translation, p. 7, NSF 73 (Kennedy Library).

62. Macmillan, *At the End of the Day*, p. 367, diary entry for Jan. 28, 1963.

63. Sir Michael Wright, in Nunnerley, *President Kennedy and Britain*, p. 109.

64. Glenn T. Seaborg, with Benjamin S. Loeb, *Kennedy, Khrushchev and the Test Ban* (Berkeley: University of California Press, 1981), p. 208. Seaborg was chairman of the U.S. Atomic Energy Commission.

65. Gore to Kennedy, Aug. 2, 1963, President's Office File, POF 31 (Kennedy Library).

Background Reading

Biographical

The official biography of Macmillan is still being written by Alistair Horne, but Macmillan's memoirs provide a good deal of useful material: *Riding the Storm, 1955–1959* (London: Macmillan, 1971); *Pointing the Way, 1959–1961* (1972); and *At the End of the Day, 1961–1963* (1973).

On Eisenhower, see the memoirs, Dwight D. Eisenhower, *The White House Years: Waging Peace, 1956–1961* (Garden City, N.Y.: Doubleday, 1966) and Stephen Ambrose's biography cited in ch. 10.

On Kennedy, the study originally published by insider-historian Arthur M. Schlesinger, in 1965, *A Thousand Days: John F. Kennedy in the White House* (New York: Fawcett ed., 1971), remains essential reading, but see also Herbert S. Parmet, *JFK: The Presidency of John F. Kennedy* (New York: Penguin, 1984).

Studies of the Anglo-American Relationship

David Nunnerley, *President Kennedy and Britain* (London: Bodley Head, 1972). An excellent study of Anglo-American relations, 1961–63, based on extensive interviews, which still holds up well.

Andrew J. Pierre, *Nuclear Politics: The British Experience with an Independent Strategic Force, 1939–1970* (London: Oxford University Press, 1972). Written by a former U.S. diplomat, much involved in nuclear negotiations of the 1960s, this is a detailed study with many penetrating insights into the Anglo-American relationship.

On nuclear relations, see also the studies by John Baylis and Simon Duke (cited respectively in the reading for chapters 9 and 10).

CHAPTER 13: DRIFTING APART, 1963–1973

Notes

1. Doris Kearns, *Lyndon Johnson and the American Dream* (New York: Signet, 1976), p. 177.

2. Broadcast of July 17, 1964, in D.E. Butler and Anthony King, *The General Election of 1964* (London: Macmillan, 1964), p. 26, note 1. See also pp. 75 and 149.

3. Sir Alec Douglas-Home in Andrew J. Pierre, *Nuclear Politics: The British Experience with an Independent Strategic Force, 1939–1970* (London: Oxford University Press, 1972), p. 256.

4. Dimbleby, BBC 1 interview with Denis Healey.

5. Dimbleby, BBC 1 interview with Capt. Robert Dibble, RN.

6. Dimbleby, BBC 1 interview with Capt. Fortson, USN.

7. Dimbleby, BBC 1 interview with Dean Rusk.

8. Dimbleby—Healey interview.

9. Harold Wilson, *The Labour Government, 1964–1970: A Personal Record* (London: Weidenfeld & Nicolson, and Michael Joseph, 1971), p. 50.

10. George W. Ball, *The Past Has Another Pattern: Memoirs* (New York: W.W. Norton, 1982), p. 336.

11. Dulles to Eisenhower, memo, Feb. 10, 1956, in U.S. Dept. of State, *Foreign Relations of the United States, 1955–1957* (Washington, D.C.: U.S. Government Printing Office, 1985), vol. 1, pp. 641–42.

12. Comments of Nov. 1961 in Arthur M. Schlesinger, Jr., *A Thousand Days: John F. Kennedy in the White House* (New York: Fawcett ed., 1971), p. 505.

13. This quotation and "bitch of a war" from Kearns, *Johnson*, pp. 263–64.

14. Comments of June 1965 in George C. Herring, *America's Longest War: The United States and Vietnam, 1950–1975* (New York: John Wiley, 1979), p. 143.

15. Herring, *America's Longest War*, p. 143.

16. Leslie H. Gelb, with Richard K. Betts, *The Irony of Vietnam: The System Worked* (Washington, D.C.: Brookings Institution, 1979), p. 111.

17. Wilson, *Labour Government*, p. 48.

18. Ibid., p. 80.

19. Dimbleby, BBC 1 interview with William Bundy.

20. George C. Herring, ed., *The Secret Diplomacy of the Vietnam War: The Negotiating Volumes of the Pentagon Papers* (Austin: University of Texas Press, 1983), p. 460.

21. Richard Crossman, *The Diaries of a Cabinet Minister*, 3 vols. (London: Hamish Hamilton and Jonathan Cape, 1975–77), vol. 2, pp. 237–38, entry for Feb. 14, 1967.

22. Dimbleby—Bundy interview.

23. Lyndon B. Johnson, *The Vantage Point: Perspectives of the Presidency, 1963–1969* (London: Weidenfeld & Nicolson, 1971), p. 255.

24. Dimbleby—Bundy interview.

25. Wilson, *Labour Government*, p. 264.

26. Dimbleby, BBC 1 interview with Louis Heren.

27. International Institute of Strategic Studies (IISS), *The Strategic Balance, 1964–65* (1964), pp. 17–18, 22–24.

28. IISS, *Strategic Balance, 1972–3* (1972), p. 73.

29. *The Times*, Nov. 17, 1964, p. 6, quoting his Guildhall speech the previous evening.

30. Crossman, *Diaries*, vol. 1, p. 95, entry for Dec. 11, 1964.

31. James Callaghan, *Time and Chance* (London: Collins, 1987), p. 187.

32. Crossman, *Diaries*, vol. 2, pp. 181–82, entry for Jan. 1, 1967.

33. Callaghan, *Time and Chance*, p. 176, cf. p. 189.

34. Quoted in F. Gregory Gause, "British and American Policies in the Persian Gulf, 1968–1973," *Review of International Studies*, vol. 11 (1985), p. 252.

35. Callaghan, *Time and Chance*, p. 211.

36. Crossman, *Diaries*, vol. 2, p. 646.

37. Dimbleby—Healey interview.

38. Dimbleby—Rusk interview.

39. Lady Bird Johnson, *A White House Diary* (London: Weidenfeld & Nicolson, 1970), pp. 629–32, entry for Feb. 8, 1968.

40. Kathleen J. Turner, *Lyndon Johnson's Dual War: Vietnam and the Press* (Chicago: University of Chicago Press, 1985), p. 231.

41. Townsend Hoopes, *The Limits of Intervention* (New York: David McKay, 1969), p. 219.

42. LBJ to Congress in 1966, in Herbert Y. Schandler, *The Unmaking of a President: Lyndon Johnson and Vietnam* (Princeton: Princeton University Press, 1977), p. 225.

43. Roger Morris, *Uncertain Greatness: Henry Kissinger and American Foreign Policy* (London: Quartet Books, 1977), p. 164.

44. Herring, *America's Longest War*, pp. 146, 250.

45. Article in *Foreign Affairs*, Oct. 1967, in Robert S. Litwak, *Detente and the Nixon Doctrine: American Foreign Policy and the Pursuit of Stability, 1969–1976* (Cambridge: Cambridge University Press, 1984), p. 55.

46. *The Memoirs of Richard Nixon* (London: Arrow Books, 1978), p. 560.

47. Interview in *Time*, Jan. 3, 1972, quoted in Seyom Brown, *The Faces of Power: Constancy and Change in United States Foreign Policy from Truman to Reagan* (New York: Columbia University Press, 1983), pp. 328–29.

48. Speech of Jan. 23, 1970, in Phil Williams, *The Senate and US Troops in Europe* (London: Macmillan, 1985), pp. 163–64.

49. "Year of Europe" speech, April 23, 1973, in Henry A. Kissinger, *American Foreign Policy* (New York: W.W. Norton, 1974), pp. 165–77.

50. Dimbleby, BBC 1 interview with Henry Kissinger.

51. Dimbleby, BBC 1 interview with Edward Heath.

52. Henry Kissinger, *Years of Upheaval* (London: Weidenfeld & Nicolson, and Michael Joseph, 1982), p. 191.

53. *The Times*, Oct. 29, 1973, p. 6.

54. Kissinger, *Years of Upheaval*, p. 709.

55. Dimbleby—Kissinger interview.

56. Dimbleby—Heath interview.

57. Kissinger, *Years of Upheaval*, p. 588.

58. House of Commons, *Debates*, vol. 863, col. 969, Nov. 7, 1963 (emphasis added). Heath had made a similar distinction on Oct. 30 (see col. 36). This appears to be in line with a policy articulated back in July 1960 when the U.S. defense secretary assured the British minister of defence that "I should be happy to ensure that you are notified of any decision to alert US forces in the UK." In other words, this would be an act of good neighborliness, but not one required under the Truman-Churchill understanding about the use of bases. See Simon Duke, *US Defence Bases in the United Kingdom* (London: Macmillan, 1987), pp. 164–65.

59. Dimbleby—Heath interview.

60. Dimbleby—Kissinger interview.

61. Dimbleby—Kissinger interview.

Background Reading

It is indicative of the declining importance of the Anglo-American relationship by this period, as well as the paucity of primary sources, that there are few studies specifically on Anglo-American relations in the later 1960s and 1970s. Baylis,

Anglo-American Defence Relations, and Louis and Bull, eds., *The 'Special Relationship'* (both cited in reading to chapter 9) remain useful.

Alfred Grosser, *The Western Alliance: European-American Relations since 1945* (London: Macmillan, 1980). A good general study of transatlantic connections up to about 1973—diplomatic, military, economic and cultural—though stronger on France and Germany than on Britain.

Richard J. Barnet, *Allies: America, Europe and Japan since the War* (New York: Simon & Schuster, 1983), is a more recent survey, covering the 1970s and stronger than Grosser on U.S. policy.

Henry Kissinger, *The White House Years* and *Years of Upheaval* (Boston: Little, Brown, 1979, 1982) are essential sources on U.S. policy—a mix of memoir, apologia and history.

CHAPTER 14: LIVING IN THE AMERICAN AGE
BUSINESS AND SOCIETY FROM THE 1940s TO THE 1970s

Notes

1. Maldwyn A. Jones, *The Growth of Liberty: American History, 1607–1980* (Oxford: Oxford University Press, 1983), p. 578.

2. William E. Leuchtenburg, *A Troubled Feast: American Society since 1945* (Boston: Little, Brown, 1973), p. 88.

3. Quoted in Walter A. McDougall, *The Heavens and the Earth: A Political History of the Space Age* (New York: Basic Books, 1985), p. 320.

4. Quotations from James T. Patterson, *America's Struggle against Poverty, 1900–1980* (Cambridge, Mass.: Harvard University Press, 1981), p. 80.

5. David Pichaske, *A Generation in Motion: Popular Music and Culture in the Sixties* (New York: Schirmer Books, 1979), p. xvi.

6. Robert M. Collins, *The Business Response to Keynes, 1929–1964* (New York: Columbia University Press, 1981), pp. 184–85.

7. *Time*, Dec. 31, 1965, pp. 46–47.

8. Michael Stewart, *Keynes and After* (Harmondsworth: Penguin, 1972), p. 287.

9. John Osborne, *Look Back in Anger* (London: Faber & Faber, 1957), p. 17.

10. Quoted in Mike Jahn, *Rock: From Elvis Presley to the Rolling Stones* (New York: Quadrangle/New York Times Book Co., 1973), p. 42.

11. *The Times*, Sept. 12, 1956, p. 4.

12. Ibid., Sept. 15, 1956, p. 4.

13. Steve Chapple and Reebee Carofalo, *Rock 'n' Roll Is Here to Pay: The History and Politics of the Music Industry* (Chicago: Nelson-Hall, 1977), p. 187.

14. Dimbleby, BBC 1 interview with Donald Griffiths.

15. George G. Giarchi, *Between McAlpine and Polaris* (London: Routledge & Kegan Paul, 1984), p. 115.

16. Dimbleby, BBC 1 interview with Richard Laning.

17. Simon Duke, *US Defence Bases in the United Kingdom: A Matter for Joint Decision?* (London: Macmillan, 1987), Table A2.2, p. 199. During the 1950s the figure was around 80,000. (These figures tend to overstate the American presence because they include some British citizens employed by the U.S. forces.)

18. For details in this paragraph, see John H. Dunning, "The Role of American Investment in the British Economy," *PEP Broadsheet*, 507 (Feb. 1969), esp. pp. 119, 126.

19. Francis Williams, *The American Invasion* (London: Anthony Blond, 1962), p. 11.

20. James McMillan and Bernard Harris, *The American Take-Over of Britain* (London: Leslie Frewin, 1968), p. 6.

21. *The Brain Drain: Report of the Working Group on Migration*, Cmnd. 3417, Oct. 1967 (London: HMSO, 1967), pp. 8, 10, 13.

22. House of Commons, *Debates*, Feb. 13, 1967, vol. 741, cols 125–26.

23. Quoted in *The Times*, Feb. 27, 1967, p. 2.

24. *The Brain Drain*, p. 98.

25. Charles Iffland and Henri Reuben, "The Multilateral Aspects: The U.S., Europe, and the 'Poorer' Economies," in Walter Adams, ed., *The Brain Drain* (New York: Macmillan, 1968), p. 63. ("Western Europe" here signifies the Six plus the UK.)

26. Speech of Nov. 13, 1967, in Jack N. Behrman, *National Interests and the Multinational Enterprise: Tensions among the North Atlantic Countries* (Englewood Cliffs, N.J.: Prentice Hall, 1970), p. 56, note 1.

27. Dimbleby, BBC 1 interview with Julian Amery. For similar claims, see Sir Stephen Hastings, *The Murder of TSR2* (London: MacDonald, 1966), pp. 110–11; Bruce Reed and Geoffrey Williams, *Denis Healey and the Policies of Power* (London: Sidgwick and Jackson, 1971), pp. 171–72; Charles Gardner, *British Aircraft Corporation: A History* (London: B.T. Batsford, 1981), pp. 108–9.

28. Dimbleby, BBC 1 interview with Denis Healey.

29. L.J. Williams, *Britain and the World Economy, 1919–1970* (London: Fontana, 1971), p. 126.

30. J.J. Servan-Schreiber, *The American Challenge* (New York: Avon, 1969), pp. 148–49.

31. *The Times*, Jan. 24, 1967, p. 8, quoting Wilson's speech of the previous day.

32. Anthony Sampson, *The New Anatomy of Britain* (London: Hodder & Stoughton, 1971), p. 326.

33. Dunning, "The Role of American Investment," pp. 140–41.

34. *New York Times*, Feb. 8, 1964, p. 25. Also the source for the following Starr quotation.

35. Ibid., Feb. 16, 1964, p. 3.

36. This and subsequent quotations from *Time*, April 15, 1966, pp. 32–42.

37. David Cannadine, "The Context, Performance and Meaning of Ritual: The British Monarchy and the 'Invention of Tradition,' c. 1820–1977," in Eric Hobsbawm and Terence Ranger, eds., *The Invention of Tradition* (Cambridge: Cambridge University Press, 1983), p. 155.

38. Philip Ziegler, *Crown and People* (London: Collins, 1978), p. 127.

39. Statistics from James Walvin, *Passage to Britain: Immigration in British History and Politics* (Harmondsworth: Penguin, 1984), pp. 199–200.

Background Reading

For surveys of American and British social history since World War II, see William E. Leuchtenburg, *A Troubled Feast: American Society since 1945* (Boston: Little,

Brown, 1979), and Arthur Marwick, *British Society since 1945* (Harmondsworth: Penguin, 1982).

An attempt to examine the social interrelationships is Daniel Snowman, *Britain and America: An Interpretation of their Culture, 1945–1975* (New York: Harper & Row/Torch, 1977).

CHAPTER 15: ALL AT SEA, 1973–1980

Notes

1. James Callaghan, *Time and Chance* (London: Collins, 1978), p. 295.
2. *New York Times*, March 20, 1974, pp. 1, 6.
3. Barbara Castle, *The Castle Diaries, 1974–1976* (London: Weidenfeld & Nicolson, 1980), p. 227, entry on Cabinet meeting of Nov. 20, 1974.
4. *The Castle Diaries*, p. 305, entry for Feb. 6, 1975.
5. Henry A. Kissinger, "Reflections on a Partnership: British and American Attitudes to Postwar Foreign Policy," *International Affairs*, vol. 58 (1982), p. 577.
6. Haig Simonian, *The Privileged Partnership: Franco-German Relations in the European Community, 1969–1984* (Oxford: Clarendon Press, 1985), p. 266.
7. *The Castle Diaries*, p. 357, entry for March 27, 1975.
8. Harold Wilson, *Final Term: The Labour Government, 1974–1976* (London: Weidenfeld & Nicolson and Michael Joseph, 1979), p. 108.
9. Alfred Grosser, *The Western Alliance: European-American Relations since 1945* (London: Macmillan, 1980), p. 277.
10. Jimmy Carter, *Keeping Faith: Memoirs of a President* (New York: Bantam Books, 1982), quoting respectively from pp. 22 and 18.
11. Jules Witcover, *Marathon: The Pursuit of the Presidency, 1972–1976* (New York: Viking Press, 1977), p. 402.
12. Zbigniew Brzezinski, *Power and Principle: Memoirs of the National Security Adviser, 1977–1981* (London: Weidenfeld & Nicolson, 1983), p. 520.
13. Carter, *Keeping Faith*, p. 472.
14. Raymond L. Garthoff, *Detente and Confrontation: American-Soviet Relations from Nixon to Reagan* (Washington, D.C.: Brookings Institution, 1985), quoting respectively from pp. 967–68 and 950.
15. Quoted in Strobe Talbott, *Deadly Gambits: The Reagan Administration and the Stalemate in Nuclear Arms Control* (New York: Vintage Books, 1985), p. 33.
16. Richard J. Barnet, *Allies: America, Europe and Japan since the War* (London: Jonathan Cape, 1984), pp. 408–9.
17. John L. Palmer and Isabel V. Sawhill, eds., *The Reagan Experiment: An Examination of Economic and Social Policies under the Reagan Administration* (Washington: Urban Institute Press, 1982), pp. 33–34.
18. Phil Williams, "The United States' Commitment to Western Europe: Strategic Ambiguity and Political Disintegration?" *International Affairs*, vol. 59 (1983), p. 200.
19. See David Reynolds, "A 'special relationship'?: America, Britain and the International Order since the Second World War," *International Affairs*, vol. 62 (1986), p. 17.

20. Dorothy Waggoner, "Statistics on Language Use," in Charles A. Ferguson and Shirley Brice Heath, eds., *Language in the USA* (Cambridge: Cambridge University Press, 1981), pp. 490–91.

21. Sevareid and Friedman quoted in Bernard D. Nossiter, *Britain: A Future That Works* (London: Andre Deutsch, 1978), pp. 12–13.

22. R. Emmett Tyrrell, Jr., ed., *The Future That Doesn't Work: Social Democracy's Failure in Britain* (Garden City, N.Y.: Doubleday, 1977), p. 2.

23. Richard Rose, *Politics in England*, quoted in Dennis Kavanagh, "An American Science of British Politics," *Political Studies*, vol. 22 (1974), pp. 251–52—a very useful article on which much of the previous paragraph is based.

24. Samuel H. Beer, *Britain Against Itself: The Contradictions of Collectivism* (London: Faber & Faber, 1982), p. xv.

25. Arthur M. Schlesinger, Jr., *The Imperial Presidency* (New York: Popular Library, 1974), p. 462.

26. Statistics from British Tourist Authority Market Guide, *USA, 1986/7* (London: BTA, 1986), esp. pp. 12–13.

27. Andrew Faulds, article in *The Times*, Jan. 19, 1976, quoted in David Lowenthal, *The Past Is a Foreign Country* (Cambridge: Cambridge University Press, 1985), p. 402.

Background Reading

Richard J. Barnet, *Allies: America, Europe and Japan since the War* (New York: Simon & Schuster, 1983), surveys transatlantic relations during the period, though, significantly, with little reference to Britain.

R. Emmett Tyrrell, Jr., ed., *The Future That Doesn't Work: Social Democracy's Failure in Britain* (Garden City, N.Y.: Doubleday, 1977), provides a sample of American criticism of Britain in the seventies.

M. Glenn Abernathy, Dilys M. Hill, and Phil Williams, eds., *The Carter Years: The President and Policy Making* (New York: St. Martin's Press, 1984). An early but useful scholarly attempt to evaluate the Carter presidency.

CHAPTER 16: A RELATIONSHIP RENEWED, 1981–1987

Notes

1. *Observer*, Feb. 25, 1979, in Denis Kavanagh, *Thatcherism and British Politics: The End of Consensus?* (Oxford: Oxford University Press, 1987), p. 253.

2. Remarks at British embassy dinner, Feb. 27, 1981, in *Public Papers of the Presidents of the United States: Ronald Reagan, 1981* (Washington, D.C.: U.S. Government Printing Office, 1982), p. 174.

3. Speech at White House dinner, Feb. 26, 1981, in Reagan, *Public Papers, 1981*, p. 168.

4. *Sunday Times*, May 3, 1981, in Martin Holmes, *The First Thatcher Government, 1979–1983: Contemporary Conservatism and Economic Change* (Brighton: Wheatsheaf Books, 1985), p. 209.

5. BBC 1, "Panorama," July 11, 1977, in Bernard D. Nossiter, *Britain: A Future That Works* (London: Andre Deutsch, 1978), p. 42.

6. *Economist,* Nov. 7, 1987, p. 15.

7. Peter Holmes, "The Thatcher Government's Overall Economic Performance," in David S. Bell, ed., *The Conservative Government, 1979–1984: An Interim Report* (London: Croom Helm, 1985), esp. pp. 22–26.

8. Ronnie Dugger, *On Reagan: The Man and His Presidency* (New York: McGraw-Hill, 1983), p. 102.

9. David A. Stockman, *The Triumph of Politics: The Inside Story of the Reagan Revolution* (New York: Avon Books, 1986), pp. 88, 92.

10. Ibid., pp. 116–18.

11. Ibid., pp. 119, 135.

12. Hugo Young and Anne Sloman, *The Thatcher Phenomenon* (London: BBC Publications, 1986), p. 110.

13. Kavanagh, *Thatcherism*, p. 250.

14. Helmut Schmidt, "Saving the Western Alliance," *New York Review of Books,* May 31, 1984, p. 25.

15. Thatcher to Reagan, March 11, 1982, in John Baylis, *Anglo-American Defence Relations, 1939–1984: The Special Relationship* (London: Macmillan, 1984), p. 202.

16. Reagan to Thatcher, March 11, 1982, in Baylis, *Anglo-American Defence Relations,* p. 203.

17. Ministry of Defence, "The Future United Kingdom Strategic Nuclear Deterrent Force," Defence Open Government Document 80/23 (July 1980), par. 5.

18. In the House of Commons, Jan. 24, 1980, quoted in Lawrence Freedman, *Britain and Nuclear Weapons* (London: Macmillan, 1980), p. 140.

19. Timothy Garton Ash, "The Trouble with Trident," *The Spectator,* April 12, 1986, p. 12.

20. Peter Clausen, Allan Krass, and Robert Zirkle, *In Search of Stability: An Assessment of New U.S. Nuclear Forces* (Cambridge, Mass.: Union of Concerned Scientists, 1986), ch. 3.

21. Paul Eddy and Magnus Linklater, with Peter Gillman, *The Falklands War* (London: Sphere Books, 1982), p. 53.

22. Reagan, *Public Papers, 1982* (1983), remarks to reporters, April 5, 1982, pp. 428, 431.

23. Quoted in *Time,* May 17, 1982, p. 22.

24. Alexander M. Haig, Jr., *Caveat: Realism, Reagan, and Foreign Policy* (London: Weidenfeld & Nicolson, 1984), p. 269.

25. Max Hastings and Simon Jenkins, *The Battle for the Falklands* (London: Pan Books, 1983), p. 295.

26. Reagan, *Public Papers, 1982* (1983), remarks to reporters, April 30, 1982, p. 540.

27. See "America's Falklands War," *Economist,* March 3, 1984, pp. 23–25.

28. Dimbleby, BBC 1 interview with Dr. John Lehman.

29. Reagan, *Public Papers, 1982* (1983), remarks to reporters, May 24, 1982, p. 669.

30. Dimbleby—Lehman interview.

31. Eddy, Linklater and Gillman, *The Falklands War*, p. 262.

32. Hastings and Jenkins, *The Battle for the Falklands*, p. 379.

33. Dimbleby, BBC 1 interview with Langhorn Motley.

34. House of Commons, *Debates*, 6th series, vol. 47, col. 294, Oct. 26, 1983.

35. Speech at White House dinner, Feb. 26, 1981, in Reagan, *Public Papers, 1981*, p. 170.

36. Reagan, *Public Papers, 1981*, p. 57, press conference of Jan. 29, 1981.

37. Robert Dallek, *Ronald Reagan: The Politics of Symbolism* (Cambridge, Mass.: Harvard University Press, 1984), p. 141.

38. BBC 1 "Panorama" interview with Sir Robin Day, June 6, 1983, in Michael Foot, *Another Heart and Other Pulses: The Alternative to the Thatcher Society* (London: Collins, 1984), p. 199.

39. Dimbleby, BBC 1 interview with Richard Perle.

40. Dimbleby, BBC 1 interview with General Bernard Rogers.

41. Dimbleby—Rogers interview.

42. Reagan, *Public Papers, 1983* (1984), p. 443, address of March 23, 1983.

43. Union of Concerned Scientists, *Star Wars: Myth and Reality* (Washington, D.C.: Union of Concerned Scientists, 1986), p. 27, citing poll of March 1986.

44. *Time*, June 23, 1986, p. 6.

45. *New York Times*, Nov. 5, 1985, quoted in Frank Barnaby, *What on Earth Is Star Wars?: A Guide to the Strategic Defense Initiative* (London: Fourth Estate, 1986), p. 157.

46. Foreign and Commonwealth Office, *Arms Control and Disarmament Newsletter*, no. 22 (Oct.–Dec. 1984), p. 31.

47. *Daily Telegraph*, Feb. 14, 1987, p. 1; *The Times*, Feb. 14, 1987, p. 1.

48. Magnus Linklater and David Leigh, with Ian Mather, *Not With Honour: The Inside Story of the Westland Scandal* (London: Sphere Books, 1986), p. 90, quoting "a note on the Whitehall files."

49. *New York Times*, Jan. 11, 1986, p. 1.

50. Dimbleby, BBC 1 interview with John Hughes.

51. Cf. Simon Duke, *US Defence Bases in the United Kingdom: A Matter for Joint Decision?* (London: Macmillan, 1987), pp. xvii–xx.

52. House of Commons, *Debates*, April 15, 1986, vol. 95, col. 726.

53. Dimbleby, BBC 1 interview with General Vernon Walters.

54. *Observer*, April 20, 1986, p. 12.

55. Speech in Brussels, March 16, 1987, in Sir Geoffrey Howe, *East-West Relations* (London: Central Office of Information, 1987), pp. 20–21.

56. Young and Sloman, *The Thatcher Phenomenon*, p. 111.

57. Statement of Nov. 15, 1986, in Foreign and Commonwealth Office, *Arms Control and Disarmament: Quarterly Review*, no. 4 (Jan. 1987), p. 3.

58. Dimbleby—Perle interview.

59. Dimbleby—Rogers interview.

Background Reading

Joel Krieger, *Reagan, Thatcher, and the Politics of Decline* (Cambridge: Polity Press, 1986). A rare attempt to compare the two leaders' policies and to place them in the context of an interpretation of recent history.

Peter Jenkins, *Mrs. Thatcher's Revolution: The Ending of the Socialist Era* (London: Jonathan Cape, 1987.) A major interpretation of the Thatcher years, more detailed on domestic than on foreign policy.

Garry Wills, *Reagan's America: Innocence at Home* (New York: Doubleday, 1987). Limited on the presidency but full of insights into Reagan's personality and prepresidential years.

INDEX

DAVID DIMBLEBY is BBC television's senior anchorman and main presenter of BBC's coverage of political events ranging from British and American elections to special programs on a wide range of current affairs. As a political interviewer he has talked with many heads of state and prime ministers. He worked for a time in the late 1960s as a special correspondent for CBS Television, making a CBS special on Britain and Texas with Dan Rather, and reporting for *60 Minutes*. His TV documentary series *The White Tribe of Africa*, a history of the Afrikaner, which was shown on PBS, won the Supreme Documentary Award of the Royal Television Society in 1979. He has reported regularly from the United States on presidential primaries and on election nights. He has also made documentary films on a range of topics in the United States, including the Ku Klux Klan, American university education, life in Kentucky, and the space race. For the BBC-PBS TV series *An Ocean Apart* he traveled extensively in the United States, talking to participants in the main events of this century, from doughboys to arms negotiators, from intelligence officers to GI brides. In addition to his television work, he is a newspaper proprietor, with a group of local papers in London, where he lives with his wife and three children.

DAVID REYNOLDS, thirty-six, is a Fellow of Christ's College, Cambridge University, where he teaches twentieth-century international relations and American history. He acted as principal historical adviser for the TV series related to this book, writing the background papers on which the films were based. He has lectured, researched and traveled extensively in the United States, including a year as Charles Warren Fellow at Harvard. An earlier book, *The Creation of the Anglo-American Alliance, 1937–41*, was awarded the Stuart L. Bernath Prize by the Society for Historians of American Foreign Relations—the only non-American so honored.